We Will Shoot Back

We Will Shoot Back

*Armed Resistance in the Mississippi
Freedom Movement*

Akinyele Omowale Umoja

NEW YORK UNIVERSITY PRESS

New York and London

NEW YORK UNIVERSITY PRESS
New York and London
www.nyupress.org

References to Internet websites (URLs) were accurate at the time of writing.
Neither the author nor New York University Press is responsible for URLs that
may have expired or changed since the manuscript was prepared.

Library of Congress Cataloging-in-Publication Data
Umoja, Akinyele Omowale.
We will shoot back : armed resistance in the Mississippi Freedom Movement / Akinyele
Omowale Umoja.
p. cm.
Includes bibliographical references and index.
ISBN 978-1-4798-8603-6 (pb : alk. paper)
ISBN 978-0-8147-2524-5 (cl : alk. paper)
1. Self-defense—Political aspects—Mississippi—History—20th century. 2. Mississippi
Freedom Project. 3. African Americans—Civil rights—Mississippi—History—20th century.
4. African Americans—Suffrage—Mississippi—History—20th century. 5. Civil rights
workers—Mississippi—History—20th century. 6. Civil rights movements—Mississippi—
History—20th century. 7. Mississippi—Race relations—History—20th century. I. Title.
E185.93.M6U46 2013
323.1196'0730762—dc23
                               2012046909

New York University Press books are printed on acid-free paper,
and their binding materials are chosen for strength and durability.
We strive to use environmentally responsible suppliers and materials
to the greatest extent possible in publishing our books.

Manufactured in the United States of America
10 9 8 7 6 5 4 3 2

I salute my Ancestors and the Elders still living, who fought and died in Mississippi, throughout the United States, and throughout the western hemisphere to assert our humanity in the fight for liberation and social justice.

Ase!!!! Free the Land!!!

Contents

Acknowledgments

This book would not have been possible without the example and influence of my ancestors and elders. My family oral tradition and other information I obtained informed me of my roots in West, West-Central, and East Africa. My ancestors survived the Middle Passage and were captives in Virginia, Georgia, and Louisiana. My Mississippi connection comes from the Delta, where my grandparents, Oscar Eugene Lewis and Carrie Freeman, were sharecroppers, and which was the birthplace of my father. I salute my parents, Vanderbilt ("Van") and Dimple Theola (Watts) Lewis. My father worked as a sharecropper from his childhood until he was thirty years old, when he finally had the opportunity to go to high school. He completed high school at the age of thirty-four, and completed an associate's degree at Southwestern Christian College in Texas. He went on to achieve a bachelor of arts degree and enter graduate school at Pepperdine College in Los Angeles. My mother was the valedictorian at Frederick Douglass High School in Wewoka, Oklahoma, and moved to Los Angeles, where she was a clerical worker and civil servant for the federal government. My parents emphasized education and literacy for my siblings and me. Books were always a part of our household. I also had the influence of my Uncle Joe Carter and older cousin, Ronald Boone. They always encouraged me to read books like James Baldwin's *The Fire Next Time*[1] and *The Autobiography of Malcolm X*.[2] Much of my introduction to the Black Power Movement comes from my older sister, Angela Lewis. "Angie," three years my senior, was a student at the University of California at Los Angeles in the late 1960s and early 1970s. She shared with me her African American history texts (including literature from Professor Angela Davis's class), turned me on to the music of Pharoah Sanders, and encouraged me to wear an "Afro." Growing up in Compton, California, during the late 1960s and being influenced by the consciousness and culture of my community were powerful forces in shaping me and this project.

I became active at the tail end of the Black Power Movement in the early 1970s. The Movement served as a New African university for me. My guides in the Movement are too numerous to mention here, as there are many individuals who influenced my development or played a role that contributed to this project. The relationships I developed in the Movement were critical in giving me access to much of the information in this book. I particularly want to acknowledge two of my political education instructors in the Movement, Mamadou Lumumba-Umoja and Adewole Umoja, for emphasizing the importance of the insurgent activism in the southern Black Freedom Struggle and urging me to pay attention to the resistance of laborers and farmers. I was given the assignment of accompanying Queen Mother Audley Moore to speaking engagements in Southern California when I was eighteen years old. Queen Mother Moore often told the story of how she and other Louisiana members of the Universal Negro Improvement Association came to New Orleans to force the police and local officials to allow Marcus Garvey to speak to their assembly in the 1920s. Conversations with and feedback from my Mississippi-born comrades, Watani Tyehimba and Makungu Akinyela, also helped to shape this work. My traveling to Mississippi with Ahmed Obafemi also helped provide background for this work. Tamu and Hekima Kanyama provided valuable first-hand accounts of their ordeal in Mississippi, as well as editorial support.

Friends in Mississippi, particularly in Jackson, provided shelter, food, and companionship that sustained my research trips there. Chokwe Lumumba, his late wife, Nubia, and their children provided a "home away from home" for me in Jackson. Demetri Marshall and his family openly welcomed me in Claiborne County and treated me as a brother. My comrades Akil and Gwen Bakari, Hondo Lumumba, Mikea Kambui, Halima Olufemi, Safiya Omari, and the rest of my Jackson, Mississippi, family always cared for me. Several people led me to folks to support my work, but I particularly want to recognize Charles Tisdale, Howard Gunn, Hollis Watkins, Willie Owens, Herman Leach, James Miller, Ser Sesh Boxley, Moriba Lumumba, and Tyrone "Fat Daddy" Davis for their assistance and contribution to this book. One person who helped put me on the right track was Ken Lawrence, who did preliminary work on this project and knew as well as worked with many of the subjects of this text.

Much respect to the community of scholars who gave timely feedback and encouragement. It was at Emory University that I first pursued this topic in Allen Tullos's seminar on southern culture. Professor Tullos encouraged me to pursue the idea of researching armed self-defense in the southern Black Freedom Struggle. Robin D. G. Kelly mentored and guided me even after leaving Emory. Dana White, Dan Carter, and Leroy Davis spent quality time to nurture and challenge me in the dissertation process. Paula Dressel and Marcellus Barksdale also provided significant input and encouragement. Charles E. Jones was "crazy enough" for hiring me and made sure I had support to continue this work at Georgia State University (GSU). Beatrice Morales and Jacqueline Rouse also provided collegial comments and inspiration. A number of GSU graduate and undergraduate students as well as staff also contributed to this work through archival research, transcription, and other forms of support. My student assistants and volunteers who worked on this project include DeMarcus McCarthy, Andrea Linnear, Tywanda Richardson, Nandi Crosby, Michael Cooper, Nafeesa Muhammad, Latrice Wright, Tiara Banks, and Mawuli Davis. The editing of Kaniqua Robinson was essential to the completion of this project. I will always be indebted to her. I also thank Belinda Futrell and Tiffany Bullock for the administrative support.

Colleagues at other institutions also offered advice and resources that were critical to the completion of the project. Emilye Crosby's interchange and sharing of resources since graduate school is part of a rare collegial relationship that I hope will continue through other mutual projects. University of Southern Mississippi graduate student and journalist Leesha Faulkner shared her personal archives, which included Mississippi State records of police surveillance of civil and human rights activists before they were officially released. Sundiata Cha-Jua offered historiographic advice throughout the project. The encouragement of scholar-activist Gwendolyn Hall helped to motivate me. Other historians who offered critical support include John Dittmer, Curtis Austin, and Kwame Hasan Jeffries.

No historian can complete quality work without archival resources. Several archives and archivists must be mentioned. The Moorland Spingarn Collections at Howard University, the archives at Tougalou College, the Mississippi Department of Archives and History (MDAH), and the University of Southern Mississippi Special Collections and the Oral History Project provided many of the primary documents of this work. Joellen El Bashir at Moorland Spingarn was very helpful in locating interviews from the Civil Rights Documentation Project. The collections at Emory University were also helpful. Clarence Hunter and Caroline Primer of MDAH (and her husband William) were both critical in finding evidence for corroboration and even informants to be interviewed. Activist archivist

Jan Hillegas and the Freedom Information Center also provided valuable support and directed me to Mississippi freedom fighters to be interviewed. The papers of the Southern Conference Educational Fund at GSU's Southern Labor History archives were essential in tracking down corroboration on the activism in northern Mississippi in the late 1970s. Finally, I was blessed to access the papers of the Student Nonviolent Coordinating Committee, the Mississippi Freedom Democratic Party, and the Congress of Racial Equality at the archives of the Martin Luther King Jr. Center for Nonviolent Social Change. A special thanks to Kayin Shabazz for tracking articles down for me at the Woodruff Library at the Atlanta University Center.

Finally, the love and support of my household cannot be underestimated. My family sacrificed greatly in terms of time and money to make sure this project became a reality. Thanks to my wife, Aminata, for listening to my revelations and ideas about this project and being excited after reading and editing some of the chapters. Thanks for the feedback, prayers, and inspiration for me to keep pushing until I could see daylight. Thanks to my children, Tashiya, Ayinde (son-in-law), and Chinua, as well as my grandchildren, Ire and Bem, for listening to my ideas and supporting me as I focused on this work. While I was the primary vessel, *We Will Shoot Back* took a community to complete. I pray that it meets the family and community expectations and helps tell the stories of the ancestors and elders.

Introduction

My father was born in 1915 to a sharecropping family in the Bolivar County village of Alligator in the Mississippi Delta. Dad told me stories about Mississippi when I was growing up in Compton, California. These stories were full of examples of White terrorism and intimidation. One story I heard invoked mixed feelings of fear and pride. My father remembered seeing a Black man hanging from a Delta water tower, apparently after being lynched by White supremacists. Angered by this visible assault on Black humanity, my grandfather grabbed a rifle and intended to shoot the first White man he saw. My father, his siblings, and his stepmother tackled my grandfather and disarmed him. After hearing this story, I was proud that my grandfather wanted to fight back against the terrorists who lynched one of our people. On the other hand, I understood the fear in the hearts and minds of my father, uncles, and grandmother as they visualized the retaliation that would have been inflicted on the family if my grandfather had carried out his plans.

Fear and intimidation were essential elements of the system of subordination of Black people and the maintenance of White power in Mississippi and the South during the times of racial slavery and segregation. White supremacist violence was the primary cause of fear and intimidation. The primary social function of this violence was to maintain White political and economic power and the color line during segregation. My grandfather would have most likely been a lone warrior on the day he was disarmed by his loved ones. His anger overcame his fear and motivated him to fight back to confront the perpetrators of this lynching. This book is about Black people in Mississippi who picked up guns or other weapons and decided to use force to fight back against those who would deny their human rights and dignity. Ultimately, the Black Freedom Struggle in Mississippi and the South was a fight to overcome fear. Blacks overcame fear and asserted their humanity through a variety of tactics. This story documents the role that armed resistance played in overcoming fear and intimidation and engendering Black political, economic, and social liberation.

The central argument in *We Will Shoot Back: Armed Resistance in the Mississippi Freedom Struggle* is that armed resistance was critical to the efficacy of the southern freedom struggle and the dismantling of segregation and Black disenfranchisement. Intimidation by White supremacists was intended to bring fear to the Black population and its allies and sympathizers in the White community. To overcome the legal system of apartheid, Black people had to overcome fear to present a significant challenge to White domination. Armed self-defense had been a major tool of survival in allowing some Black southern communities to maintain their integrity and existence in the face of White supremacist terror. By 1965, armed resistance, particularly self-defense, was a significant factor in the effort made by the sons and daughters of enslaved Africans to overturn fear and intimidation and develop different political and social relationships between Black and White Mississippians.

We Will Shoot Back argues that without armed resistance, primarily organized by local people, the National Association for the Advancement of Colored People (NAACP), the Congress of Racial Equality (CORE), and the Student Nonviolent Coordinating Committee (SNCC) activists would not have been able to organize in Mississippi. After organizing by SNCC and CORE, armed resistance served as a complement to self-proclaimed nonviolent organizers and organizations from 1961 through 1964. By 1965, armed self-defense and militant rhetoric was chosen by a growing number of Mississippi human rights activists as the alternative to the nonviolent tactics and posture of the early 1960s. This study argues that a tradition of armed resistance existed in the culture of southern Blacks that produced a variety of organizational forms to respond to the necessity of protecting Black communities, their leaders, allies, and institutions. The way armed resistance was organized varied in different stages of the freedom struggle in Mississippi. Armed self-defense tended to be informal and loosely organized by community activists and supporters from the 1950s through 1964 in Mississippi. After 1964, paramilitary groups with a specific chain of command and discipline emerged in some Mississippi communities and Movement centers. The open advocacy of armed resistance and the abandonment of the rhetoric of nonviolence also became the common practice of Movement spokespersons after 1964.

Historiography and Armed Resistance in the
Southern Black Freedom Struggle

I completed my dissertation, entitled "'Eye for an Eye': The Role of Armed Resistance in the Mississippi Freedom Movement," in 1996. The question of armed resistance in the southern Black Freedom Struggle was under-developed in previous literature. "Eye for an Eye" and other works have turned the tide on the historiography of the Civil Rights Movement with respect to the question of armed resistance in the southern Black Freedom Struggle. Historian Emilye Crosby has pointed out the importance of lo-cal studies of the Civil Rights Movement revealing the role of armed self-defense in a way that was ignored by previous literature that emphasized a national "top-down" narrative.[1] The two seminal books on the Mississippi Civil Rights Movement, John Dittmer's *Local People: The Struggle for Civil Rights in Mississippi*[2] and Charles Payne's *I've Got the Light of Freedom*,[3] ac-knowledged the role of armed self-defense in the Civil Rights Movement. Books like Adam Fairclough's *Race and Democracy*,[4] David Beito and Linda Royster Beito's *Black Maverick*,[5] Emilye Crosby's *Common Courtesy*,[6] Hasan Kwame Jeffries' *Bloody Lowndes*,[7] and Wesley Hogan's *Many Hearts, One Mind*[8] seriously represent the role of armed self-defense in their accounts of the southern Black Freedom Struggle. Recent publications, particularly Timothy Tyson's *Radio Free Dixie*[9] and Lance Hill's *Deacons for Defense*,[10] illuminate the role of armed self-defense in the southern freedom struggles of the 1950s and '60s. Christopher Strain's *Pure Fire*[11] and Simon Wendt's *Spirit and the Shotgun*[12] connect the southern tradition of self-defense to the general Black Freedom Struggle, including the Black Power Movement.

We Will Shoot Back continues the study of the armed self-defense and armed resistance tradition in the southern Black Freedom Struggle. Prior to the intervention of the trend represented by the abovementioned au-thors, Robert Williams and the Deacons for Defense were seen as excep-tions in the Civil Rights Movement. My work demonstrates that armed resistance was persistent and pervasive in the Civil Rights Movement in Mississippi and played a critical role in the survival and success of the Movement. Tyson's award-winning work on Robert Williams is a much-needed biography on the most popular advocate of armed resistance in the southern Black Freedom Struggle. My work is different from *Radio Free Dixie* in that it is not a biography of one individual but primarily focuses on virtually unknown activists from local movements who played critical roles in the southern struggle in campaigns that had local, regional, and national significance. *We Will Shoot Back* also distinguishes the overt practice of Williams from that of his contemporaries in the late 1950s and early 1960s, who tended to play a more covert and conciliatory role in their advocacy and use of weapons. Medgar Evers was the most well-known of Williams's contemporaries who engaged in armed self-defense. This book also places the Deacons in the context of the tradition of armed Black resistance. I will also demonstrate how the Deacons played a part in changing political culture and efficacy in the Mississippi Black Freedom Struggle.

Another contribution *We Will Shoot Back* makes to the historiography of the Civil Rights Movement is that it offers another layer to the story of Freedom Summer. During the summer of 1964, in the face of intensified racial terror and limited federal protection, local community residents organized themselves to protect their communities and hundreds of volunteers who came to support voter and human rights efforts in the state. Armed resistance by local people was a common feature and practice during Freedom Summer.

Strain's and Wendt's contributions to this dialogue discuss the continuity of the armed resistance tradition in northern urban centers during the Black Power Movement. Their accounts are consistent with the general trend in the proliferation of recent literature on the Black Power Movement. Most accounts acknowledge the role of the southern Black Freedom Struggle in ushering in the term "Black Power" in association with the growing militancy and radicalization of activism in the 1960s. The dominant narrative of Black Power shifts away from the South to the northern and western regions of the United States after the popularization of the term "Black Power" in the 1966 Meredith March in Mississippi. *We Will Shoot Back* demonstrates the continuity of the armed resistance tradition during and beyond this period of the Black Power Movement in the Freedom Struggle in Mississippi. Wendt argues that federal intervention made it unnecessary for Blacks to utilize armed self-defense in the post–Civil Rights Era. He argues after 1967, "defense squads that emerged in Alabama, Louisiana, and Mississippi outlived their usefulness."[13] While some paramilitary groups and defense networks demobilized after 1967, campaigns for human rights persisted in rural communities in Mississippi and the South, as did the need for local communities and activists to protect themselves from White terror and intimidation. Some Black activists and communities continued to see the need for armed resistance in spite of the passage of the Civil Rights Act of 1964 and Voting Rights Act of 1965. This work documents the continuity of collective self-defense activities until the late 1970s, particularly in the campaigns organized by the United League in northern Mississippi. Elements of the Mississippi Black Power Movement would even engage in retaliatory violence and guerilla warfare.

Strain frames the political content of armed self-defense in the context of the "fight for full citizenship and full American-ness." He also discusses the philosophical context of the right and practice of self-defense in European philosophy and mainstream U.S. political culture.[14] Black resistance in the United States cannot be solely interpreted through the lens of Western philosophical constructs. I argued in my dissertation that the Black armed resistance legacy was rooted in retention of African military tradition.[15] Colin Palmer asserted that the first enslaved Africans (born in West and West-Central Africa) established the "cultural underpinnings" of African descendant life in the United States.[16] Michael Gomez offered that enslaved Africans created a polycultural matrix in which they enacted one culture when visible by slaveholding society and another when in their own social space. Gomez's interpretation postulates enslaved Africans negotiating within the slave quarters, forests, and swamps to design their own New African cultural matrix borrowing on West and West-Central African institutions.[17] I argue that this New African matrix in the United States must be considered as a significant and foundational factor in the identity, social life, and political culture, including insurgent resistance, of Black people in the United States. The work of Black Atlantic World historians John Thornton and Walter Rucker establishes African influences on enslaved African rebels in colonial British North America and pre-emancipation United States.[18] Mississippi-born activists like Hollis Watkins and MacArthur Cotton told me that they were protected in Mississippi during the early 1960s by Black men who were connected through secret societies. Former Black Panther and political prisoner Geronimo ji Jaga (Pratt) often shared that his elders in Morgan City, Louisiana, had a clandestine network for armed self-defense of the Black community that originated with Marcus Garvey's Universal Negro Improvement Association of the 1920s and continued through the Deacons for Defense of the 1960s.[19] The UNIA and the Deacons in Louisiana and Mississippi relied on the secret society tradition to provide themselves with organizational cohesiveness and a chain of command. Gomez also informs us that the proclivity to organize social and political activities through fraternal organizations was a tradition our enslaved ancestors remembered from their African heritage.[20]

The work of Gomez and Cedric Robinson establishes the heterogeneous character of African descendant political culture in the United

States. Gomez asserts that by 1830 "two distinct and divergent visions of the African presence in America" surfaced. Some African Americans' vision was to achieve inclusion within the United States as "full participants in the American political experiment." Others were less hopeful of inclusion as equal partners within the U.S. power structure and held as "close to the bosom of Africa as they could get."[21] Robinson also argued that "two alternate Black political cultures" emerged by the 1850s, one assimilationist and elitist, another separatist (or nationalistic) and communitarian. Robinson argues that the two Black political cultures reached "their closet accommodation" during the Civil Rights Movement of the 1960s. He argues that political repression of civil rights militants and Black nationalists contributed to a divide between the two historic Black political orientations in the culmination of the 1960s political insurgency. The African political experience in the United States has diverse ideological currents, ranging from assimilation to pluralism to autonomy to radical transformation to nationalism. The desire for "first-class" U.S. citizenship was one political objective of the Black Freedom Struggle, but aspirations for self-determination and autonomy also compete and coexist with liberal pluralist expressions. This study focuses on the Civil Rights and Black Power Movements. The orientation of the Civil Rights Movement was a fight for first-class citizenship and basic human rights. The Black Power Movement included activist fighting for pluralism and citizenship rights, but also the desire for an independent Republic of New Africa, the socialist transformation of U.S. society, and pan-African revolution. The emphasis on self-determination is what primarily distinguishes the Black Power Movement from the Civil Rights Movement. In this sense, the Black Freedom Struggle and armed resistance cannot be confined to the fight for "full citizenship and full American-ness."

We Will Shoot Back also treats the Civil Rights and Black Power Movements as two related but distinct periods of social movement in the historic Black Freedom Struggle for human rights and against racial oppression. This study does not view the Black Freedom Struggle as one long social movement.[22] I utilize the term "Black Freedom Struggle" to identify the historic fight of African descendants for liberation and human rights. The Black Freedom Struggle includes both the fight for emancipation from racial slavery that was waged from the seventeenth to the nineteenth century and the fight for human rights, social and economic justice, and political power that was waged from the late nineteenth century through contemporary times. Several social movements rose and declined through the Black Freedom Struggle, including the Civil Rights and Black Power Movements.

New social forces emerge in different periods but often rely on traditions and resources of previous movements. The strategic objective of the Civil Rights Movement was the inclusion of African Americans in citizenship rights and the dismantling of U.S. apartheid barriers to Black humanity and dignity. The Black Power Movement had several ideological expressions, including revolutionary nationalism, cultural nationalism, political pluralism, Black capitalism, and Pan-Africanism. All of these ideological expressions emphasized Black identity and consciousness, self-determination, and self-reliance. Some of the activists of the Civil Rights Movement became Black Power militants. Other civil rights advocates became critics and opponents of the new, often more radical ideological direction of their former comrades who embraced Black Power and the emerging social forces it represented in the late 1960s and early '70s. While armed self-defense was debated in the Civil Rights Movement, it was virtually accepted in the Black Power Movement, and the rhetoric of nonviolence was virtually unused by its activists. Challenges to segregation continued to occur during the Black Power Movement in Mississippi. Unlike in the civil rights period of the struggle, demands for Black self-determination, community control, and Black pride emerged in the desegregation struggle. For example, many Mississippi Black communities demanded Black representation in decision making in school desegregation plans and that African American history be required in school curricula in the 1970s.

Terminology

How do I define "armed resistance"? Emilye Crosby points out "a lack of consistency" in the use of the term "armed resistance" in recent scholarship.[23] I define "armed resistance" as individual and collective use of force for protection, protest, or other goals of insurgent political action and in defense of human rights. Armed resistance includes armed self-defense, retaliatory violence, spontaneous rebellion, guerilla warfare, armed vigilance/enforcement, and armed struggle. "Armed self-defense" is the protection of life, persons, and property from aggressive assault through the application of force necessary to thwart or neutralize attack. "Retaliatory violence" is physical reprisal for attacks on people or institutions associated with the Movement. "Spontaneous rebellion" is unplanned, unorganized, politically motivated collective violence intended to redress injustice. "Guerilla warfare" refers to irregular military-tactic efforts utilized by small groups to harass, attack, and strike a larger, better-resourced opponent. "Armed vigilance/ enforcement" is the use of coercive force by a social movement to assert its authority among its constituency and community and to counter the loyalty its population may have for the dominant power structure. Finally, "armed struggle" is a strategy utilized by an insurgent movement to gain state power through military means.

All of the forms of armed resistance defined above were employed in Mississippi during the Civil Rights and Black Power Movements, with the exception of armed struggle. The use of guns is not necessary in my definition, only the use of force. Guns are merely technology utilized during a particular moment in history. Fists, feet, stones, bricks, blades, and gasoline firebombs may all be employed to defend, protect, or protest. "Armed resistance" is utilized in this study as a broad term that includes different forms of insurgent force.

We Will Shoot Back: Chapters

This study focuses on the Black Freedom Struggle in Mississippi from the post–World War II era through the late 1970s. Chapter 1 provides a historical and cultural background to the Civil Rights Movement in Mississippi. This chapter reconstructs the political and social climate in the state, describing the nature of segregation, the character of White terrorist violence, and the collective and individual acts of armed resistance to racial oppression prior to the birth of the modern Civil Rights Movement in the state. The social function of White supremacist violence during the Reconstruction and Nadir period was to suppress Black political aspirations and maintain Black workers as a servile labor force. Post–Civil War Black insurgency, particularly armed resistance, is placed in a cultural construct of the "Bad Negro," public defiance of White supremacy, and "Bruh Rabbit" (covert resistance).

Chapter 2, "'I'm Here, Not Backing Up': Emergence of Grassroots Militancy and Armed Self-Defense in the 1950s," focuses on the role of self-defense in the Mississippi Black Freedom Struggle in the 1950s. This period provided the network and infrastructure for the dismantling of apartheid in the 1960s and '70s. The development and role of the Regional Council for Negro Leadership (RCNL) and its primary spokesperson, Dr. T. R. M.

Howard, is highlighted, as well as Howard's assertive self-defense posture. Finally, the chapter highlights the prevalence of armed self-defense utilized by grassroots activists as reflected in Medgar Evers's attitudes and practices concerning armed resistance.

"'Can't Give Up My Stuff': Nonviolent Organizations and Armed Resistance," chapter 3, examines the initial organizing efforts of the Student Nonviolent Coordinating Committee (SNCC) and the Congress of Racial Equality (CORE) in Mississippi and the interaction with organizers from these groups with local leaders and people who engaged in armed resistance. SNCC's and CORE's origins were rooted in the strategy, methods, and philosophy of nonviolence. When their organizers initiated and ignited voter registration campaigns, they encountered a host of local leaders who utilized guns as a means of survival in political and everyday life. This chapter highlights the tension and cooperation between the nonviolent organizations and the indigenous armed resistance tradition in Mississippi.

Chapter 4, "'Local People Carry the Day': Freedom Summer and Challenges to Nonviolence in Mississippi," focuses on the events leading up to, during, and after the historic Freedom Summer voter registration campaign of 1964 and the impact of armed resistance on that period. The chapter describes the informal organization of armed self-defense in a variety of communities across the state during Freedom Summer. I also draw attention to how spontaneous rebellion in McComb put pressure on federal and state government to intervene to suppress racial terrorism by the Klan. A particular focus is the first national debate within SNCC on self-defense, as well as the impact of armed resistance by local people on SNCC's and CORE's ideology and practice, which eventually led to both organizations embracing the concept of armed self-defense.

Chapter 5, "Ready to Die and Defend: Natchez and the Advocacy and Emergence of Armed Resistance in Mississippi," explores the transition from informal self-defense groups to formal paramilitary organizations, particularly the Deacons for Defense and the open advocacy of armed resistance. In Mississippi, the development of paramilitary organization was parallel to the emphasis on consumer boycotts as a method to coerce local White power structures to concede to demands of the Movement. The campaign led by the state and local NAACP in Natchez, Mississippi, provides the model for this collaboration of consumer boycott and paramilitary organization. Consistent with this model is the development of enforcer squads to gain accountability from local Blacks during the boycott. The open advocacy of armed resistance by activists signified a shift in rhetoric that would be modeled until the late 1970s in the state. Chapter 6, entitled "'We Didn't Turn No Jaws': Black Power, Boycotts, and the Growing Debate on Armed Resistance," explains how the "March against Fear" from Memphis to Jackson was significant in igniting local initiatives in many communities. SNCC's promotion of the slogan "Black Power" signaled a shift in attitude and emphasis of the freedom struggle. This chapter examines how the Black consciousness/Black Power emphasis interacted with the Natchez paramilitary model in Mississippi in two towns impacted by the march, Belzoni and Yazoo City. These boycotts were organized by Rudy Shields in Humphries and Yazoo counties and emphasized armed resistance.

Chapter 7, "'Black Revolution Has Come': Armed Insurgency, Black Power, and Revolutionary Nationalism in the Mississippi Freedom Struggle," continues the story of the Black Power Movement in Mississippi and the role of armed resistance in it. One focus is the boycott organizer, Rudy Shields, and his transition to Black Nationalism in campaigns in Aberdeen and West Point in northeast Mississippi. West Point experienced retaliatory violence organized by an armed clandestine unit of the Black Power Movement months prior to Shields's involvement there. Shields was also active in organizing college students in the aftermath of the campus shootings and deaths at Jackson State College in 1970. Finally, this chapter examines the ordeal of the Republic of New Africa in Mississippi and the involvement of Mississippi Black Power militants with the nationalist formation. Finally, in chapter 8, "'No Longer Afraid': The United League, Activist Litigation, Armed Self-Defense, and Insurgent Resilience in Northern Mississippi," I look at the United League of Mississippi, self-described as a "priestly, human rights organization" that organized boycotts in the state from 1974 through 1979. In a period generally considered a low point of Black insurgency, the United League organized successful boycotts utilizing self-defense and bold rhetoric embracing armed resistance. The United League represents a continuity of the Natchez model and its last expression in Mississippi politics in the twentieth century.

1

Terror and Resistance

Foundations of the Civil Rights Insurgency

On Christmas Day in 1875, state senator Charles Caldwell, a freedman, was invited by Buck Cabell, a White associate, to a store for a friendly drink. Because of his political activity and actions in defense of his people's liberty, Caldwell's life had been threatened by local White citizens. Due to these threats, Caldwell's wife, Mary, cautioned him against leaving home and traveling to town. Not wanting to offend someone he had known and respected for years, Caldwell disregarded the concern of his wife and accepted the invitation of Cabell, one of the few White men he trusted. In fact, Cabell insisted they have the drink together and escorted the Black politician to Chilton's store in Clinton. They went to the store cellar to enjoy their drink. The two men toasted each other by tapping their glasses. With the clink of the glasses, a shot was fired from the window of the store and Caldwell fell to the floor. Suddenly, armed White men surrounded Caldwell. He recognized them, "community leaders, judges, politicians, men of substance."[1] Not wanting to "die like a dog closed up,"[2] the wounded man asked to be taken from the cellar to the street. In his last act of courage, the proud politician declared, "Remember when you kill me you kill a gentleman and a brave man. Never say you killed a coward. I want you to remember it when I'm gone."[3] Christmas in Clinton was not a silent night. Dozens of shots riveted the body of Caldwell.

In the beginning of the nineteenth century, Mississippi, a territory of the United States (acquired in the Louisiana Purchase), consisted of only a few thousand White settlers and captive Africans, as well as the indigenous population. In 1817, Mississippi was granted the status of a state in the U.S. federal union. Demand for land for White settlement and expansion of commercial farming meant the expulsion of the indigenous population and the increased demand for captive African labor. Particularly due to the expansion of "King Cotton," Mississippi had increased in population. The region east of the Mississippi River was overwhelmingly populated, with over 55 percent consisting of enslaved people of African descent. By 1860, the state had a population of 353,899 Whites and 437,404 Blacks, with a very small "free" population (773).[4] The Mississippi economy was dependent on the system of racial slavery. The end of the Civil War and the corresponding policy of "emancipation" potentially undermined the White planter class, who relied on a servile and oppressed Black labor force for their livelihood, privilege, and power.

Charles Caldwell, White Terror, and the Defeat of Reconstruction

The assassination of Caldwell is symbolic of the reign of terror that defeated Reconstruction, democracy, Black political participation, as well as human rights in Mississippi and the South in the mid-1870s. Violence was central to the establishment of White domination, not only to seize power for White supremacists but also to instill fear and intimidation in the Black population and their allies. In a state with a Black majority, to secure White supremacy and to maintain Black labor, particularly rural workers, as a servile labor force, it was necessary to institutionalize fear and intimidation. Men like Caldwell represented hope for Black progress and resistance to White domination.

Who was Charles Caldwell, and why was he a threat? Caldwell was an enslaved person—a blacksmith—living in Hinds County, Mississippi, who became a leader in his community during emancipation. After the end of the Civil War, Caldwell aligned himself with the Republican Party and, in 1868, was one of sixteen Black Republican delegates to the state Constitutional Convention. Congressional invention placed the former Confederate states under martial law and would form new governments that would prevent the Confederates from securing power. To neutralize the power of the former Confederates in the South, particularly the southern elite, it was necessary to include Black people in the franchise. In Mississippi, including Black males in the body politic meant that the majority of the voting population would be people of African descent. In this political environment, Charles Caldwell emerged and was elected to the 1868 Mississippi Constitutional Convention.

With sixteen Black delegates (out of a total of ninety-four), the convention drafted the most democratic constitution in the history of Mississippi until the Civil Rights Era of the 1960s and '70s. It made all persons residing in the state citizens, with rights of trial by jury and other rights provided to U.S. citizens by the Constitution and Bill of Rights. The Mississippi Constitution of 1868 eliminated property criteria for holding office, jury service, and suffrage. As with other Reconstruction assemblies during this period, the Mississippi Constitution of 1868 provided for public education, the elimination of segregation in public accommodations and institutions, and universal adult male suffrage. On the other hand, Whites who were linked to the Confederate rebellion against the union were disenfranchised. This policy resulted in twenty thousand Whites, mostly elite, being denied the right to vote or hold office.[5] Caldwell was an active participant in the four-month process of drafting a Reconstruction constitution for his home state.

Subsequent to the convention, Caldwell was involved in a shooting incident in Jackson, the Mississippi state capital. In "broad daylight," a White man, who was the son of a Mississippi judge, attempted to shoot Caldwell, but in self-defense, the Black leader shot and killed his attacker. Caldwell was tried and acquitted, achieving the distinction of becoming the first, *and possibly only*, Black person to win an acquittal after killing a White man in Mississippi.[6]

Following the convention, the successful defense of his life, and acquittal in Jackson, Caldwell became involved in the Hinds County government. In 1870, he was elected to the state Senate. Caldwell and other Black politicians participated in state government. After the election of 1873, Black men were elected to the offices of lieutenant governor, secretary of state, superintendent of education, and speaker of the House. While Caldwell and other Black legislators did not possess the numbers to control either body of the state legislature, their interests were reflected in the policies developed by state government. The Mississippi Reconstruction legislatures instituted elements of the 1868 Mississippi Constitution, including universal male suffrage, elimination of chattel slavery, eradication of codes related to racial servitude and control, and establishment of public education. Vagrancy laws were eliminated and taxes for mechanics and artisans lowered. The right of married women to control their own income, autonomous from their spouses, was implemented. Husbands were also required to receive consent from their spouses on the sale of family domiciles.

In response to the democratic agenda of the Mississippi Reconstruction government, former Confederates, the White planter class, and their allies worked to undermine and ultimately defeat the Republican government. With the Democratic Party as their electoral arm and White supremacy as a mobilizing tool, they used extra-legal violence as a major vehicle to achieve their interests. According to John Lynch, U.S. congressman and first Black Mississippi State speaker of the House, "Nearly all Democratic clubs in the state were converted into armed military companies. Funds with which to purchase arms were believed to have been contributed by the national Democratic organization."[7] Lynch also stated that the paramilitary forces, primarily former Confederate military, were "tried and experienced soldiers" and "fully armed and equipped for the work before them."[8] The development and use of White terrorist organizations to neutralize and defeat Republican and Black politicians by any means necessary was the order of the day. For the Bourbon White elite and their allies, the intimidation of the Black laborers and farmers was necessary to prevent their political involvement and to maintain their subjugated location in the economy. The White elite could not maintain its interests and position without the subordination of the Black majority. Determined Black leaders like Caldwell served as obstacles to White elite power in Mississippi and throughout the South.

During the 1875 elections, the White supremacist forces intensified their offensive to undermine and harass the Reconstruction government of Mississippi. Race riots occurred in Vicksburg, Water Valley, Louisville, Macon, Friars Point, Columbus, Rolling Fork, and Yazoo City. White supremacists initiated race riots to intimidate Black voters and disrupt Republican political campaigns. In Macon, for example, twelve Blacks were killed by White vigilantes imported from Alabama. In Vicksburg, as recently emancipated Blacks celebrated their new citizenship at a Fourth of July parade, White terrorists killed large numbers of the Black population. In Yazoo City, White supremacist violence forced the Republican sheriff to leave town and took the lives of several Blacks.[9]

Terrorist violence disrupted an election debate on September 4, 1875, in Clinton. Caldwell, running for reelection to the state Senate, was a participant in the debate, which was witnessed by more than one thousand Blacks and approximately one hundred Whites. The Democratic candidate spoke first with no incident, but after Caldwell began his speech, heckling and other disruptive behavior by Whites escalated into shooting at the predominantly Black and Republican audience, resulting in the death of four people (two Whites, two Blacks) and injury to nine others (four Whites, five Blacks). Blacks fled Clinton, seeking refuge in Jackson—a Republican stronghold—or the swamps and woods. Caldwell, along with others who retreated to Jackson, demanded that Governor Ames provide weapons so they could protect themselves.[10]

In subsequent days, the terror continued, targeting Republicans, Black and White, in Clinton, with dozens of people killed. The reign of terror spread throughout Hinds County. Without a significant response from President Ulysses Grant or the Union military to suppress the terrorist onslaught, Mississippi Republican governor Adelbert Ames mobilized citizens loyal to the state Reconstruction government to form seven companies of the state militia. Recognizing the level of genocidal violence being waged on their leadership and communities, Black people answered the call for forming a militia for defense from the White supremacist onslaught. Recently emancipated Blacks were willing to defend their liberty, lives, and newly acquired political and human rights. Caldwell, who had previously defended himself on the streets of Jackson, was one of those citizens demanding arms to protect the state government as well as the freedom and humanity of his people. Five of the companies consisted exclusively of Black men. The first militia company mobilized, Company A of the Second Regiment of Mississippi Infantry, was commanded by Caldwell, who was appointed the rank of captain.

While some Black militia members possessed military experience as Union soldiers from the U.S. Civil War, the Black militias were not as well equipped or trained as the former Confederate, pro-Democratic paramilitary forces.[11] However, they did possess the determination and will to maintain their newly won freedom. In an interview several decades later, Black Mississippi state senator and militia leader George Washington Albright remembered, "Our militia helped to fight off the Klan which was organized by the old slave owners to try and make us slaves again in all but name."[12]

On October 9, 1875, a little more than a month after the attack on the Clinton political debate and the raid on his home, Caldwell carried out a significant military campaign. The company under Caldwell's command had the responsibility of transporting "several wagon loads of weapons"[13] to another militia company composed of Black men in the town of Edwards Station (southwest of Clinton). Returning from this mission, Caldwell consolidated his forces with two other predominantly Black companies, leading three hundred soldiers (approximately two hundred armed) into Jackson. Recognizing Caldwell's determination and that a major engagement might encourage federal intervention, Democratic leaders ordered their paramilitary forces not to engage the troops under the captain's command.

While they did not defeat the Black militia on the battlefield, the Democrats were able to defeat them in the courts. One month prior to Caldwell's march through Hinds County, Democratic lawyers filed motions to prevent the state from allocating resources for the organization of state-supported militias. The state supreme court ruled in favor of the Democrats, and on October 12, 1875, three days after Caldwell and his forces initiated their march, Governor Ames demobilized the state militias. The disbanding of the predominantly Black militias significantly weakened the defense and resources available to Mississippi's Black communities ten years after the end of chattel slavery. A Reconstruction based upon democracy and radical reform was doomed to failure in the face of a White supremacist armed rebellion, insufficient federal intervention, and the decision not to provide arms to the Black majority. White supremacy would be the order of the day in Mississippi for nearly a century. Within ten weeks of the decision to disarm Black militias, Caldwell was assassinated.

During the 1870s, Black political participation was the primary motivation for White supremacist violence. Black political participation accounted for 83 percent of the recorded mob violence of the period.[14] The federal government allowed its southern adversaries back into the union through the violence, terror, and disenfranchisement of people of African descent. The U.S. government and national Republican Party proved unreliable allies as valiant men like Caldwell were assassinated, Black political officials were deposed, and the Black masses were forced into agrarian peonage.

With the Hayes-Tilden Compromise of 1877, any pretense of federal intervention in Mississippi and the former Confederacy was dropped for decades. A war was waged in the South to place emancipated Blacks, in the words of Du Bois, "back towards slavery."[15] Terrorist violence was unleashed to secure the White planter elite in power and to perpetuate a system based on White supremacy. The specter of violence remained as a means of intimidation and social control. In the decades following Reconstruction, lynching became common in the state. Between 1882 and 1940, 534 Black people were lynched in Mississippi—the highest total in the United States during that period.[16] The federal government ignored terrorism waged against Black people: "Congress and the president took no action to prevent lynching, and the federal government did not prosecute the perpetrators, even when the event was publicized at least a day in advance."[17] With White supremacist violence as a major vehicle used to intimidate and suppress, within decades Blacks were excluded from representation and participation in electoral politics and apartheid was institutionalized in civil society.

Survival: Accommodation under Apartheid

As tenancy increased and White planter hegemony and apartheid consolidated itself in Mississippi politics and civil society, Blacks responded to White domination and violence in a variety of ways. Leaving Mississippi and the South was one option to escape terror.[18] Of those who stayed in Mississippi and the South, some attempted to survive through accommodation to White domination and to build institutions without coming into direct confrontation with White power. Isaiah Montgomery—a prosperous Black farmer, entrepreneur, and founder of the Black town of Mound Bayou—proclaimed, "This is a white man's country . . . let them run it."[19] Montgomery was the lone Black delegate to the 1890 state constitutional convention; he argued that disenfranchising Blacks was a "fearful sacrifice" to maintain peace between the races. The convention would implement a literacy provision that was liberally used to disqualify potential Black voters.[20]

While Montgomery was in the minority of Mississippi's Black leadership, accommodation did characterize most of the direction of the state's Black politics in the decades between Reconstruction and the Civil Rights Movement of the 1950s and '60s. Prior to the 1940s, few leaders attempted legal challenges to disenfranchisement. Similarly, direct-action protests were not the order of the day, as the 1904 streetcar boycott was the only documented civil disobedience campaign that occurred prior to the actions organized by SNCC in the early 1960s.[21]

While Black Mississippians did not openly protest, the existence of National Association for the Advancement of Colored People (NAACP) and Universal Negro Improvement Association (UNIA) chapters is evidence that elements of the African-descendant community aspired to do more than live by accommodation under apartheid. Mary Rolinson argues that while the NAACP, from its inception in 1910 until 1920, received a significant amount of correspondence from Mississippi, the organization had difficulty organizing in Mississippi due to the fact that it had to have fifty members, who had to pay a dollar a year, in order to establish a chapter. She also argues that Klan terror disrupted the attempt to organize the NAACP in Mississippi. NAACP chapters were initiated in Vicksburg in 1918 and Mound Bayou in 1919, but floundered shortly after starting.[22]

Neil McMillen reports that in the 1920s and 1930s, every concentration of Blacks throughout the state expressed interest in the NAACP. However, by 1929, only Jackson had established a branch, which would also collapse and be reorganized twice in 1930 and 1934. In 1940, a resurgence of the organization took place, with chapters in Meridian, Vicksburg, New Albany, and Natchez, followed by a decline in NAACP state membership the following year, from 377 to 100.[23] While efforts to organize NAACP chapters in Mississippi were meager compared to those in other southern states, the continued attempts in the context of Mississippi's intense racial terror also reflect the determination of some Blacks not to completely submit to White domination. In a manner that Nan Woodruff argues is consistent with democratic, anticolonial movements globally, NAACP activity would increase in the state after World War II.[24]

In contrast, during the 1920s, fifty-six UNIA chapters were organized in Mississippi, thirty-five of them in the Delta. The contiguous Arkansas/Mississippi Delta was the "most purely pro-Garvey region in the United States."[25] In 1923, a local UNIA convention in Merigold, Mississippi, attracted fifteen hundred participants. Unlike the NAACP, the UNIA required only seven people to begin a chapter. The height of UNIA activity in the state was from 1922 to 1928. The arrest and deportation of UNIA leader Marcus Garvey and the little attention its southern base received from the national leadership and the organization's newspaper, *Negro World*, resulted in a decline in its membership in the South.[26]

Other developments occurred between the post-Reconstruction era and the 1940s that would serve to nurture the upsurge of activism during the 1950s. While this was a period when direct confrontation with White power was not common, the development of economic and social institutions as well as organizations within the Black community was essential to the activist campaigns and the armed resistance of the 1960s and 1970s. The community building and economic and social development of Black Mississippians have just as much significance to the Civil Rights Movement as the NAACP and UNIA, if not more. While not openly in contradiction to White domination, the building of churches, civic organizations, lodges, educational and financial institutions, as well as businesses during this period provided resources for the Black Freedom Struggle and for armed resistance in the later period.

Armed Resistance in the Heyday of Apartheid Terror

Collective armed resistance was not common after the defeat of Reconstruction. The Black uprising in Tunica County in 1874 and the militant armed defiance of Leflore County Black farmers in 1889 are examples of collective armed resistance in the decades after the Civil War in Missis-sippi. The armed resistance of the post-Reconstruction period does not generally manifest as intentionally organized collective action but rather as emergency self-defense, often in the form of individual acts, in response to the threat of White violence. In 1889 in Greenville, a Black man, Moses Wesson, was ordered to leave a White saloon. In response to the demand to leave, Wesson asserted his right to do business where he chose. When a White man attempted to forcibly move Wesson from the bar, the Black man shot and killed him. After his individual act of resistance, Wesson was shot and killed by the saloon owner.[27]

In June of 1920, a Simpson County Black tenant farmer, Jim Brady, questioned his account with the landlord. Whites flogged him, resulting in three Blacks and one White killed.[28] In the same year, a Hinds County farmer, Sandy Thompson, provided labor to a White planter, E. B. Hobson, in exchange for a hog. A dispute ensued when Hobson came to Thomp-son's home and demanded the pig back, citing dissatisfaction with the Black farmer's work. Thompson shot and killed his White adversary and sought refuge in the woods anticipating revenge from local Whites. Not only was Thompson captured and lynched by local Whites for his act of defiance, but his mother-in-law, Rachel Moore, was also hung by the mob in Rankin, a neighboring county.[29]

One of the most dynamic stories of Black sharecropper defiance was the case of Joe Pullen. In 1923, Pullen, a forty-year-old Black tenant farmer from the Delta town of Drew, disputed owing a fifty-dollar debt to White planter W. T. Sanders. Sanders, accompanied by another White man, J. D. Manning, came to the home of Pullen to collect the debt. Pullen defiantly responded to the White men's approach to him by sullenly talking to Sand-ers with his hands in his pockets. Considering this an act of disrespect, in the midst of the debate Sanders demanded that Pullen remove his hands from his pocket. Pullen appeared to comply, but was holding a handgun as he removed his hands from his pocket. Pullen then fired and shot the White farmer through the heart.

After shooting Sanders, Pullen retreated to his mother's home to ac-cess more weapons and ammunition. Seeking refuge in a ditch, Pullen ambushed the pursuing White mob of more than one hundred men. Pul-len killed nine Whites and wounded nine others in a seven-hour-long gun battle. Reinforcements had to come from neighboring Coahoma County, armed with a fully automatic "machine" gun, to subdue and kill Pullen. The mob tied the corpse of Pullen to a car and dragged his body to Drew to terrorize Black farmers. In the savage ritual of lynching, Pullen's ear was severed from his body and displayed in a jar. The White supremacist posse also showed off Pullen's shotgun as if it were a trophy awarded after an athletic event.[30] Some Blacks heralded Pullen's actions as heroic and exemplary. The January 19, 1924, issue of the UNIA's *Negro World* reprinted an article from the *Richmond Planet* headlined "Negro Tenant Farmer Shot to Kill and Should Have a Monument." The article hails Pullen's resistance as "one of the most remarkable fights that has ever been recorded in this southern country of ours."[31]

The attention the UNIA gave to the Joe Pullen incident was reflective of the interests that its southern membership had in defending their humanity and communities from White supremacists. Garveyites in the Deep South considered strategies to confront White terrorist violence. On August 12, 1922, during a UNIA international convention in New York, Marcus Garvey presided over a special session titled "Lynching and How to Correct It." The *Negro World* reported that the special session on August 12, 1922, reflected the beliefs of the southern convention delegates that lynching would be eliminated by meeting "force with force." Recognizing the historic strategy of White mobilization of reinforcements in neighboring states and counties to overwhelm Black resistance in the southern Black Belt, UNIA member Harry W. Kirby of Chicago insisted that a higher level of coordination and organization on the part of rural Blacks was necessary. Kirby argued,

> The characteristic of the white man was to impose on others who were unable to protect themselves. . . . When lynching is contemplated [white people] organized nearly the entire community to get one black man. The remedy . . . was better organization of Negroes through the U.N.I.A. . . . [I]f some means were devised whereby the various divisions [of the UNIA] in a certain radius could get in rapid communication with each other the moment any trouble was brooding and confront the lynchers with an organized force of blacks there would be no lynching.[32]

The fact that UNIA members were considering such tactics demonstrates that they recognized the insurgent potential of their organization in the Black-majority counties of the Deep South.

Some Garveyites articulated a strategy of global Black solidarity to fight lynching. Possibly referring to the antilynching campaign of the NAACP, S. R. Wheat, a delegate from the southern border state of Missouri, argued that lynching would be eliminated by collective armed resistance, "not by legislation." Wheat argued that if Black men could fight in Europe during World War I, "the black man in the United States and other countries . . . can by uniting himself . . . settle and do away forever with the evil of lynching, the greatest and most monstrous curse of the age."[33] Southern Garveyites envisioned Joe Pullen not fighting alone but joined by other heroic figures to smash lynching and White terror. The heroic Black man challenging and defying White domination is a historic construct of Black culture and consciousness.

Southern Folk Culture and Black Resistance

Black southern folk culture produced two gendered cultural constructs, the Bad Negro and Bruh Rabbit, which are useful in analyzing Black resistance to White violence and domination. These cultural prototypes have origins in traditional African society but were constructed in slavery and are active in contemporary Black experience and U.S. culture.[34] Reinforced by the individual and informal actions of legendary Black resisters, these cultural constructs contributed to maintaining Black insurgent consciousness in an era when accommodation was a dominant ideology in southern Black communities.

The "Bad Negro" construct is very important in Black folklore and southern culture. In White southern culture, "Bad Negroes" were those who openly defied segregationist customs and were not deferential to Whites, as was expected in White supremacist social etiquette. To White segregationist society, the behavior of "Bad Negroes" was considered "uppity," "sullen," and "dangerous" to the security of the social order. Blacks had an ambivalent response to "Bad Negroes," who were seen by some as "troublemakers" and revered and respected by others. Some lived vicariously through the actions of "Bad Negroes" who sometimes behaved and lived as some Blacks dreamed and wished they could. In Black folk culture, the "Bad Negro" is revered and depicted in an honorific manner.[35]

In the context of segregationist ethics, Blacks who possessed the resources or physical space to avoid being constantly subjected to the humiliation imposed on the majority of Black southerners were also considered "Bad Negroes." This is particularly true of Blacks who, due to their resources, could, unlike their sharecropping brothers and sisters, live an existence semi-autonomous from segregationist society. Particularly in rural areas, "Bad

Negroes" were often those who owned enough land to survive and support their households without being involved in agrarian peonage.

In 1964, there were one million acres of land owned by Mississippians of African descent. In Black-majority counties or in contiguous African-descendant communities, Black landowners and their offspring proved to be more defiant to White supremacist codes of behavior. Ed Cole, a 1960s civil rights activist who later became a state Democratic Party official, grew up in a landowning family in Black-majority Jefferson County in southwest Mississippi. Cole remembers that his father would not allow his children to work for White planters. Often privileged Blacks would restrict their offspring from working for Whites so as to protect their children from racial indignities and disrespect.[36] During the dominance of apartheid, White domination was so attached to the concept of Black servile labor that Black men could not wear a white dress shirt downtown during weekdays in Fayette, the Jefferson county seat. Wearing a white dress shirt was equated with not engaging in servile labor and was reserved for privileged Whites during the week and Blacks only on the weekend, which was the only time when Blacks had periods of leisure during daylight hours.[37] Providing an example of his father's defiance, Cole cited a time when his father confronted Whites who were hunting on his property without his permission. Cole spoke with pride about his father's stance to protect his family and the courage he displayed in a White supremacist environment.[38]

Often guns were necessary to preserve the dignity and security of landowning "Bad Negroes" facing reprisals from Whites. Oral testimonies of several Black Mississippians reveal a collective memory of the armed resistance of landowning "Bad Negroes" challenging racist Whites. SNCC activist MacArthur Cotton remembered Black landowners in his home county of Attalla cooperating to defend their community from nightriders. After the emancipation and the Civil War, Blacks began to occupy land, one-third of the county, and form contiguous communities in the hills of Attalla. Cotton remembers Black landowners setting traps to protect their communities from nightriders.[39]

In Madison, a Black-majority county in the central region of the state, C. O. Chinn was a revered "Bad Negro" of the Black community and the Freedom Struggle. Chinn acknowledged that his reputation as a "Bad" or "Crazy Negro" began with an incident that occurred when he was a teenager. Chinn was born into a family that owned 154 acres of land. Since his family was privileged, as a young man Chinn did not have to engage in labor during the week and was often observed wearing dress clothes.

In keeping with Cole's description of apartheid in Jefferson County, the thought of a young Black male not engaged in servile labor was unsettling for some Whites, many of whom believed Chinn was a bad example for other young Blacks. C. O. Chinn's mother told him that a local White planter approached her and insisted that the young man either find work during the week, preferably with a White employer, or leave the county.

Upon hearing of the White planter's demand, Chinn asked his mother, "Mama, do you owe this man any money?" After learning that neither she nor the family owed the White planter anything, he asked his elder permission to resolve the problem. According to Chinn, he went to the White farmer's plantation and surprised him with a .38 handgun and politely warned him to stay out of the Chinn family's business. Chinn stated that this incident won him the reputation of being a "Crazy Nigga," thereby arousing the fear of local Whites and the admiration of local Blacks.[40] As an adult, Mr. Chinn would become one of the most revered activists in the Mississippi Civil Rights Movement.

Ms. Annie Colton (Reeves)[41] grew up during the Depression years in the Algiers community of Pike County, in the southern part of the state. Her parents owned several firearms, including a Winchester rifle, a .22 rifle, a shotgun, and two handguns. Her father would say, "It's better to have ammunition than have food." She and her siblings, two brothers and four sisters, were all taught by their father to use firearms. It was important to the Colton patriarch that his daughters become proficient in the use of weapons to protect themselves from White rapists. According to Annie Colton, her family was known in their community for being a defiant family that stood up to "White folks."[42]

Defiant Blacks in the vein of Joe Pullen were acknowledged as "Bad Negroes" solely due to their exceptional acts of armed resistance. One of the most extraordinary examples of this type of "Bad Negro" is the case of Eddie Noel in Holmes County. Holmes was a Black-majority county in the southeastern part of the Delta in the central region of the state. In January of 1954, Eddie Noel, a 28-year-old Black man, shot and killed the son of a White store owner as a result of a dispute in Ebenezer, near the county seat of Lexington. Noel was ordered by the owner to leave his store. After Noel left the store he noticed the owner and his son approaching the porch; believing they were coming to shoot him, Noel shot and killed the store owner's son, thirty-year-old Willie Dickard.[43]

Noel was a U.S. Army veteran and a sharpshooter. Local lore suggests that the army veteran had a reputation for shooting matches and cigarettes

out of his wife's mouth without harming her. Newspaper accounts and local oral history seem to differ on what occurred after he killed the store
owner. Newspapers, generally based on sheriff's reports, asserted that
when Whites attempted to apprehend Noel, the Black sharpshooter killed
two more Whites, including a deputy sheriff, John Malone, and wounded
two others in separate shootouts. The "official" newspaper account said
that after three weeks surviving in the woods, Noel turned himself in after
being pursued by a posse that included the county sheriff, the state Highway Patrol, and over one hundred "volunteers." While Noel was a fugitive,
terror gripped the county's Whites. White Holmes County journalist Hazel Brannon Smith remembered,

> It was bedlam. Nurses and other female employees, many of whom lived
> in the area between the hospital and the manhunt area, were afraid to go
> home, even in daylight. Their families were worried and frightened. A
> floor of the hospital was made comfortable for the women who did not
> want to leave.[44]

Black oral accounts claim that Noel out-dueled and scattered a posse
of Whites organized to kill him. In this version of the incident, the White
posse worked in coordination with five hundred members of the National
Guard, supported by the Highway Patrol, and the FBI with surveillance
airplanes, all participating in a manhunt attempting to capture and murder Noel in his refuge in the woods. Using search and destroy tactics, the
White posse harassed Holmes County Blacks, believing they were providing assistance to Noel.

Fearing his survival was becoming an embarrassment, state officials offered a deal to Noel if he would turn himself in to authorities. After surren-
dering, Noel would receive protection and be taken from Holmes County
to Jackson to ensure a fair trial. Noel accepted the offer. Both accounts
agreed that Noel was declared unfit to serve trial due to mental illness and
sentenced to the state mental hospital in Jackson.[45] Reflecting the pride of
Black folks in "Bad Negroes," Holmes County activist T. C. Johnson reflected on the impact of Noel on Holmes County Blacks:

> It did give some of the black peoples the idea that they didn't have to take
> the beatin' and runnin' and that abusement like they had been. I've heard
> a lot of 'em say it was good that somebody had the courage and the nerve
> to stand tall like a man than be treated like an animal.[46]

Johnson's statement implies that "Bad Negroes" served as inspirations for the developing Civil Rights Movement. The actions of "Bad Negroes" served as examples of courage necessary for activism in the Struggle.

While Black resistance was often recognized and honored in the form of defiant "Bad Negroes," insurgent actions and consciousness were often not visible and public but covert. "Bad Negroes" like Joe Pullen and Eddie Noel were exceptional. In southern Black folklore, whether they be animal characters like Bruh Rabbit or personages like High John the Conqueror, Black folk tricksters used deception and manipulation to overwhelm powerful foes. Like such tricksters of Black folklore, most Black folks feigned deference while maintaining an oppositional consciousness, quietly rejecting the assumptions of White supremacy. It was more common for Blacks to show disdain for segregation and White people in general in the privacy of their own communities, hidden from the eyes of White society. Based upon his experiences growing up in apartheid Mississippi, the prolific Black novelist Richard Wright described this phenomenon:

> The white South said it knew "niggers." . . . Well, the white South had never known me—never known what I thought, what I felt. The white South said that I had a place in life. Well . . . my deepest instincts had always made me reject the "place" to which the white South had assigned me. It had never occurred to me that I was in any way an inferior being. And no word that I have ever heard fall from the lips of southern white men ever made me doubt the worth of my humanity.[47]

The majority of southern Blacks generally maintained two selves: one persona for White society and another within their own world. Historian Neil McMillen described the dual consciousness and behavior of the apartheid-era Mississippi Blacks as "an accommodative demeanor [that] often masked a resentful spirit."[48]

Some actualized their oppositional consciousness in the form of clandestine oppositional action. In the South, where Blacks lived under White supremacist terror, Black freedom activities were often concealed from White people. Mary Rolinson argues that the UNIA military, the African Legion, possessed a more clandestine character in the rural South than did its urban and northern counterparts.[49] The thought of Blacks openly organizing defensive violence could not be tolerated in a system of White domination.

Along with the church, much of the organizational life of the African-descendant community took place through secretive fraternal organizations.

Fraternal organizations provided a means of group solidarity and cohesiveness in southern Black communities. Fraternal orders provided resources (such as leadership development, cooperative financing, meeting places, and access to membership) for Black freedom and other social justice organizing in the South, including the NAACP, the UNIA, and sharecropper unions.[50]

Due to their sense of solidarity and clandestine practices, lodges also provided local, regional, and national networks and relationships, which could be useful in escaping lynch mobs and law enforcement as well as in organizing self-defense.[51]

Like the folkloric trickster, the Black Freedom Struggle utilized "sleight of hand" to evade the power of their adversary—White terrorism. To fight segregation, rather than engage in direct confrontation or acquiescence, some Black southerners chose to "hit a straight lick with a crooked stick"—a New World African proverb meaning to utilize deception to meet your objectives. Unable to rely upon law enforcement and the courts, Black southerners were forced to develop clandestine networks for protection and survival.

Black oral tradition and journalistic accounts speak of an underground railroad or "Negro underground," which helped Blacks evade southern lynch mobs and secure safe passage outside of "Jim Crow" territory.[52] In 1958, Black journalist Arrington High arrived in Chicago claiming he had escaped from the Mississippi state mental hospital with the assistance of the "Negro underground." According to High, he had been confined in the state mental hospital for his public advocacy of school integration and his exposure, in his newspaper, the *Eagle Eye*, of segregationist White male sexual trysts with Black women. High escaped the state institution and was transported out of Mississippi concealed in a casket.[53] Utilizing secrecy and deception was necessary to ensure the success of an underground network.

Those Black Mississippians who decided to stay and live in Mississippi had to endure the terror of apartheid. From Reconstruction until after World War II, the global, national, regional, and local political landscape did not provide the opportunity to overcome White supremacy and segregation. While the end of Reconstruction represented a significant defeat of the Black Freedom Struggle, there was still hope. Blacks' preparations through community and institution building as well as their maintenance of a culture of resistance would serve as the foundations of a movement in the next period.

2

"I'm Here, Not Backing Up"

Emergence of Grassroots Militancy and Armed Self-Defense in the 1950s

"Bad Negroes" spoke loudly and defiantly in Mound Bayou at a massive camp meeting in April of 1955. The accommodationist Booker T. Washington had dedicated this town fifty years previously, but resistance, not accommodation, was preached at the gathering. Thirteen thousand Black people from the Delta assembled to participate in the mass rally. This massive camp meeting was organized by Dr. T. R. M. Howard and the Regional Council for Negro Leadership (RCNL). Advocating voting, civil, and other human rights, the rally also encouraged Blacks to persevere and overcome fear and intimidation.

The spirit exhibited by the RCNL mass meeting was truly a break with the strategy of accommodation. The defiant tone of the rally represented what Ebony magazine described as "The New Fighting South": "Today in Dixie there is emerging a new militant Negro. He is a fearless, fighting man who openly campaigns for his civil rights, who refuses to migrate to the North, in search of justice and dignity, and is determined to stay in his own backyard and fight."[1]

Something new was happening in Mississippi. Although White terror was still formidable, Black people were willing to rally in the thousands for their freedom and human rights. Accommodationist Black leadership still had significant control over Black institutions, but they were being challenged by new, assertive activists who attracted and articulated the aspirations of a growing constituency. Black leaders emerged to demand the rights of citizenship and to express the grievances of the Black masses. What was occurring in Mississippi was connected to the struggles of people of color throughout the world.

The decades following World War II represented a crisis for Western imperialism. Combined with the realignment of the international balance of power, new social forces among colonized and subject peoples asserted themselves. Internationally militant voices emerged from the intellectual and professional sectors of oppressed nations. The end of World War II ushered in an upsurge in nationalist movements among oppressed people across the globe, particularly in Africa and Asia. The Black Freedom Struggle in Mississippi, and the rest of the South, was part of an international movement to dismantle racialism, colonial rule, and apartheid as well as to achieve democracy for oppressed people. Like anticolonial leaders in Africa and Asia, African descendants in the United States emerged and demanded human rights for their communities living under apartheid. The rise of the activist leadership from the Mississippi Black professional class is a consequence of the segregated economy. In the 1950s, Black professionals—including doctors, members of the clergy, and entrepreneurs—serving an almost exclusively Black clientele became Movement spokespersons and organizers.

Like colonized troops returning to subject African and Asian nations following World War II, U.S. soldiers of color returned to U.S. apartheid from Europe and Asia. (Later they would return from the Korean conflict.) Mississippi activist Amzie Moore was a World War II army veteran when the U.S. armed forces were still segregated. Moore stated that Black U.S. soldiers involved in the conflict wondered "why are we fighting? Why were we there? If we were fighting four [sic] freedoms that Roosevelt and Churchill had talked about."[2] Moore returned to the Mississippi Delta, where some Whites had mobilized to protect their communities from Black G.I.s.

Human rights activists in Mississippi did not miss the opportunity to point out the contradiction of U.S. troops of African descent fighting for "freedom" abroad while they and their communities remained oppressed in the southern apartheid states. Mississippi activist T. R. M. Howard asserted that "Black soldiers from Mississippi are fighting and dying for a democracy that they don't know one single thing about back home on the plantations of the Mississippi Delta."[3]

Another factor in global politics contributed to challenging the apartheid system in Mississippi and the South. The accelerating conflict and competition between the United States and other Western capitalist regimes, the Soviet Union, as well as other socialist countries affected U.S. domestic politics. Quick to expose the contradictions of its adversaries, the "Cold War" utilized propaganda to achieve an advantage in the global chess game between capitalism and communism. In this context, racial oppression was an obvious liability in the United States, gaining leverage in the propaganda war. Historian Mary Duriak argued,

> At a time when the United States hoped to reshape the postwar world in
> its own image, the international attention given to racial segregation was

troublesome and embarrassing. . . . The need to address international criticism gave the federal government an incentive to promote social change at home.[4]

The necessity of achieving an advantage over socialist competitors and re-inforcing its image as a democratic state motivated the United States to pay attention to the civil rights of the oppressed Black population in the South.

In concert with the international situation, changes in the domestic political environment signaled new possibilities for Black Mississippians and encouraged a new assertiveness in the face of White terror and domination. After decades of virtually ignoring racial oppression in the South, the federal government began to initiate a gradual policy shift. Federal courts began to challenge elements of White domination in the South. In 1944, the U.S. Supreme Court outlawed the Mississippi White primary in the case of *Smith v. Allwright*. The White-only primary was a key pillar of White political power—and an important way of denying the franchise to Black Mississippians. The Court's decision in *Smith v. Allwright* set the stage for challenges to racial voting restrictions in the state.

White resistance mounted, as White supremacists would not acquiesce to gradual desegregation by federal officials. In the 1946 elections, the first statewide poll since *Smith v. Allwright,* White supremacists, including U.S. senator Theodore Bilbo, mobilized to prevent Black political participation. Law enforcement officials and vigilantes physically attacked Blacks attempting to register as well as the small number of registered Blacks who attempted to vote in the 1946 election. Nearly two hundred Blacks testified at a U.S. Senate committee hearing about the White supremacist "reign of terror" during the 1946 elections.[5]

The internal social development of local Black communities, combined with the changes in international and domestic political environments, allowed for a visible Black Freedom Struggle in the state. The development of institutions, organizations, and resources in Black communities were significant factors supporting the emergence of an insurgent movement. NAACP activity in the state was affected by the political environment that existed in the decade of the 1940s. The organization possessed only one hundred members in 1940. By 1949, NAACP membership increased to one thousand.[6] Black voter registration also increased from two thousand to twenty thousand between 1940 and 1949. However, the number of Black voter registrants must be put in context: half a million potential Black voters resided in the state of Mississippi.[7]

Although White domination and racial violence was still commonplace, Black efficacy increased. The development of the Regional Council of Negro Leadership (RCNL) in the Mississippi Delta was the cornerstone of the surfacing Black Freedom Struggle in the early 1950s. The appearance of a militant, public leadership of the Mississippi Freedom Movement meant that it was necessary to protect the organizers and spokespersons of the Movement if it was to survive.

From Accommodation to Activism

Dr. T. R. M. Howard was the charismatic leader of the RCNL. A native Kentuckian, the Black physician moved to the Black town of Mound Bayou in 1942. Mound Bayou was founded in 1887 by Isaiah Montgomery, the accommodationist Black leader. Howard came to the Delta town to serve as the surgeon for the Taborian Hospital, a medical institution founded by a Black mutual aid and secret society, the Knights and Daughters of Tabor. The Taborian Hospital served the Black Delta population; it is an example of efforts by Black secret orders to use cooperative economics to develop viable financial, economic, and social institutions for Black communities in the apartheid southern United States.[8]

Dr. Howard became one of the wealthiest Blacks in Mississippi. Across the highway from the Taborian Hospital, Howard established his own clinic. The Mound Bayou physician owned a construction firm, a farm, and an insurance company in addition to his medical practice. A "race man" and an advocate of Black self-help and economic development, Howard built a park, a zoo, and the first swimming pool for Black Mississippians. Howard's efforts certainly contributed to the vision and hope of Black Mississippians by developing a Black oasis in the Delta.

For many moderate Whites, Howard and the self-help efforts in Mound Bayou represented racial progress. Southern liberal journalist Hodding Carter described Howard's endeavors as a "one man uplift movement" in a 1946 article titled "He's Doing Something about the Race Problem." Howard's demeanor in the article does not suggest the posture of a confrontational, activist agitator but rather that of a racial pragmatist. In the Carter article, Howard stated,

> I don't spend much time worrying about racial problems or tensions, because I'm too busy trying to do something about them. Not much

speechmaking, but doing things. . . . And I think the Negro who is fortunate enough to be able to do something about the animosity should do
it . . . instead of putting all the blame on the white men.[9]

Carter's portrayal of Howard acknowledges the Black physician's desire to
bring progress for his fellows of African descent. However, according to
Carter's portrayal, Howard did not believe in a militant challenge to Mississippi's version of apartheid.

Howard and Perry Smith, leader of the Knights of Tabor, became embroiled in a factional dispute inside the society in 1946. Howard was
charged with being "power hungry" and attempting to enrich himself at
the expense of his patients. Smith was accused of being autocratic and
elitist and engaging in nepotism. After a contentious election, Smith re-
gained control of the organization and Howard, his allies, and his supporters founded a new fraternal organization, the United Order of Friendship
(UOF), in 1947. The UOF opened the Friendship Clinic in Mound Bayou
in 1948.[10]

At the 1951 UOF convention, the Regional Council of Negro Leadership was founded. The initial political posture of RCNL was neither radical
nor confrontational. During the founding of the RCNL, Howard remained
consistent with his seemingly accommodationist public image. He called
for cooperation with the White power structure, not confrontation or
resistance to it. In the published prospectus of the organization, Howard
stated, "All I ask is that we be consulted on matters that affect members of
our race. We are not organizing to work against our white citizens . . . but
to work with them."[11]

The RCNL's accommodationist public stance would soon fade as the
organization began to organize voter registration campaigns, call for equity
in Black public educational resources, challenge police brutality, and boycott gas stations that did not provide restrooms to Blacks. The "Don't Buy
Gas Where You Can't Use the Restroom" campaign demanded not integration but use of facilities, even if separate, by Black patrons.[12]

The RCNL began to attract brilliant young Black professionals; many
of them were NAACP members from the Delta, propelled into leadership
and activism. Clarksdale pharmacist Aaron Henry, Cleveland entrepreneur and postal worker Amzie Moore, Belzoni minister and businessman
George Lee, and Medgar Evers, a college-educated insurance agent, all
joined and become officers in the new organization. Most of the RCNL
and new NAACP leaders were professionals and entrepreneurs serving

Black people in the segregated economy. Activist Charles Evers stated that the RCNL and state and local NAACP leadership were "mostly independent people who had their own businesses. We couldn't afford to work for White folks. They'd fire us."[13]

Those dependent on Whites for employment could not represent or be associated with the RCNL or NAACP without fearing reprisal. Henry, Moore, and both Everses were also World War II veterans. After fighting for "democracy" abroad, they were determined to have it in Mississippi. The new militancy and optimism invigorated the Black Freedom Struggle. With independent farmers, professionals, entrepreneurs, and World War II veterans taking the lead, the RCNL and the NAACP began to function openly and to coordinate statewide efforts for voting rights and desegregation.

The popularity of the RCNL swelled among Delta Blacks. The primary evidence of RCNL's popularity was the organization's annual tent meeting and rally in Mound Bayou. The first RCNL rally took place in 1952, with U.S. representative William Dawson of Chicago as the keynote speaker and an appearance by gospel singer Mahalia Jackson. More than seven thousand Delta Blacks arrived in Mound Bayou to attend the event. A similar number attended the next year to hear Black Chicago jurist and politician Archibald Carey at the 1953 rally. In 1954, ten thousand Black Mississippians came to hear NAACP attorney Thurgood Marshall. Thirteen thousand assembled in Mound Bayou to hear U.S. congressman Charles Diggs from Detroit. The annual RCNL tent meeting was a combination of political rally and cultural festival. One Black journalist described the RCNL rally as "a show all by itself" with "barbecue and soda pop, high school and college choruses and bands . . . and the speeches."[14]

The RCNL also utilized the large gatherings to raise funds. The organization reportedly raised three thousand dollars at its 1955 mass meeting. The *Pittsburg Courier* reported that concessions at the event sold "three hundred tons of barbecue, hundreds of chickens, 500 cases of soft drinks and 800 gallons of ice cream." Howard also served free "barbecued ribs and chicken" to "hundreds" of Delta Blacks who attended the event.[15]

In addition to the growth of the crowds, the militant posture of the RCNL also increased over the years, which is evidenced by the 1955 Mound Bayou rally. One speaker, the militant minister George W. Lee from the Delta town Belzoni, told the audience, "Pray not for your mom and pop. . . . They've gone to heaven. Pray that you can make it through this hell."[16]

The RCNL encouraged the desires of Mississippi Blacks to achieve the political franchise and, ultimately, political power and participation. Over six decades since the state's Blacks had been successfully disenfranchised with the endorsement of the founder of Mound Bayou, Lee challenged the audience to visualize elected Black representation. Reverend Lee exhorted, "Do you believe you can elect a Negro?" Recognizing Black voting potential in the Mississippi Delta, Lee predicted, that "someday the Delta would send a Negro to Congress."[17]

The RCNL invited U.S. representative Charles Diggs of Detroit to address the rally. A state with dozens of Black-majority counties had not produced a Black representative to U.S. Congress since John Lynch in 1883. Diggs spoke militantly to the forces of White domination, stating, "Time is running out in Mississippi. It is two minutes to midnight."[18] When Amzie Moore passed out instructions for voting, he was mobbed by dozens in the audience desiring the material.[19]

T. R. M. Howard's demeanor at the rally could be interpreted as significantly different from his accommodationist statement in the 1946 *Saturday Evening Post* article. Howard's powerful and charismatic oratory could not be confused as conciliatory. Howard jokingly told the rally that the deceased segregationist Senator Theodore Bilbo was now in hell and had "sent a direct message to the capital at Jackson asking them to stop treating the Negroes so badly in Mississippi and to give them a break, because they have a Negro fireman down there that keeps the fire mighty hot."[20]

White supremacists intensified their economic harassment of Black activists in response to the increased Black activism and the 1954 U.S. Supreme Court's decision in the case of *Brown v. Board of Education.* The White Citizens' Council was founded in 1954 to coordinate economic harassment. The RCNL and the NAACP, however, would not be intimidated by economic pressure placed on them by the state's White power structure. In response to the White supremacist financial campaign, a national effort was initiated to establish a fund to support targeted Black activists.[21] Dr. Howard bragged, "We are definitely whipping the economic freeze." At the same time, the Black leader warned, "When it develops as a real flop, the next round will be violence."[22]

Violent Terror Attacks Emergent Movement

Howard's warning was not without precedent. Dr. Emmett Stringer, president of the state Conference of Branches NAACP, who was by this time a target of economic intimidation, experienced escalating threats of violence after the U.S. Supreme Court's decision in *Brown*. Stringer, who practiced dentistry in the east Mississippi city of Columbus, was a focus of pressure applied by state and local White racists coordinated through the White Citizens' Council. Stringer's spouse, Flora, a teacher in a Columbus public school, was fired. The Stringers also experienced physical threats, as well as threatening phone calls and letters. In response, Stringer began carrying weapons in his daily travel and was armed at home as well as in his office.[23]

A list of nine key NAACP, RCNL, and other Mississippi activists was published as a full-page ad in a Delta newspaper. This list was distributed at Citizens' Council meetings throughout the state. The list included Stringer, George Lee, T. R. M. Howard, and Medgar Evers. The Citizens' Council coordinated the financial harassment of those on the list, which included denying credit and mortgage renewals and demanding that debt from an existing loan be immediately paid. Violent terror, including assassination, led forces of the Black Freedom Struggle to believe that the Citizens' Council list was a White terrorist "death list."[24]

RCNL vice president and local NAACP leader Reverend George Lee was ambushed and murdered in the streets of Belzoni on May 7, 1955, two weeks after Howard's warning at the 1955 RCNL mass rally. Acknowledged as "the most militant Negro minister in Mississippi," Lee was the first Black to qualify to vote since Reconstruction. Belzoni was the seat of the Black-majority Humphreys County. The Belzoni clergyman was planning to vote in the upcoming Democratic primary. Lee received threats from local Whites after he refused to persuade thirty recently registered Humphreys County Blacks to remove their names from the voting registration rolls. Two thousand mourners attended the three-and-a-half-hour funeral for Lee at Belzoni's Green Grove Church.[25] At the funeral, Howard declared, "We are not afraid. We are not fearful. . . . Some of the rest of us here may join him, but we will join him as courageous warriors and not as cringing cowards."[26]

U.S. representative Charles Diggs, the national leadership of the NAACP, and the American Civil Liberties Union all demanded a federal investigation of the murder of Lee. Humphreys County sheriff Ike Shelton proclaimed that Lee's killing was a "freak accident." Movement activists and the Lee family felt the U.S. Justice Department and local authorities never really attempted to find the assassins of the charismatic minister.[27]

Another Belzoni activist would be attacked by White supremacists months later. Belzoni NAACP leader, entrepreneur, and grocer Gus Courts was warned after the murder of Lee that he would be "next on the list to go." Courts was distinguished from his peers by organizing a contingent of Humphreys County Blacks to pay their poll taxes and register to vote in 1953. After being harassed by the Humphreys County Citizens' Council, Courts appealed to the state government for protection. Instead of receiving protection, Courts was confronted in his store by a local Citizens' Council member who possessed a copy of his letter appealing for protection.[28]

After the November 1955 elections, Courts was shot in his store. Friends took the wounded Courts two counties away to the hospital in Mound Bayou, due to concerns about the care Lee received in the Belzoni hospital after his assault. Courts recovered from the attack in Mound Bayou. Following advice from Medgar Evers, Courts decided to leave the state. Escorted by an armed Evers, Courts fled the Delta to Jackson. After stints in Texas and California, Courts and his family would eventually move to Chicago. An FBI investigation of the Courts shooting ended with no arrests.[29] In Chicago, Courts was clearly a political exile of Mississippi apartheid. During a 1968 interview, Courts reflected,

> I had to leave my $15,000 a year grocery business, my trucking business and my home and everything—my wife and I—thousands of us Mississippians had to run away. We had to flee in the night. We are American refugees from the terror in the South all because we wanted to vote.[30]

The inability or unwillingness of the federal and state governments to find the terrorists who murdered Lee or shot Courts demonstrated that Mississippi freedom fighters would have to rely on their own resources for protection. Notwithstanding the executive and judicial efforts toward gradual desegregation, some realized that the federal government could not be depended on for the survival of the Mississippi Black Freedom Struggle.

T. R. M. Howard and Armed Protection

Howard had previously instituted precautions due to the increased level of violence. As his profile and militant activism increased, so did his willingness to practice armed self-defense. Howard's friends and associates knew he was willing to protect himself. Howard was known to have an "a cache of rifles and pistols" in his home, which included a Thompson submachine gun. One visitor to the Howard residence had difficulty bringing a suitcase into a room due to the "small arsenal" that was blocking the door. The Mound Bayou doctor wore a "pistol strapped to his waist."[31] Howard associate and journalist Robert Ratcliffe said, "He was looking for gunmen to fire into his home. 'When they come,' he once said, 'I'll be ready for them.'"[32]

In addition to having guns to protect his home, Howard traveled the highways of Mississippi armed. One could only carry handguns with a highway "special permit," which Blacks were generally denied. Charles Evers described this policy as "gun control only for Blacks."[33] Blacks were randomly stopped and searched on Mississippi highways by state patrolmen. Howard was also often searched but had a secret hiding place for his handgun and was never caught. Howard commonly rode with his handgun "cocked" on his lap.[34] It was common for rural Mississippians to travel with rifles in public view in their vehicles; Howard was not an exception to this custom. Memphis activist attorney Ben Hooks remembered, "[M]any times he had high powered rifles in his car; three, four, five, big huge rifles."[35]

In addition to concealing his handgun, Howard would use deception in other ways to protect himself on the highways. He would often travel to his destination via circuitous routes, including traveling through Louisiana from Mound Bayou to get to another Mississippi location. He believed traveling out of state was less dangerous than traveling in Mississippi. On one occasion, Howard rode in a hearse to conceal himself from potential attackers.[36]

Howard also hired bodyguards to protect himself and his family. He had round-the-clock armed protection of his home, an armed chauffeur, and security at his clinic. Even Blacks who approached the activist doctor were often searched by his security people for weapons. Journalist Simeon Booker described Howard's security as "a model of dispatch and efficiency."[37]

RCNL members and supporters were also willing to participate in the protection of Howard. On one occasion, when he was warned that a White mob was preparing to attack his home, Howard received a call from a Mound Bayou Black farmer. "Don't worry about a thing, Doc. Me and a gang of fellows will surround your house tonight and we all have guns."[38] A rumor that White terrorists had assaulted Howard's wife, Helen, resulted in a rapid response of fifteen vehicles filled with armed Blacks.[39]

The Emmett Till Case and Armed Security

The Emmett Till case created an increased need for protection in the Black Freedom Struggle. Emmett Till was a fourteen-year-old Black Chicago resident visiting family in Mississippi in the summer of 1955. On August 28th, at approximately 12:30 a.m., two Delta White men, Roy Bryant and J. W. Milam, kidnapped Till for the purpose of punishing the young man for allegedly whistling at Bryant's wife. Till's body—he had been lynched—was found in the Tallahatchie River, three days after being taken from his uncle's home.[40]

After Till's body was found, NAACP southern regional director Ruby Hurley, Medgar Evers, and Amzie Moore combed the Delta as part of an investigation. The three activists disguised themselves as sharecroppers, all wearing overalls and "beat up shoes," with Hurley wearing a red bandanna. Moore borrowed a car with registration and license plates from a Delta town.[41] Armed security was organized to protect the three activists. "Protection was there for me all the way," Hurley stated. "There were men around with shotguns standing in various spots to be sure that I got where I was going and got back," she added.[42] T. R. M. Howard also participated in the effort to find evidence and witnesses in the Till case. Delta Blacks contacted Howard with information concerning the lynching of Till. Howard utilized his resources to locate and provide refuge and protection for witnesses in the hostile environment.[43]

Howard also played a role in the case by providing logistical support, security, and housing for people connected to the case, including Till's mother, Mamie Till-Mobley. Traveling to the Delta to attend the trial, Mobley received support from the clandestine network of the Freedom Struggle. She was escorted to a series of "safe houses" rather than taken directly from Memphis to Mound Bayou. She flew from Chicago to Memphis, where she was housed by a local Black doctor. From Memphis, she was transported to Clarksdale, Mississippi. In Clarksdale, Bishop Louis Henry Ford, a Chicago clergyman with Mississippi Delta roots, facilitated shelter and protection for Mobley. From Clarksdale, Till-Mobley was taken to Howard's residence in Mound Bayou.[44]

Howard's home was described as a "Black command center" and "haven" during the travel. The prosperous Black activist offered protection, shelter, and hospitality for Mobley as well as Black dignitaries and journalists attending the trial, including congressman Charles Diggs. Legal and political "strategy sessions" took place each evening during trial, and included Mobley, Diggs, and Ruby Hurley, as well as Mississippi activists Howard, Medgar Evers, Amzie Moore, and Aaron Henry.[45]

Special security measures were taken to protect Howard's guests. Approaching the Howard residence, one visitor noted that "[y]ou had to go through a checkpoint to get to Howard."[46] Delta Movement supporters and RCNL leaders hired bodyguards who provided security for Howard, his family, and his guests. Mobley observed, "The people in Mound Bayou didn't tolerate any invasion of any kind. If you were there, you had to state your business. And if they didn't agree with your reasons for being there, you were asked to leave and that would be enforced."[47]

Mobley wished to attend the trial in Sumner, Mississippi, riding in Howard's convertible Cadillac. For her safety, she was instructed to travel in another car, which Howard told her was "bulletproof" and not as identifiable as his Cadillac. Flowers were placed in the back of the vehicle escorting Mobley and others, who required special security, so observers could not see who was riding in the car.[48]

The efforts of Mobley, the RCNL, the NAACP, and other activists and supporters to achieve justice through convictions of the murderers of Till were not successful. The trial lasted five days, from September 19th to the 23rd. An all-White jury acquitted Milam and Bryant after a 67-minute deliberation. The acquittals were considered a victory for White supremacists but evoked cries of outrage throughout the United States and internationally. Howard continued to campaign for justice through a national speaking tour highlighting the Till case and other examples of White terror.[49]

Howard decided to move his family out of Mississippi in December 1955. Escalating harassment and threats of violence against the RCNL leader motivated the move.[50] Despite his being well-armed and protected, the tension of living in such a hostile environment became too much for his family. One reporter suggested that the Howard household was paying an emotional price for its participation. Visiting the Howard home during the Till trial, Robert Ratcliffe of the *Pittsburg Courier* observed, "Mrs. Howard was worried. Fear was etched all over her pretty face. 'It's awful down here,' she said. 'I don't know what is going to happen.'... One could see Mrs. Howard, a native of California, was concerned about her two children, her husband, and herself."[51] Howard continued to aid the Mississippi Movement from exile in Chicago. He returned to the South in 1958 to assist in the escape of militant journalist Arrington High from the state mental hospital (see chapter 1). According High, Howard initiated plans with leaders of the "Negro 'underground'" who facilitated High's escape. He also criticized the FBI for its failure to properly investigate White supremacist violence in Mississippi.[52]

During his national speaking tour, Howard pressed for a federal intervention to prevent the escalation of violence in Mississippi. On a national speaking tour in October 1955, Howard told a Pittsburg audience,

[I]t is practically impossible for a Negro to get justice where races are involved . . . [U]nless the Federal Government can be made to realize how
extremely serious the situation is in Mississippi . . . with tension mount-
ing by the moment in the hearts of both Negroes and Whites . . . there is
going to be an outbreak of violence in Mississippi which will shock the
imagination of the American people and the entire civilized world.

Howard warned, "The Negro fear in my state today is a rather dangerous
fear complex because he feels now that there is absolutely no justice he can
expect at the hand of whites. He is going to have to be the one to see that
he gets justice."[53]

Medgar Evers Emerges

After the exile of T. R. M. Howard, Medgar Evers emerged as the most visible freedom activist in the state. Evers was born in Decatur, Mississippi, in
1925. World War II began during his sophomore year at Newton County
High School. The next year, he decided to leave high school—at age seventeen—and enlist in the U.S. Army, along with his older brother, Charles.
The Evers brothers fought in Europe during World War II and were dis-
charged in 1945. Medgar returned to Decatur and found employment.

The year following his discharge, an incident revealed his future as a freedom fighter. With the 1944 U.S. Supreme Court decision undermining the
all-White primary, Medgar and Charles decided to register to vote in Decatur.
The Evers brothers organized four other Black World War II veterans from
Decatur to vote during the 1946 primary. Word traveled throughout Decatur
that the men planned to register and vote. White supremacists threatened
the six Blacks. On the day of the primary, the six Black veterans were met at
the courthouse by a group of "some fifteen or twenty armed white men" who
prevented them from entering the building. The White supremacist group
grew in number to a mob of two hundred. The Black veterans retreated to
their homes to arm themselves and returned to the courthouse with their
guns in their vehicles. The veterans again attempted to enter the courthouse
and were prevented by the mob. To prevent a blood bath the veterans decided not to pursue registering on that day. The mob followed the men, but
according to one account, Charles Evers brandished his weapon to slow the
Whites' pursuit. That evening Medgar and Charles Evers stood guard at their
parents' home waiting for nightriders, who never came.[54]

After the incident at the Newton County courthouse, Evers decided to finish high school at an experimental secondary program at Alcorn A&M (a state-funded, historically Black college), where his brother Charles was enrolled. After he completed the Alcorn secondary program, Evers enrolled in the undergraduate school in 1948. At Alcorn A&M, he met Myrlie Beasley, whom he married in December 1951. After graduating from Alcorn in 1952, Medgar and Myrlie moved to the all-Black Delta town of Mound Bayou. In Mound Bayou, Evers became an RCNL and NAACP activist.

The college-educated Medgar and Myrlie Evers became employees of T. R. M. Howard's Magnolia Mutual Insurance Company. His work as an insurance agent and salesman prepared Evers for the grassroots organizing he was to do when building the NAACP chapters throughout the state. Traveling throughout the Delta, Evers witnessed and studied Black life in the Delta. The poverty, hunger, hopelessness, and squalor horrified Evers. Through his employment with Magnolia Mutual, Evers began to blend selling insurance with recruiting members and organizing chapters for the NAACP. Evers became a principal organizer of the RCNL's "Don't Buy Gas Where You Can't Use the Restroom" campaign.[55]

Evers first received statewide and national attention when he applied to the University of Mississippi ("Ole Miss") Law School in 1954 as part of an NAACP legal challenge to segregated education. His decision was motivated by a passionate speech by NAACP state leader Dr. Emmett Stringer. Evers also believed that the Civil Rights Movement needed more Black attorneys committed to justice. NAACP attorney Thurgood Marshall also encouraged Evers to apply.[56]

Evers became the target of threats of violence and harassment due to his decision to apply to "Ole Miss." The university denied his application, claiming his recommendations came from Bolivar County as opposed to the county of his birth, Newton. This denial led to Evers becoming the principal plaintiff in litigation to desegregate the "Ole Miss" law school. Ultimately, the NAACP decided not to pursue the suit because they had another task that would occupy a great amount of his time.[57]

A primary focus of the development of the Citizens' Council and White supremacist violence of 1954–55 was to undermine the momentum created by the RCNL and NAACP in Mississippi. The economic harassment and terror was directed at the emerging Movement to force it underground or out of existence.[58] In October of 1954, the NAACP national leadership made an assessment of the development of its organization in the state:

The leadership in the state conference is aggressive and intelligent. The leadership at the local level, however, is typical of NAACP leadership in small towns and cities, in addition, [it] faces the problem of threats of violence which has made it difficult for the Association to function without continued direction and supervision.[59]

The organization decided to make maintaining and building its presence in Mississippi a priority. This would mean committing resources to employ staff members in the state and maintaining a visible presence in spite of its economic harassment and intimidation by the White Citizens' Council and the violent terror of White supremacists.

In December of 1954, the NAACP director of branches announced the hiring of a field secretary and the establishment of a full-time office. The motivation for committing these resources was as follows:

With the threatened violence, acts of intimidation, economic boycotts, and the other activities on the part of those who oppose the desegregation program, it is essential that the Association, through this office, convey to Mississippians that we are prepared to conduct a high level program which will enable us to direct and coordinate the various phases of our work including education and legal action.[60]

On December 15, 1954, Medgar Evers assumed the position of field secretary. Evers became the official NAACP spokesperson and organizer in the state. He and his family, which now included two children, moved to Jackson, the state capital. Myrlie Evers took the job of secretary of the Mississippi field office in Jackson.[61] The NAACP national leadership also supported the proposal of T. R. M. Howard to establish a fund in a Memphis Black-owned bank to support those targeted by the Citizens' Council's economic intimidation campaign.

The decision to hire Medgar Evers as an organizer and make Mississippi a national priority was a smart one. He had previously proven himself as a good recruiter and chapter builder in his work in the Mississippi Delta. The NAACP membership increased in the state during the early days of his employment as field secretary. After the *Brown* decision, all Deep South states experienced a significant decline in NAACP membership, with the exceptions of Georgia and Mississippi. This was the result of escalating campaigns of repression, harassment, intimidation, and violence by White supremacists. An NAACP memorandum disclosed that between

January 1954 and April 1955, Mississippi's NAACP membership increased from 874 to 1,481. The organizational membership declined in Louisiana (-1,347), South Carolina (-171), Florida (-369), and Alabama (-587).[62]

Being an NAACP leader in apartheid Mississippi was a hazardous venture. With Howard leaving Mississippi, the NAACP became the central human rights organization in the state. Before the post–World War II Movement upsurge, the organization operated in a virtually clandestine way in most places in the state. Evers's new visibility made him a primary target of White supremacist terrorists. In the bastion of racist violence, his survival was a tenuous question.

Mississippi "Mau Mau": The Prospect of Retaliatory Violence

During Evers's years in Mound Bayou, he began to follow African independence movements, particularly the nationalist struggle in Kenya. Prior to assuming the position of NAACP field secretary, Evers envisioned the development of guerrilla warfare. He dreamed of forming a clandestine Black commando unit based on the Kikuyu Land and Freedom Army, popularly known as the "Mau Mau." The Mau Mau was an underground, peasant-based resistance movement that led a popular uprising between 1953 and 1956 in British colonial Kenya. Although the Mau Mau was defeated militarily, their revolt was credited with breaking the British resolve to directly colonize Kenya.[63]

After the outbreak of the revolt, Evers closely followed the Mau Mau uprising in the press and greatly admired Kenyan nationalist and suspected Mau Mau leader Jomo Kenyatta. Evers shared his plan to establish a Mississippi Mau Mau with close friends, family, and NAACP officials. The Mississippi Mau Mau would retaliate against perpetrators of racist violence on Blacks. Evers's strategy was to use guerrilla warfare to bring national and international attention to the Freedom Struggle and the horrors of segregation, not to defeat White supremacy in Mississippi militarily. Evers did not win much support for this idea and focused his energies on the traditional NAACP methods, exposing the violations of White supremacy in the media and promoting litigation.[64]

As NAACP field secretary, Evers would come to distance himself from his ideas about retaliatory violence. John Salter, Jackson activist and advisor to the NAACP youth council, described Evers as being in "the middle"—he was between local activists, who wanted to engage in civil disobedience, and the conservative national NAACP. The strategy of NAACP national leadership was to rely on litigation and efforts to influence public opinion, which would ultimately affect politicians—particularly on the federal level—and the commercial community. Their position often subordinated and discouraged the tactics and initiative of local activists, but controlled campaigns coordinated on a national level by utilizing lobbying, media campaigns, and litigation. Local militants were more inclined to utilize disruptive tactics, particularly civil disobedience and boycotts, in order to pressure local White power structures. The conciliatory posture of the NAACP national leadership created tension with local militants. Evers often identified and sympathized with local leadership, but, due to his organizational position, he was compelled to publicly articulate the perspective of the NAACP national leadership.

Likewise, Evers's position constrained his public posture on armed resistance. The NAACP had historically supported the right of Black people to self-defense. Certainly, the national leadership in New York knew and supported Evers and other southern NAACP functionaries employing methods of armed self-defense as a means of survival in a hostile environment. In 1957, the NAACP paid for armed security for one of its local leaders, Daisy Bates, during a school desegregation campaign, which drew national attention.[65] On the other hand, the national leadership of the organization was careful not to be identified with insurgent politics and militant armed resistance.

The posture of the national leadership concerning armed resistance advocate Robert Williams is an example of its caution on the issue of retaliatory and insurgent violence. In 1959, the NAACP leadership suspended Williams for six months for telling the press that Black activists should meet "violence with violence." Williams's suspension became the focus of a debate at the 1959 NAACP national convention. The NAACP counsel even visited FBI offices in New York to encourage the Bureau to investigate Williams. In 1961, Williams was forced into exile after charges of kidnapping, and a national manhunt was initiated against him.[66] Although never speaking publicly on the issue, Evers expressed sympathy for the exiled advocate of armed resistance.[67]

Consistent with his silence on Robert Williams, Evers was publicly deceptive about his previous plans for a Mississippi Mau Mau. In a 1958 interview in *Ebony* magazine, Evers is quoted as stating that he studied the Mau Mau and Kenyatta when he was in the U.S. Army. However, Evers was enlisted in the U.S. military between 1941 and 1945, whereas the Mau Mau uprising did not begin until 1953, only five years prior to the *Ebony* interview. Evers says in the interview that the Bible convinced him "that two wrongs would not make a situation any different, and that I couldn't hate the white man and at the same time hope to convert him." Due to his role as the official voice of the NAACP in Mississippi, Evers was required to distance himself from advocating armed resistance. The emerging popularity and influence of nonviolence advocate Martin Luther King Jr. and the conciliatory posture of the national NAACP leadership made articulating armed insurgence a marginal position in mainstream Black politics.

Nevertheless, Evers's pro–Mau Mau position was known among some national NAACP leaders. According to southern regional director Ruby Hurley, "Talk about nonviolent; he was anything but nonviolent; anything but! And he always wanted to go at it in Mau Mau fashion."[68] It is certain that NAACP national leadership discouraged Evers from articulating retaliatory violence and convinced him that a conciliatory approach was best for advancing the freedom movement.

Evers was also conscious of public relations and image.[69] He understood that to win federal and northern liberal support it was not good public relations to publicly demonstrate anger toward racists. He believed it was necessary to publicize Mississippi's crimes against people of African descent to win support outside the state and to pressure the White power structure to eliminate segregation. Evers wanted to project the image of Mississippi Blacks as victims of White terrorist violence.

Like Howard, Evers played a significant role in bringing national and international attention to the Emmett Till case. He would investigate and publicize many other offenses against Mississippi Blacks, including the 1959 lynching of Mack Parker in the small Mississippi town of Poplarville. He also played a leading role in assisting individuals and communities of color to take action in order to gain access to educational institutions that had been designated "White only," including the successful effort to admit James Meredith to the University of Mississippi in 1962.[70]

Movement leaders believed retaliatory violence could jeopardize White liberal support for the Civil Rights Movement and inspire increased reactionary violence from White supremacists. Evers and the NAACP state conference condemned Black retaliatory violence in the northern Mississippi towns of Tupelo and New Albany in November 1958. On Halloween of that year, eight White teenagers armed with a shotguns murdered one Black youth and wounded another. It was suspected that a series of stabbings of Whites, which occurred on November 15th and 16th, in Tupelo were responses to the Halloween shootings. On November 17th, three Black youths—T. L. Caruthers, J. B. Little, and Otto Jones—were arrested for the stabbings. The youths were reportedly members of a youth organization called the "Jayhawkers," named for a pre–Civil War antislavery movement in Kansas and Missouri. Around the same time, in New Albany, it was reported that the Black youth were throwing rocks at a young White female.[71]

The Mississippi chapter of the NAACP responded on the day of the arrests of Caruthers, Little, and Jones. Evers and his colleagues stated, "We deplore violence in Tupelo and New Albany, allegedly by Negroes, as we do violence in Corinth, Poplarville and Money by Whites." The NAACP was also concerned with the mobilization of White civilians in response to Black retaliatory violence: "We also deplore the use of private White citizens, armed to carry out the functions of duly elected and appointed law enforcement officers, in solving the incidents in Tupelo and New Albany."[72]

Evers himself understood the anger of Blacks in response to White terrorist violence. After the lynching of Mack Parker, Evers told his wife Myrlie, "I'd like to get a gun and just start shooting."[73] On the other hand, Evers's perspectives and actions were restrained due to his accountability to the NAACP national leadership and his understanding that spontaneous and reactive violence could retard the Movement.

Evers and Armed Self-Defense

Although Evers abandoned his plans to build a secret Black commando unit, he continued to practice armed self-defense in his organizing. Like T. R. M. Howard, Evers and other NAACP activists realized they had to rely on their own resources to protect themselves. Evers was a known and targeted activist throughout the state. His field work had him driving all over the state. In urban and rural places, he facilitated the building of new chapters and strengthening existing ones, as well as investigating atrocities of White supremacists. Wherever Evers went he was armed. He commonly rode with a .45 semi-automatic handgun. Ruby Hurley spent many days with Evers driving on Mississippi roads investigating violations of civil and human rights. "Many times when Medgar and I would drive together, Medgar would tell about carrying his gun. . . . He used to sit on it, under his pillow," Hurley remembered. The NAACP southeast regional director was uncomfortable with Evers's routine possession of firearms.[74]

Evers not only needed security in the field, but his Jackson family home required protection. A security network was formed in the state capital to protect Evers and local NAACP leaders, including Sam Bailey and Robert T. Smith. Carolyn Tyler was Smith's secretary and the Jackson NAACP's chair of voter registration for women. Tyler stated that Evers, Bailey, and Smith were routinely assigned armed security. She remembered, "They were never supposed to go anywhere alone. . . . There was always someone with them." She described the security team as "big burly guys, provided for by the NAACP."[75] According to Bailey, Evers's detail was composed of three to four men to secure his home and to travel with him.[76]

A veteran of the NAACP since the 1940s, Sam Bailey described the home protection. Bailey explained that security was placed on alert after information was received that an attack was imminent. Armed guards protected the homes of targeted individuals during the evenings. Bailey believed White terrorist "nightriders" raided in the evening "cause they wasn't coming in the daytime." The visible presence of Whites would naturally draw attention in a segregated environment, particularly when racial tensions were high. The security team would place armed guards in automobiles across the street from the home they were protecting. Other defense guards sat on the porch of the house. The armed guard would look for "stray cars coming" down the street. The visibility of security would deter the invading terrorists, who noticed the presence of armed guards. "That White man, he wasn't gonna get no blood if he can help it, cause they know we would shoot," reminisced Bailey over thirty years later. Armed security was also organized to protect special guests and the NAACP leaders such as Roy Wilkins, NAACP president; Gloster Current, director of branches; attorney Thurgood Marshall; and Lena Horne, entertainer and friend of the Civil Rights Movement.[77] Besides personal security, protection was also organized for Jackson NAACP mass meetings. The entrances were secured and sentries posted near the podium between the audience and the leadership, who generally sat facing members and supporters in attendance.[78]

In addition to assistance from local NAACP members and supporters, Evers, who owned several guns, was also prepared to defend his family and home from violent racists. NAACP activists were on alert at this time due to the White supremacist violent response that erupted at the University of Mississippi due to the admission of James Meredith to the university. John Salter remembered coming to the Evers home in 1962. Evers greeted Salter at the door with a weapon, stating, "We were expecting the wrong type of people." Upon entering the house, Salter observed "half a dozen guns in the kitchen and living room." Furniture was stacked behind each window in the house. The Evers household also had windows with "bullet-proof blinds." Myrlie and the three Evers children were instructed to "immediately fall to the floor" if they heard the screech of car brakes outside the home. The Everses also purchased a German shepherd for protection.[79]

A week before his fatal shooting, the Evers household was once again on alert. Evers would instinctively vault from bed, armed with one of his many rifles, when awakened by the barks of his guard dog. Myrlie Evers also slept with a small revolver on the nightstand of her bed. The Everses had good reason to believe the family was in danger. They received threatening phone calls and mail, and a firebomb was tossed at their home in spring 1963.[80]

Unfortunately, the precautions and defenses practiced by Evers, his family, and his comrades could not save him from the bullet of his assassin, Byron De La Beckwith. Witnesses observed De La Beckwith at a Jackson NAACP mass meeting on June 11, 1963. The White supremacist had attended NAACP mass meetings before, sitting with the media.[81]

Around midnight that evening, Evers returned home by himself after a Jackson NAACP mass meeting. Myrlie and the Everses' children were at home waiting up for him. Unfortunately, Evers had no personal security trailing him. The Jackson police, who often followed him home, were nowhere to be found. Evers was shot by a high-powered rifle immediately after leaving his car. A neighbor, Houston Wells, after hearing the shots and the screams of Myrlie Evers, went to his bedroom window to see Evers lying on the ground bleeding. Wells got his handgun and fired a shot in the air for the purpose of frightening away the sniper. Evers somehow was able to stagger to his kitchen door, where he collapsed by the steps. Wells and other neighbors, after covering Evers with a blanket and placing him in a station wagon, transported him to the hospital. Evers died shortly after arriving at the hospital. It is possible that having security that evening might have prevented Beckwith's assassination plans, and it is unclear why he was not accompanied by bodyguards. Sam Bailey lamented, "[Evers] was supposed to have a bodyguard carry him home. I don't know what happened to him. I guess he got careless."[82]

Mississippi Negroes with Guns

Chicago-based journalist Simeon Booker visited Mississippi to observe the RCNL rallies and the Emmett Till trials. From Booker's perspective, Howard's and Evers's armed preparedness with weapons and security posture were not exceptions in the Mississippi Black Freedom Struggle. "Firearms, protection and security are ingredients of a successful civil rights program in Mississippi," wrote the Black journalist. Booker's observations recognized the role of armed resistance in the survival of the Struggle. The journalist reflected,

> The Negro social reformer must defend himself, because he has no protection from police, sheriffs or state troopers. He must be ready to die at any moment. . . . The reason many more Negro civil righters are not killed is because they are armed to defend themselves and their families.[83]

Booker's observations reveal that armed self-defense was common practice for southern Black activists.

The practices of Howard and Evers demonstrate that Robert Williams's incorporation of armed resistance in North Carolina was not exceptional in the southern Black Freedom Struggle. Evers, like Williams, had views that were potentially radical and less optimistic about the possibility of peaceful integration. Both Evers and Williams believed in the possibility of a "race war" and were prepared for it. The escalation of violent hostility by White supremacists led Evers and Williams to question the possibility of a peaceful transition to human rights and dismantling of apartheid. Years before Williams, Evers considered the possibility of an independent Black state in the southern Black Belt to prevent genocide. Myrlie Evers said her husband considered,

> If white structural racism . . . was relatively "permanent," what practical options or alternatives did African Americans have? Perhaps blacks should consider demanding a separate, all-black state of their own, based on a territorial separation between the races. . . . Medgar believed "you must always be prepared for whatever comes our way." And we were talking about guns, the arms, collecting what we need to fight if by chance we ended up in a race war. Which he felt could possibly happen. . . . [H]e was thinking about building a nation . . . of black people.[84]

Evers's perspective was obviously private, given his position with the NAACP. More autonomous from the national leadership, Williams openly advocated armed self-defense and retaliatory violence. Issuing statements from exile in Cuba, China, and Tanzania, Williams would echo Evers's private thoughts and called for armed guerrilla warfare to protect Black people from a White supremacist genocidal pogrom. Williams would embrace the demand of the nationalist Republic of New Africa to establish an independent Black nation-state in the Deep South.

Evers became the symbolic martyr of the Mississippi Movement. His was a complex personality, his public persona contrasting with his private comments and practices concerning armed resistance. The image-conscious leader created a public portrait of himself as a tireless soldier who did not hate his enemy. Although this image is not inconsistent with armed self-defense, he realized that the majority of the White American public, whether in the North or in the South, was threatened by the image of "Negroes with guns." The image of Evers as an armed militant was inconsistent with the strategy and objectives of the national NAACP leadership. The perception of "Negroes with guns" would not win White liberal or federal support. It was necessary for Evers to have an image of one who was willing to sit down and resolve problems with segregationists to bring racial harmony.

To White supremacists, Howard and Evers were "Bad Negroes" who had to be killed or exiled. Although he certainly lived as a "Bad Negro" in defiance of White domination, Evers was also a trickster. He concealed his belief in and practice of armed resistance, as well as his dissatisfaction with nonviolence. Although Evers realized that the image of armed Blacks was not "good public relations," he possessed weapons as a matter of survival.

3

"Can't Give Up My Stuff"

Nonviolent Organizations and Armed Resistance

In 1961, activists of the Student Nonviolent Coordinating Committee (SNCC) were the first organizers to advocate the philosophy of nonviolence and to practice nonviolent direct action in Mississippi. Medgar Evers never publicly disavowed nonviolence. On the other hand, he would privately express his disagreement with the philosophy of nonviolence to SNCC organizers. SNCC activist MacArthur Cotton often traveled with Medgar in the early 1960s. Reflecting on his travels with Evers around the state, Cotton commented, "Medgar used to carry a gun. . . . He always talked about how crazy we was, talking about nonviolence."[1]

The NAACP never overtly promoted armed resistance. The organization's national leadership also never advocated nonviolent direct action as a primary method of struggle. The Student Nonviolent Coordinating Committee (SNCC), which began organizing in Mississippi in 1961, became the first activist organization to advocate nonviolence as a philosophy, strategy, or tactical approach in the Mississippi Black Freedom Struggle. Within two years, another nonviolent activist group, the Congress of Racial Equality (CORE), also became active in the state. A natural tension developed when nonviolent activists began to organize in communities where indigenous leadership and sympathizers believed in and practiced armed self-defense on a normal basis. The interaction between nonviolent and armed activists would be at times tense and in other instances complementary.

The successful Montgomery Bus Boycott (December 1, 1955, to December 20, 1956) and the dynamic sit-in campaigns of 1960 propelled nonviolent direct action as a primary tactic in the struggle to dismantle U.S. apartheid. The philosophy of nonviolence ascended as the preeminent orientation of the organized movement, particularly on the national level. Indigenous activists and local people tended to continue the practice of armed self-defense as the struggle advanced in Mississippi and other southern communities.

Origins of Nonviolence and the Black Freedom Struggle

In the 1960s, nonviolence had recently emerged as an orientation, strategy, and practice. CORE was the first national organization to advocate and practice nonviolence as a primary philosophy and strategy in the Black liberation movement. CORE's origins emanate from the legacy of U.S. pacifist activism. In 1941, the Christian pacifist organization Fellowship of Reconciliation (FOR), which began as a pacifist group during World War I, developed a special project at the University of Chicago aimed at challenging racism.[2] Activist confrontation without the use of violent force was the exclusive tactic of CORE. The organization's statement of purpose read, "CORE has one method . . . interracial nonviolent direct action."[3] By December 1942, CORE grew from a campus-based "peace team" at the University of Chicago to a small federation of local direct action groups committed to nonviolence. In 1943, the federation officially named itself the Congress of Racial Equality.[4]

The Montgomery Bus Boycott captured the attention and imagination of the Black Freedom Struggle. The momentum of the Montgomery Bus Boycott yielded another important player in the nonviolent movement in 1957. On January 10th and 11th, the first meeting of the Southern Leadership Conference (SLC) took place at Ebenezer Baptist Church in Atlanta, Georgia. The purpose of this meeting was to create a regional organization of local church-based desegregation movements, which had emerged in several southern urban centers. The Reverend Dr. Martin Luther King Jr. emerged as the popular leader of this new organization. The leadership of SLC emphasized the philosophy of nonviolent direct action as the central weapon necessary to desegregate institutions in the South. In their initial statement to the press, the SLC expressed the following message to the Black community to discourage any use of force in the freedom movement: "We call upon them to accept Christian Love in its full power to defy. . . . Nonviolence is not a symbol of weakness or cowardice, but, as Jesus and Gandhi demonstrated, resistance transforms weakness into strength and breeds courage in the face of danger."[5] While calling for Black people to confront segregation, "[E]ven in the face of death," the SLC declared, "not one hair of one head of one white person shall be harmed."[6]

Soon after its founding, the SLC announced that it would be identified as the Southern Christian Leadership Conference (SCLC). The predominance of clerical leadership in its membership and the sensitivity to being labeled communist motivated the addition of "Christian" to the organization's name. SCLC's approach was to utilize confrontational, but nonviolent, tactics in campaigns to oppose segregation in local communities. The goal of SCLC's nonviolent direct action campaign was to create a local crisis that could draw the attention of the national media and the executive and legislative branches of the federal government, and sway U.S. public opinion to the side of the Black Freedom Struggle. In order to win the public opinion fight with White segregationists and particularly to gain the support of White liberals, SCLC leaders felt it necessary to disassociate themselves from any acts of retaliatory violence or form of armed self-defense by local Black activists or supporters of the Struggle. In this sense, nonviolence was an important ideological weapon in SCLC's strategy. SCLC leaders believed that the use of force by Black people would only serve to alienate White liberals and the general White U.S. public.[7]

The February 1, 1960, sit-in at a segregated lunch counter in Greensboro, North Carolina, led to an explosion of nonviolent demonstrations by student activists throughout the South. This student-initiated movement was pivotal in the creation of SNCC. Ella Baker, then the executive director of SCLC, convened a conference on April 16-18, 1960, at Shaw College in Raleigh, North Carolina. The purpose of this conference was to coordinate the activities of various student groups that had blossomed throughout the South after the Greensboro sit-in. The Raleigh conference would become the founding convention of SNCC.

SCLC, CORE, and FOR were all represented at the Raleigh conference. Martin Luther King Jr., by this time a nationally recognized leader of the Civil Rights Movement, addressed the conference, but a lesser-known activist would have a greater philosophical influence on the direction of the new organization. James Lawson, a committed Gandhian and nonviolent activist, made convincing arguments for protests based on moral and spiritual foundations. Lawson, a theology student and southern field secretary of FOR, had a rich history of pacifist activism. As a missionary in India, he studied Mahatma Gandhi's method of nonviolent activism. As an activist, Lawson involved himself with the Nashville student movement's efforts to desegregate lunch counters in the spring of 1960. Lawson's influence was critical to the adoption of a nonviolent philosophy based on Christian principles.[8]

Philosophical commitment to nonviolence was reflected in SNCC's statement of purpose.[9] However, in the early years within the organization, this perspective competed for ideological hegemony with the point of view of activists who saw nonviolence as a political tactic. The leadership of the Nashville student movement advocated philosophical nonviolence as a way of life. This group included SNCC founders James Lawson, John

Lewis, Diane Nash, and James Bevel. The Nashville group favored confrontational, nonviolent action along the line of the sit-ins to disrupt the institutions of segregation. They believed that nonviolence, based upon Gandhian and Christian principles, would be a powerful moral force to defeat racist violence and attitudes.

The competing point of view saw organizing around voting rights, not direct action in public institutions, as the primary focus of SNCC's activism. This point of view was articulated in SNCC's early years by activists Chuck McDew, Tim Jenkins, Charles Jones, and, later on, Bob Moses. This group believed that SNCC's priority should be the massive registration of Black voters in southern states in which the voting rights of African descendants were denied. This group viewed nonviolence as a tactical weapon to be used by organizers for protection. These activists, similar to the leadership of SCLC, believed that the perception of armed Black organizers would not encourage federal intervention or garner support from White liberals for the Civil Rights Movement.[10]

In SNCC's early years, no debate took place within the national leadership over embracing nonviolence. While it is possible that some SNCC workers carried weapons in the early years of the organization, armed self-defense was not overtly advocated. In local chapters, some young activists were indifferent to nonviolence; others openly challenged the concept as a strategy and philosophy. In Nashville, where philosophical nonviolence was reputed to be most entrenched, student activists debated the methods of nonviolence versus self-defense. The "Young Turks" of the Nashville student movement protected nonviolent demonstrators from White attackers in that city.[11] On a few occasions in the early years, some SNCC workers were armed or advocated use of force for self-defense.[12]

Some SNCC and CORE activists also came in contact with local Movement activists or supporters who participated in armed self-defense. Most practiced some form of self-defense covertly. The only exception was Robert Williams in Monroe, North Carolina. Under Williams's leadership, Monroe Blacks organized armed patrols that had discouraged Klan caravans from harassing and terrorizing their community. Williams's "meeting violence with violence" statement received national headlines. He was considered the primary advocate for armed self-defense by Movement activists and observers. Williams published a newsletter, *The Crusader*, with national distribution for the purpose of spreading his views on the Movement, including his views about armed self-defense. From exile in Cuba, Williams also produced a radio program, *Radio Free Dixie*.[13]

Williams's open advocacy of armed resistance was an exception in the southern Black Freedom Movement of the late 1950s and early 1960s. Most SNCC and CORE activists came into contact with activists and Movement supporters who practiced armed self-defense without seeking or receiving publicity. Michael Flug, a CORE worker from Brooklyn, New York, remembered armed sentries protecting CORE Freedom Houses throughout the South from 1962 through 1964. The Freedom Houses were the center of activity, particularly voter registration, and the residences of some field workers and staff in southern communities. Mostly local people would be involved in the sentries, with occasional participation from some CORE workers. While CORE members were bound to practice nonviolence by CORE's Rules of Action, local people were not obligated to be pacifists. Flug remembered that local Black southerners would be shown passages in CORE's Rules of Action and comment, "I didn't see that." Flug also recalled that those who were willing to provide security for him and other CORE workers were not interested in publicly advocating armed self-defense. In response to Williams's public advocacy of armed resistance, the covert protectors of Freedom House and CORE staff asked, "Why you want to put that out in the public?" Consistent with the public relations strategy of nonviolent leaders like Martin Luther King Jr., some armed participants in the Movement agreed to decrease the visibility of Blacks with guns to win the support of the federal government and White liberals. Flug argued, "We're playing to the media, tactically it wasn't a good idea [to advocate or project an armed presence]."[14]

SNCC activists also received covert armed support in Black southern communities. For instance, SNCC workers were protected by Black snipers in a section of the Black community of Danville, Virginia, in 1963. White supremacist civilians and police would not follow SNCC activists into the Black neighborhood for fear of engaging the snipers. While the SNCC statement of purpose committed them to the practice of nonviolence, SNCC organizers appreciated and often depended on the "blanket of protection" they received from local people in Danville and other places in the South, particularly in Mississippi.[15]

The Genesis of SNCC in Mississippi and Armed Self-Defense

In the summer of 1960, SNCC volunteer and Harvard doctoral student Bob Moses was sent on a tour of the South to identify areas where the young organization could expand its work. Moses had taken time from his studies to make a contribution to the human rights movement in the South. Mississippi was not represented in the gathering of southern Black college students who came together to form SNCC in April of 1960, and Moses volunteered for the assignment of organizational reconnaissance in Mississippi. He was sent on this mission in August of 1960.

SNCC advisor Ella Baker possessed a wealth of experience and contacts from her work with the NAACP, the SCLC, and the leftist Southern Conference Educational Fund. Baker provided Moses with a list of contacts that could provide room, board, and information. The most valuable contact that Baker gave Moses was RCNL and NAACP organizer Amzie Moore. Moore owned a gas station and resided in the Delta town of Cleveland. He was a World War II veteran who organized RCNL voter registration and "Don't Buy Gas Where You Can't Use the Restroom" efforts. He assisted Ruby Hurley and Medgar Evers in the investigation of the Till murder (see chapter 2). Moore had survived the financial harassment of the White Citizens' Council, in which local White financial institutions refused to extend credit to his business and his hours at his post office job were cut. The national NAACP, the American Friends Service Committee, as well as Bayard Rustin and Ella Baker's New York–based "In Friendship" network provided financial assistance to Moore.[16]

Moore's posture toward armed protection was similar to that of his comrades T. R. M. Howard and Medgar Evers. In addition to economic pressure, Moore was the target of threats of violence.[17] The Delta activist was often armed and believed that self-defense was a necessary posture for activists to take for organizing and surviving in Mississippi. Historian Charles Payne described Moore's home as "well armed" and said that "at night the area around his home may have been the best-lit spot in Cleveland."[18] Three years after Moses' initial Mississippi trip, guests of Moore's home would be offered a loaded Luger handgun by the Movement veteran. Artist and writer Tracy Sugarman recalled Moore placing the handgun on the nightstand, stating, "This is in case of emergency." When Sugarman and another guest declined, Moore picked up the weapon and courteously replied, "Just as you say. . . . Good night."[19] Moore would provide security for SNCC activists. SNCC organizer Lawrence Guyot remembered, "Whenever anyone was threatened, Amzie Moore was sort of an individual protection agency."[20]

Moses resided with Moore during his 1960 Mississippi trip. Along with Baker's perspectives on developing indigenous leadership and grassroots

NAACP leader and SNCC advisor Amzie Moore was once described as a "one man protection agency." (Courtesy of Estuary Press.)

organizing, Moses' discussions with Moore provided the basic orientation of SNCC organizing in Mississippi. Moore was fed up with the litigation-based campaigns of the NAACP. He also believed that nonviolent activism directed at segregated public facilities would not be effective in Mississippi. Moore argued that a massive voter registration campaign challenging Mississippi Black disenfranchisement was the best vehicle to crush White supremacy and ensure African American civil and human rights.[21]

Moses developed Moore's views into a proposal for SNCC activists to come to Mississippi to assist indigenous leadership and cultivate new leaders for a massive voter registration project in the state. Moore was invited to a SNCC leadership conference later that year to discuss the idea of a statewide voter registration campaign. The next summer, Moses returned to Cleveland to report to Moore and begin organizing in Mississippi. Moore's contacts throughout the state would become invaluable to SNCC.[22]

Agitation of and confrontation with apartheid institutions through non-violent direct action would not be the primary activity of SNCC in Missis-sippi. Nonviolence would be an important part of the orientation and prac-tice of Moses in his organizing in the state. Moses was aligned with the "voter registration" group within SNCC that believed nonviolent direct actions to desegregate public facilities should be deemphasized in favor of organizing Black citizens to challenge racist voting restrictions. Moses believed "non-violence was a tool" that could allow organizers to assume an offensive pos-ture. He believed that if SNCC organizers commonly carried weapons, they would be constantly stopped by law enforcement and indicted with weapons charges. Moses also did not believe that SNCC organizers had the authority to demand that local Black Mississippians disarm and adopt nonviolent tac-tics. While Moses embraced nonviolence, he believed that quietly organizing disenfranchised Blacks to register to vote was the major method by which to involve Mississippians in the Movement, not confrontational, direct action.[23]

The internal debate within the SNCC over whether the emphasis should be nonviolent direct action or voter registration led to a compromise that allowed those committed to civil disobedience to organize projects in Mis-sissippi. The voter registration faction's strategy relied on the perceived commitment of federal intervention, particularly through the Department of Justice, to prevent potential White supremacist violence or to punish the perpetrators of racist violence. In the summer and fall of 1961, SNCC lead-ers, including Tim Jenkins and Lonnie King, and other Movement activists were involved in a series of meetings with federal officials—including Assis-tant Attorney General Burke Marshall and Harris Wofford, special assistant to President Kennedy on civil rights—as well as representatives from liberal foundations. The purpose of these meetings was to develop an apparatus to accelerate Black voter registration in the South. The Kennedy administration preferred voter registration efforts to confrontational nonviolent direct ac-tion. The federal executive branch hoped that diverting the activity of the Black Freedom Struggle from nonviolent confrontation to voter registration would reduce the agitation of southern White supremacists while winning the support of newly registered Blacks for the Democratic Party. Nonviolent confrontation was often disruptive and led to open violent reaction from White racists. Federal officials wished to avoid civil disobedience and White reaction, both of which challenged civic order.[24]

The ultimate result of these meetings was the formation of the Voter Ed-ucation Project (VEP), which was administered by the Southern Regional Council (SRC) and funded by the liberal Taconic, Field, and Stern family foundations. Not only were SNCC workers and other Movement activists to receive financial support through the VEP, but they also believed, as a result of statements made by federal officials, that federal law enforcement would provide protection for voter rights workers in the South. Federal officials later denied making these commitments.[25]

Southwest Mississippi became the region where Moses would first initiate a voter registration project in the state. Southwest Mississippi was selected on the basis of Amzie Moore's recommendation. Moore assessed that Movement forces in the Delta did not yet possess the resources to provide the necessary support for a sustained voter registration effort. Agreeing with Moore's assessment, southwest Mississippi NAACP leaders Claude Bryant and E. W. Steptoe requested a SNCC project in that part of the state.[26]

The Southwest Mississippi Black community of McComb possessed a network of indigenous leaders with sufficient resources to support the SNCC voter registration project. McComb was located in Pike County, midway between the Mississippi state capital of Jackson and New Orleans. Due to its location, the town was founded as a railroad nexus to serve the Illinois Central Railroad. The railroad provided Blacks with stable union employment. The protection of the union and a small core of Black businesses based on the segregated economy allowed the McComb movement spaces for organizing, which did not exist in the Delta. McComb had 6,936 Blacks of voting age, with only 250 Blacks actually registered to vote in 1961.[27]

Moses and SNCC were convinced that the local NAACP possessed the necessary resources to initiate a voter registration campaign in McComb. Pike County NAACP president C. C. Bryant formally invited Moses and solicited local clergy and entrepreneurs for resources to support staff for a voter registration campaign. Two other SNCC workers, Reginald Robinson and John Hardy, joined Moses within weeks of his arrival there. A voter registration class was established at the local Masonic temple. The course attracted Blacks not only from McComb and other parts of Pike County but also from neighboring counties Amite and Walthall. A contingent of SNCC workers—including John Hardy, and recent recruits MacArthur Cotton, Jimmie Travis, and George Lowe—were assigned to set up voter registration classes in Walthall. There was not one registered Black citizen out of a population of 2,490 voting-aged Blacks in Walthall in 1961.[28]

MacArthur Cotton had been recruited by Moses in the summer of 1961. Cotton, a native of Attala County, had just finished his freshman year at Tougaloo College (near Jackson). Cotton and other SNCC workers came to the Walthall municipality of Tylertown in 1961. Local people told Cotton and his comrades about "some of the old brothers" who prevented night-riders from terrorizing a Black community outside of the Tylertown city limits. Several months prior to SNCC coming to Tylertown, nightriders had repeatedly come across the bridge at Magee's Creek, which separated this Black community from predominantly White neighborhoods of the city. To no avail, members of the Black community warned that the terrorism must stop. Local Blacks told Cotton that during a raid by nightriders, a group of "brothers with . . . ancient connections" captured a White supremacist marauder. "Ancient connections" suggested that the Black captors were a part of a fraternal order. The nightrider's head was severed from his body and placed on the bridge as a warning to White terrorists. After this act of counterterrorism, no White person crossed the Magee's Creek bridge unless "on business and treated [Black] people in a respectful manner." This Walthall County Black enclave served as a "haven" for SNCC workers. As in the Black neighborhood in Danville, Virginia, which was protected by snipers, nonviolent activists could receive protection and refuge. The identification of haven communities for protection throughout the state was essential to SNCC's work in the state.[29]

E. W. Steptoe: "A Fearless Warrior"

To the west of Pike County was the Black-majority Amite County. Amite was considered a bastion of racial violence. Black political representation and land ownership emerged in the county during Reconstruction, but white terror was successful in eliminating the emerging Black presence in the county government and in driving the majority of Black landowners to agrarian peonage or to flight away from Amite to what was perceived as "greener pastures." Some Black farmers fought to maintain their land and stayed in the county. Eldridge Willie Steptoe (known as E. W. Steptoe) descended from the Black landowners who endured a racially hostile environment.[30]

Bob Moses personally traveled to Amite to organize voter registration efforts. Fifty-three-year-old dairy and cotton farmer E. W. Steptoe was president of the county's chapter of NAACP. Steptoe's 240-acre farm overlooked the Mississippi/Louisiana border. He descended from a lineage of independent farmers and entrepreneurs who were respected by Amite Blacks and Whites alike.[31] Steptoe often traveled across the Louisiana state line for financial survival, as doing so allowed the crafty Amite farmer to outmaneuver the economic pressure of the Mississippi Citizens' Council.[32]

The Steptoe farm served as housing for SNCC organizers and was often used for meetings and voter registration classes.[33]

The youthful SNCC workers admired and respected Steptoe. While small in physical size, Steptoe was revered for his courage and determination. One SNCC activist remembered Steptoe as "a fearless warrior. . . . [J]ust being around him inspired you." In describing Steptoe, writer Jack Newfield stated, "His courage, his common-sense wisdom, his bittersweet wit and love, are the special qualities of the rural Mississippi Negro, who lives by his wits to survive." Newfield also described Steptoe as "a violent man." Movement people knew Steptoe to be well armed in order to protect his household, associates, and himself from the violence of White racists.[34] SNCC activist Chuck McDew remembers,

> You go to Steptoe's house and Steptoe just had guns aplenty. . . . [A]s you went to bed he would open up the night table and there would be a large .45 automatic sitting next to you, just guns all over the house, under pillows, under chairs. It was just marvelous.[35]

One journalist noted "three rifles and a .45 caliber pistol" at the Steptoe home "to ward off night attacks."[36]

Steptoe was also generally armed when away from home. SNCC workers would joke about him carrying a small derringer handgun and about how Steptoe's wife would search him before he went downtown to attempt to register to vote. On different occasions, Steptoe was known to hide handguns in hats he wore, in his sock, or in the crotch of his pants.[37] When Steptoe traveled to Washington, D.C., to meet with federal officials, SNCC workers had to convince him not to go to the meeting armed, but to leave his weapon in his hotel room. Chuck McDew commented that the Mississippi farmer came to Washington armed "like Poncho Villa."[38]

In 1961, Moses was beaten in the Amite county seat, ironically named Liberty, after attempting to take a group of local Blacks to register. Moses returned to the Steptoe farm bloody and injured. An angered Steptoe had to be restrained from "shooting up the town." Steptoe's son, E. W. Jr., reflecting on his father's belief in retaliatory violence, stated, "[H]e didn't believe in nonviolence. He didn't believe in seeing people get beat up and not doing anything about it. He didn't let anybody push him around."[39]

Many SNCC workers depended upon the protection of and were inspired by Black farmers like Steptoe. On the other hand, Moses was uncomfortable about Steptoe's guns and his willingness to use them. McDew commented,

E. W. Steptoe, an Amite County farmer described as a "fearless warrior" for his vigilant defense of his life, family, and supporters of the Movement. (Courtesy of Matt Herron.)

"Bob Moses . . . was always very, very nonviolent and would not touch a gun. But there were some others of us who felt very comfortable staying at Steptoe's."[40] On one occasion, Moses noticed that Steptoe was armed when they were entering the elder's vehicle. Moses protested Steptoe being armed and stated, "No, I'm not going. I'm not going with you if you're going to carry a gun." Steptoe replied, "You don't know these people around here." Grudgingly, Steptoe took the gun back to his house.[41]

Steptoe was often deceptive about being armed. Moses offered, "I asked Mr. E. W. Steptoe not to carry guns when we got together at night. So, instead, he just hid his gun, and then I find out later."[42] On the way to the airport for the previously mentioned trip to Washington, D.C., Moses was said to have told the rural NAACP activist, "Mr. Steptoe, you have a gun. You can't carry guns on the airplane." In response to Moses' request, Steptoe "surrendered his weapon." However, Steptoe had again fooled his younger comrades. McDew commented, "When we got to Washington we discovered he had two or three others on him."[43]

Moses ultimately learned not to debate with the elder activist about the virtues or tactical advantages of nonviolence. Neither did the perceptive Mississippian debate the necessity of armed resistance with Moses and other young activists committed to nonviolence. Each seemed to silently acknowledge each other's approach. Moses' experiences with Steptoe prepared him for future encounters with Black Mississippians and their attitudes about guns and armed self-defense. While Moses would insist that SNCC workers maintain a nonviolent and unarmed posture, he would not attempt to commit local Blacks to nonviolence. Moses argued, "Self-defense is so deeply ingrained in rural southern America that we as a small group can't affect it." The young activist would articulate, "The difference . . . is that we on [SNCC] staff have committed ourselves not to carry guns."[44]

Steptoe's precautions were based on real, not imaginary, threats. As was experienced by Moses, it was common that Blacks could be randomly beaten in downtown Liberty.[45] While Amite had a majority-Black population, it only had one registered Black voter (who never voted) out of a total of 3,560 voting-age Blacks in 1960. Steptoe had first attempted to register in Amite in 1953, with subsequent attempts in 1954, 1956, and 1957. Steptoe also initiated the Amite County NAACP in 1954. Local law enforcement and other White supremacists disrupted an NAACP meeting advocating Black voter registration. Sheriff E. L. Caston and his deputies, Klan members, as well as other White civilians raided an NAACP meeting at Mount Pilgrim's Baptist Church and seized the local membership rolls. The Amite NAACP membership totaled nearly two hundred at that time. Only after FBI intervention were the membership rolls returned. The White terrorist raid on the Amite NAACP and subsequent intimidation and harassment of individuals on the membership list was effective. Fearing reprisal from White supremacists after the attack on the church, Steptoe's uncle fled to the woods for a week, surviving on raw food. Like many Amite Blacks after Reconstruction, he left the county in fear of economic harassment, bodily harm, or death. Only the determined persistence of Steptoe prevented the chapter from completely folding after the repression of county White supremacist forces.[46]

On September 24, 1961, Steptoe informed John Doar of the civil rights division of the federal Department of Justice that his and other Amite County NAACP leaders' lives were in danger. Doar left Mississippi for D.C. immediately after his meeting with Steptoe, and the day after his departure, White Mississippi state legislator E. H. Hurst shot and killed a charter member and vice president of the Amite NAACP, Herbert Lee, in downtown Liberty. Lee had transported Moses and Steptoe around the county in their organizing efforts. A coroner's jury ruled that the shooting was self-defense and acquitted Hurst the day after Lee's death.[47]

Moses and Steptoe found three Black witnesses willing to testify that Hurst murdered a defenseless Lee. One of these witnesses, Louis Allen, had been coerced into corroborating Hurst's claims of self-defense at the coroner's inquest. With the guarantee of protection, Allen informed Moses of his willingness to admit that his previous testimony was coerced and false. Allen would acknowledge to a grand jury that Hurst murdered Lee. Moses appealed to federal officials for Allen to receive protection. Moses was informed by Department of Justice officials "that there was no way possible" to provide security for Allen. Without federal protection, local White supremacists constantly harassed Allen for years. On the eve of planning to leave the state to escape the harassment, Allen was shot in the driveway of his farm on January 31, 1964. The lack of intervention by federal officials somewhat stymied the voter registration efforts in Amite.[48]

Steptoe was quite familiar with Hurst since the White politician lived down the road from his farm. He had witnessed and been involved in disputes with the Hurst family as he grew up.[49] The day prior to Lee's death, Hurst was identified by Steptoe to Doar as a potential threat. Steptoe continued in his attempt to organize local Blacks to challenge Amite's White power structure in spite of Lee's murder and the lack of federal protection for human rights activists. Steptoe and his family recognized the inadequacy of relying on federal protection after the lack of justice in the death of Lee. The male members of the Steptoe family—including himself and his five sons—established their own sentry around the Steptoe farm.[50] He continued to organize and maintain his relationship with Moses and SNCC. Steptoe remained an inspiration and elder to the young activists.

McComb: Nonviolence and Armed Protection

Protection was also needed for the voter registration efforts in McComb. Moses and other SNCC organizers were given shelter and support from three Black neighborhoods in McComb: Burgland, Algiers, and Beartown. SNCC organizers were monitored and harassed by the local police and the Klan. Moses and his comrades depended on indigenous networks to avoid the surveillance and persecution of local White supremacists.[51]

The Black-owned Nobles Brothers Cleaners was one place of refuge in the Burgland community of McComb. Ernest Nobles was the primary owner of the cleaners. Nobles was a World War II veteran, local NAACP leader, and one of the McComb business owners supporting the voter registration campaign. SNCC workers would enter the side entrance of Nobles Cleaners to evade the pursuit of White supremacists. They would hide behind the machinery or in the office of the cleaners. The cleaners' personnel would transport Moses and others away to safety in the company vehicle.[52]

Nobles Cleaners itself became a target for White supremacists. Ernest Nobles and his brothers kept weapons in the business for protection. A sentry was maintained at a Black-owned taxi stand across the street from the cleaners during times when hostilities increased in McComb, as White supremacists reacted to Movement activities.[53]

Moses' voter registration efforts in McComb created opportunity for SNCC's nonviolent direct action wing to initiate activity in the state. Indeed, the emergent McComb Movement would provide the first test for nonviolent direct action in Mississippi. In August of 1961, SNCC's direct action wing sent Marion Barry to McComb to recruit and organize nonviolent confrontation. Barry, a veteran of nonviolent campaigns in Nashville, facilitated nonviolent workshops in McComb and organized local activists under the umbrella of the Pike County Nonviolent Movement. Two local teenage males "sat in" at the segregated Woolworth's lunch counter in downtown McComb weeks after Barry's arrival in the city. The two young men, Hollis Watkins and Curtis Hayes, were SNCC's first two recruits in Mississippi. Watkins and Hayes were arrested after refusing to comply with police orders to move from the lunch counter. They were charged with breach of the peace and incarcerated for thirty-four days.[54] The nonviolent campaign in McComb led to the involvement of high school students and arrests of local youth and SNCC activists engaged in direct action.[55]

Hollis Watkins exemplified the attitude of many southern Black youth toward nonviolence. Watkins grew up in the nearby county of Lincoln, in the Chisholm Mission community. As in most rural Black communities in the South, in Chisholm Mission most households owned a rifle or shotgun for hunting and protection. Watkins himself carried a knife for protection. He was Moses' first recruit into the ranks of SNCC. Watkins wanted to see change in his local community, in the South, and throughout the United States.[56]

Watkins's family had to make choices due to his decision to participate in the McComb Movement. After his arrest for participation in the inaugural McComb sit-in, White segregationists sent a local Black man to Watkins's father offering money if his son left the Movement. Watkins's parents were not responsive to the offer. In turn, the segregationists sent their Black representative back to the Watkins's household. He stated that the White supremacists threatened to set fire to the Watkinses' home and bring physical harm to the family patriarch. The elder Watkins replied that his son was old enough to make decisions for himself and that he was willing to retaliate against any intruders. The Watkins patriarch responded, "[I]f people wanted to 'meet him,' he was 'prepared to meet them.'"[57]

Watkins was willing to try nonviolence, even though the philosophy was not consistent with his background or personal inclinations. He went through nonviolence training in Barry's McComb nonviolent workshops, but even after the training, he doubted he could be nonviolent if physically attacked at the Woolworth's sit-in or any other nonviolent action. Because Watkins wanted to be involved in action to change his community, he subordinated his personal reservations and differences with pacifist activism and chose to participate in the nonviolent action at Woolworth's. However, he would never totally commit himself to nonviolence. His perspective reflected that of numerous grassroots southerners of his generation who joined nonviolent organizations.[58]

Forrest County and Vernon Dahmer

Forrest County NAACP leader Vernon Dahmer made a request for SNCC workers to come to build a voter registration campaign there. In response to Dahmer's request, Watkins and Hayes were sent to Forrest County months after their release from the McComb jail and the decline of the Pike County campaign.[59] Forrest County is located in the south central Piney Woods region of Mississippi. Its county seat, Hattiesburg, had a population of around thirty-five thousand, with the Black community comprising a third of the total. Hattiesburg was considered moderate as compared to other parts of the state like Amite and the Delta, where Blacks experienced violent terror. In spite of its reputation for moderation, however, Hattiesburg and Forrest County Blacks still experienced apartheid-segregation and denial of civil and human rights. Only twenty-five Blacks were registered out of 7,495 persons of African descent eligible to vote.[60]

Vernon Dahmer had been a significant NAACP leader in Forrest County and the state since the early 1950s, when he achieved notoriety for suing the Forrest County sheriff for preventing Blacks from voting. Dahmer was born in 1908 in Kelly's Settlement, a small, rural Forrest County Black community just northwest of Hattiesburg. The community was named for Dahmer's White great-grandfather, John Kelly. Dahmer was of multiracial heritage and could "pass" for White, but he passionately identified with the Black community and was a determined fighter willing to use his resources for civil and human rights. Dahmer never completed high school but was considered wealthy by the standards of his time and community. He owned a 200-acre commercial farm, producing cotton and raising cattle, as well as a sawmill and a small grocery store. Dahmer's enterprises provided employment for many of Forrest County's Black population.[61]

Dahmer requested that SNCC send personnel to invigorate Forrest County's voter registration campaign. He needed assistance to get the voter drive moving since most of his time was occupied running his enterprises. Watkins and Hayes relied on Dahmer for economic support. SNCC had only provided the two young activists with fifty dollars to run a three-month campaign. Watkins and Hayes lived with the Dahmer family, were employed at Dahmer's sawmill, and had the use of one of Dahmer's vehicles. Watkins considered Dahmer "a real down-to-earth father."[62]

Dahmer provided the two activists with protection, as well as economic subsistence. According to Watkins, "[T]here is no doubt about it, Vernon Dahmer believed in self-defense." The Dahmer residence was well armed with "guns, pistols and rifles," similar to the Evers and Steptoe households. Due to his vocal leadership of the Forrest County NAACP, he was targeted by state and local segregationist forces. Like Steptoe, Dahmer "strategically had guns placed throughout his house." While living with the Forrest County farmer, Watkins observed Dahmer engaging in a unique practice. To warn potential nightriders of his preparedness for attackers, Dahmer would "every so often, as he would go about his property . . . just take one of his guns and shoot in the air, just to let folks know he was alive, well, and intended to protect his property."[63]

Dahmer and his wife, Ellie, began to take turns sleeping at night to watch for intruders in response to anonymous threats received from White supremacists in 1961. For years, the Dahmers would maintain the practice of an evening watch for nightriders. Dahmer also had a network of supporters who helped protect him and his family. This support network included other NAACP members and local businesspeople. This network was involved in protecting voter registration activities in Forrest County.[64]

Vernon Dahmer, the Forrest County farmer who died after defending his home and family from nightriders in 1966. Dahmer provided security for SNCC workers in his community. (Courtesy of Matt Herron.)

Getting the "Word Out" in Greenwood

SNCC personnel and energy shifted to the Mississippi Delta in 1962. The first SNCC organizer in the Delta was Sam Block. Block was recommended to Moses for the task of organizing in the Delta by Amzie Moore, who had known him most of his life. Block was a 23-year-old resident of Cleveland, Mississippi. His father was a construction worker and his mother was a maid. Block was an air force veteran and attended Mississippi Vocational College (now Mississippi Valley State) in the Delta town Itta Bena. Block was assigned by Moses to organize a voter registration campaign in Leflore County.[65]

Leflore County and its county seat, Greenwood, would be the primary SNCC beachhead in the Delta. Greenwood was an important center of Mississippi's Delta cotton belt and a bastion of White supremacist power. With a population of forty-seven thousand, the Delta city was the state headquarters of the Citizens' Council. Although Leflore was a Black-majority county with over two-thirds of the population being of African descent, it possessed only 250 Black registered voters. Ninety-five percent of Leflore's eligible Whites were registered in contrast to only 2 percent of eligible Blacks. Consequently, all of the elected officials were White in this Black-majority county.[66] Poverty was also a significant issue in Leflore County. The median income for Whites was fifty-two hundred dollars, while for Blacks it was fifteen hundred dollars. White farmers also owned 90 percent of the county's land.[67]

Block arrived in Greenwood on June 18, 1962,[68] and was identified and targeted by White supremacist forces within weeks of his arrival.[69] In spite of being evicted from his initial meeting place and being homeless, Block was persistent, organizing Greenwood residents to register. His efforts led a group of twenty-one Black Greenwood citizens to conquer fear and intimidation and go downtown to the Leflore County courthouse to register. After being refused service by the registrar, Block and the group were confronted by the sheriff. The sheriff singled Block out, spat in his face, and told the young activist to get out of town. Block militantly responded, "If you don't want to see me here, I think the best thing for you to do is pack your clothes and leave, get out of town."[70] Block's courage inspired those with him. In the face of being harassed by police officers while leaving downtown, some of the would-be registrants retorted, "You don't scare me no more. You don't scare me no more."[71]

In the coming weeks, Block would return with other Leflore Blacks wishing to register. Block also became more of a target for local White supremacists and police by encouraging a young Greenwood Black man to file charges of police brutality to federal officials. The SNCC activist submitted an affidavit, photos, and other evidence to the Department of Justice. Bob Moses commented that after Block's attempt to solicit federal intervention for this victim of police terror, "From then on . . . it was Sam versus the police."[72]

White supremacists were angered by Block's courage and militancy. The level of terror increased from harassment to physical brutality. On August 13th, three White males accosted Block on a Greenwood street, forced him into an alley, and beat him. SNCC soon sent reinforcements. Tougaloo College student Lawrence Guyot and eighteen-year-old SNCC field secretary Lavaughn Brown joined Block on August 16th, three days after Block was beaten.[73]

SNCC intentionally sent Guyot and Brown to Greenwood to communicate its resolve to the African American residents of Leflore. White supremacists would again take terror to a new level. On the evening following Guyot and Brown's arrival, the SNCC workers were in their new office, located upstairs in a building in Greenwood's Black community. Block and the new arrivals noticed eight men leaving vehicles and armed with shotguns, ropes, bricks, and chains. Block immediately called Department of Justice official John Doar. While Doar offered no immediate protection, he advised the activists to leave the office. Block, Brown, and Guyot escaped through the office bathroom window, climbed over the roof, and jumped to another roof to find refuge with a supporter in the Black community of Greenwood.[74]

The Greenwood SNCC contingent returned the next day to find their office ransacked; Moses and a new comrade were waiting for them. Willie Peacock, a graduate of Rust College (located in Holly Springs, Mississippi), was another recruit of Amzie Moore. Local police would soon pressure the Black owner of the building where SNCC's Greenwood office was located to evict the organization. SNCC workers rooted themselves in the Greenwood Black community and slowly gained support in spite of the repression, the lack of resources, and the fear of some Leflore Blacks of being associated with the Movement.[75]

White supremacist attacks on SNCC voter registration workers in the Delta intensified in 1963. On February 28th, three White supremacists armed with a submachine gun and riding in a 1962 Buick carried out a drive-by shooting on Moses and two other activists. Moses and Randall Blackwell of the Voter Education Project were being driven by SNCC worker Jimmy Travis on their way from Greenwood to another Delta town, Greenville. This assault left SNCC activist Jimmy Travis wounded in his shoulder and in the back of his neck. Travis immediately received medical attention in Greenville. He was then taken to the Greenwood hospital and finally to a Jackson hospital where the bullet lodged behind his spinal cord was removed.[76]

The shooting of Travis became a catalyst for the Leflore County movement. Movement forces throughout the state and from the national leadership mobilized to Greenwood after this vicious attack. Voter Education Project executive director and civil rights attorney Wiley Branton made a call for all voter registration workers in the state to converge on Greenwood. SNCC voted for its entire Mississippi staff to answer Branton's call.[77] Since 1962, SNCC, CORE, the NAACP, and the SCLC coordinated efforts in Mississippi through the umbrella of the Council of Federated Organizations (COFO). Other voter registration projects also sent reinforcements through the COFO vehicle.[78]

One month prior to the shooting of Travis, Bob Moses and six other Mississippi SNCC activists filed suit in Washington, D.C., against several Mississippi officials. The suit charged the state officials with responsibility for the violent acts directed against Black Mississippians and Movement activists. The complaint noted that President Kennedy and FBI director J. Edgar Hoover had been consistently informed of the violence and harassment of local Blacks and activists in the South in 1961 and 1962. The suit failed in court, and federal officials gave little indication that they were willing to intervene on the basis of legality, moral conscience, or goodwill.[79]

In March of 1963, White supremacist assaults on SNCC workers continued and intensified. Peacock, Block, and two other comrades, Essie Broom and Peggy Maryne, were the targets of a terrorist attack on March 6th. The four activists were assaulted by shotgun blasts as they were parking in front of the SNCC office. Fortunately, they escaped with only minor cuts after nightriders fired on their car. Greenwood mayor Charles Sampson charged that SNCC created the incident to gain publicity for its campaign. On March 24th, terrorists set the SNCC office on fire, destroying all of the office equipment.[80]

The response to White terror increased again after nightriders shot into the home of COFO worker and local NAACP president Dewey Greene on March 26th. Greene and his family were in the center of the Leflore County Movement. Greene's son, Dewey Jr., was Block's first Leflore County recruit. Four children of the Greene household were involved with COFO and the local voter registration campaign. One of them, George, returning home from a mass meeting, was nearly shot when nightriders fired a shotgun blast, shattering a window in the house.[81]

The Greene patriarch immediately contacted local law enforcement and communicated that he was armed and was prepared for anyone wishing to attack his household. Greene warned, "[I]f anybody else came shooting at his house, the police could just come and collect the bodies."[82] The attack on the well-liked Greene family angered Greenwood's Black community and sparked more Leflore County residents into action. SNCC executive secretary James Forman stated that many in the Black community "felt they now had nothing to lose. They were ready to move."[83]

A large crowd gathered at Wesley Chapel Methodist Church the next morning, angered by the attack on the Greene household. Moses passionately exhorted the crowd to march to the Leflore County courthouse

downtown in honor of Greene and his family, who had committed themselves to the voter registration campaign. Speaking after Moses, James Forman offered a different option. Forman called for the crowd to march to
city hall and demand that Greenwood's mayor utilize his authority to stop
the violence against the Black citizens of the city. The gathering enthusiastically supported both suggestions. Forman and Moses privately huddled
and compromised. The demonstration would first go to city hall and then
to the courthouse to register to vote.[84]

Over 150 people participated in the march. Anyone participating had
to commit to nonviolence; however, many local Blacks were not willing
to make that commitment. Hollis Watkins recalled, "[S]ome of the local brothers and sisters said 'I can't give up my stuff so I won't be on the
march, I'll just be on the side.'" The presence of armed bystanders accompanying nonviolent demonstrations was not isolated to Greenwood and
would become a common occurrence during Movement demonstrations.[85]
SNCC activists led other confrontational activism, including a demonstration and voter registration contingent to the Leflore County Courthouse.[86]

The SNCC strategy to force the federal government to "take a side"
proved to be successful in the case of Greenwood. On March 31st, five days
after the attack on the Greene household, a federal district court ordered
Greenwood officials to allow Blacks to peacefully protest. The judge, responding to a Department of Justice petition, also ordered the release of
incarcerated SNCC activists. Coverage of the police attacks on demonstrators from the *New York Times* and the *Chicago Defender* and other national
media played a significant role in motivating the federal government to
act.[87]

Local officials resisted federal intervention. The interned SNCC activists remained incarcerated. On April 3rd, three days after the injunction,
Greenwood police prevented a small demonstration of forty people from
marching. Nineteen of the marchers were arrested. One local activist broke
the vow of nonviolence during the confrontation between the marchers
and the police. Mrs. Laura McGhee defended herself after being shoved by
a police officer's nightstick. McGhee wrestled with the officer's nightstick.
Entertainer and activist Dick Gregory had to restrain her from further
action.[88]

Like the Greene family, Laura McGhee and her family were in the center of the Leflore County freedom movement. Mrs. McGhee was a widow,
a small farmer, and one of the first county residents to support the SNCC
voter registration campaign in Leflore. She was the sister of Gus Courts,

who was shot in Belzoni and ultimately exiled from Mississippi. McGhee's land was used for voter registration classes, meetings, rallies, refuge for tenants displaced for supporting the voter registration campaign, as well as collateral to bail out Movement activists.

The McGhee family was reputed to "take no shit," while they also "gave shit out." Mrs. McGhee was a clear example of the fact that the Black armed resistance tradition was not exclusively male. She was an active participant in the defense of her household and property. Mrs. McGhee would sleep in the day so that she could conduct a watch from her porch at night, armed with a Winchester rifle.[89]

Her sons—Silas, Jake, and Clarence—were also active in the voter registration campaign and like their mother, actively defended their family. One evening, after an explosion from a "cherry bomb," the McGhee brothers witnessed nightriders leaving the area. The nightriders shot the McGhee family dog as it ran toward the car. The McGhee sons fired their weapons at and hit the marauders' vehicle as it left their property. The FBI and the Leflore sheriff came to the McGhee matriarch to demand that her sons not shoot at intruders. According to historian Charles Payne (who interviewed Laura McGhee), she told them not to worry, "she'd do all the rest of the shooting herself."[90]

Local police presented themselves as the primary nemesis to nonviolent demonstrators in Greenwood "direct action" demonstrations. In other southern cities and towns, White civilians attacked human rights demonstrations that occurred in the spring of 1963. Hollis Watkins analyzed that once "the word got out" that there were armed Black bystanders at marches and demonstrations, it served to prevent violence by civilians. Watkins argued that due to the presence of armed Blacks, the police had to "worry about making sure these crazy white folks don't come and attempt to do nothing 'cause some of them could be killed in the process." Local law enforcement discouraged White terrorism to prevent the loss of White life and the escalation of violence. The police did not respond when SNCC workers were shot at and harassed. However, after Blacks like Dewey Greene and Laura McGhee vocally announced that they would meet violence with violence and the "word got out" that there was covert armed Black protection at the nonviolent marches, police attempted to deter White civilian terrorism.[91]

The federal government and Greenwood officials reached a compromise on April 3rd. The Department of Justice compromised on its initial position by rescinding its injunction against the Greenwood government.

In turn, the local Greenwood authorities agreed not to press charges against those in the initial arrest on March 27th. This grant of amnesty did not apply to Laura McGhee and the eighteen other activists arrested on April 3rd. Greenwood officials and local segregationists viewed the compromise as a victory, as they had successfully resisted northern liberal and Black agitators.[92]

The compromise was a blow to the notion that the federal government could be relied upon to neutralize the power of White supremacy and apartheid in the South. The Kennedy administration succumbed to pressure from the segregationist U.S. senators from Mississippi, James Eastland and John Stennis. The Kennedy government did not want to alienate White southerners while making overtures to potential Black voters. The Department of Justice compromise was viewed as a sellout by Movement activists and the Greenwood Black community. The ambivalence of the federal government would eventually have an effect on the commitment to tactical nonviolence and the anticipation of federal intervention to curtail White supremacist violence, whether state or civilian. Some in the Movement would be convinced of the necessity to rely on their own resources to sustain and protect the Black community, including armed self-defense.

"Just Protecting My Wife and Family": Holmes County and Hartman Turnbow

Directly south of Leflore is Holmes County. Black residents of Holmes County traveled to Greenwood to support the civil rights demonstrations and make contacts with the Movement. Holmes also possessed a Black majority, with people of African descent constituting 72 percent of the population. The western quarter of Holmes County is Delta country: physically, politically, and culturally. In keeping with the political culture of the rest of the Delta region, people of African descent were denied the right to vote, in spite of Holmes's Black majority.

Holmes's high percentage of Black-owned farms made it unique compared to other Delta counties. Black land ownership increased in the early 1940s due to two developments in the county. First, Black World War II veterans utilized the G.I. Bill to purchase land to increase their personal economic independence. Secondly, 107 tenant families were able to purchase 9,850 acres of Delta farmland in the Mileston community on long-term, low-interest loans through a New Deal program, the Farm Security Administration.[93]

SNCC was invited to initiate a voter registration campaign in Holmes after local residents visited Greenwood. SNCC sent John Ball to initiate a voter registration school there. The Mileston farming community provided the location and most of the participants in the Holmes County voter registration school. Mileston, a community of independent Black landowners, would become one of the haven communities in Mississippi. SNCC and other activists could venture to Mileston for protection and refuge from hostile White terror.[94]

Fourteen Holmes County Blacks went to downtown Lexington (the Holmes County seat) and attempted to register on April 9, 1963. This group consisted primarily of Black landowners over the age of forty. The group was met at the courthouse by county sheriff Andrew Smith, county and city police, as well as nearly thirty deputized Whites. Smith and his armed contingent attempted to intimidate the group through a show of force. The sheriff cursed and shouted at the group while slapping one hand on his sidearm and the other on his club. A Black farmer named Hartman Turnbow humbly appealed that the group was "only here to vote . . . to *redish* [register]." Seeking to avoid publicity or federal intervention, Smith decided to comply with Turnbow's request and barked, "Who will be first?" Turnbow was the first to respond, and one by one the group entered to apply. Turnbow and one other farmer, John Wesley, were allowed to take the complicated Mississippi voter registration test. Wesley and Turnbow failed the test, and the other twelve applications were denied. The group was encouraged that it survived the ordeal, seeing it as the beginning of a long struggle.[95]

The White supremacist forces in Holmes would respond swiftly to this violation of the institution of apartheid and White supremacy. The names of each of the fourteen who sought registration were published in the local newspaper. Reverend Nelson Trent, who was part of the group, left town after being threatened by local police. One Holmes County activist recalled that Trent was given "thirty minutes to get outta town."[96]

Hartman Turnbow was identified as the leader of the group due to his willingness to humbly ask to register and go first. Turnbow was named in the local press as an "integration leader." One month after the journey to Lexington, on May 8, 1963, nightriders tossed Molotov cocktails and shot several rounds into the home of Hartman Turnbow in the hamlet of Tchula. The nightriders waited for Turnbow to escape from the front of his burning house so they could assassinate him. Turnbow's wife and daughter escaped the burning house first and were not harmed by the nightriders. Turnbow emerged from the burning house with his sixteen-round .22 semiautomatic rifle. The nightriders fired at Turnbow and he returned the fire, expending every round. Turnbow's response forced the terrorists to retreat. Holmes County Blacks believed that Turnbow shot and killed one of the nightriders, but to protect the identity of the terrorist, local authorities claimed the cause of death was a heart attack.[97]

The Turnbow family turned their attention to putting out the fire, and the house was saved, in spite of severe damage. Turnbow was arrested the following day on charges of arson by Sheriff Smith. Local authorities accused Turnbow of setting his own home on fire to "work up sympathy and excitement" for the voter registration campaign. Bob Moses and three other SNCC workers came the next morning to investigate the attack on the Turnbow home. Moses and his comrades were immediately arrested for "obstructing the sheriff's investigation" by taking pictures of the crime scene. Due to federal intervention, charges against Turnbow and the SNCC activists were dropped six months after the arrests.[98]

Turnbow's successful defense of his life and his inspirational leadership made him a legendary figure within the Holmes County Black community and the Mississippi Movement. Similar to militant grassroots leaders like Steptoe, Dahmer, Greene, and McGhee, Turnbow won the admiration and respect of young SNCC activists. It was widely known within the Movement that Turnbow did not practice or advocate nonviolence. According to Charles Cobb, Turnbow would joke about his act of armed resistance in defense of his family and home. He was known to say, "I wasn't being non-nonviolent. I was just protecting my wife and family." In one interview, Turnbow took pride in the fact that he publicly disagreed with Martin Luther King Jr.'s advocacy of nonviolence on two occasions. At a meeting during the 1964 Democratic Convention, Turnbow made the following response to statements by King: "[T]his nonviolent stuff ain't no good. It'll get you killed." The same day Turnbow told a young female activist, "[E]ver what the Mississippi white man pose with, he got to be met with. . . . Meet him with ever he pose with, if he pose with a smile, meet him with a smile, and if he pose with a gun, meet him with a gun." Turnbow generally came to SNCC/COFO meetings with a briefcase that concealed his .38 handgun. The Tchula farmer exhorted, "This [his handgun] is for folks who might try and come in here and do something to us. They ain't gonna come up in here and take us, not as long as I'm here and alive."[99]

Hartman Turnbow, who was arrested for setting his own house on fire after defending his family from nightriders. Turnbow stated that he "wasn't being non-nonviolent. I was just protecting my family." (Courtesy of Matt Herron.)

In spite of White violence and intransigence, Turnbow and the Black community of Holmes would continue their fight for basic civil and human rights. The Holmes County movement was very self-reliant and maintained its momentum after COFO/ SNCC organizers relocated to other counties.[100] Holmes County became a significant base for the Mississippi Movement. The Mileston farming community was particularly important to the maintenance of the Movement. Part of Mileston's significance was its ability to provide a protective ring around its community. The armed presence of independent Black farmers in Holmes County was greatly appreciated by activists committed to nonviolence. From their experiences in Pike and Leflore counties, many SNCC and COFO activists were beginning to believe that federal law enforcement could not be relied on for protection.

CORE in Canton: Protected by "Badass" C. O. Chinn

CORE also experienced challenges to its nonviolent philosophy in the rural Deep South. SNCC, the first organization to apply Gandhian principles to the Mississippi anti-apartheid movement, engaged Black southerners who practiced armed self-defense as a way of life. CORE organizers would also rely upon rural Blacks for protection.

CORE sent its first full-time organizer to Mississippi in 1962. A veteran of the Freedom Rides, New Orleans CORE member Dave Dennis went to Mississippi as CORE's sole representative in the state. His presence in the state was initially facilitated by a Voter Education Project grant shared by CORE, SNCC, and the NAACP. Dennis would convince CORE to allow him to continue in Mississippi after the grant ended. He traveled to communities around the state involved in voter registration. Dennis became one of COFO's principal leaders, as cochair along with Bob Moses. CORE assumed responsibility to organize COFO's voter registration project in Mississippi's Fourth Congressional District, which primarily consisted of five central Mississippi counties: Madison, Rankin, Leake, Neshoba, and Lauderdale. Similar to his comrades in SNCC, Dennis and the group of people he organized became targets of harassment and White terrorism. The young organizer appealed to others in CORE to join him in the fight for voting rights in Mississippi. Another Freedom Rider and New Orleans CORE member, George Raymond, was sent to Mississippi to join Dennis in 1963.[101]

Dennis felt that Madison County, and its county seat of Canton, had good potential as a CORE base. Blacks constituted nearly 75 percent of the county's population and owned 40 percent of the land in Madison. In spite of their numbers and economic strength, Blacks were denied the right to vote. Less than two hundred people of African descent were registered to vote, from a population of twenty-nine thousand Blacks. While Blacks controlled a significant amount of the county's land, their economic independence was very limited. Cotton was the primary crop in the county, as in the Delta region, and cotton production was subsidized by the federal government. State officials determined which farmers would receive federal allotments, and, due to racial discrimination, Black farmers rarely received allowances. Madison County's Black farmers also found themselves constantly in debt, often having to pledge their crop in advance. Despite their large numerical majority and the percentage of Black-owned land, Madison County's Blacks found themselves in the status of "second-class citizens." Madison also provided the Movement with Tougaloo College as a resource. Tougaloo was a private Black institution located in the south-west corner of the county. It was an important recruiting zone for the Mississippi Black Freedom Struggle.[102]

George Raymond came to Canton (the county seat of Madison) in June of 1963. Raymond had participated in the Freedom Rides and had organized in the Mississippi Delta before coming to Madison. Dennis described Canton as "a hot bed area. . . . Like the 'Old West.'"[103] In 1963, Canton was a frontier town controlled by a segregationist White elite and enforced by a strongman, Sheriff Billy Noble. Noble fulfilled all the stereo-types of a White southern sheriff. He was brash and brutal and a staunch segregationist. Any Movement activism in Madison would find Noble a formidable adversary.[104]

The survival of CORE and the Movement in Madison depended on the involvement and support of a man whose reputation was at least as formidable as Billy Noble's; "Badass" C. O. Chinn fit the description. Chinn developed his reputation years before the Movement came to Canton, when he confronted a White planter who made demands that he work on a White-owned plantation (see chapter 1). As a young adult, Chinn participated in the U.S. military. Ironically, he served in the same military with Sheriff Noble. Upon leaving the military, Chinn and his young wife, Minnie, began to build their family in Canton. He became an enterprising businessman, opening a café and bar and "bootlegging" liquor on the side. The White power structure and Noble did not interfere with Chinn's legal or illegal enterprises, allowing him the space to exist. In return, Chinn paid a tribute to the local White elite in order to operate his illegal alcohol business.[105]

As in other Mississippi towns, George Raymond and CORE were avoided by local people when they initially came to Canton. Most Canton Black citizens feared reprisal from Canton's White power structure. Chinn made a decision to embrace Raymond, and doors began to open for Raymond after the well-respected Chinn's endorsement of the young activist. Chinn's embrace of Raymond and CORE extended beyond his endorsement and goodwill. CORE was able to utilize office space in the Chinn Café, and Chinn also provided CORE workers with transportation and protection. He began to use his connections to get CORE forums at churches and other public gatherings and often spoke in support of the voting rights campaign. In response to his support for CORE activism, Chinn was targeted for economic reprisal and political repression by the local White supremacists. The cordial relationship that had developed between Chinn and Noble since their days in the military soured after Chinn openly supported CORE. He eventually lost his liquor license and was forced to close his bar.[106]

C. O. Chinn is a legendary figure in the history of the Mississippi Black Freedom Struggle. If Billy Noble was the stereotypic White southern sheriff, Chinn was definitely the quintessential "crazy Negro." He certainly did not fit the stereotype of servile and deferential behavior that has been identified with southern Blacks of his generation. He crossed lines that other Blacks only dreamed of crossing. He was revered by the local Blacks and feared by local Whites. Chinn also did not fit most popular images of a southern civil rights leader. He was not a clergyman or an idealistic intellectual like many of the personalities projected as leaders of the Civil Rights Movement in the popular narrative. While Chinn was a Christian, his lifestyle could not be confused with that of a devout religious leader or layperson. In fact, his wife, Mrs. Minnie Chinn, who also loved and respected her husband, described Chinn as a "devil."[107] Black people in Madison County respected Chinn because he openly spoke his mind and was not intimidated by White racists. Chinn's moral authority in the Black community was based on his courage and willingness to openly oppose the White power structure.

Chinn was also respected by Blacks because Whites, including the police and the White power structure, actually feared him. CORE activist Matthew Suarez remembered that "every White man in that town knew that you didn't fuck with C. O. Chinn." Chinn also received respect and special treatment from Billy Noble and the police that was not afforded to other local Blacks. According to CORE leader Rudy Lombard, the intimidating Noble would taunt Black protesters, yelling, "[A]in't but two bad sons of bitches in this county, me and that nigger C. O. Chinn." Lombard recalls, "They treated him and they approached him very gingerly. . . .They would ask for his permission to proceed or to talk to him or to do something that he might consider a violation of his space or his rights." It is also suggested by many Movement activists that Billy Noble was the only Madison County official that Chinn would allow to arrest him. One observer claimed that when a young deputy attempted to arrest Chinn, the Black activist apparently laughed at the youthful deputy and demanded that if he was to be arrested, only Billy Noble could arrest him. The young officer left and returned with Noble. Noble took off his gun and told Chinn that if he could whip him hand to hand, Chinn would not be arrested. If Chinn lost the battle, he was expected to go to jail. Movement veterans claim this scenario occurred several times, with the sheriff winning some of the matches but Chinn often emerging as the victor.[108]

CORE workers' admiration for Chinn parallels the respect SNCC workers had for Steptoe, Dahmer, McGhee, and Turnbow. According to Dave Dennis, Chinn was "assertive, aggressive and didn't take no shit." CORE activist Anne Moody recalled, "[H]e [Chinn] was the type of person that didn't take shit from anyone. If he was with you he was all for you. If he didn't like you that was it. . . . He was in position to speak his mind."[109]

Chinn's reputation was an asset to CORE's organizing effort. His intervention often struck fear into local Whites, preventing them from attacking CORE activists. At times, Chinn openly carried a handgun on his person, which was legal in Mississippi. Chinn was also the inspirational leader of a group of "protective guys," who provided armed security for CORE and other voter registration workers. CORE workers realized that Chinn not only provided them legitimacy in order to speak to the community but also acted as the catalyst to a local network that provided protection from nightriders. According to Lombard, Chinn "wasn't solo, he was just the inspirational leader. He gave other people heart . . . and the courage to step to it." Chinn's protective guys and other defense networks of this period were informal, not structured and organized paramilitary groups, as Lombard explains:

> There were no organized groups that were professionally committed to self-defense. But there were these individuals and their friends who took it on themselves to do it without publicizing it, without serving public notice in any way whatsoever. They just did it as a matter of a part of the way they normally lived.

In the Mississippi Movement, organized paramilitary groups dedicated to armed self-defense were not common in the late 1950s and early 1960s. On the other hand, Lombard argued that Chinn, his colleagues, and other informal networks in the South would serve as the inspiration for and as forerunners of the subsequent development of such militant paramilitary formations in later periods as the Deacons for Defense and Justice and the Black Panthers.[110]

Besides the network of protective guys, Chinn's defiant attitude inspired support for the Movement and a growing militancy in certain working-class and poor communities. Similar to haven communities in Walthall, Mileston, and Danville, Virginia, certain Canton neighborhoods were feared by local Whites. Dennis remembered, "Black folks said you [nightriders] don't come into this area." With this in mind, the CORE Freedom House was strategically located across the street from a housing project. The residents of the project organized to protect CORE workers and the Freedom House. Local people even provided "nonviolent" CORE workers with a rifle to protect themselves.[111]

Closing Chinn's business was not enough for the segregationists. After warnings and economic reprisal, Chinn refused to bend or compromise and remained an inspiration to Movement forces and the Black community. The CORE voter registration campaign was beginning to develop steam, recruiting young people and winning the support of adults. Less than a month after the campaign began, in late June 1963, twelve Blacks succeeded in registering in one week. Another eighteen Blacks were turned away by county officials. It was obvious to the White power structure that Chinn's presence and influence had to be neutralized. Chinn was stopped by police while driving his pickup truck one summer evening in 1963. Police observed Chinn's .45 caliber automatic handgun on the front seat of the truck, which was legal by Mississippi law. Chinn was arrested on felony charges of carrying a concealed weapon, was convicted, and spent six months in prison. In spite of Chinn's internment, the Canton Movement continued and new leaders like former schoolteacher Annie Devine joined the voter registration campaign.[112]

To exist and to mobilize the Black population of Canton and Madison County, CORE had to rely on indigenous Blacks who were immersed in the Black armed resistance tradition. CORE also would come across other local Movement activists who utilized armed self-defense in the Harmony community of Leake County and in the city of Meridian and would rely on them for protection. This was ironic since CORE pioneered the concept and practice of nonviolence in the struggle for Black human rights. The reality of danger in Mississippi and the example of Chinn and the Black community of Canton did create a debate within the CORE staff in Canton about the necessity of arming themselves.[113] This debate within an organization that was so committed to nonviolence is a compelling statement of the influence and persuasiveness of the armed resistance tradition within the South, particularly in rural communities.

Initial Engagement: Nonviolence and the Armed Resistance Tradition

SNCC's and CORE's initial experience in Mississippi illuminates the existence and role of the armed "eye for an eye" tradition in the Deep South. Significant local leaders and/or contiguous neighborhoods that practiced armed self-defense were present in virtually every community SNCC and CORE organized. Nonviolent activists encountered and received protection from informal community networks of Blacks in Walthall, Leflore, Madison, and Holmes counties. Indigenous Mississippi Black leaders Medgar Evers, E. W. Steptoe, Ernest Nobles, Vernon Dahmer, Hartman Turnbow, C. O. Chinn, Dewey Greene, and Laura McGhee were clearly not nonviolent.

It was difficult for young, nonviolent activists to challenge the practice of armed self-defense in Black Mississippi communities. First, many of the activists from organizations committed to nonviolence depended on Black people who were immersed in the "eye for an eye" tradition for survival and protection. Secondly, SNCC and CORE began to recruit young Black Mississippians like Hollis Watkins, MacArthur Cotton, and Anne Moody, who grew up familiar with the armed resistance tradition within their local communities. These two factors would have a major impact on the perspectives concerning the utility of nonviolence in the Civil Rights Movement. SNCC and CORE would move from compromise with the "eye for an eye" tradition to debate within their organizations over support for the right of armed self-defense.

4

"Local People Carry the Day"

Freedom Summer and Challenges to Nonviolence in Mississippi

SNCC activist Margaret Block was assigned to organize in Tallahatchie County for Freedom Summer. In Tallahatchie, Block resided with 86-year-old Janie Brewer.

> *Mrs. Brewer asked me what did SNCC mean and I told her the Student Non-violent Coordinating Committee. And she stopped me. [She said,] "You said nonviolent. If somebody come at you, you ain't gonna do nothing." . . . She pulled up a big ole rifle. . . . She kept a big rifle behind the chair. . . . [Brewer said,] "Shit, we ain't nonviolent." . . . Since I was living with them [the Brewers], I had to be what the family was.[1]*

The Origins of Mississippi Freedom Summer

By 1964, CORE and SNCC organizers in Mississippi were confronted with the dilemma of continuing their voter registration efforts in the face of increasing violence from White supremacists against the activists and communities they organized. SNCC's and CORE's initial years in Mississippi had demonstrated that White supremacists would respond violently to protect the system of segregation. The Kennedy administration, particularly the Department of Justice, proved an inconsistent partner with respect to its ability or willingness to protect COFO activists from the violence of Mississippi racists. COFO activists, some of whom had come to Mississippi with the expectation of federal protection, were dismayed by their inability to guarantee security for local Blacks in Mississippi. Since the arrival of Moses, Black Mississippi and its Freedom Struggle experienced a reign of terror, which included the assassination of Medgar Evers in 1963. In spite of the willingness of local Blacks to protect themselves and their communities, nightriders continued their bombings, drive-by shootings, as well as other acts of harassment and intimidation. COFO activists were concerned that the growing level of White supremacist violence would paralyze Movement activity in Mississippi.[2]

By the fall of 1963, in response to the reign of terror, a debate developed within COFO and SNCC concerning how to proceed with the Movement in Mississippi. Concerned about the organization's inability to protect Black Mississippians, Bob Moses proposed that COFO bring a massive number of White volunteers from northern colleges and universities.[3] Moses was impressed by the involvement of nearly one hundred White volunteers from Yale and Stanford during the successful "Freedom Vote" campaign in the fall of 1963. During the Freedom Vote campaign, a decrease of violence occurred in the areas where the White volunteers were present. The decrease in violence led to the perception that bringing in White volunteers from privileged backgrounds would motivate White supremacists to suppress terrorist violence.[4]

SNCC had not encouraged massive numbers of White volunteers in Mississippi. Moses had felt that the involvement of large numbers of Whites in rural Mississippi might violate the security of the local projects and their organizers. In the spring of 1964, a SNCC field report from Mississippi stated that it was "too dangerous for whites to participate in the project in Mississippi—too dangerous for them and too dangerous for the Negroes who would be working with them."[5] Prior to the involvement of Whites in the Freedom Vote, Moses had also been an advocate for local Blacks to be the primary recruits and workers in the local projects to ensure the development of indigenous leadership.[6]

Despite the good impressions left with Moses from the White participation in the Freedom Vote, he was primarily concerned about the security of local people and the Movement. Moses was convinced federal intervention was necessary to prevent racist violence by nightriders as well as state and local law enforcement. In spite of appeals by Moses and other SNCC leaders, most COFO workers active in Mississippi believed the Kennedy administration provided an inadequate response to the assassination of activists like Medgar Evers, as well as to other shootings, bombings, and attacks on other activists and local Mississippians. Since the federal government did not seem to place priority on Black lives, Moses proposed that bringing large numbers of Whites from privileged northern families would force the Department of Justice and the FBI to play an assertive role in protecting voter registration personnel.[7]

On the other hand, the majority of the SNCC Mississippi field staff, particularly local recruits, opposed the inclusion of Whites in projects in Black Mississippi communities. Mississippi field organizers—including Hollis Watkins, MacArthur Cotton, Willie Peacock, and Sam Block—believed that the involvement of White college students would interrupt the process of developing indigenous leadership and organization in Mississippi communities of African descent.[8] They believed it was necessary to continue to organize new forces, particularly young people, and to unite with the indigenous networks, which had been in local communities, like the local NAACP chapters, the informal intelligence systems[9] and defense groups. In many Mississippi communities, COFO had not yet initiated any organizing. Some argued that having northern Whites as the first contact these communities would have with the Movement might not encourage Black initiative and self-reliance. Some maintained that the Mississippi Blacks with little formal education might be intimidated by northern Whites with a college education. SNCC activist Charles Cobb (a Howard University student from Massachusetts) feared that—due to their experiences, contacts, and administrative skill—privileged White students would "take over" the local COFO projects from indigenous Blacks.[10]

On November 14, 1963, in a COFO staff meeting in Greenville, Mississippi, Moses presented the idea of a Mississippi Summer Project. The Mississippi Summer Project would include a massive statewide voter registration of disenfranchised Black voters, the organization of the Mississippi Freedom Democratic Party (MFDP), and the organization of freedom schools to enhance the academic skills as well as political and social consciousness of Mississippi Black youth. The MFDP was projected to be a multiracial political party that would challenge the legitimacy of the Mississippi Democratic Party at the National Democratic Convention. Moses' proposal, supported by Dave Dennis and Lawrence Guyot, included the mobilization of large numbers of White students to participate in the Summer Project. Primarily indigenous Black Mississippians involved in COFO and SNCC—like Watkins, Cotton, Block, and Peacock—opposed Moses' proposal. After a heated debate and three votes, the COFO staff agreed to a compromise, which allowed the participation of one hundred White volunteers.[11] On December 30, 1963, Moses presented the idea to SNCC's national executive committee, which enthusiastically supported it. In this meeting, SNCC veterans like John Lewis, Marion Barry, and James Forman supported Moses' proposal, agreeing that involving large numbers of White students would compel the federal government to protect Movement workers in Mississippi. SNCC's executive committee agreed to expand the number of White volunteers decided upon by the COFO staff. SNCC's national leadership decided to send representatives to a COFO meeting in January 1964 to provide Moses with support in convincing COFO staff to accept the large number of White volunteers they planned to recruit.[12]

Armed Self-Defense vs. Nonviolence:
Internal Debate within SNCC and CORE

On June 10, 1964, six months after Moses and SNCC national leadership convinced COFO staff to agree to bring a large number of White volunteers to participate in the Summer Project, another issue created debate within SNCC. At a national SNCC staff meeting in Atlanta during the preparation for Freedom Summer, the question of armed self-defense was argued on the national level within SNCC. This was the first time carrying or using weapons was discussed or debated at a national meeting of SNCC.

The same group who opposed the inclusion of a large number of Whites in the Summer Project presented the argument that SNCC activists should be allowed to protect themselves and their offices with guns. The debate began after SNCC staff working out of the organization's Greenwood office, the Freedom House, informed the participants in the meeting that they had made a decision to "protect the people around the office and [to prevent] people from breaking in and bombing the office." Since January 1964, guns had been kept in the Freedom House in Greenwood. Charles Cobb informed the meeting that Amzie Moore had received information from the "grapevine" (the informal intelligence network) that he (Moore), Bob Moses, Fannie Lou Hamer, Dave Dennis, and Aaron Henry were targeted for assassination. SNCC staff members in Greenwood also believed their lives were in jeopardy. They were informed that Whites in the Delta were arming themselves to terrorize COFO. SNCC staff also received information about a truckload of arms and ammunition, which was intercepted in Illinois before being delivered to White supremacists in Mississippi. Besides the threat to their personal security, staff members were concerned about burglaries, which had occurred at the office. Due to the potential for violence, the staff of the Greenwood office decided to obtain guns for their protection. The Greenwood staff and other Delta organizers also reported that local Blacks in the Delta were also arming themselves and advising SNCC activists to do likewise. Willie Peacock pointed out that since the "FBI was unwilling to track down" the perpetrators of White supremacist violence, rural Blacks established a "self-defense structure." As a result, attacks on the Black community were prevented because Whites were aware that they were armed.[13]

The reality of the position and recent practices of SNCC organizers in Greenwood sparked a lively and heated discussion on the question of armed self-defense versus nonviolence. Various questions were raised: Should SNCC workers in the Deep South arm themselves? Should armed sentries be placed around SNCC and COFO Freedom Houses in the South? What relationship should SNCC have with indigenous Black southerners who practiced armed self-defense? What were the consequences of Black communities defending themselves through armed resistance? SNCC staff passionately debated these questions.

In the debate, many offered arguments that supported a strategy of nonviolence and questioned the practicality of armed resistance. Frank Smith, an indigenous Mississippian who organized in Greenwood and Holly Springs (Mississippi), encouraged his comrades to maintain a non-violent posture. Smith supported the view that only the federal government could provide adequate protection for local Blacks and Movement people in Mississippi. Courtland Cox, an activist in the Nonviolent Action Group (SNCC affiliate group at Howard University in Washington, D.C.), believed that the advocacy and practice of armed resistance would isolate SNCC from the majority of the Black population. One of SNCC veterans of the 1961 sit-in movement and a Spelman College student, Ruby Doris Smith, wondered if SNCC should allow local Blacks to provide ostensibly nonviolent organizers with protection. One of the most passionate arguments in opposition to armed self-defense was made by Prathia Hall, an activist and theology student from Philadelphia. Hall was no stranger to the violence of southern segregationists, as she had been wounded in Dawson, Georgia, in 1962. On the philosophical level, Hall argued that by "destroying life [through violence] we don't preserve them." From a pragmatic point of view, she argued that the talk of Black self-defense was suicidal. Hall believed that "if you kill an attacker . . . you will lose your home anyway because the [White] townsmen will come to the aid of the attacker and take everything [life and property] away from you." Bob Moses argued that while SNCC could not expect local Blacks to commit themselves to nonviolence, SNCC workers were obligated to be unarmed. Moses recognized that being armed was a way of life in Black southern culture and that to most local Blacks, nonviolence was a foreign concept. On the other hand, SNCC as an organization had made a commitment to nonviolence, and its organizers were required to practice Christian pacifism.[14]

The advocates of armed self-defense also argued passionately and persuasively. Sam Block testified that armed Blacks had deterred Whites intending to do harm to the SNCC office. Block also invoked the example of Laura McGhee, who had prevented attacks on her Greenwood home by openly being armed. In response to Hall's assertion that armed self-defense would be suicidal for Black southern communities, Mike Sayer, a White activist from New York, reminded his colleagues about Robert Williams and the armed Black community in Monroe, North Carolina. To Sayer, the deterrence of the Klan by armed patrols in Monroe suggested that armed Black resistance would not necessarily lead to a holocaust and massacre, as implied by Hall. Other SNCC projects were also affected by this debate. Donald Harris, a SNCC organizer in Albany, Georgia, questioned whether SNCC activists should discourage local Blacks from participating in acts of retaliatory violence. In 1964, SNCC workers had also encountered armed Blacks in a fierce struggle that had exploded in Cambridge, Maryland.[15]

In a critical moment in the debate, Charles Cobb then asked a critical question: "Where does SNCC stand when Mr. [E. W.] Steptoe is killed while defending his home, with his two daughters there and his rifle laying on the floor?" He continued, "Where does SNCC stand when I pick up his gun . . . as I will . . . and, then, when the police arrest me?"[16] After a long silence, SNCC's elder advisor Ella Baker offered her perspective to break the impasse. Baker rarely intervened in the internal debates of her junior comrades in SNCC, but in response to Cobb's questions, Baker stated, "I can't conceive of the SNCC I thought I was associated with not defending Charlie Cobb. . . . In my book, Charlie would not be operating out of SNCC if he did what he said." All factions within SNCC respected Ella Baker. While she did not affirmatively advocate armed self-defense, Baker's support for Cobb's position was a critical acknowledgment of support for SNCC staff desiring more flexibility around the organization's position on the use of force. After Baker's affirmation and several other comments, Cobb asserted, "I won't carry a gun . . . but what's different here is the presence of Mr. Steptoe's daughters. If I was there alone, I'd head out the back door. The question to me is purely one of protection of the daughters."[17]

After the lengthy debate, a consensus was reached that no guns were to be kept in any "Freedom House or office in any SNCC project" and that "no one on [the SNCC] staff is to carry guns or weapons." It was also resolved that SNCC as an organization would not take any public position on armed self-defense and that "volunteers recruited for the Mississippi Summer Project who carry weapons will be asked to leave."[18]

Revolutionary Nationalism in the Mississippi Civil Rights Movement

The decision concerning armed volunteers was motivated by the presence and influence of members of a northern-based radical nationalist organization, the Revolutionary Action Movement (RAM), in the Greenwood Freedom House. The presence of RAM in Greenwood was an issue raised in the June 10th SNCC leadership debate on armed self-defense. The influence of "ideas brought in [to the Greenwood COFO project] by outside groups [in reference to RAM]" was raised as a concern by opponents of SNCC members engaging in armed self-defense.[19] RAM defined its ideology as revolutionary Black nationalism and was seeking to organize a liberation movement to free the "colonized Black nation" in the United States. Black student activists initiated the Revolutionary Action Movement on the campus of Central State College in Ohio during 1962. The founders of RAM came together due to a "need for a 'Third Force' . . . somewhere between the Nation of Islam [fundamental Black nationalism] . . . and SNCC [activist/militant reform]." RAM was politically to the left of SNCC and CORE and saw armed struggle as the primary means by which Black liberation would come about. RAM described itself as being in league with "Robert Williams and the concept of organized violence."[20] The leadership of RAM believed it was necessary to build a Black liberation army to wage guerilla warfare in the United States. Ultimately, RAM believed that a revolutionary situation would be created through a "strategy of chaos" utilizing mass civil disobedience to disrupt the U.S. economic and social order and enable organized revolutionaries to seize state power through armed struggle. Robert Williams, the Monroe (North Carolina) NAACP activist and advocate of armed resistance, would be appointed the international chairman of RAM in the summer of 1964, while he was in exile in Cuba. The association with Williams, considered a living hero by many, helped gain legitimacy for RAM in some freedom circles. While RAM identified with the militant confrontation tactics of SNCC and other nonviolent activists, it was critical of what it labeled the "bourgeois reformism" of the Civil Rights Movement. The revolutionary nationalists believed that with the exception of SNCC, which organized southern "grassroots" people, the rest of the Civil Rights Movement was "bourgeois in orientation." RAM argued that most integrationists were "seeking upward mobility" within the U.S. political and economic system rather than a "structural transformation of the system." RAM founder Donald Freeman articulated that the organization embraced "W. E. B. Du Bois' conviction that 'capitalism cannot reform itself, a system that enslaves you cannot free you.'" The revolutionary nationalists agreed that "full integration" of the masses of Black people "within the capitalist system" was "impossible." Thus, RAM opposed integration as a solution and advocated radical Black self-government in the context of dismantling capitalism and U.S. constitutional order.[21]

RAM's first organizing venture in the South was the "Afro-American Student Conference on Black Nationalism" at Fisk University in Nashville, May 1-2, 1964. The purpose of this conference was to consolidate Black college students who were leaning toward Black nationalism and radical politics into a force in the southern Black Freedom Struggle. The Nashville Student Movement (NSM), considered the vanguard of nonviolence and multiracialism in SNCC, came to the RAM gathering to confront the Black radicals, labeling them as "black racists." NSM was so concerned by RAM's conference that it invited Martin Luther King Jr. to speak in Nashville the same weekend. King blasted the RAM conference as "hate in reverse." A few Mississippi SNCC staff members attended the Nashville RAM gathering in solidarity, in contrast to their comrades in the NSM.[22]

Conceding to the requests of a few Mississippi staff members, John Lewis agreed to allow two avowed radical nationalist organizers, RAM field chairman Max Stanford and Harlem-based Black writer/activist Roland Snellings (aka Askia Ture), to participate in the SNCC project in Greenwood. Stanford was raised in Philadelphia with family members who had been involved in the NAACP, the Nation of Islam, and the organized Left. His father was a vocal supporter of Robert Williams's efforts at self-defense in Monroe, North Carolina. After engaging in student activism at Central State, Stanford left college and established relationships with a network of Black radicals, including Harlem's Malcolm X and reparations advocate "Queen Mother" Audley Moore, Detroit-based Marxists James and Grace Boggs, and Robert and Mabel Williams, in exile in Cuba. Stanford was secretly "smuggled" into Mississippi in 1963 through SNCC activist Willie Peacock. Snellings, a veteran of the U.S. military, joined RAM after becoming a central participant in what would eventually become the Black Arts Movement in Harlem. He also dialogued with and was influenced by Malcolm X.[23]

Revolutionary Action Movement chairman Max Stanford advocating armed self-defense at the 1963 NAACP national convention in Chicago. He also advocated armed self-defense while a volunteer in Greenwood and attempted to acquire resources to support a statewide defense structure in Mississippi. (Courtesy of Allen Koss.)

Stanford and Snellings went to Greenwood in May 1964. Both participated in the COFO freedom school in Greenwood. Snellings focused on
instruction in African and African American history and Stanford on political education and voter registration. Besides their official role in the
project, they planned to wage ideological struggle within the ranks of the
SNCC field staff. RAM's objective in the Mississippi Civil Rights Movement was to win the Black field organizers over to Black nationalism and
armed self-defense and to "push the bourgeois reformists 'up temp' as fast
as possible" to radicalize the southern Black Freedom Struggle. Stanford
and Snellings emphasized the need for Black leadership in the projects,
which resonated with the Mississippi-born field staff, many of whom opposed the drive to bring hundreds of northern White students from elite
colleges and universities to Mississippi Freedom Summer. RAM argued
that White friends of the Civil Rights Movement should organize in White
communities to confront White supremacists. Stanford and Snellings also
believed that Black male activists often compromised their advocacy for
Black indigenous leadership and autonomy after sexual trysts with White
female staff and volunteers.[24]

Stanford and Snellings also found that SNCC organizers had previously
established an armed watch of the Greenwood Freedom House. SNCC
staff member and close friend of Stanford and RAM, Willie Peacock initiated the arming of the Freedom House as early as January of 1964, five
months prior to RAM's official presence in Greenwood. Snellings reported
that the Greenwood Freedom House was armed with carbine rifles and
shotguns. The RAM organizers came into contact with indigenous Black
Mississippians who they thought were interested in meeting White supremacist violence with armed force. The RAM members vocally advocated armed patrols of the community after White terrorist threats accelerated in the wake of Freedom Summer and Laura McGhee's home was firebombed by White supremacists. RAM found that local Blacks in Leflore
County were "strapped" (armed) and prepared to initiate armed patrols
in response to the threats. When Stanford and Snelling went to a regional
COFO gathering in Greenville, Mississippi, they met Black youth in a local
pool hall who expressed their conflict with nonviolence. Snellings remembered the youth stating, "We don't believe in that nonviolent stuff. We ain't
with that." This encounter encouraged the RAM organizers to believe that
Mississippi's Black youth could be organized for armed resistance.[25]

Stanford, Snellings, and members of the Mississippi field staff met with
Amzie Moore at the SNCC elder's home to discuss the organization of

armed self-defense in Mississippi. RAM found that the Mississippi organizers were ready "to establish a state-wide self-defense system." Arms and funds would be necessary for such an undertaking. Stanford pledged to solicit support from his northern revolutionary networks for this development. Shortly after the meeting, Stanford left Mississippi to meet with friends of RAM and its leadership to obtain resources and plan a broad strategy to include fellow travelers within SNCC. He was also advised to leave Mississippi after excerpts of a report he wrote titled "Towards a Revolutionary Action Movement Manifesto" was published in an editorial of the left journal *Monthly Review*. Stanford's statement was highlighted in tandem with Robert Williams's treatise on urban guerilla warfare from exile in Cuba ("Revolution without Violence?") in the May 1964 *Monthly Review* editorial entitled "The Colonial War at Home." An interview with Malcolm X appeared in the issue. Older activists like Williams advised Stanford that his safety was compromised due to the publication of the editorial in a nationally circulated journal, making him an elevated target for White supremacists in Mississippi.[26]

Many of the SNCC field staff were receptive to RAM's Black nationalist orientation. Concerning the field staff's relations with RAM, MacArthur Cotton remembered, "[T]he majority of the local SNCC people didn't have a problem with RAM." According to Cotton, most of the Mississippi-born field staff believed "that other philosophy [integration and non-violence] was foreign," not radical Black nationalism. On the other hand, some Black organizers, particularly Bob Moses, opposed Black nationalism. They believed that RAM's nationalist ideology and advocacy of armed resistance were a disruptive force in the Mississippi SNCC. Moses was concerned about reports of Snellings' interpretation of African American history in the Greenwood freedom school. RAM's revolutionary perspective that the U.S. government was a colonial government and the enemy of Black people also ran counter to SNCC's liberal reformist view, which saw elements of the Democratic Party and the federal government as allies. Liberal Whites and some White radicals associated with SNCC and COFO also viewed RAM as a divisive force in the development of multiracial harmony. Another concern was that the charismatic Stanford was exerting "a great deal of influence" among Black activists in Mississippi.[27]

Opponents of armed self-defense in the June 10th debates noted RAM's presence in Greenwood. Bob Moses dispatched Stokely Carmichael to Greenwood after the decision was made to remove the guns from all Freedom Houses as well as SNCC offices and to disassociate from any volunteer who was armed. Carmichael was to remove the guns from the Greenwood office and ask that RAM forces also leave the Freedom House and not participate in any SNCC project.[28] Snellings remembered Carmichael telling James Jones, the head of the Greenwood project, "[I]f you want to remain head of this project, you need to get these guns out of here. . . . This is SNCC not RAM." Writing about his experience in Mississippi, Snellings stated that the Greenwood staff was told that "SNCC . . . is nonviolent, and when one becomes 'influenced' by another philosophy, one should leave." After the purge of RAM from Greenwood, Snellings left to connect with Stanford and RAM leadership in Detroit.[29] This signaled the end of RAM organizers being directly involved in Mississippi. Ironically, during Freedom Summer, many SNCC militants did carry and use weapon. SNCC executive secretary James Forman, who opposed the guns being in the Greenwood Freedom House, placed an armed sentry around the Greenwood office. RAM's ideological position on the role of Whites in the Civil Rights Movement would also ultimately become the dominant position within SNCC during the two years in which the revolutionary nationalist organization was present in Mississippi, when "Black Power" became its official position.[30]

The June 1964 staff meeting represented the first national debate for SNCC on the issue of armed self-defense. While the SNCC field staff reached a consensus on this issue on the eve of Freedom Summer, support for armed self-defense and the practice of carrying weapons grew within the organization. In fact, the Freedom Summer experience played a significant role in diminishing nonviolence as a philosophy and practice of the organization.

CORE, the Neshoba Murders, and Challenges to Nonviolence in the Southern Black Freedom Struggle

CORE also was engaged in debate concerning its position on armed self-defense. As early as 1962, CORE national leadership became concerned about the commitment of the CORE field staff to nonviolence and the difficulties of getting southern Blacks not to utilize weapons in response to segregationists' violence. At the 1963 CORE national convention, a special workshop on mass violence and nonviolent philosophy was organized. A primary reason for the organization of this workshop was the reports of

CORE field organizers that spoke of the common practices of southern Blacks being armed. In Deep South Movement centers like Canton, Mississippi, as well as Plaquemines and West Feliciana parishes in Louisiana, CORE workers received protection from armed Black civilians. In West Feliciana, meetings organized by CORE staff received armed protection from local Blacks. In a report from West Feliciana, a CORE worker stated, "We cannot tell someone not to defend his property and the lives of his family, and let me assure you, those 15-20 shotguns guarding our meetings are very assuring."[31] James Farmer, the national director of CORE, feared that as the Black Freedom Struggle intensified, it would be difficult to restrain CORE members from participating in acts of armed resistance. In one instance, Farmer reported that after police had raided a local CORE office in the South, CORE members were arming themselves "to shoot it out with the police the next time they came to the office." At the 1963 convention, many delegates reported that they had to disarm southern Blacks "who had come to mass meetings and demonstrations with revolvers and knives."[32] Farmer spoke directly to the perceived dangers of CORE members and Movement activists and supporters embracing armed resistance. Fearing the effects that the association of the Movement with armed resistance would have on White support, Farmer stated, "[W]idespread violence by the freedom fighters would sever from the struggle all but a few of our allies." He also noted that "it would also provoke and, to many, justify such repressive measures as would stymie the movement."[33]

Farmer's fears of CORE members abandoning nonviolence as a way of life and primary strategy were not imagined or exaggerated. In the South, many key CORE activists began to recognize the utility of armed resistance as a complement or alternative to nonviolent direct action. Young CORE leaders from the New Orleans group were so committed to Gandhian principles that in 1961, they spoke of "preparing to die if necessary."[34] In 1963 and 1964, they recognized armed resistance as legitimate and in some cases used its potential as a bargaining measure. One example of this occurred in May 1963 during a heated exchange between CORE activist Jerome Smith and Attorney General Robert Kennedy. Smith, once a committed Gandhian and mentor of the New Orleans group, asserted that if the federal government could not protect Movement activists, he could not promise a continued commitment to nonviolence. Smith told Kennedy, "When I pull the trigger, kiss it [nonviolence] good-by."[35] COFO leader and CORE representative in Mississippi Dave Dennis also began to change his total commitment to nonviolence. In January 1964, Dennis cautioned Robert Kennedy that due to a lack of federal protection, Blacks "shall not watch their families starve, be jailed, beaten, and killed without responding to protect themselves. You have proven by your refusal to act that we have no other recourse but to defend ourselves with whatever means we have at our disposal."[36]

On the eve of Freedom Summer, an incident occurred that would move Dennis to an emotional and political break from the philosophy of nonviolence. On June 21, 1964, two CORE volunteers, James Chaney and Mickey Schwerner, and one Freedom Summer volunteer, Andrew Goodman, were missing after being released by Neshoba County deputy sheriff Cecil Price. Chaney was a Black Mississippian from Meridian. Schwerner was a White New Yorker who had come to Meridian in 1963 to run the CORE office there. Goodman was a college student from New York. The three workers were in Neshoba County to find housing for Freedom Summer volunteers. Dennis was to travel with them but did not go due to a bout with bronchitis. For security purposes, COFO workers were required to call in to their local headquarters (in this case Meridian) every two hours to communicate their location and the status of their well-being. When no call was received from them, an alert was sent out. SNCC, CORE, and COFO workers and supporters in Mississippi as well as across the United States mobilized to Neshoba County to locate them.[37]

Pressure was directed at the federal authorities, particularly the FBI, to join in the search for Chaney, Schwerner, and Goodman. COFO workers were very critical of the response of federal authorities. The FBI was contacted on the evening the three activists came up missing but responded to the case twenty-four hours after their call from COFO. President Lyndon Johnson also inquired into the whereabouts of Chaney, Schwerner, and Goodman. Johnson expressed his concern with U.S. senator James Eastland and Mississippi governor Paul Johnson and sent former Central Intelligence Agency director Allen Dulles to meet with Mississippi officials. COFO activists were dismayed that Dulles did not make time on his schedule to meet with Rita Schwerner, the wife of Mickey. On July 10, 1964, the FBI opened a field office in Jackson, Mississippi. On that occasion, FBI director J. Edgar Hoover, not a supporter of the Civil Rights Movement, made statements that did not invoke feelings of security from COFO forces. Assuring segregationist forces in Mississippi, Hoover stated, "[W]e most certainly do not and will not give protection to civil rights workers." Hoover also declared, "[P]rotection is in the hands of local authorities."[38] The existence of two White northerners from prominent families did create public outcry, which pressured the FBI and federal authorities not only to investigate the case but also to provide some security for human rights activists and supporters, particularly the hundreds of White volunteers involved in the Summer Project. By the end of the summer, over 150 agents were assigned to the Jackson FBI office.[39]

It was not until the early days of August that the bodies of the three activists were found and identified. The corpses of the three men were located in a bulldozed trench in a dam's base and covered by two feet of dirt. Dennis, the director of CORE activity in the state, took personal responsibility for the disappearance and subsequent lynching of the three activists. Dennis was at his mother's home in Shreveport, Louisiana, suffering from bronchitis on the evening of the three Movement workers' disappearance. Due to the absence of Dennis, inexperienced volunteers were staffing the Meridian COFO office. Chaney, Schwerner, and Goodman were expected to return to the office by 4:00 p.m. While the COFO office in Meridian did call the state headquarters in Jackson and called six jails in eastern Mississippi to inquire about their comrades' whereabouts, they did not immediately contact federal officials, including the FBI, until 9:00 p.m. that same evening. Dennis later expressed remorse that he was not in Meridian that evening to give his leadership and experience to initiating swift action in searching for his missing comrades. Dennis also believed that if federal officials had been contacted earlier, they might have intervened and saved the lives of Chaney, Schwerner, and Goodman. Another element of this case that profoundly affected Dennis was that during the federal search for Chaney, Schwerner, and Goodman, federal officials found several dead bodies in remote areas of Mississippi. One of these corpses was the body of a fourteen-year-old boy found in the Big Black River clad in a CORE t-shirt. While the search for his three comrades was important, Dennis was distraught by the fact that no serious effort was being made to investigate the cause of death and, if the cause was determined to be murder, to pursue the perpetrators of these crimes.[40]

Dennis, as a result of this experience, began to disassociate himself from an adherence to nonviolence. In fact Dennis, when asked to speak at the memorial service for James Chaney, either consciously disobeyed or unintentionally disregarded an order from CORE national leadership to preach reconciliation and nonviolence at the commemoration ceremony in honor of Chaney. At the service, Dennis gave an emotional address. He was quoted by the press as stating, "I'm sick and tired of going to the funerals of Black men who have been murdered by white men. . . . I've got vengeance in my heart tonight." Dennis also told the audience, "If you go back home and take what these white men in Mississippi are doing to us . . . if you take it and don't do something about it . . . then God damn your souls."[41] Years later, reflecting on his emotional comments that day, Dennis attempted to explain his intent:

> I felt then that there was only one solution. If we're gonna have a war, let's have it. And people say, "Let's leave it up to the government to take care of this. . . ." Let's go in there ourselves, let's go on and get it over with, one way or another. That's the emotion I felt. I was just tired of going to funerals . . . I never did . . . try to deal with anyone on nonviolence again.[42]

Even after his abandoning nonviolence, Dennis was never armed in his work in Mississippi. The fundamental change in his practice was that prior to the abduction and subsequent murders of Chaney, Schwerner, and Goodman, Dennis was a confirmed pacifist who believed that not retaliating against the violence of White racists would eventually change their hearts. After the tragedy of Neshoba County, Dennis and other CORE workers in Mississippi did not discourage anyone from defending himself or herself. In fact, Dennis wondered whether, if his three deceased comrades and other victims of racist violence whom he had encouraged to be nonviolent had perhaps been armed, the results would have been different.[43]

The events leading up to Freedom Summer reveal serious differences in the Movement around the role of nonviolence and the use of weapons. Certainly, though, SNCC and CORE members in Mississippi were becoming more receptive to, and in some cases participants in, armed self-defense. At the same time nonviolence was becoming less popular within the ranks of the southern Black Freedom Struggle. These trends would be strengthened by the occurrences of the summer of 1964.

Freedom Summer

In spite of the abduction and murders of Chaney, Schwerner, and Goodman, as well as the threat of violence by Mississippi segregationists, the Mississippi Summer Project went on as planned. Over three thousand students were recruited to volunteer in local COFO projects in thirty-eight communities. In each of these communities, COFO attempted to

revitalize its voter registration efforts. In twenty-three Mississippi localities, community centers were constructed and organized. Also as a result
of the Mississippi Summer Project, freedom schools that taught Black history, Movement politics, as well as literacy and math skills to Mississippi
youth were organized in thirty communities in the state.[44]

As predicted by Moses and Dennis, the massive involvement of White
students in COFO projects did put Mississippi in the national media spot-
light and, particularly after the abduction of the three COFO activists in
Neshoba County, increased the presence of federal law enforcement. In
spite of the increased FBI presence in the state and national media attention, White supremacists continued their campaign of violent terror on
Mississippi communities and activists. Between June and October 1964,
over one thousand activists and Movement supporters had been arrested
by Mississippi police, thirty-seven churches bombed or burned to the
ground, and fifteen people murdered due to the segregationist offensive of
violent terror.[45] Due to the inability of the increased federal presence and
media attention to prevent White supremacist violence, local Blacks in
Mississippi communities attempted to meet the security demands of the
Movement. Black communities across the state of Mississippi activated
defense networks for the protection of their lives, property, and the Black
Freedom Struggle.

Haven Communities

Throughout Mississippi there were localities that were known for providing a safe haven for Movement workers. These haven communities were
essential for the statewide campaign. These localities were generally communities in which Black landowners held farms contiguous to each other.
Due to the organized armed presence in these communities, nightriders
were not as likely to conduct raids into them. Movement workers, particularly field organizers, had a relative sense of security if they could make it
to the haven communities, such as Harmony, before dark.

Harmony was a small farming community in Leake County. It was located fourteen miles from Carthage, the county seat. Leake County was in
Mississippi's Fourth Congressional District (CORE's domain in the state),
east of Madison County and west of Neshoba County. Harmony's location
in the heart of the Fourth District made it a natural safe haven for activists going from one center to another. Harmony was composed of "several
hundred [Black] families who own their own farms."[46] The Harmony community was organized after Emancipation around a school that had been

built by local resident Blacks with assistance from the philanthropic Rosenwald Fund. The school was a central institution and a source of community pride for Harmony residents.[47]

Freedom Summer was not Harmony's first episode in the Black Freedom Struggle. Armed resistance was an essential element of the Freedom Struggle in Harmony. Leake County, as well as its eastern neighbor, Neshoba, was a center for the Klan. Due to its location in the midst of White supremacy, Harmony residents "would look out for one another."[48] The males, in particular, were concerned about the possibility of White men sexually violating the womenfolk of Harmony and were prepared to retaliate against White rapists. Harmony officially linked up with the statewide Freedom Struggle when NAACP field secretary for the state of Mississippi, Medgar Evers, visited the small hamlet in the late 1950s. Evers came to assist local residents with organizing the Leake County NAACP. Given the threats to the lives of Medgar and other Mississippi activists, Harmony residents organized protection for Evers anytime he was in Leake County. In 1962, residents filed a desegregation suit against the Leake County school system. The suit was initiated after county officials closed the Harmony school and bused its youth to a segregated school in Carthage. After the local NAACP filed suit, nightriders retaliated on Harmony residents. In turn, Blacks in Harmony organized vigilante teams and initiated retaliatory violence on Leake County Whites. Following a couple of forays by vigilantes from both "sides of the tracks," Leake County officials thought it might be better to negotiate a truce between the warring factions. Even though the truce was in effect, Blacks realized "you better not get caught out of the community."[49] In 1964, federal courts forced the Leake County schools, as well as those in Jackson and Biloxi, to desegregate.

As a haven community, Harmony had a tradition of armed resistance that was probably more important than its strategic location in the Fourth Congressional District. Giving his impressions of this proud community, CORE activist Jerome Smith called Harmony "a together community" of "powerful people who would defend themselves."[50] Adult men and women and the youth were all involved in a community defense system. In the evening, young men took turns participating in an armed watch of the Harmony community center, which housed the local freedom school and COFO headquarters, and the main roads entering Harmony. Signals utilizing car horns and blinking headlights were developed to identify when intruders were approaching the general community or individual farms. So as not to violate their security, signals were changed periodically. Volunteer

Von Hoffman commented, "[I]t is dangerous to drive off the paved highway into the Harmony area after sundown if your car is unfamiliar there."[51] Husbands and wives took turns during the evening staying awake and participating in an armed watch of their individual property.[52]

Remembering an incident that exemplifies Harmony's tradition of armed resistance, local NAACP activist Dovie Hudson recalled hearing that White vigilantes were traveling down the road placing bombs in mailboxes of Harmony residents. After Hudson called her "boys," "one got one gun and one got the other one." As the White vigilantes drove up and got ready to place the bomb in Hudson's mailbox, in her words, "[M]y boys started shooting. . . . They just lined that car with bullets up and down."[53] This incident also illustrates why Harmony residents called their community "the lion's mouth." As stated by Dovie Hudson's sister, Winson, the nightriders who came into Harmony "wouldn't get out."[54]

Due to Harmony's cooperative spirit in terms of supporting and protecting its friends and neighbors as well as its determination to combat its enemy's movement, Movement workers felt very secure in this hamlet. The experience of Harmony was definitely not that of a nonviolent community but, rather, the epitome of collective armed resistance. An essential element of the armed resistance tradition in Harmony was a collective attitude of defiance and militancy. As Winson Hudson stated, "[T]he more [White terrorists] did to us . . . the meaner we got."[55] Since White supremacists understood the risks of marauding Harmony, COFO activists were relatively safe in this small community.

The Mileston farming district in Holmes County was one of the most important haven communities in Mississippi. Like Harmony, Mileston was a Black landowning community. The Black landowners of Mileston had a strong sense of community solidarity and cooperation. Mileston farmers shared tools and helped their neighbors with planting and harvest. A cooperatively owned cotton gin also served to make the Mileston farmers more self-reliant.[56]

As in Harmony, the cooperative spirit Mileston farmers showed in the economic arena was also displayed in the area of self-defense and community protection. As a result of the potential for violence during the Summer Project, in the summer of 1964, the Mileston community formed a community patrol. In terms of defending their community, Mileston folk took responsibility for their own security, also relying on the informal networks and bonds they had established in agricultural production. The self-reliance and cooperative spirit of the Mileston community on the issue of armed defense gave COFO/SNCC activists and summer volunteers a sense of security in that section of Holmes County.[57] Concerning Mileston's preparedness for segregationist violence, SNCC activist Ed Brown, who worked in Holmes County during the Summer Project, stated that "when there were instances of confrontation there was sufficient organizational strength behind us to make whites think twice before doing anything."[58] Brown remembered an incident in 1964 when Mileston and neighboring Tchula residents demonstrated their might. Dozens of Black farmers came downtown visibly armed after a series of threats by White supremacists to the effect that "they didn't want any freedom riders around there [in Holmes County]." Brown stated, "Those Negroes showed up in town the next day with their pistols. . . . They [the White supremacists] realized they was ready for war."[59]

COFO/SNCC organizer Hollis Watkins, who was assigned to Holmes County for the Summer Project, participated in the Mileston armed patrol. Watkins's participation in the armed patrol of the Mileston community was in direct violation of SNCC policy that no SNCC activists would be armed for the Summer Project. Since Watkins was relying on families in the Mileston community, particularly the household of farmer Dave Howard, he felt obligated to participate in the defense of the community. Watkins described, in great detail, the system that was set up to "make sure strangers didn't venture" into the Mileston community. Describing the system, Watkins stated,

> If a vehicle came across the tracks down into the community and didn't give the proper signals, after a certain hour, you know after dark, then the telephone messages would be relayed and ultimately that vehicle would be approached from the front and the rear and checked to see who it was. In most cases it would be met head on with headlights . . . with two people in a car. And generally being approached by 4 people in a pickup truck from behind . . . two of the people would generally be in the cab. And two would generally be in the back with the guns raised over the cab.[60]

As in Harmony, the system included signals for incoming friendly vehicles, including blinking one's headlights or "honking" the automobile horn a certain number of time. In case intruders had observed the signal and figured out its purpose, the signals would periodically change. According to Watkins, the evening hours were divided, and community residents volunteered for different shifts. Only adult males participated in the armed watch of the community.[61]

Armed sentry at the Mileston Freedom House. SNCC workers acknowledged Mileston as a "haven" community due to its members' readiness to defend themselves. (Courtesy of Matt Herron.)

Besides the general watch of the community, particular attention was given to the homes of Mileston residents who were considered local Movement leaders, people who were housing summer volunteers, churches, and other institutions identified with the Movement. Describing the watch on targeted people and places, a Mileston resident, Shadrach Davis, remembered,

> [W]e would have to watch different ones' houses here at night. . . . Two or three of us would set in the trucks wit' guns at this driveway. Then we'd leave an' ride over to the other areas of the community . . . one, and two o'clock at night . . . n' see how was everythang goin'.[62]

COFO organizers believed that Holmes County, particularly Mileston, was a safe area. Just as in Harmony, COFO activists believed they could rely on, in Brown's words, the "organizational strength" of the Mileston farmers for protection.[63] In fact, early in the summer, when it was determined that it was too dangerous for the White volunteers to go directly

SNCC member Hollis Watkins participated in an armed watch in Mileston in 1964. (Courtesy of Estuary Press.)

to southwest Mississippi, summer volunteers were instead sent to Holmes County. In Holmes County, the volunteers could adjust to Mississippi and receive some of the best protection in the state.

Of course, Mileston farmers had a great example of the efficacy of armed self-defense in their neighbor Hartman Turnbow. Turnbow became a living legend in the Holmes County and Mississippi Black Freedom Struggle after his successful defense of his life and his family from segregationist invaders in 1963. A poem written by a participant in a Mileston freedom school is an example of the admiration Black resident of Holmes County reserved for Turnbow. A Holmes County youth, Lorenzo Wesley, wrote his poem about the legendary Turnbow during Freedom Summer. Titled "Turnbow," Wesley's poem reads as follows:

I know a man who has no foe
His name is Mr. Turnbow

He is about five feet six
Every time you see him he has a gun or a brick
If you want to keep your head
Then you'd better not come tripping around his bed
When he talks to you
His fingers talk too
Some people might not understand
But Mr. Turnbow is a good old man.[64]

Wesley's poem demonstrates that it was general knowledge that Turnbow was always prepared to defend himself. This fact was also shared among COFO staff and volunteers. Most evenings after the 1963 defense of his home, Turnbow, armed with his rifle, stood watch. In instructions for volunteers coming to work with Turnbow, SNCC staff member Mary King wrote that when approaching the Turnbow house, volunteers should "get directions or an escort as he may shoot."[65]

Due to his role in the local and statewide Black Freedom Struggle and his act of armed resistance that spring 1963 evening, Turnbow was one of the Holmes County leaders who were targeted for terrorist violence. Providing shelter to two White female volunteers increased the danger facing the Turnbow family. One of these women, Martha Honey, a student from Oberlin, remembers that after returning to Mileston from the funeral of James Chaney, she found that the Turnbow farm "had been converted into an armed camp."[66] While Honey and others had been in Meridian at Chaney's funeral, Turnbow's home had been attacked again. Honey, whose father was a Quaker, was influenced by the philosophy of pacifism and supported nonviolence as the principal tactic of the Movement. Since Turnbow had previously concealed weapons around her, Honey was "shocked to see other people and guns" for the first time.[67] The "other people" Honey referred to were two White volunteers who were labor activists and veterans from the Abraham Lincoln Brigade in the Spanish Civil War. The vehicle of one volunteer, Abe Osheroff, was bombed as soon as he arrived in Holmes County. Osheroff and his other comrade assisted Turnbow in the security of his home by participating in a 24-hour armed watch of the farm as well as designing and installing an electric alarm system around the house. The alarm system was composed of wires around the house, which would alert the Turnbows and their guests if intruders were approaching. The Turnbows also had a two-way radio to maintain intelligence of local police activity and to communicate with the local Movement patrol

Freedom Summer volunteers in the home of Hartman and Sweet Turnbow. *Left to right:* Edie Black, Ms. Sweet Turnbow, Abe Osheroff, Martha Honey, Jim Boebel. Osheroff participated in armed security of the Turnbow home. (Courtesy of Matt Herron.)

if necessary. Honey commented that in the Mississippi Black Freedom Struggle,

> [T]here was a fine line. There was a general commitment to non-violence as the appropriate tactic. . . . They were realistic enough to know that in certain circumstances, like when Hartman's house was attacked for the second time for his own safety and our safety, they felt they needed armed guards.[68]

Turnbow "lived day to day with Mississippi violence"; he and his counterparts in Mileston realized, despite the nonviolence of their guest, that armed defense was necessary for their survival and the success of the Black Freedom Struggle.[69]

Armed Defense in Projects throughout the State

While other communities did not achieve the same level of organization as haven communities like Mileston and Harmony, armed defense was an essential practice of the Movement in projects throughout the state. One feature that distinguished haven communities from other rural communities was the high level of group solidarity in places like Harmony and Mileston. In other communities, small numbers of isolated but committed freedom fighters bonded together to support one another. These communities often lacked the high concentration of Black landowners in a contiguous area, unlike the rural haven communities. One example is the Old Pilgrim's Rest community in Holmes County, where three households providing shelter for volunteers also worked together to provide security for the voter registration workers and each other.[70]

Black urban communities that possessed a critical mass also had the capability to protect Movement leaders and Black institutions and businesses. One clear example of this is the Mississippi city of Meridian. During the dominance of rail transport, Meridian was a transportation hub and retail center for Mississippi. Though experiencing segregation and the threat of White supremacist violence, many in the Meridian Black community perceived Black life in Meridian as being better than in other parts of the state. At the same time, while they had pride in their community and achievements, citizens of Black Meridian were not satisfied with the restrictions on voting and political participation and the unavailability of economic opportunities for Blacks, as well as the constant threat of racist violence.[71]

The First Union Baptist Church was a primary center of the Meridian Movement, and its pastor, Reverend R. S. Porter, was a vocal leader of the Movement. Union Baptist hosted most of Meridian's Movement meetings, and its members formed the core of the armed sentry for the Meridian Black community. Porter, who was known as a "man who liked his rifle," also participated in the self-defense group. The purpose of the Meridian self-defense group was the protection of key Movement leaders and institutions, particularly churches, which were targeted by white supremacist terrorists. Meridian was located in Lauderdale County, which had more churches bombed than any other county. Members of Union Baptist generally rotated participation in an armed guard located in the church loft. The presence of their visible security group prevented an attack on the edifice of the Union Baptist Church. The Meridian group was also responsible for protecting high-profile activists who visited Meridian, including Martin Luther King Jr. and Roy Wilkins.[72]

Consistent with the reports of Greenwood SNCC organizers in the June 1964 debate, during Freedom Summer Delta Blacks were arming and preparing themselves for White supremacist violence. While not exhibiting the same level of organized armed response as their comrades in Harmony and Mileston, some local Blacks demonstrated the will to defend their lives and property with guns from racist violence. The SNCC Freedom House and mass meetings also received armed protection from a small group of Black Greenwood residents. Elements of the Greenwood Black community maintained an armed presence throughout Freedom Summer.[73]

While other Delta communities may not have been as organized as Greenwood, guns were certainly part of the culture of survival and resistance. Community leader of the Delta town of Mayerville, Unita Blackwell, took turns sleeping in the evenings with her husband, so someone would be awake, armed, and on alert for nightriders.[74] Hosts making weapons available to volunteers was not an unusual occurrence. SNCC organizer Kwame Ture (formerly known as Stokely Carmichael) remembers being handed a revolver by MFDP leader Fannie Lou Hamer when staying at her home in Ruleville, Mississippi. A young Black activist living in New York, Sundiata Acoli (formerly known as Clark Squire) volunteered to come to Mississippi to participate in Freedom Summer after hearing about the murders of Chaney, Schwerner, and Goodman. He was assigned to Batesville, a small town in the Delta county of Panola. Acoli was housed by an "older sister" who was one of the Movement leaders in Batesville. When entering his bedroom, which was in the rear of the house, he noticed "a loaded 12 gauge [shotgun] leaned against the corner and a box of shells on the bureau."[75]

"They Didn't Get a Chance to Shoot at Us": Ambush in Tallahatchie County

One of the most dynamic examples of armed resistance during Freedom Summer took place during August of 1964 in Tallahatchie County, where the Emmett Till murder had taken place. Margaret Block, the sister of Sam Block, was assigned to organize in Tallahatchie in January of 1964. Like her brother, Margaret was recruited into the Black Freedom Struggle by their neighbor Amzie Moore. After joining SNCC in 1963, she had organized mass meetings for voting rights in Ruleville and Cleveland. She began to make contacts in Tallahatchie County in the early months of 1964. Block was the only COFO staff person appointed to Tallahatchie on the eve of Freedom Summer.[76]

The 1960 census reveals that 8,580 Whites resided in a county with a Black majority of 15,400. No Blacks were registered to vote in Tallahatchie, which was considered a dangerous county. The awareness of the Till lynch-ing invoked fear in the Black residents and Movement personnel alike.[77]

In June 1964, Block was forced to flee Tallahatchie due to White su-premacist harassment. Her security was in jeopardy after local White su-premacists found out she was in the county to organize a voter registra-tion campaign. County NAACP president Birdia Keglar facilitated the SNCC worker's temporary exodus from the county in a hearse to conceal her rendezvous with COFO staff Charles Cobb and Ivanhoe Donaldson. Cobb and Donaldson transported Block to the COFO district headquar-ters in Greenwood. She returned weeks later and was hosted by 89-year-old Janie Brewer in the unincorporated Swan Lake community in the rural southwestern section of Tallahatchie. Mrs. Brewer was the matriarch of a farming, landowning family who solidly supported the voter registration effort. Several of the Brewers' children and grandchildren lived on the fam-ily land in what Block described as a "colony." The Brewer family became the core of Block's support in Tallahatchie. Since the family did not own a telephone, Block had to go four miles away to the village of Glendora to use a pay phone in order to report to the Greenwood district headquarters. One evening, while in a phone booth reporting to Greenwood, she was surrounded and threatened by a small mob of White men. Block dispersed the mob by claiming she was on the phone with the Department of Justice. The mob did not notice Mrs. Brewer's children, Jesse, Lee, and Essie, posi-tioned nearby with guns to protect Block.[78]

District coordinator Stokely Carmichael sent reinforcements in July 1964 to Tallahatchie after the groundwork was established by Block and the Brewers and other rural residents demonstrated the capacity to sup-port a project in the county. Carmichael appointed his Howard University classmate Fred Mangrum to head the project. Mangrum was accompanied by Ed Brown, Tina Lawrence, Gwen Gilliam, and Len Edwards (son of California congressman Don Edwards), all of whom resided at the Brewer farm. A citizens band radio was also allocated to the Brewer residence so the project participants could communicate with the Greenwood head-quarters and other Movement-supporting residences in the area. The local authorities constantly jammed the radio to prevent communication and also monitored it for surveillance purposes.[79]

On August 5, 1964, four of Janie Brewer's sons and one other Black local resident unsuccessfully attempted to register at the Tallahatchie County courthouse. Three days later, Len Edwards sent a report to COFO head-quarters and the SNCC national office in Atlanta stating, "Their lives are in grave danger." Edwards continued, declaring that one of the Brewer sons, Eugene, had experienced Whites "coming by his house with guns every day since he tried to register." Eugene, the only son of Janie Brewer not residing on her Swan Lake farm land, was afraid to leave his residence to go to work after the threats. On August 10th, the threats continued as three cars full of armed White supremacists continuously circled the Brewer home while local authorities jammed radio transmissions from the residence.[80]

The Brewer family and the COFO staff and volunteers persisted in their efforts to be registered in spite of the terrorism and harassment. On August 11th, a small contingent of Black Tallahatchie residents, COFO staff, and volunteers caravanned to the county courthouse in Charleston (one of Tallahatchie's two county seats) to attempt to register. They were met near the courthouse by a mob of over ninety Whites and multiple trucks with a "considerable number of guns." A portion of the mob attempted to attack the small delegation of local Blacks and civil rights activists. A Department of Justice official on the scene had to intervene to prevent a member of the mob from striking Margaret Block with a blade.[81]

The activists and the local Blacks noticed that their caravan of two vehicles was being pursued by three truckloads of Whites as they headed back to Swan Lake and the Brewer farm. Sheriff E. R. Dogan was among the Whites following them. Anticipating that they would be followed, the Brewers and their neighbors came up with a plan for protection of the COFO activists and local Blacks in the procession back to Swan Lake. Jesse Brewer radioed back to the farm. As their group approached a turn in the road before the Brewer farm, a surprise was waiting for their White supremacist pursuers.[82] Margaret Block described the situation:

> We lived in the country. . . . So we had to go way back to the country. It was two cars. The white people they were following us. They thought they were going to ambush us. Little did they know, we had a whole caravan of cars around the bend waiting for us to come back. . . . All those farmers and everybody . . . car pool of people with guns . . . about ten cars [of local residents organized to protect the local Blacks and civil rights workers]. When they saw all those people . . . they turned around and went back to town.[83]

Mrs. Brewer realized that the attacks would not end so easily. She initiated a plan to ambush the nightriders who would inevitably come in the evening. The Brewer matriarch instructed her children, grandchildren, and guests to conceal themselves, with firearms, in the cotton fields and shrubbery near the farm that evening. COFO workers Margaret Block and Tina Lawrence assisted Janie Brewer inside the kitchen preparing gasoline bombs—Molotov cocktails—in anticipation of White supremacist attackers that evening.[84] Block remembered,

> The night we were making those Molotov cocktails, we had a lot of bottles. And Mrs. Brewer was in the kitchen trying to pour the gas in the bottles . . . and was spilling gas all everywhere. And I'm like "Damn if we get burned up in here, everyone was going to swear the Klan did it. It's going to be Ms. Brewer blowing us up."[85]

Sheriff Dogan returned that evening with a truckload of local Whites. Dogan and his associates did not notice members of the Brewer family, another local resident, Mangrum, and Brown concealed near and around the farm with rifles and shotguns.[86] According to Block,

> By the time we let them get not halfway to the house, somebody got up and shined a great big ole flood light on them and shot up in the air. We were going to let them get closer to the house so we were going to set them on fire. . . . When we shot . . . up in the air they got out of there.[87]

Mrs. Brewer came out of the house ready to hurl a Molotov cocktail at the nightriders. Ed Brown, who was armed with a 30.06 rifle in the perimeter of the house, remembered Fred Mangrum revealing himself to Sheriff Dogan and the nightriders. Mangrum came forward to negotiate and prevent a shootout. He proclaimed to the sheriff, "Y'all back out here where we live. We ain't out there in Charleston." Realizing he was in a trap, Sheriff Dogan ordered his team to "get on out of here, everybody back in their car." The Tallahatchie County road crew came to Swan Lake two days later and destroyed the gravel road leading to the Brewer farm as punishment for this act of resistance. Nightriders never returned to the Brewer farm again after the evening of August 11, 1964.[88]

McComb Movement Responds to the Racial Terror

While the level of violence was intense throughout the state in 1964, the Black community and the Movement were certainly challenged in McComb during the summer and early fall months of the year. McComb became popularly known as the "bombing capital of the world" in 1964.[89]

There were twelve bombings of homes, churches, and businesses in the Black community of McComb between June 22nd and August 12th. The perpetrators of the rash of bombing were the local Klavern of the United Klans of America. With access to guns, ammunition, as well as dynamite, the local United Klans group initiated a campaign to terrorize McComb's Black community. The goal of this campaign was to instill so much fear into McComb's Blacks that they would not support the voter registration program of COFO.[90] In 1963, a Black domestic worker in the household of members of the White power structure came upon an important revelation. Serving her function as part of the informal intelligence apparatus of the Black Freedom Struggle, the domestic uncovered that the local segregationist forces had developed a "hit list" of local NAACP and COFO leaders that local Blacks believed were targeted for assassination.[91] SNCC had initially begun a voter registration and desegregation campaign in Pike County in 1961, but an increase of terrorist violence initiated by the Klan and harassment by local police had occurred in McComb even prior to SNCC activity there. The increased anti-Black violence in McComb was a vehicle of social control in response to a rapid influx of Black people to the city from rural Mississippi, particularly neighboring Amite County. Freedom Summer only accelerated the campaign of terror.

COFO activists and many in the Black community believed that the local and state police never seriously pursued the bombers and were in fact in conspiracy with them. Local and state police investigated COFO members for the bombings and on occasion publicly blamed Movement activists for the terrorism. In response to the violence, individual households and Movement people prepared to defend themselves. While they did not possess the firepower of their enemies, McComb's local Black activists were also armed. While armed Black patrols did not prevent much of the bombing, they did often provide an armed response to the Klan attacks. On June 22nd, the White supremacist terrorists attempted to bomb the home of McComb NAACP leader Claude Bryant, also bombing two other homes that evening. Like many other local NAACP members, Bryant worked at the Illinois Central Railroad and was the owner of a local barber shop. On April 23, 1964, Bryant's barber shop was bombed. A resident of the politically active Beartown community of McComb, Bryant was considered by many to be the principal leader of the McComb Movement. The dynamite did not reach Bryant's house, exploding twenty-five yards from the NAACP leader's property. After the impact of the explosion jarred his house, Bryant grabbed his rifle and fired at the vehicle of the perpetrators. An armed patrol composed of local male NAACP members was established around Bryant's home in the evenings. This sentry was maintained from the day of the bombing of the barber shop until the bombing campaign ceased. Bryant also purchased a high-powered rifle to more adequately protect himself.[92]

On July 26th, Bryant's brother, Charlie, and his wife, Ora "Miss Dago" Bryant, were awakened by the sound of a car pulling into the driveway of the house. "Miss Dago," considered a significant local Movement leader, grabbed her shotgun and fired at the vehicle at the moment a perpetrator threw a bundle of explosives at the home of the Bryant family. The explosion broke the front windows and tore the asbestos siding off the house. Responding to the attack on his brother's home, Claude Bryant, armed with his new high-powered rifle, and other neighbors traded gunfire with the perpetrators.[93] Remembering that evening, McComb resident and Movement supporter Johnnie Nobles gave his account of the eventful night:

> It was a white man that got desperately shot that night . . . he got shot. . . . She [Ora Bryant] shot somebody. . . .That car was fired on so many times coming out of there . . . by people straight up the street all through there. . . . And he was shot at when he turned the curb, coming back towards town. . . . And you could hear people hollering "here he come."[94]

Some local Blacks believe the bullets of Mrs. Bryant's and her neighbors' weapons hit one of the perpetrators, who was possibly taken across the border to Louisiana or Tennessee for treatment in order to escape suspicion. From that evening on, for the rest of the summer, Charles and Ora Bryant took turns guarding their home with their shotgun.[95]

Like the Bryants, families throughout the Black neighborhoods of McComb, particularly those involved in the Black Freedom Struggle, began to conduct a nightly armed watch of their homes. In the Algiers community of McComb, the Reeves[96] family had a history of being "Bad Negroes."[97] Mr. and Mrs. Reeves had reputations for being outspoken as well as participating in the NAACP. The Reeveses also housed COFO workers and volunteers participating in the Summer Project. The Reeves family also received threats from White supremacists due to their reputation and involvement in the local movement. The family patriarch, Carl Reeves, participated in the patrol of Bryant's home for three months after the bombing of the McComb NAACP leader's home. Mrs. Annie Reeves and son

William took responsibility for the defense of their home in the evening, with assistance from neighbors. After receiving threats, the Reeveses contacted the local police and proclaimed, "[Y]'all won't catch 'em, but we'll catch 'em." Responding to the counterthreats of the Reeveses, the police instructed the family, "[D]on't shoot the man, shoot the tires [of the vehicle of the nightriders]."[98] Mrs. Reeves, armed with a rifle, watched with the lights out from her living room in the evenings. Her teenage son, William, participated in an armed watch of the house from the porch. The Reeveses' teenaged neighbor Eddie Williams and other young neighbors patrolled the perimeter of their house with rifles.[99]

The Reeveses were just one example of families working together to protect their lives and property in the face of segregationist terror. NAACP member Matthew Nobles slept on the roof of his house with a rifle to anticipate nightriders. While Nobles was on the roof, his wife slept with a rifle at her side and the window open so the sound of any vehicle in their neighborhood would wake her up.[100] The Reeveses, the Nobleses, as well as Charles and Ora Bryant are examples of how households became virtual militia units to defend the Black communities of McComb.

An armed community watch was also organized to protect Black-owned businesses in McComb, particularly those owned by local Movement activists. Particular attention was paid to the café owned by Aylene Quin and the cleaners owned by Ernest Nobles. Quin and Nobles were the backbone of the group of Black entrepreneurs who provided housing, food, and transportation for COFO activists and volunteers in Pike County. COFO workers were provided meals at Aylene Quin's café and the Nobles Cleaners truck often clandestinely transported Movement workers from one point in the city to another. Nobles Cleaners was also a place of refuge for activists being pursued by police in the Burgland section of McComb. In the evenings, Nobles, his brothers, and friends took turns participating in an armed watch of the business.[101]

Armed Black men watched Nobles's business all night long during the Freedom Summer from a loft across the street, above a Black-owned cab stand. Despite the patrol, one evening someone set a fire in the back of the business, which caused minor damage. On another occasion, Nobles's brother almost shot a man distributing the newspaper to the cleaners, thinking the "paper man" was throwing dynamite. Johnnie Nobles remembered, "[W]hen he threw that paper we threw the door open and had guns on him." Fortunately, the "paper man" was recognized before there were fatal consequences.[102]

COFO was also targeted during the bombing campaign. The COFO Freedom House was dynamited on July 8, 1964.[103] SNCC activist Curtis Hayes was severely cut by glass shattering from the explosion. McComb residents rushed with guns to the scene of the explosion. McComb project director Jesse Harris established a watch of the Freedom House and new security measures for the project after the July 8th bombing. While SNCC members in the McComb project remained nonviolent, McComb youth who participated in the watch were armed.[104] Commenting on the response to the bombing of the Freedom House, Harris recalled,

> We had to change our whole security thing. Especially with the White people on the project had to be in by a certain time at night. The Black people on the project, they didn't have a time to be in, because we could be residents. . . . We had to have some form of security. I didn't have no weapon. But other people in the community, that man ain't going to stand over on that corner or sit in his car in that corner without some weapon for security for us. Can't nobody argue that.[105]

SNCC activists continued the COFO project in McComb. After the official end of the Summer Project, Harris and two hundred volunteers remained in McComb, determined to complete the tasks of the Movement.[106] However, the forces of segregation and White supremacist terrorism also continued in order to intimidate, harass, and neutralize the Black communities and Movement activists of McComb. The bombings and other violent forms of terrorism continued.

The Black community and Movement activists had little confidence that the federal government was seriously trying to prevent the continued terrorism and repression in McComb. There was certainly a belief by McComb Blacks that the FBI had not seriously attempted to find and punish the perpetrators of the proliferation of bombings that had occurred since June of 1964. In fact, in August of 1964, the FBI contingent in McComb had been reduced from sixteen to four. In a letter sent to Department of Justice official Burke Marshall, dated September 9, 1964, Jessie Harris appealed to the federal government "to take action before it was too late." Harris concluded his letter by stating, "[U]nless responsible forces are brought to bear in McComb, what happened in Neshoba County [Philadelphia, Mississippi, where three civil rights workers were murdered] will happen here."[107] In spite of the appeals of Harris and others, the federal government took no substantive action to make the Black community feel more secure.

The Black community of McComb became an armed camp in the face of continued threats of racist violence and without assurances of federal protection. Besides being armed and on alert, the Black neighborhoods of McComb were angered and tense during the late summer and early fall of 1964. The Klan's use of segregationist violence and intimidation to instill fear in Blacks and drive a wedge between the Black Freedom Struggle and the Black community was basically unsuccessful. The violence had increased the potential for retaliatory violent action from large numbers of McComb Blacks, particularly among the working class, the poor, and youth.[108] Remembering the climate in McComb's Black neighborhoods in September of 1964, SNCC activist Joe Martin stated,

> The thing that was threatening white folks, was thinking they was putting fear in Blacks. The fear turned into anger, but it was turning the wrong way [from what white supremacists intended]. They [many McComb Blacks] was ready to start shooting people who was white. . . . Deacon [Claude] Bryant and the other older guys went to them [the white power structure and the FBI] and told them "some peoples fixin' to be killed. And ain't all of them going to be Black."[109]

The fuse of the explosive element within the McComb Black community was lit and the explosive ignited on the evening of September 20, 1964. That evening, the residence of Aylene Quin was bombed, injuring her two children, a nine-year-old girl, Jacqueline, and a five-year-old boy, Anthony. The politically active Society Hill Baptist Church of the Beartown community was bombed and almost completely destroyed later the same night. These two bombings, particularly the assault on the home of the well-loved and respected Quin, brought an immediate reaction from angry Blacks. Hundreds of Black McComb residents poured into the streets armed with guns, Molotov cocktails, bricks, and any other weapon that was available to them. Roving mobs of youth marched down McComb's streets looking for White people or White-owned property and establishments to attack. Johnnie Nobles, remembering the effect the Quin bombing had on him, said, "I was hateful and mean and I wanted to do something."[110] Leaving his shift guarding his brother's cleaners from nightriders, Nobles, armed with his .32 handgun, was stopped for speeding in his vehicle and arrested on his way to Quin's neighborhood. In order not be charged with possession of a concealed weapon, Nobles called a friend to the car and passed his weapon pretending he was only passing a wallet. In Quin's neighborhood, Nobles spoke of the retaliatory Black violence in response to the bombing. "If a white[-owned] vehicle come into that section, Miss Aylene Quin's neighborhood, [the angry Blacks] tearin' it up. . . .You could hear them bustin' windows out of cars."[111] Black snipers also shot at passing cars driven and occupied by whites, including police vehicles. "People start[ed] taking 'pot shots' at white people's cars and stuff," remembered Joe Martin.[112] Due to the fury of the spontaneous Black uprising, McComb's police and the legion of Whites who were deputized stayed on the perimeter of the Black community. The rebellion was calmed by the persistent persuasion of COFO workers, who walked the streets talking to the roving mobs.[113]

The federal government turned its attention to the volatile situation in McComb after this violent response from the Black community. On September 21, 1964, Aylene Quin, Ora Bryant, and another activist whose property was the target of terrorist bombers, Matti Dillion, went to Washington, D.C. The three female freedom fighters from McComb not only met with Department of Justice officials but convened with President Lyndon Johnson. After this meeting, President Johnson personally contacted Mississippi governor Paul Johnson and threatened to send federal troops to McComb. Governor Johnson in turn contacted Pike County district attorney Joseph Pigott, who had already been warned about the possibility of federal intervention by Department of Justice officials. Not only had the federal government taken notice, but the *New York Times* and national network news media reported the violence in McComb. The bombing in McComb suddenly become a national issue after the specter of an armed Black uprising.[114]

On September 29, 1964, Governor Johnson and state highway patrolman T. B. Birdsong convened with McComb and Pike County officials. Governor Johnson also warned that he was on the verge of mobilizing the Mississippi National Guard to McComb. Local officials appealed for forty-eight hours to resolve the situation themselves. Within twenty-four hours, Klansmen were being arrested for the bombings. One week later, eleven Klansmen had been arrested for participating in arson and the bombing of homes and institutions in the Black community. Nine of these men were tried on October 23, 1964. After they pled guilty and were sentenced to five years of incarceration, Judge W. H. Watkins granted them probation, stating that the bombers had been "unduly provoked."[115]

The Black community felt betrayed again by the virtual release of the White terrorists. While legal action proved to lead to a dead end, the commercial leadership of the White power structure began to champion

toleration and compromise. The White commercial elite of McComb realized that in a changing climate, for the city to be known as "the bombing
capital of the world" was not good business. They also realized the bombing and racist violence had not terrorized the Black community into sub-
mission but instead, if continued, could potentially lead to a racial uprising. The outrage and retaliatory violence of September 29, 1964, played a
significant role in forcing the federal and state governments to intervene
and in making the commercial elite "blink."[116]

Armed self-defense and armed resistance played a role in virtually every community where COFO projects were organized during Freedom
Summer. Armed defense was organized according to the nature of each
community. The extensiveness of the organization of community patrols
seemed to depend on how developed the social organization and cohesiveness of each community was. In communities that had a strong sense of
solidarity and self-reliance, like Harmony and Mileston, collective armed
organization was more developed. At the same time, whether in Black
landowning "haven" communities, in town or country in the Delta, or in
cities like McComb or Meridian, armed self-defense was a component
part of Freedom Summer and the overall Black Freedom Struggle for civil
and human rights.

The Beginning of the End of Nonviolence

As mentioned earlier in this chapter, in June 1964, SNCC had its first national organizational debate on the issue of armed self-defense. CORE's
national leadership had been challenged by this same issue as early as
1963. While both organizations maintained a public posture of nonviolence, many of its members and volunteers began to be armed during
1964. It could also be argued that in Mississippi and other parts of the
South, these organizations could not function without the armed protection of local people.

Despite the ban on SNCC organizers being armed during the Summer
Project, several SNCC and COFO staff members were armed during Freedom Summer. SNCC organizer Hollis Watkins participated in armed patrols in Mileston. SNCC activists Fred Mangrum and Ed Brown were part
of an ambush in Tallahatchie County, while their comrades Margaret Block
and Tina Lawrence helped prepare Molotov cocktails. Sundiata Acoli commented that his COFO escorts were armed when he was transported from

Jackson to his assignment for the Summer Project at Batesville.[117] After receiving an unsatisfactory response from federal authorities when their Freedom House was bombed and after being the victims of harassment and violence on several occasions, Jesse Harris and other SNCC staff consented to an armed patrol of the McComb Freedom House.[118] McComb SNCC organizer Joe Martin, who also participated in an armed watch of the home of Ora and Charles Bryant, stated that "it was against SNCC's policy, but we had weapons."[119]

Much of the SNCC and COFO staff were from Mississippi and southern communities where armed self-defense had a longer tradition than nonviolence. Many others were influenced by the local Movement leaders with whom they came in contact, like E. W. Steptoe, Hartman Turnbow, Laura McGhee, Ora Bryant, Janie Brewer, R. S. Porter, and many others whose practice could not be confused with philosophical nonviolence. Nonviolence was an alien philosophy to many Black southerners. Given the context of southern Black tradition, it was difficult for nonviolence to compete with armed self-defense. Bob Moses spoke about the importance of local people transforming SNCC's nonviolence policy in terms of the actual practice of many in its membership:

> Local people carried the day. They defined how they and the culture was going to relate to the issue of using guns, having them available and nonviolence. . . . They defined that and people fell into it. Then the question was "well, can we apply that to us as organizers?"[120]

For the strategy of nonviolence to work in Mississippi, the federal government would have to intervene with force to provide security from the forces of White supremacist terrorism. The experience of Freedom Summer left Freedom Struggle activists and Black Mississippians dissatisfied with the response of the federal government to their safety concerns. This dissatisfaction culminated in the unsuccessful attempt by the Mississippi Freedom Democratic Party to challenge the credentials of the segregationist Mississippi Democratic Party at the 1964 National Democratic Convention. The failure of the national Democratic Party leadership to seat the multiracial delegates of the MFDP and to support the MFDP's challenge to the legitimacy of segregationist Mississippi Democrats was a serious disappointment to Movement activists. National Democratic leadership, including President Lyndon Johnson, did not want to offend southern Democrats and White voters. After all the bombings, deaths, and other forms of terrorism endured by Mississippi Blacks and the Black Freedom Struggle, combined with the failure to unseat the segregationist Democrats, many activists lost faith in cooperation with White liberals and the Democratic Party as a means to secure the goals of the Struggle. The experiences of Freedom Summer and the Democratic convention moved many SNCC and CORE activists away from any belief that the federal government could be relied on for protection or as a strategic ally in the Struggle.[121] These activists generally believed that the Movement and Black people in general would have to rely upon themselves and their own resources for their own protection.

The de facto change in the practice of SNCC membership on the question of armed self-defense was illustrated in a SNCC staff retreat at Waveland, Mississippi, in November 1964. The purpose of this retreat was to evaluate SNCC's direction and program. An important event occurred during the retreat that reflected the new directions in SNCC and the Movement overall. Waveland is located near the Mississippi Gulf, and the retreat was near the beach. Retreat participants were alerted when they heard a low-flying plane soaring near their facilities. Later that evening, a vehicle drove near their meeting place and threw a Molotov cocktail on a nearby pier. Suddenly several male members of SNCC ran from the meeting carrying arms, and the nightriders were abducted and released after a warning from the young freedom fighters. Lorne Cress, a Chicago native and SNCC staffer in McComb, was surprised by the armed response from her comrades. Up until that day, she had believed she was a member of a nonviolent organization. She turned to Howard Zinn—a college professor, historian, and advisor to SNCC—and stated, "You have just witnessed the end of the nonviolent movement."[122]

5

"Ready to Die and Defend"

Natchez and the Advocacy and Emergence of Armed Resistance in Mississippi

Charles Sims of the Bogalusa-based Deacons for Defense and Justice was con-
tacted and arrived on August 29, 1965, with ten Louisiana Deacons at a Jack-
son MFDP meeting one week after the shooting of the Unitarian minister Don-
ald Thompson. MFDP representatives from the city of Jackson and the rest of
Hinds County, Madison County, and Forrest County (in southern Mississippi)
were present at the rally. Sims and his Deacon delegation were well received by
a predominantly Black Mississippi audience. Reports of the size of the audience
ranged between 175 and 300 people.

Sims pledged that the Deacons would come to the state whenever needed.
The organization's Bogalusa spokesperson argued that a Deacon's chapter could
have prevented the shooting of Thompson. If the Deacons could not stop the
shooting of the human rights activists, they had the capacity to find the perpe-
trators, argued Sims. He declared that southern Whites wouldn't respect Black
people until "Negroes were ready to die for their families and for their beliefs."
The Bogalusa leader challenged the local audience, stating, "It is time for you
men in Jackson to wake up and be men." Sims's speech received several standing
ovations from his Mississippi audience.[1]

The years following the Freedom Summer of 1964 represent a significant shift in the tactics of the Civil Rights Movement in Mississippi. The
COFO coalition was unable to maintain its momentum in terms of providing statewide direction and coordination for the Mississippi Movement
after Freedom Summer and the failure and disappointment of the MFDP's
challenge in Atlantic City. There were several reasons for COFO's decline
as a statewide vanguard for the Mississippi Civil Rights Movement. The
primary entities of COFO, CORE, and SNCC went through a crisis of
direction after the major campaigns of 1964. CORE and SNCC experienced internal debates on the role of Whites within the Movement and on
each organization's commitment to nonviolence. SNCC began to debate

the very nature of its organization. From the Waveland conference in November 1964 to the election of Stokely Carmichael as its chairman in 1966, SNCC debated whether it was to maintain its consensus-oriented structure, which allowed for local autonomy and for individuals to determine their roles and assignments. Some SNCC members believed the organization needed a more centralized structure. SNCC had also previously contributed most of the COFO staff but now began to focus more attention and resources in the Alabama Black Belt. Many experienced SNCC workers left Mississippi to do work building freedom organizations in Alabama.

NAACP state field secretary Charles Evers began to assert his leadership as the primary spokesperson for the Mississippi Civil Rights Movement. Evers filled the leadership vacuum that was created by the crisis in the COFO alliance. Under Evers's leadership, the local NAACP chapters in various parts of the state began to mobilize and organize local Mississippi Black communities to challenge the segregationist power structure throughout the state. This new momentum followed a different posture than that of COFO. The boycott of White enterprises and central business districts was the primary tactic used to undermine local White power structures so as to achieve the demands of the Movement.

Another significant difference in this stage of the Movement was the open advocacy of armed resistance. Prior to 1965, Black activists in Mississippi practiced armed self-defense but did not openly advocate its exercise. Monroe, North Carolina's Robert Williams was the exceptional Black southerner who openly declared that African Americans should meet "violence with violence." The conciliatory approach of practitioners of armed resistance allowed SNCC and CORE organizers to depend upon the protection of armed Blacks while maintaining a public stance of nonviolence. After 1964, Mississippi Movement leaders openly embraced armed resistance.

The nature of the armed resistance at this stage of the Mississippi Movement took on a different character than in the previous stage. Previously, Mississippi Movement activists and supporters functioned as a civilian militia, participating in armed defense on an ad hoc basis in times of emergency or when information was provided of a potential threat. It was often composed of an informal group of neighbors and/or family members. On the contrary, paramilitary groups, by definition, are also composed of civilians, not professional military personnel, but are organized similarly to the formal military or law enforcement and possess a specific chain of command. Paramilitary groups operate in coordination with or in the role of regular military or police groups. Unlike previous informal defense networks in the Mississippi Civil Rights Movement, paramilitary organizations were organized with a clear chain of command and viewed themselves as filling the vacuum left in the African American community by federal, state, and local law enforcement that was either sympathetic to or neutral about White supremacist violence.

The function of armed defense was often placed in the hands of a paramilitary group whose role in the Movement was the protection of its leaders, demonstrations, and the Black community in general in the years following Freedom Summer. When a paramilitary force was not developed, its existence was often deceptively claimed in order to instill confidence in the African American community and fear among White supremacists, the local White power structure, and other enemies of the Movement. In addition, enforcer squads were developed to support the economic boycott strategy. The development of a coercive enforcer group gave the Movement the capacity to effectively harass or punish violators of the boycott and Black collaborators with the White power structure.

Natchez: History, Demographics, and White Supremacist Terror

The first place where the formula of open advocacy of armed resistance, promotion of a paramilitary force, and use of an enforcer squad in a consumer boycott was employed was in Natchez, Mississippi, in 1965. The "Natchez model" became the basis for social movement change in Mississippi from 1965 until 1979. Natchez is an important center in the history of Mississippi. Located in the southwest corner of the state, on the banks of the Mississippi River, Natchez is the commercial center and seat of Adams County. The city became the oldest European settlement on the Mississippi River when French settlers established a trading post there in 1716. The city's ensuing expansion resulted in conflict with the indigenous Natchez people. Black resistance was rooted in the colonial origins of Natchez as enslaved Africans, primarily from Mali (the Bamana ethnic group), collaborated with the indigenous Natchez nation to defeat French settlers in 1729. The Natchez/Bamana alliance was defeated when the French employed soldiers from the Choctaw nation and a militia of emancipated Blacks. Natchez became British territory as a result of the Treaty of 1763, after which Anglo settlers began to occupy the town, making it the British hub for England's southwest colonial possessions in North America.

The Natchez White settler elites were important players in Mississippi in the transition from territory to state in 1817, at which time Natchez was the state capital. While Jackson became the state capital in 1822, the Natchez elite remained significant players in state politics. Natchez was the heart of the antebellum plantation economy of Mississippi, and the homes of wealthy Natchez plantation owners and commercial captains became tourist attractions decades later. The Natchez elite's power and influence in the state diminished due to several factors in the late nineteenth century and early twentieth century: natural calamities, including floods and the boll weevil, the depletion of the soil from repeated cotton crops, as well as the development of the Delta as a center of wealth and privilege.[2]

Natchez acquired a manufacturing base with industries like Armstrong Tire and Rubber, the International Paper Company, and the Johns Manville Corporation being located in this "New South" city by the 1960s. The development of these industries in Natchez after World War II sparked the economy and population growth. The development of an industrial economy did not eliminate the institutionalized racism, which had its roots in slavery and peonage. In 1965, Adams County had a population of 37,730, and the city of Natchez had nearly 24,000 residents. People of African descent comprised 50 percent of the population of Adams County, where the median income for Whites was $5,600 per year and $1,994 for African descendants. The large gap in median family income in the county between the White and Black communities clearly demonstrates the continuity of White supremacy in "New South" Natchez.[3]

Ku Klux Klan activity in Natchez accelerated in the middle 1960s. Adams County and surrounding areas were key strongholds of the Ku Klux Klan, and the Klan in Natchez was among the most violent and organized in the state. Two major Klan organizations functioned in Natchez and competed for members in the middle 1960s. The United Klans of America (UKA) was the largest Klan faction in the United States and in Natchez, which hosted the state convention of the UKA in May of 1965. Local factory worker E. L. McDaniel was the grand dragon of the UKA in Natchez. The White Knights of the Ku Klux Klan also had members and supporters in Natchez but began to lose momentum and members to the UKA in the middle 1960s. McDaniel was initially a member of the more militant White Knights but defected to the UKA in 1964.

Two major factors account for the rise of White supremacist violence in the southwest Mississippi urban center. First, the population growth in Adams County intensified White supremacy as White privilege was

evoked to eliminate Black labor in competition for the best jobs in growing industries in the area. Federal contracts with Armstrong Tire motivated the firm to employ more African Americans, which motivated Klan
recruitment. Armstrong Tire and the International Paper Company employed several Klansmen. A report from congressional hearings revealed
that in 1966 seventy current or former Klan members were employed at
the International Paper Company. A 1965 magazine article reported, "With
some four hundred local Klansmen, Natchez has possibly the highest per
capita Klan population anywhere in the South."[4]

The other major factor in the growth of Klan activity in Adams County
and environs was the advance of activism by local Blacks and the Civil
Rights Movement. The Klan presence in Adams County historically served
as a vehicle to prevent African American pursuit of the franchise and civil
rights. Natchez Blacks who attempted to register to vote in 1954 received
death threats. COFO initiated a voter registration campaign in Adams
County in 1963. The Klan reacted to the increase of voter registration organizing and civil rights activism sparked by COFO. Hundreds of Whites
were attracted to Klan rallies in Natchez during the mid-1960s. Civil rights
activists and local residents also were the targets of beatings, kidnapping,
church bombings, and murder. From February 18th through the 20th in
1964, the Klan abducted and physically assaulted sixteen Black men in Adams County. The victims of this campaign included Alfred Whitley, a jani-
tor at the Armstrong Rubber Company; local mortician and voting rights
activist Archie Curtis; and his employee Willie Jackson. The home of
Leonard Russell, active in the Negro Pulp and Sulfite Worker's local, was
also bombed. Clinton Walker, an International Paper Company worker,
was fatally shot in the back on the night of February 28th.[5]

The local police seemed to offer no significant protection from the
Klan. No arrests occurred for any of these acts of violence. The Klan had
infiltrated law enforcement in Adams County. The Natchez police chief, J.
T. Robinson, was also a vocal advocate of White supremacy and had no
problems using force to uphold the system of segregation. Natchez mayor
John Nosser called for racial tolerance but had no effective control over the
Natchez police or Chief Robinson. Indeed, Mayor Nosser himself became
a target of Klan violence. On one Saturday evening in September of 1964,
explosions jarred the homes of Mayor Nosser and Black contractor Willie
Washington. Nosser, an American of Lebanese origin, believed his home
was bombed because he attempted to serve as a "peacemaker" during the
racial hostilities of Freedom Summer.[6]

Charles Evers, Advocacy of Armed Resistance, and the Natchez Boycott

NAACP state field secretary Charles Evers came to Natchez on March 3, 1965, to moderate Adams County's first NAACP meeting. Evers's presence in Natchez was part of an effort to assert the NAACP's visibility and presence throughout the state. Evers became a major leader in the Mississippi Black Freedom Struggle after the assassination of his brother, Medgar, on June 11, 1963, by White supremacist Byron De La Beckwith. Charles Evers had migrated to Chicago after a brief stint of activism in the Regional Council of Negro Leadership and as an NAACP organizer in Neshoba County. Evers was employed as a teacher and tavern owner in Chicago, where he supplemented his income through the underground economy, including bootlegging, numbers running, and petty theft. He returned to Mississippi as an honored dignitary after his younger brother's death.

Charles Evers returned to Mississippi campaigning for and virtually seizing his brother's post as the NAACP state field secretary. Evers assumed Medgar's position within days of the assassination. NAACP officials were uneasy about Charles Evers becoming their primary representative in the state, but did not feel it was appropriate to deny him the position so soon after his brother's assassination. Furthermore, given the reign of terror in Mississippi, there were few competitors for the position.

Charles Evers did not initially appear to be as conciliatory as his brother Medgar. Evers actually admitted to associates that his desire to replace his brother was motivated by his desire for revenge against White supremacists and complacent Blacks. Medgar Evers's widow, Myrlie, commented, "Charles sought the job with one thing in mind. He wanted vengeance. . . . He wanted to show them [White racists and accommodating Blacks] you couldn't get rid of an Evers that easily."

Charles Evers would openly advocate armed resistance, unlike his brother and previous African American human rights spokespersons in Mississippi. Evers made a controversial speech on February 15, 1964, at the NAACP Freedom Fund banquet in Nashville, Tennessee. His message went beyond armed self-defense to retaliatory violence. Evers proclaimed,

I have the greatest respect for Mr. Martin Luther King, but non-violence won't work in Mississippi. . . . We made up our minds . . . that if a white man shoots at a Negro in Mississippi, we will shoot back.

> If they bomb a Negro Church and kill our children we are going to bomb a white church and kill some of their children
>
> We have served notice in Mississippi . . . that before we be slaves anymore, we'll die and go to our graves.[7]

This statement certainly got the attention of Roy Wilkins and the conservative national leadership of the NAACP. Wilkins had sanctioned and suspended local NAACP leader Robert Williams in 1959 for a similar endorsement of retaliatory violence. Evers revised his statement two weeks later in a national NAACP press release, removing the first-person "we" and adopting a more distant approach to Black retaliatory violence. Evers's revision stated,

> There are white extremist who do not understand the non-violent movement. And they will shoot into your home if you are on your knees praying for democracy.
>
> And there are Negroes who have said and believe that the only thing these extremists understand is if you shoot into my home, they will shoot back, and if you bomb our churches, we will bomb yours.
>
> But I hope and trust the day will never come when either the extremist whites or the extremist Negroes will have to resort to this type of thing.[8]

Evers's use of rhetoric threatening armed Black response became a common feature in the summer of 1965 in Natchez.

Evers's involvement in the Natchez Movement also meant a more visible defense presence to counter the violent terror of the local Klan. According to NAACP activist Milton Cooper, a security team had developed in Jackson to protect Evers after his return to the state in 1963. Evers led a campaign to desegregate the hotels of Natchez after the initiation of an NAACP chapter in Natchez in the spring of 1965. During this campaign, White hostility grew to the point where Evers's security team had to position snipers at the Holiday Inn where the NAACP leader was residing in Adams County. Later that same summer, an incident occurred that sparked an acceleration of activity in Natchez.[9]

On August 27, 1965, NAACP leader George Metcalf was seriously injured after a bomb hidden beneath the hood of his car exploded when he turned on the ignition. While Metcalf was fortunate enough to survive the blast, he had to be hospitalized, suffering from facial lacerations, a broken arm and leg, as well as other assorted cuts and burns. The explosion of

Metcalf's vehicle had occurred in the parking lot of the local Armstrong Tire plant, where Metcalf had just finished a shift. The explosive was so potent it completely demolished Metcalf's vehicle and damaged several other cars nearby.

George Metcalf was a 53-year-old native of Natchez who housed Freedom Summer volunteers in 1964. He began to receive threats after his support for COFO efforts. His home was also sprayed with gunfire from nightriders in January of 1965. Metcalf was elected president of the Natchez NAACP chapter months before the bombing, at the same March meeting where Evers presided. Wharlest Jackson—Metcalf's good friend, Korean war veteran, and coworker at Armstrong—was selected to be treasurer of the local NAACP chapter at the same meeting. Since Metcalf was asked to work overtime on the evening of the bombing, some local Blacks believed that his supervisors had collaborated with the perpetrators of the bombing. The attack on Metcalf occurred eight days after the NAACP submitted a petition on behalf of Metcalf and eleven other Natchez Blacks to the local school board to desegregate Natchez public schools on the basis of the 1954 U.S. Supreme Court *Brown* case. Metcalf had also recently contacted the Adams County chancery clerk to seek compliance with federal voter registration legislation. Members of the Black community also thought he was targeted because he had recently received a promotion to a position as a shipping clerk at Armstrong—in other words, "taking a job reserved for a White man." The day of the bombing was his first in the new position. Most Blacks at Armstrong were concentrated in low-paying, unskilled positions. Armstrong desegregated its cafeteria shortly before the bombing.[10]

The terrorist assault on Metcalf was a part of the series of attacks, including house and church bombings, that had been initiated since the arrival of COFO in Adams County. COFO remained in Adams County after Freedom Summer and attempted to build a local campaign to register voters in spite of the terrorist intimidation of the Klan. The NAACP leader had been the target of several acts of harassment and intimidation at his home and his place of employment prior to the bombing of his car.[11]

The bombing attack on Metcalf seemed to incite Natchez Blacks to action like none of the previous acts of terror had done. Hundreds of Natchez Blacks swarmed the city's streets "threatening revenge." Evers and other activists, calling a rally on the streets in the heart of the Natchez Black community, prevented a spontaneous rebellion. Chants of "we going to kill for freedom" and "we going to kill Mayor Nosser, no matter what we do" came from the angered crowd during the rally. A police car window was shattered by a rock hurled at the vehicle after the rally. Four police officers armed with shotguns faced off a crowd of Blacks after the assault on their vehicle until activists were able to divert the crowd. Movement forces walked the streets calling for tranquility.[12]

While Evers received credit from the media for directing the angered African American mob away from spontaneous violence, his tone and rhetoric that evening and in subsequent days was anything but nonviolent. Evers publicly acknowledged the possession of guns and endorsed their use. On the day of the bombing, Evers was quoted as saying, "There is going to be trouble, no question about that . . . [T]he Negroes have armed themselves." On the same day, Evers spoke to a rally in Natchez. While cautioning Natchez Blacks not to initiate violence against Whites, Evers stated, "[I]f they do it anymore, we're going to get those responsible. We're armed, every last one of us, and we are not going to take it." Evers's statements were not idle rhetoric. Journalists noted that hundreds of Blacks in the streets of Natchez were armed that evening. The increase in Black gun ownership was sparked by the recent growth of White supremacist violence.[13]

Evers expressed frustration with the federal government's lack of protection for Movement activists in Mississippi and other parts of the South. He told a *Washington Post* reporter,

The Negroes have taken all they can take. We've armed ourselves and we are going to fight back, I informed the Justice Department many times this was going to happen. We have asked many times for protection. Every time we do the Justice Department says, "We'll look into it." . . . Nothing happens except that we keep on being shot at and murdered.[14]

Evers's statement laid the basis for an argument for armed self-defense. The failure of the federal government to protect Blacks from White supremacist violence meant that African Americans would have to rely upon their own resources for survival and to assert their civil and human rights.

The bombing attack on Metcalf occurred weeks after the spontaneous rebellion in the Watts section of south-central Los Angeles, and there was a great deal of speculation about a racial explosion in the Mississippi town. Evers also responded to the possibility of a spontaneous rebellion in Natchez: "We're not going to take it any longer. We're not going to start any riots, but we got guns and we're going to fight back. I might be fired [from the NAACP] for saying this, but that's what we are going to do."[15]

Evers was correct in his assumption that his fiery rhetoric might create problems with the national leadership of the NAACP, which reported that Evers's open advocacy of armed resistance was not received well in the national headquarters in New York. The NAACP national leadership was concerned about the national attention and visibility Evers possessed without being under their discipline. After the bombing attack on Metcalf, Evers assumed control of NAACP activity in Natchez and seized the leadership of the local Movement. Historian John Dittmer argues that Evers's central role in the Natchez Movement may have delayed the organization's national hierarchy proceeding to dismiss him.[16]

Evers's tough talk may have also been motivated by a growing militancy among elements of the Black community in Natchez. Evers was also in competition for leadership of the local Movement with younger activists from COFO/MFDP. In this period, militant speech replaced the rhetoric of the "beloved community" in much of the southern Black Freedom Struggle. Evers either realized the moment or was consistent with the growing radicalization and participation of working-class and young Blacks in the Movement.

Natchez and the Mississippi Deacons for Defense and Justice

Another example of the growing militant response in the African American community to White terror was the development of a paramilitary group in Natchez. Weeks prior to the bomb attack on George Metcalf, a small group of Black men met secretly in Natchez to form a paramilitary organization. The acceleration of White supremacist violence and Klan activity in Adams County provided motivation to organize to protect the lives and property of the African American community. According to Natchez Movement activist James Stokes, the Natchez paramilitary group was formed due to the perception among local Movement activists and supporters that they could not rely on the police for protection. Most of the men were Black workers who had grown up in Adams County and had known each other most of their lives. These men were also either members or supporters of the local NAACP. Members of the developing Natchez paramilitary group and others in the local Movement began to protect Metcalf, his family members, and his home prior to the bombing. Members of the local Elks lodge played an important role in providing personnel, weapons, and ammunition for the security of Metcalf and Movement activity in Natchez. Local NAACP leader Wharlest Jackson was an important member of the Elks Lodge. Jackson also played a role in Metcalf's security.[17]

The activity and the size of the Natchez group accelerated after the attack on Metcalf. On August 28th, one day after the attack, James Jackson, a local barber and one of the leaders of the Natchez paramilitary group, publicly announced that a chapter of the Deacons for Defense and Justice was formed in Natchez. Jackson had a reputation in Natchez for being tough and defiant. One local activist stated, "You step up on Jackson and he was going to lay you flat. . . . He wasn't going to turn the other cheek." One local leader, John Fitzgerald, had attempted to organize a Deacons chapter earlier that year but had been unsuccessful. The 25-year-old Jackson and other young Black workers took responsibility for the development of a Natchez Deacons group. Under Jackson's leadership the group accelerated their plans after the attempted murder of Metcalf. The Natchez group had heard of the success of the paramilitary Deacons for Defense and Justice in Louisiana, which had received national attention by neutralizing White terrorists in Bogalusa and Jonesboro, Louisiana.[18] According to Bogalusa leader Robert Hicks, Charles Evers requested that some of the Louisiana Deacons come to Natchez and help establish the organization there. A spokesperson of the Bogalusa Deacons was in Jackson, Mississippi, speaking to an MFDP forum the same day that Jackson announced the formation of a Natchez Deacons chapter. On August 29th, Charles Sims arrived in Natchez to discuss the formation of the Deacons for Defense in Adams County.[19]

According to Natchez Deacons James Stokes and James Young, the Natchez paramilitary group decided not to affiliate with the Louisiana Deacons. While Sims offered advice on how to set up a paramilitary organization, the Natchez group felt they had little to gain from a formal affiliation with the Deacons. Stokes remembered Sims offering no significant material aid to the Natchez paramilitary group other than the use of the name "Deacons for Defense and Justice." Sims stated that in order to use the Deacons' name, the Natchez group had to pay a percentage of their dues to the Louisiana Deacons. The Natchez group rejected Sims's offer.[20]

While the Natchez paramilitary group decided not to officially affiliate with the Louisiana Deacons, they had no problem using their name. The Natchez group was known throughout the Movement and the state, to friend and foe alike, as the Natchez Deacons for Defense and Justice. The Natchez group helped form the Mississippi Deacons for Defense and

Justice as they began to assist the establishment of affiliates across the state. By early October 1965, a little over a month after the attack on Metcalf, the Natchez Deacons were visible on the streets of Natchez providing security at marches and demonstrations. Visible members of the Natchez Deacons wore overalls and a white shirt while conducting the organization's business of protecting the Movement and the Black community.[21]

The Natchez Deacons never revealed the size of the group's membership. This policy followed the approach of the Louisiana Deacons. The nondisclosure of all of its membership kept the Klan, local police, and the FBI confused about the actual size and capability of the group. Organized much like a secret society, the Deacons realized that the less their enemies knew about them the better. James Young, who joined shortly after the attack on Metcalf, revealed decades later that the Natchez Deacons' actual size was about ten to twelve men. As in Jonesboro and Bogalusa, a few central leaders were identified to represent the Deacons to the public. James Stokes was appointed spokesman. James Jackson was the first president of the Natchez Deacons. James Young was selected as secretary and was responsible for the development of the by-laws and the charter for the Deacons and the Sportsmen Club. According to Stokes, "The strongest thing we had going for ourselves is that nobody knew, not even some of our members, how many men there were in the organization." The Deacons' concealing their size served as a weapon to instill doubt and concern in White supremacists since they did not know what to expect from the Natchez paramilitary group.[22] Movement folks outside of the Deacons were not privy to the identities of the entire Deacon membership.[23]

Secrecy was essential for the mission of the Deacons. It was important that the organization selectively recruit its members and that its membership not reveal its secrets. Since trust was an important factor for recruitment, the initial group only recruited men they had grown up with and whose background and character they knew. "Everybody we had, we knew," said James Young. A Deacon recruit had to be sponsored by someone currently in the group. Anyone with a history of abusing alcohol or a criminal past was not allowed to join. The Deacons did not want to have members who could be easily compromised by police pressure.[24] Before induction into the organization, a member was informed of the seriousness of joining the Deacons.

The Deacons informed their recruits that revealing organizational secrets could result in death for the informant.[25] The Deacons' internal security methods were apparently effective and prevented the Mississippi State

Sovereignty Commission, the FBI, local police, and the Klan from receiving an adequate assessment of the size and capability of the Deacons. In order to maintain security, a small group within the membership made all of the plans. Individual members knew their assignments, but not the entire security plan. This also prevented information from leaking to the opposition.

As earlier stated, there was a proliferation of arms in the Black community in Natchez in response to a White supremacist reign of terror, which accelerated in Adams County around 1963. The Natchez Deacons believed that it was important for them to be well armed in order to meet the demands of protecting the Black community as well as the leadership and workers of the Movement. One unidentified source in the Natchez Deacons revealed that the organization possessed "hand grenades, machine guns, whatever we needed." According to this source, only one store in Natchez would sell ammunition to the Deacons. If White supremacists knew that the Deacons had a limited supply of ammunition, the Deacons' efforts would be compromised. The Natchez Deacons received ammunition from external sources to counter efforts by local Whites to prevent Blacks from obtaining ammo.[26]

Clifford Boxley, a Natchez native residing in northern California, became an important contact for the Deacons. Boxley left Natchez for California in 1960. He did not involve himself in Movement activism until after hearing and reading about the brutal bombing of the 16th Street Church in 1963. Boxley then decided to involve himself in the northern California Civil Rights Movement. He visited Natchez in 1965 during the boycott and remembered that on "[o]ne side of the street was the Klan and other side was the Deacons of Defense." Boxley returned to California and organized a speaking tour for James Stokes, who was joined by another Natchez Deacon, Richard Lewis. The funds raised in northern California enabled Stokes and Lewis to purchase weapons and communication equipment, some of which they took back to Mississippi with them in Boxley's 1956 Oldsmobile.[27]

Mississippi law allowed for civilians to openly carry loaded weapons in public. Citizens could also carry a loaded firearm in their vehicle as long as it was not concealed. This allowed the Deacons to openly carry guns to protect demonstrations, mass meetings, and community institutions. The public display of weapons by Black freedom fighters served to prevent attacks from White supremacists. The Deacons openly carried their weapons on marches and demonstrations to protect Movement activists and supporters from attack.[28]

On September 4, 1967, in Centerville, a small town in the southwest Mississippi county of Wilkerson, the Natchez Deacons, aligned with the Wilkerson County chapter of the Deacons for Defense, scattered a mob of White supremacists. After a member of the racist mob trained his weapon on participants in a demonstration for Black voting rights, twenty-five armed Deacons responded to prevent the demonstrators from harm.[29] Deacon James Young, describing the situation that day, stated, "We pulled in there and started unloading all of this heavy artillery and they loaded up and left."[30] SNCC activist Hollis Watkins, who was also there that day, remembered the leader of the Deacon stating, "We represent the Deacons for Defense, if you come in here with that you're going to be in trouble." According to Watkins, hearing the name "Deacons for Defense" invoked was almost as effective in scattering the racist mob as the guns.[31]

The Deacons were not hesitant about using their weapons also. According to Stokes, Young, and Jefferson County NAACP activists Lillie Brown and Ed Cole, one evening in the late 1960s, the Natchez Deacons were asked to provide security in Jefferson County, just north of Adams, at a mass meeting in a rural church. An armed watch was placed on the perimeter of the church. Any White person coming after dark was considered suspicious, so White allies of the Movement were asked to come to the meeting early. After the meeting started, a car approached the scene of the meeting. The security patrol observed some Whites in the automobile coming down the road leading to the church with the vehicle lights out. One of the Whites in the vehicle was observed preparing to throw a Molotov cocktail. A Deacons' security team, armed with a dozen shotguns, bombarded the vehicle, preventing the firebomb from even being propelled from the vehicle.[32] The armed presence and preparedness of the Deacons prevented the Movement in Natchez, and in southwest Mississippi in general, from being terrorized and intimidated. White supremacist terrorists also were on alert that any foray into the Black community or in the vicinity of Movement activity was not without consequence.

Mississippi state officials opposed to the Movement wished to find means to disarm the Deacons. On September 3, 1967, FBI documents reveal, a proposal was forwarded by an unnamed source to the governor of Mississippi to make it illegal for members of the Deacons for Defense in the state to possess firearms. On September 4, 1967, the same day as the confrontation between Deacons and the White mob in Centreville, three members of the Deacons were arrested for illegal possession of firearms. The state district attorney for the Southwestern District of Mississippi gave the Mississippi State Highway Patrol the "authority to disarm all members of the Deacons for Defense and Justice."[33] Mississippi and other southern states made it illegal for anyone to transport rifles and shotguns in the cab of a car. These laws required that rifles and shotguns be carried on a rack on the back of a vehicle.

Even though the Deacons experienced repression concerning their possession of firearms, being armed as an organized force served as an asset to the organization and the Movement. The armed, organized presence of the Deacons and their preparedness for combat, as well as the uncertainty on the part of Whites as to the Deacons' capabilities, provided the Movement with a serious bartering chip. Combined with effective boycotts, the presence of the Deacons gave Evers and local leaders a position of strength from which to negotiate.[34]

The Natchez Deacons became an essential ingredient in the Natchez Movement and the Mississippi Black Freedom Struggle. The Deacons provided the Movement with an instrument to neutralize the violence of the Klan and other White supremacist civilians. The potential of the Deacons for Defense also gave Evers and other leaders more potency in their negotiating position with the White power structure and more boldness in their public statements. Without a doubt, the Deacons made the Natchez Movement and the Mississippi Black Freedom Struggle more effective.

Natchez, the Boycott, and Enforcing the Movement

The day after the attack on Metcalf on August 28, 1965, Evers and local leaders of the Black community presented "A Declaration of the Negro Citizens of Natchez" to Mayor Nosser and the Natchez city government. "A Declaration of the Negro Citizens of Natchez" was a list of twelve demands for civil and human rights for local Blacks. The twelve demands included the desegregation of local schools, a denunciation by city officials of the Ku Klux Klan and other White supremacist groups, expanded employment opportunities for Blacks (particularly store clerks and police officers), police escort for Black funerals, and the requirement that local police and civil servants address Black adults as "Mr.," "Mrs.," or "Miss" as opposed to "Boy," "Girl," or "Auntie." The Black delegation gave Nosser and the city government until September 1st, four days, to respond to their demands before the Natchez Black community would apply coercive action. According to journalistic accounts of the meeting, one Black participant in the meeting threatened that "violence might ensue unless City government acted favorably on matters contained in the declaration."[35]

On September 1, 1965, the Natchez Board of Aldermen rejected the demands of the Black leaders.[36] To ensure that no uprising occurred in the Black community, the Natchez government imposed a curfew from 10 p.m. to 5 a.m. to restrict activity in the city during the evening and early morning hours. All alcohol sales were also banned during this time. Stating that Natchez was in "imminent danger of a riot," Governor Paul Johnson ordered 650 armed National Guardsmen to the city.[37]

Upon hearing the decision of the Board of Aldermen and the restrictions imposed by the state and local government, debate ensued within the Natchez Movement on how to respond to the challenge. COFO and MFDP forces wanted to immediately challenge the curfew with marches and demonstrations. There had been nightly mass meetings from the time of the bombing attack on Metcalf until the evening after the city government rendered its rejection of the Black leaders' demands. At each of the mass meetings, the consensus was that a demonstration would take place if the demands were not met. Charles Evers, who announced a boycott of all-White businesses on the evening of August 28th, wanted to place emphasis on the boycott rather than demonstrate. Evers believed that the presence of the National Guard and the potential for violence created an unfavorable environment for demonstrations. Evers told those assembled that evening, "[T]here is too much chance of bloodshed to ask you to walk down the streets of Natchez."[38] Evers won the debate and was able in the coming weeks to cement himself as the leader of the Natchez Movement. When the National Guard left Natchez the following weekend, Evers approved demonstrations in Natchez, even in opposition to court order. By October 6, 1965, the Natchez Deacons secured the marches.[39]

While demonstrations were an important aspect of the Natchez Movement, local NAACP leaders would credit the economic boycott with being the decisive element of the Natchez campaign. The NAACP-organized boycott was very successful; indeed, Movement leaders claimed that the Black community boycott of White businesses was nearly 100 percent effective. Names of Blacks who violated the NAACP boycott were announced at mass meetings.[40] Violators of the boycott were not only isolated, but were harassed by the enforcer squad, which was organized by Rudy Shields. Shields, a Korean War veteran, had moved to Mississippi from Chicago at the request of Charles Evers.[41] Evers called Shields to Natchez from Belzoni, Mississippi, where he was working with the local

NAACP. Shields's primary responsibility was to make the boycott successful. As one Movement participant stated, "Rudy was mostly a boycott man. . . . [W]henever you had a boycott, he was right up front."[42]

Just as it was the Deacons' role to protect the Movement and the community from external enemies, it was the responsibility of Shields and his squad to deal with internal enemies. The Natchez Movement resorted to terror within the Black community to enforce its decisions. For those in the Black community who did not take seriously the edict of the NAACP and the Natchez Movement, Shields and his squad would provide coercive violence as an incentive. Movement activist Ed Cole offered, "Folks go shop, break the boycott, they didn't get home with the damn groceries . . . cause somebody was waiting for them when they got there."[43] The Movement considered breaking the boycott a serious offense and felt that violators had to be disciplined. With the sanction of the Movement's leadership, Shields and his team were committed to punishing the violators. As Evers stated, "We didn't go around bragging about it, but we were ready to enforce those boycotts, to die if necessary."[44]

State and local officials, law enforcement, and local press often stated that the Deacons were responsible for the enforcement of boycotts. There seems, though, to have been a division of labor between the Deacons, who were solely responsible for the defense of the Black community and the Movement from external enemies, and Shields's enforcer squad, which was particularly responsible for harassing and terrorizing Black people who violated the boycott. When asked if the Deacons enforced boycotts, Natchez Deacon James Young responded, "We had another team out there. If you went in there [a White-owned business] this time, after [the enforcer squad] got through with you, you weren't hardly going back any more."[45]

The Deacons and the enforcer squad recruited different types of people for each organization. The Deacons tended to be adult males over thirty years of age who were considered disciplined, stable, and respected in the community. The enforcer squad tended to utilize working-class males in their late teens to early twenties. As opposed to the older Deacons, the recruits of the enforcer squad tended to be less stable and from the more volatile elements of the community.[46]

While women were not recruited into the Deacons, females did play a significant role in enforcing sanctions on internal enemies. Women, young or old, were not included in Shields's boycott enforcers but were involved in punishing suspected female informers. The Movement suspected that certain Black domestics were providing, either voluntarily or through

Boycott organizer Rudolph "Rudy" Shields leads a demonstration confronting the Claiborne County sheriff at Alcorn A & M. (Courtesy Mississippi Cultural Crossroads.)

coercion, information to the White power structure. A team of NAACP women was organized to physically discipline the suspected informants.[47]

The vigilance of enforcer groups certainly aided the Natchez Movement in maintaining an effective boycott. On October 12, 1965, an NAACP delegation met with Natchez city officials. The NAACP delegation came from the meeting claiming victory, announcing that the mayor and the Board of Aldermen had agreed to most of their demands. Two days later, Natchez city officials denied agreeing to the NAACP's proposals. The boycott and marches continued. Within a two-month period, six White-owned enterprises went out of business. Concerned that the boycott would affect the Christmas season, a significant number of White merchants gave their consent to the White power structure to negotiate with the NAACP. On November 29, 1965, the NAACP and the White power structure came to an agreement. The NAACP agreed to lift the boycott on twenty-three White-owned businesses in Natchez. In turn, the city of Natchez hired six

Black policemen, desegregated municipal public facilities, and agreed to appoint a "qualified Negro" to the school board. The twenty-three White businesses conceded to hiring or promoting Black workers to the position of clerk. While some in the local Movement, particularly COFO and FDP forces, did not believe the agreement went far enough, the settlement was hailed nationally. The Natchez boycott strategy would be replicated in communities throughout southwest Mississippi.

Though not as visible as Evers, the Deacons, or the NAACP, the work of the enforcer squads, both that of Shields and that of the NAACP women, was essential to the Movement. The enforcer groups ensured accountability and respect for the decisions of the Natchez Movement. If the boycott was almost 100 percent effective, recognition has to be given to the work of the enforcer groups. While this has escaped most accounts of the Mississippi Movement, the participants in the Movement, particularly those active in southwest Mississippi, recognize the significance of Rudy Shields and the enforcer groups he organized.

The Natchez Paradigm and the Mississippi Movement

The formula developed in Natchez to combat the local White power structure to win concessions toward human and civil rights was utilized throughout the state, particularly in southwest Mississippi communities. Other local communities observing the success of the Natchez boycott, under the leadership of Evers and Shields, began to organize boycotts utilizing the model developed in Natchez. The Natchez model had proven the necessity to utilize the threat of a coercive response to defeat external and internal enemies of the Mississippi Black Freedom Struggle. Chapters of the Deacons for Defense and Justice and enforcer squads were established in other local Movements.

When Evers and Shields became involved in boycott campaigns in Jefferson and Wilkerson counties, the Natchez Deacons directly became involved in these local campaigns. Since Jefferson County (north) and Wilkerson County (south) were contiguous to Adams County, the Natchez Deacons could take up a major responsibility in these counties. According to Deacon Samuel Harden, Wilkerson County activists established their own chapter of the Deacons for Defense and Justice. The Wilkerson Deacons received personnel and support from, and virtually came under the chain of command of, the Natchez Deacons. In both of these communities, Rudy Shields organized teams to enforce the boycott.[48]

When NAACP-led boycotts developed in Claiborne County and in the towns of Hazelhurst and Crystal Springs in Copiah County, Rudy Shields organized local Deacons units. In all of these communities, the Deacons and enforcer squads were organized as part of boycott campaigns to pressure the White power structure to concede to demands similar to those presented by Black leaders in Natchez. The Claiborne County Deacons for Defense and Justice was among the most visible paramilitary organizations in the state. In 1960, Claiborne County had a population of 11,000, with 8,239 (76 percent) of its residents being of African descent. During the same year, Claiborne's county seat, Port Gibson, had a population of 2,816, which was almost evenly divided between African descendants and Whites. There were no Black elected or appointed officials in the county. In 1966, prior to the initiation of the NAACP boycott of White merchants in Port Gibson, there were only seven Black registered voters in the whole county. Claiborne County is also the home of Alcorn A&M, Mississippi's first public Black college.[49]

The Deacons for Defense and the enforcer squads, now known as "Da Spirit," were organized in Claiborne County after the Black community under the leadership of Evers and the local NAACP called a boycott on April 1, 1966.[50] The Claiborne County Deacons were popularly known as "the Black Hats." Friend and foe alike in Claiborne County called the local Deacon chapter "the Black Hats" because Claiborne Deacons wore a black helmet while on duty. Khaki pants were also part of their uniform. "The Black Hats" first appeared in public on April 1, 1966, the day the boycott was initiated in Port Gibson. The Deacons came out to protect the NAACP picket of White merchants in downtown Port Gibson. The boycott of Port Gibson streets would go on for the next three years. The Deacons also patrolled the Black community during the evening, monitoring the activity of the local police, the Klan, and other White supremacist forces. According to Deacon George Walker, the Deacons for Defense and Justice were committed to preventing "another Neshoba County" (where civil rights workers James Chaney, Andrew Goodman, and Mickey Schwerner were murdered) from happening in Claiborne County.[51]

The boycott of White-owned enterprises in Port Gibson lasted over three years, driving several White merchants out of business. The boycott was definitely made more effective by the leadership of Rudy Shields and the activity of the enforcer squads. Shields organized a network of youth in neighborhoods throughout the county to harass violators of the boycott in their community.

Due to the solidarity of the Black community and the enforcement of the boycott, by 1969, several White merchants acquiesced and consented to hire Black workers. By this point, tensions had calmed and the local movement decided to demobilize the Deacons. In April of 1969, the shooting of a Black man by White police sparked a near uprising by the Black community and the resumption of a full-fledged boycott. After the second boycott was called, the local Movement leaders did not see the need to mobilize the paramilitary Deacons. In this year, local Blacks had won several concessions from the White power structure and were beginning to participate in local government. While the organized defense wing of the first boycott was no longer seen as necessary after 1969, the organization of the Deacons in Claiborne County is partially responsible for Black political gains in the county.[52]

In a few cases, the Bogalusa Deacons were active in local Mississippi campaigns. In 1965, the Bogalusa group unsuccessfully attempted to establish Mississippi chapters of the original Louisiana Deacons for Defense and Justice in a variety of towns in the state.[53] That year they organized one chapter in Marion county, and in the early months of 1966, Bogalusa Deacon leader Charles Sims and other Louisiana Deacons became active in a community campaign in Hattiesburg, Mississippi. The campaign was sparked by the murder of NAACP leader Vernon Dahmer on January 10, 1966, by nightriding Klansmen. Dahmer returned fire and scattered a group of approximately fourteen Klansmen, who firebombed and shot into his home. While Dahmer's response allowed his wife and daughter to escape their domicile, the NAACP leader was severely burned from the waist up before his escape from the burning house, and he died the following day.[54]

In response to this brutal slaying, Charles Evers urged an economic boycott to achieve the basic rights to which Dahmer had committed his life. Citing Natchez as an example, Evers stated, "The only thing the white man understands is the ballot and the dollar. . . . We're going to get both of them."[55] Weeks later, local leaders presented Hattiesburg and Forrest County officials with a list of demands, including employment opportunities in the public sector, the desegregation of public facilities, and implementation of federal civil rights and voting legislation.

The Bogalusa Deacons established a chapter of the paramilitary organization in Hattiesburg. Like Deacons groups in other southern towns, their basic responsibility was the protection of Movement leaders, activists, and the Black community in general. Through contacts in the Deacons group in Hattiesburg, the Bogalusa paramilitary organization was able to establish a Deacons chapter in Laurel, Mississippi. In Laurel, the Deacons supported voter registration efforts and became the basis of the paramilitary organization of a labor movement in Laurel.[56]

While the Deacons were initiated in Louisiana, as in other communities implementing the Natchez model, Rudy Shields was involved in organizing the boycott enforcer squad in Hattiesburg. By the summer of 1967, Mississippi law enforcement surveillance revealed that the Black economic boycott in Hattiesburg was 100 percent effective. It was in Hattiesburg that the enforcer squad received its name "Da Spirit." James Nix, Hattiesburg organizer of "Da Spirit," stated, "[A] spirit is something that you don't see. This is the reason for it. . . . [W]e would harass people. . . . And this was our job." In Hattiesburg, "Da Spirit" also aided in providing covert security for local Movement leaders. The pressure of the boycott gradually won concessions from the Hattiesburg White power structure. As in other Mississippi communities, White merchants in Hattiesburg pressured political elites to negotiate with NAACP leaders to end the economic boycott.[57]

The Natchez model was applied throughout the state, particularly in southwest Mississippi. The threat of retaliatory violence and the rhetoric of self-defense were openly advocated. Whether the effort was organized by the Mississippi or the Louisiana Deacons, Black Mississippians organized or deceptively projected the formation of paramilitary organizations to protect Movement leaders and activists and the Black community during economic boycotts designed to win basic civil and human rights. Additionally, local leaders recognized, on the basis of the Natchez experience, the necessity of an enforcer squad, generally separate from the defense organization, to ensure accountability and solidarity in the boycott effort. The armed aspect of the Natchez model was essential for gaining basic rights in communities throughout the state.

The Impact of the Natchez Model on the Mississippi Freedom Struggle

The development of paramilitary organizations in the Mississippi Black Freedom Struggle signaled a new day in Black communities throughout the state. The capacity of the Movement to protect itself and the Black community as well as to retaliate against White supremacist terrorists gave Evers and other Black leaders more leverage in negotiating with local

White power structures. The ability of Movement leaders to maintain effective economic boycotts through solidarity and intimidation gave the NAACP even more negotiating strength. The Natchez model, combining economic boycotts with paramilitary defense and the potential for retaliation, proved more effective in winning concessions and social and cultural change on the local level than nonviolent direct action or voter registration campaigns depending on federal protection.

The Natchez model served as the major paradigm for Black resistance in the state of Mississippi until the end of the decade. After Rudy Shields left Claiborne County, he helped organize economic boycotts in several Mississippi communities, including Yazoo County, Belzoni, West Point, and Indianola. In each of these communities Shields would apply the Natchez model.[58] In the late 1970s, in several communities in northern Mississippi, including Holly Springs, Okolona, Tupelo, and Byhalia, the United League of Mississippi would organize economic boycotts. The United League continued the armed tradition of the Natchez model in the economic boycott it organized in northern Mississippi. The leaders of the United League openly declared the right of Black people to protect themselves and their Movement. Members of the United League carried weapons to protect demonstrators from the Klan and other White supremacists, and in some cases engaged in gun battles with racist Whites.[59]

For more than a decade and a half after the 1964 Freedom Summer, the Black Freedom Struggle of Mississippi survived and sustained itself primarily through reliance on economic coercion and armed resistance. Born of disenchantment with federal promises and expectations for external support and intervention, the Natchez model clearly demonstrates how local communities initiated social change primarily utilizing their own resources. The Natchez model proved to be an effective disruptive campaign that forced White elites to negotiate with segregated Black communities. Along with other vehicles of collective action, the Natchez boycott strategy must be included if we are to understand the elimination of de jure segregation in Mississippi.

Another significant element of the Natchez model is what it reflected in terms of gender politics in the southern Black Freedom Movement. The development of the Deacons for Defense promoted a masculinist appeal. The notions of patriarchy and the role of men as protectors had existed within the Black Freedom Movement for centuries. The development and projection of paramilitary organization brought a call for Black men to assume the role of protectors of their families and communities. In the early

1960s, Black women participated in the defense of their homes and neighborhoods, sharing the responsibilities of armed watch of their domiciles
with their husbands and sons. Janie Brewer even organized her children
and grandchildren, as well as COFO volunteers, to defend her family com-
pound from nightriders. The Deacons' spokespersons and the advance of
the open promotion of armed resistance generally called for the involvement and organization of Black men in defense efforts. In spite of the
masculinist emphasis, several Black female activists were still armed and
engaged in politically motivated armed self-defense in Mississippi through
the late 1970s.

6

"We Didn't Turn No Jaws"

*Black Power, Boycotts, and the Growing
Debate on Armed Resistance*

*Joining the March against Fear, Deacons national organizer Ernest Thomas
told* Jet *magazine, a Black publication, "If a white man starts shooting again,
you'll know where to find him."*[1]

On June 6, 1966, Movement activist James Meredith was shot one day after
he initiated his "March against Fear." His one-man march was a challenge
to the intimidation from White supremacist terror that Blacks had had to
endure for centuries. The Mississippi-born activist stated that the march's
purpose was "to encourage the 450,000 unregistered Negroes to go to polls
and register." He argued that the march would "point out and challenge
the all-pervasive and overriding fear that dominates the day-to-day life of
the Negro in the United States—and especially in Mississippi." Meredith
would travel 220 miles south from Memphis, Tennessee, to Jackson, Mississippi. However, his march was interrupted two miles south of the northern Mississippi town of Hernando as he lay wounded from a birdshot fired
from the shotgun of sniper Aubrey James Norvell. Before firing and injuring the lone marcher, Norvell, an unemployed salesman, yelled the following from the side of the highway: "James Meredith, James Meredith . . . I
only want James Meredith."[2]

Leadership of the national Civil Rights Movement converged in Memphis in response to the shooting, which was a potential crisis for the national Civil Rights Movement. Meredith's individual March against Fear
had been suspended by a sniper's bullets. This would have been interpreted as a significant defeat of the Civil Rights Movement, particularly by
civil rights forces and their adversaries, if its leaders had not pushed forward with Meredith's march. Notable leaders rushed to Memphis where
Meredith was hospitalized: Dr. Martin Luther King Jr., representing the
Southern Christian Leadership Conference; Roy Wilkins of the NAACP;
Whitney Young of the Urban League; Floyd McKissick of CORE; and

Stokely Carmichael, Cleve Sellers, and Stanley Wise of SNCC. Meredith had reluctantly agreed that the Movement organizations would pick up his March against Fear from the point where he had been assaulted in De Soto County, Mississippi.

The national leadership of the NAACP, the Urban League, the SCLC, CORE, and SNCC met at SNCC founder Reverend James Lawson's Centenary Methodist Church in Memphis on June 9th, three days after the shooting of Meredith. Wilkins and Young proposed continuing Meredith's march with the assistance of nationally known personalities and liberal organizations. Their proposal sought collaboration with the administration of President Lyndon Johnson and emphasized drawing the attention of national media. The NAACP and Urban League leaders had been in consultation with the Johnson administration on legislative objectives, and they argued that the goal of the march should be to build support for a new civil rights bill that would guarantee federal protection for desegregation activists.[3]

Carmichael and McKissick wanted to publicly issue a statement critical of the Johnson administration for failing to protect Movement activists, including Meredith. This position contrasted with the Wilkins/Young preference for collaboration with the federal government, particularly President Johnson. SNCC also had grown weary of national marches that paraded national personalities and White liberal forces to cater to liberal public opinion. Their objective was to organize independent Black organizations for political and economic power with a focus on Black-majority counties and towns. The Mississippi Delta was the heart of the march's route. The indigenous networks that SNCC and CORE developed in Mississippi, including local NAACP chapters and leaders, would be essential to a successful march. SNCC had organized in this area since 1962, and this gave the organization some leverage in the discussion. Carmichael presented a proposal emphasizing indigenous Mississippi participation to encourage Black voter registration, local Black electoral campaigns, and promotion of local Black leaders.[4]

Carmichael also proposed that the Louisiana-based Deacons for Defense should participate in the march. He had worked with the Deacons in the effort to build an independent Black political organization, the Lowndes County Freedom Organization, in the Alabama Black Belt. The Deacons requested to participate in the march after the shooting of Meredith. Deacons founder and national spokesperson, Ernest "Chilly Willie" Thomas, arrived in Memphis with a contingent of Chicago Deacons and planned to coordinate security with Louisiana and Mississippi chapters of the organization. According to one northern Black nationalist publication, the Deacons "vowed to put trigger happy whites in the cemetery."[5]

CORE supported Carmichael's proposals to emphasize grassroots Black participation and include the Deacons in the march. SNCC and CORE perspectives on development of local leadership and organization were similar. CORE had developed a relationship with the Deacons from the inception of the Louisiana-based paramilitary formation. Dr. Martin Luther King Jr. stood at the middle of this heated debate. He was sympathetic to the criticism of the Johnson administration and Carmichael's call for a locally based emphasis for the march. King initially disagreed with including the Deacons in the march but was ultimately convinced to allow their participation if the march maintained the banner of nonviolence. Sensing a loss of their positions, Wilkins and Young abandoned the effort, left Memphis, and returned to New York.[6]

The Deacons would "patrol the perimeters of the march and protect the campsites." Their role was to protect the marchers from Klan and other White supremacist civilian attacks.[7] Speaking on the Deacons' role, SNCC's program secretary Cleve Sellers offered,

> The Deacons for Defense served as our bodyguards. Their job was to keep our people alive. We let them decide the best way to accomplish this. Whenever suspicious whites were observed loitering near the march route, the Deacons would stop them and demand they state their business. In those areas where there were hills adjacent to the road, they walked the ridges of the hills.[8]

The Deacons' inclusion in a march sponsored by national Civil Rights Movement organizations represented an important shift in the Black Freedom Struggle. While the march continued under the banner of nonviolence, the public association with and acknowledgment of the Deacons signified that the Movement had entered a new period. SNCC, CORE, and SCLC, as well as their national leadership, were relying upon organized Black militants, not the federal government, to defend their organizations and the participants in this campaign. It was an implicit statement that the security of the Movement could not rely on local, state, or federal law enforcement to protect it.

Carmichael's proposal reflected an emerging orientation that would become dominant in the Black Freedom Struggle: "Black Power." Embracing armed resistance and deemphasizing nonviolence, Black Power would also represent the ascendance of identity politics through the medium of Black identity and Black consciousness. It would also represent, particularly in the liberal-pluralist expression of Black Power, the expansion of political demands beyond the call for access to resources to a call for political representation and decision-making power in institutions that affect the cultural, economic, and social life of the Black community.

The March against Fear: Self-Defense and the Rise of Black Power

The March against Fear was considered "the last great march of the civil rights years."[9] Designed to inspire and organize Black Mississippians to register and vote, the March against Fear had varying degrees of success in organizing Black communities and mobilizing the vote. The march would register new Black voters in the state and would have a lasting impact on the political participation of Blacks in the communities along the route of the march.

In Greenwood, SNCC field organizer Willie Ricks was put on the advance team. Ricks, a charismatic exhorter, went to Greenwood Black communities and implemented an agitation/propaganda campaign promoting the slogan of "Black Power." Conflict occurred when the march arrived in Greenwood on June 16th. Local police arrested Carmichael, SNCC worker Robert Smith, and CORE organizer Bruce Baines. The charge was violating a city order that prevented marchers from setting up tents for a campsite at a Black public high school. After being bailed out, Carmichael spoke at an evening rally in Greenwood. He had been encouraged by Ricks to include and emphasize the "Black Power" slogan in his presentation. Carmichael, a gifted and skillful orator, was fervent and inspiring, speaking to a crowd of six hundred at the Leflore County Courthouse. The SNCC chairman passionately asked them, "What do you want?" Ricks, an extremely effective "hype man," responded, "Black Power!" Carmichael asked the question again and again, and each time more people in the audience of mostly local people responded enthusiastically.[10]

The inclusion of the "Black Power" slogan represented a more nationalist shift in the ranks of SNCC, CORE, and particularly in the younger generation of the Movement. The "Black Power" slogan was rejected by integrationists, including King, SCLC leaders, Charles Evers, and National Baptist Convention leader John H. Jackson. The development of incipient

Black nationalism, along with the growing rejection of nonviolence by Movement activists and the presence of the Deacons, became a concern of integrationist and nonviolent forces in the Black Freedom Struggle and a major focus of national media covering the March against Fear. SNCC and SCLC leaders offered competing chants during the march. SNCC members led the march with, "What do you want . . . Black power." In response, SCLC chanted, "What do you want . . . Freedom."[11]

The march inspired several Mississippi Black communities into political activity. Much of the media coverage and many of the scholarly accounts have emphasized the ideological difference among march participants, the emergence of the "Black Power" slogan, and the presence of the Deacons. The impact of the march on the political consciousness and participation of Mississippi Black communities and on individual Blacks in the state must not be lost. The charismatic appeal of Martin Luther King Jr. was a motivation for thousands of Black Delta residents to leave school, work, or their residences in order to march or rally at the respective county courthouses.[12] The presence of King was a tremendous asset for the success of the march.

In some communities, the March against Fear was a significant moment that inspired individuals toward political action. The march entered the Delta town of Belzoni on June 19th, and as twelve hundred marchers arrived in the city, a Black citizen proclaimed, "There has never been anything like this in Belzoni." Hundreds of plantation workers and farmers in Humphreys County joined the march, increasing the number from the 150-person core of primarily SNCC, CORE, and SCLC field workers. Black Humphreys County residents responded to the call of the marchers and demonstrated support for the Movement, in spite of the threat of economic reprisal and violence. One Humphreys County resident remembered, "We was a little afraid, but we still stepped up." In Humphreys County, marchers witnessed conditions of life on plantations reminiscent of chattel slavery. During the march activities, 150 Blacks were registered at the Humphreys County courthouse in spite of intimidation tactics by plantation owners and local White supremacists.[13]

Even those who did not register due to fear or age were inspired by the events. Fourteen-year-old Robert Davis left home in Belzoni to join the march. He traveled with the marchers from Belzoni to Yazoo City, then traveled with a contingent led by King to Philadelphia, Mississippi, and finally to Canton. After the march ended, Davis continued his activism as a boycott enforcer in Belzoni and leader in a student walkout at his high school. Ten-year-old Irvin Bradley (also known as Hondo Lumumba) had attended the freedom school in Humphreys County. His parents allowed him and his brother Tony to sleep with the marchers at Green Grove Baptist Church in Belzoni and walk the next day to the county courthouse with Meredith March participants. Bradley would grow up to be a labor organizer and human rights activist in Jackson, Mississippi, nearly two decades later.[14]

The March against Fear entered Yazoo County on June 22nd. The march and rally in the county seat, Yazoo City, would mark a turning point for many local residents. Prior to the march, Yazoo County had not been a significant Movement center in the state. The march initiated the beginning of dynamic Movement activity in the county. Nancella Hudson was a domestic and a mother of five. She went to the march with her youngest child, Rodney (an eight-month-old baby), in a stroller to shake the hand of King. She allowed her three older children, ages six, seven, and eight, to march with chaperones from the county courthouse to the Oak Grove African Methodist Episcopal Church. The church was located in the nearby Benton community (nearly seven miles away). Hudson decided to register to vote at the rally in front of the Yazoo County courthouse. Hudson remembered, "And then you know when I got home, I got scared, I said oh my goodness! You know, but at that time, you know there come a time when you just don't have no fear. I didn't have no fear." Hudson's overcoming her fear to register on that day is precisely the act Meredith had wanted to encourage when he had initiated the march weeks earlier.[15]

Arthur Clayborn was a postal worker in Yazoo County who had previously registered to vote. Clayborn did not fear losing his job for participating in the march since he was a federal employee. He was determined to see King at the march, so he carried his six children to the rally at the county courthouse for the opportunity to see the civil rights leader. Clayborn's oldest child wanted to march away from the rally to Canton. Two years later, he would actively participate in the boycott in Yazoo County.[16]

Herman Leach was a teacher at the Saint Francis School in Yazoo City. His brother Wardell was teaching at a public school in Yazoo. Hundreds of Yazoo youth prepared to march downtown. Yazoo City mayor Jeffrey Barber mobilized local police and firemen with a fire truck to prevent the young people from marching through downtown. Wardell Leach warned Barber that for city law enforcement to attack young people would have political consequences. The Leach brothers escorted the students on the march. Herman Leach would become more politically active after the march, participating in organizing boycotts in Yazoo and serving as an elected official. Wardell Leach would become Yazoo City's first African American mayor.[17]

The March, the Deacons, and the Growing
Debate on Armed Resistance

U.S. Attorney General Nicholas Katzenbach agreed to grant the state of Mississippi the responsibility of securing the marchers. Mississippi governor Paul Johnson assumed responsibility for providing protection for the marchers, despite publicly exhibiting disdain for its participants. Johnson stated that state law enforcement's protection of the march was dependent on whether "they [the marchers] behave themselves, commit no acts of violence nor take any position of provocative defiance." Johnson also discouraged White Mississippians from disrupting the march, which he characterized as consisting of "agitators and radical politicians."[18]

Governor Johnson originally provided twenty state patrol cars for this assignment. After early voter registration successes on the route, Johnson sliced the number of patrol cars to four, declaring that the march had "turned into a voter registration campaign." Johnson stated in a news conference, "We aren't going to wet-nurse a bunch of showmen." Carmichael believed that the Deacons' presence openly and legally carrying guns motivated the decision to scale the state police escort back to a token show of force. Carmichael's account also conveyed that state troopers allowed vehicles on the march route to "veer over, speed up, and zoom by, inches from where our people were walking." One evening state troopers intervened to discourage a few carloads of White hooligans who had driven dangerously close to the marchers' campsite only after the Deacons confronted the marauders.[19]

The march became a venue for the debate between nonviolence and armed resistance. One White nonviolent protestor, Reverend Theodore Seamans, argued that "the movement is no place for guns." Seamans's comments occurred after he observed a .45 handgun in a vehicle driven by one of the Deacons. Responding to Seamans's criticism, Ernest Thomas, the Deacons' spokesperson and national organizer, retorted that it was dangerous to tell Blacks not to fight back in such a violent and hostile situation. The debate between Seamans and Thomas sparked a vigorous exchange between nonviolent advocates and supporters of armed resistance. The debate caught the attention of media observers. CORE field secretary Bruce Baines intervened, saying, "[I]f you want to discuss violence and nonviolence, don't talk around the press. This march is too important." CORE chairman Floyd McKissick maintained a deceptive and conciliatory posture with the press concerning armed security. McKissick told the press he was not aware of arms around the campsite and insisted on telling all marchers, including the Deacons, "[T]he march must remain nonviolent. . . . I don't believe in no damn war."[20]

A growing number of activists appreciated the presence of the Deacons. SNCC members openly praised the Deacons' security efforts and role in the Movement. "Everyone realized that without [the Deacons], our lives would have been much less secure," declared Cleve Sellers. Willie Ricks proclaimed to an audience in Belzoni, "We don't have enough Deacons." The Deacons gave some marchers a feeling of security and confidence that they could prevent White terrorism. SNCC executive committee member Jesse Harris sensed, "Along the march we had no problems because all the white folks, Klansman and everybody, they knew if they came in with a threat, if a church got bombed along the way, boom . . . the Deacons were going to find you."[21] The Deacons' presence and posture provided confidence and confirmed to some that Blacks needed to rely on their own resources for protection.[22]

All of the spokespersons, including Thomas, insisted that the march was nonviolent. However, while the Deacons' leader acknowledged the march as nonviolent, he openly advocated armed self-defense. In a masculinist appeal, Thomas told a rally in Belzoni, "It's time for Black men to start taking care of their Black women and children."[23]

The debate within the ranks of the march represented a developing trend of the Movement toward open advocacy of armed self-defense. Seventy-one-year-old Bishop Charles Tucker of the African Methodist Episcopal Zion Church expressed a patriarchal perspective on the issue, stating, "Any Negro or white has the right to defend himself with arms. Any man who didn't ought to take off his pants and wear a skirt."[24] Other marchers considered abandoning the pledge for the march to be nonviolent. Carmichael stated that harassment from local White supremacists, provocation from local police, and lack of serious protection from state troopers had activists discussing the need for "bringing out their pieces." King and others committed to passive resistance encouraged participants to maintain vigilance and the march to remain nonviolent. King stated, "If anyone can't live with it [the discipline of nonviolence] we'll give him bus fare and let him go his merry way."[25]

Mainstream media was obsessed with and seriously concerned about the Deacons and the significance of their presence. Unlike in marches of the past, where Blacks covertly secured their comrades, observers noticed "disciplined" Black men communicating with "two-way" radios. Probably more troubling were the "bulges" detected "beneath the clothing" of young men patrolling the march. While often speaking in conciliatory terms, Deacons leader Thomas was frank with the press about the presence and purpose of the organization at the march. Thomas told the press that the Deacons were guarding the campsite "with pistols, rifles, and shotguns. . . . But we don't take guns with us when the people are marching. . . . The march is nonviolent." The Memphis *Commercial Appeal* reported that the "[a]ppearance of the 'Deacons' in the Mississippi marching column marked a significant, and to many a frightening shift in tactics of Negroes who for 10 years had been lulled and led by the non-violent oratory of Dr. Martin Luther King, Jr."[26]

A common theme in national coverage of the march emphasized contradictions between King and those embracing armed resistance. A dichotomy was constructed pitting the nonviolent King against the "violent" Deacons and Black Power militants. On June 22nd, a *New York Times* article titled "Dr. King Scores 'Deacons,'" stated that King publicly lashed out at the "Black Power" advocates SNCC and the Deacons. Close examination reveals that King's words were directed not to the protection provided by the Deacons but to the retaliatory violence advocated by other elements of the Movement. King argued,

> Some people are telling us to be like our oppressor, who has a history of using Molotov cocktails, who has a history of using the atomic bomb, who has a history of lynching Negroes. . . . Now people are telling me to stoop to that level. . . . I'm sick and tired of violence. I'm tired of the war in Vietnam. I'm tired of Molotov cocktails.[27]

While King deplored all violence, he made the distinction between "self-defense involving defensive violence and retaliatory violence." A growing number of Black Power militants embraced the spontaneous urban rebellions that were becoming common occurrences in the middle and late 1960s. One factor in their support of urban rebellions was their growing fascination with the work of Frantz Fanon and other anticolonial national liberation movements. Fanon, who had become popular among the youth of the Movement, argued that the coercive force of the oppressed was necessary and psychologically liberating. King was concerned about the advocacy of armed resistance, the embracing of Fanon's concepts on violence within the Black Freedom Struggle (particularly within SNCC), and the growing occurrence of spontaneous rebellion in Black communities inside the United States. While King may have critically examined different forms of armed resistance, mainstream media made no distinction.[28]

It is clear that King's consent to allow the Deacons in the march did not mean that he abandoned his allegiance to nonviolence. On the contrary, King was disturbed by the public advocacy of armed self-defense by the Deacons and also a growing number of young activists who had rejected nonviolence. Concerning the growing support of armed resistance, one Black publication quoted him as saying, "I'm worried about this climate." King believed a violent confrontation during the march was potentially "impractical and disastrous." He not only morally supported nonviolence but also believed that it was tactically viable. King argued that since Black people were a minority, it was impossible for them to achieve a strategic victory against a hostile majority through armed resistance. While King was not opposed to self-defense in the face of racist or oppressive violence, he believed that demonstrations utilizing nonviolence assisted activists in achieving a moral high ground from which they could expose injustice rather than be perceived as aggressive antagonists.[29] In spite of his concerns, King respected the Deacons and saw them as a viable part of the Movement. King's associate Andrew Young commented, "[King] would never resort to violence, even in defense of his life, but he would not and could not demand that of others. . . . He saw the Deacons as a defensive presence not a retaliatory one."[30]

"They Were Hit": Philadelphia and the Defense of the FDP House

Nonviolence was tested in Philadelphia, Mississippi. While the marchers were in Belzoni, King took twenty-five members of his staff and other marchers to Philadelphia to a June 21st demonstration and rally commemorating James Chaney, Andrew Goodman, and Michael Schwerner. King took his contingent to Philadelphia without a Deacons security presence. A day earlier, the Department of Justice announced that Neshoba County sheriff Lawrence Rainey and his deputy, Cecil Price, were being charged with violating the civil rights of Chaney, Goodman, and Schwerner. King and the contingent joined two hundred local Blacks in a march from Philadelphia's Mount Nebo Baptist Church to the county courthouse downtown. The group rallied at the county jail after being denied the right to assemble on the courthouse lawn by local police.[31]

A mob of three hundred White civilians attacked the commemorative march as they proceeded back to Mount Nebo in Philadelphia's Black community. The mob hurled insults, as well as "stones, bottles, clubs, firecrackers," at King and the marchers. Police only intervened after fighting broke out between six of the marchers and a small group of the mob. The mob attacked again a half a block away. After receiving a signal from Price, a White counterdemonstrator threw a cherry bomb that ignited under the feet of King. The cherry bomb explosion made a sound similar to gunfire, intended to create fear and confusion in the memorial march. One marcher was hit by a truck and media observers were assaulted by members of the mob. On the way back to the church, King commented, "This is a terrible town, the worst I've seen. . . . There is a complete reign of terror here." Upon returning to the March against Fear in the Delta, King pledged that the march would return to Philadelphia to "straighten the place out . . . using our nonviolent might."[32]

Armed self-defense would be necessary to repeal nightriders attacking the Freedom Democratic Party (FDP) headquarters that evening in Philadelphia. The FDP office also served as a residence for organizers and volunteers in Neshoba County. White terrorists made four raids on the headquarters, which contained approximately twenty occupants on the evening of June 21st. The first attack came at 8:10 p.m. from a lone White racist who fired at a group of Blacks after arguing with them. SNCC field secretary and Neshoba County project director Ralph Featherstone organized his comrades to defend themselves after the first encounter that evening. White terrorist nightriders came twice again that evening and found the occupants of the FDP house ready to return fire. FBI agents told the press that the nightriders fired around twenty shots, with the Blacks firing "more times than that." One of the attackers, forty-year-old Stanley Stewart, was wounded after being hit with "buckshot in the head and neck" by Featherstone and his comrades. Stewart was treated for his wounds at a local hospital and released, never to be arrested by local authorities. Media reports stated that nightriders returned again that evening and fired at an FBI agent who was standing near the FDP house. Federal officials denied that any agent was fired upon. In contrast to official FBI declarations, the *New York Times* reported that the FBI agent could not get his weapon out in time to return fire. At a press conference the next day, Featherstone would not confirm whether there were guns in the FDP house or not.[33]

The only arrest made that evening was made by a Black police officer. Two other Whites in the area, a predominantly Black neighborhood, were stopped, questioned, and released. Philadelphia police chief Bruce Latimer said—in reference to Whites detained in the area immediately after the shooting—"I know their mamas and papas and they are not hell raisers. I think they got to drinking . . . and somebody took a pop at them." Local officials blamed Movement activists for the day's violence. Philadelphia mayor Clayton Lewis told the media that "[i]t's just those rabble rousers and foreigners that came in here." Chief Latimer added, "We got good nigger people here. . . . What I think is we are going to accept our good niggers and they are going to fall in line."[34]

The defense of the office was considered a victory for many in the organization. One SNCC militant remembered,

> I remember white people in Philadelphia, Mississippi, coming down to the SNCC office and houses where movement people lived, shooting in houses. And one night that all stopped, because when they shot, they were shot back and they were hit. So that stopped that. . . . And for those people it was a big victory.[35]

The defense of the MFDP led by a SNCC member also signified the organization's shift from advocating nonviolence to embracing armed self-defense.

Featherstone was also revered by SNCC members for his role in the defense of the Neshoba County FDP office. One SNCC comrade remembered years later that "he was the type of guy that dealt with the situation, whatever the situation was. . . . Feather [as he was often called by his comrades] organized a group of fellas to shoot back, and they stopped it." Featherstone, a District of Columbia native and special education teacher, left his job and came to Mississippi during Freedom Summer. Featherstone was immediately assigned to work in the freedom schools in southwest Mississippi. After Freedom Summer, he remained in the state for three more years until he was elected national program director of SNCC in 1967. Described as "one of SNCC's most daring and courageous organizers," Featherstone organized in Marshall, McComb, and Neshoba counties, as well as Selma, Alabama, before being elected to the national leadership group of SNCC. He was involved in organizing economic cooperatives, voter registration, electoral campaigns, as well as freedom schools in Mississippi communities. The defense of the office did not reflect a recent change in position for Featherstone on the issue of armed self-defense. While he agreed to adhere to the tactic of nonviolence for demonstrations, Featherstone told associates in 1964 that "in any other situation [other than nonviolent protests], if someone attacked him, he would fight back."[36]

King requested federal protection when the march route continued to Philadelphia on June 24th. The SCLC leader noted in his request "the complete breakdown in law and order" in the memorial march in Philadelphia on June 21st. The federal government again agreed to allow the state of Mississippi to send additional state police to the Mississippi town to provide protection for the marchers. The defense of the MFDP office by Featherstone and his comrades intensified debate at the campsite about the saliency of nonviolence versus armed resistance. The *New York Times* again noted the debate and the armed response of Black activists to White terrorist attacks. King, McKissick, and Carmichael all made public statements confirming the march's commitment to nonviolence.[37]

Trouble erupted in Canton on June 22nd, the day before the march reached the central Mississippi town. Nightriders attempted to firebomb the Canton FDP office. The White invaders were pursued by C. O. Chinn and his "protective guys" minutes after tossing the incendiary device on the lawn of the Freedom House. Chinn was arrested after one of the White invaders, 26-year-old William Long Grear, was shot and wounded. The Canton Black activist was charged with "assault with a deadly weapon with intent to kill." One hour after the arrest, Chinn was released on a seven thousand dollar bond. Chinn insisted he was unarmed and was innocent of assaulting Grear. *New York Times* reporters again noted this act of armed resistance, along with the growing debate in the Movement, as significant trends.[38]

Violence continued when the marchers arrived in Canton on June 23rd. Despite averting injury or fatal attacks from the Klan, nightriders, or White supremacist civilians during the march, a predominantly Black assembly of twenty-five hundred marchers and Movement supporters was the target of state and local police terror. As in Greenwood, segregationist local officials refused to allow marchers to camp at McNeal Elementary, a Black public school. C. O. Chinn, SCLC leader Hosea Williams, and nine others were arrested earlier in the day for attempting to set up tents at McNeal before the main march contingent arrived. That evening, marchers

insisted on defying police orders not to set up a campsite. Sixty-one hel-
meted state police officers (who were sent by Governor Johnson to protect the marchers) armed with "carbines, automatic shotguns and pistols"
and local police propelled "tear and irritant gas" at the campsite, scattering
the marchers. Some marchers were hit by tear gas canisters. Men, women,
and children were brutally beaten and injured in what historian John Dittmer described as a "police riot." While the leaders of the march decided to
defy the police commands, the marchers were directed to adhere to nonviolence in the face of the armed Mississippi officers. Dr. King ordered the
marchers not to fight back against the state troopers. King declared to the
Movement contingent, "There is no point in fighting back. Don't do it. . . . I
don't know what they plan for us. . . . But we are not going to fight any state
troopers." CORE leader Floyd McKissick also directed the marchers not to
physically resist the state troopers. The Deacons' security team stood down
rather than engaging the Mississippi state police. SNCC organizer Hollis
Watkins remembered, "Tactically and strategically the Deacons knew they
couldn't maintain their usual posture. The Deacons' usual posture wasn't
directed toward law enforcement."[39]

A dozen marchers, including a three-year-old, passed out from the
fumes of tear gas. Fourteen-year-old Robert Davis was knocked unconscious after being struck by a police tear gas projectile and woke up days
later in a Canton medical facility. Carmichael was also injured by a tear gas
canister. Others were beaten by state troopers. King questioned the decision of the federal government to assign protection of the march to Mississippi state troopers. The SCLC president stated immediately after the
marchers were attacked, "This is the very state patrol that President Johnson said today would protect us. . . . Anyone who would use gas bombs
on women and children can't and won't protect anyone." King ultimately
reached a compromise with local officials to hold a meeting on the school
grounds, but not to set up tents there. Some of the marchers were upset
and vocally protested the compromise.[40]

The march arrived in Philadelphia on June 24th and was greeted by
the same hostile mobs that had assaulted King and his contingent three
days earlier. Journalist Lawrence Henry reported exchange of gunshots
between Deacons and nightriders on the March route near Philadelphia.
One hundred state troopers and local police prevented the mob of nearly
two thousand Whites from assaulting three hundred marchers at the Neshoba County courthouse. The mob hurled bottles, eggs, and insults at
the marchers. Two White males were arrested after racing their vehicle

through the marchers as they returned from downtown to Philadelphia's Black community.[41]

James Meredith returned from his hospital bed to rejoin the march on June 26th at Tougaloo College, on the outskirts of Jackson. Meredith was given the doctor's consent to travel the last miles of the march to the state capital. There had been concern that Meredith would be armed if he rejoined the march. While hospitalized, he told a journalist the following:

> I will return to the march . . . and I will be armed unless I have assurances I will not need arms. I believe in law and order, but if the whites continue to kill the Negro in the South, I will have no choice but to urge them [Black people] to go out and defend themselves.[42]

Meredith also expressed embarrassment for being wounded by James Norvell, the lone White supremacist sniper who shot him on June 6th. Meredith told the press, "I'm embarrassed . . . because I could have knocked the intended killer off with one shot had I been prepared." Meredith did come to the march unarmed after receiving a guarantee of his protection from the state police. "I'm not armed," Meredith told the press "because the Mississippi highway patrol chief has accepted all responsibility for security. He has given me his word."[43]

The march concluded in Jackson on June 26th. Nearly fifteen thousand people converged at the state capitol to hear King, McKissick, Carmichael, and other leaders of the Black Freedom Movement on this day. The march activities resulted in four thousand Mississippi Blacks being registered in a three-week period. The Black Freedom Struggle was reinvigorated in communities like Belzoni and Yazoo. The Movement had overcome the threat of White supremacist violence and intimidation and inspired tens of thousands of local Blacks to join the march in places where White domination was a stark reality.[44]

"Boycott Rudy" in Belzoni

Rudy Shields was in and out of county jail and organizing the Claiborne boycott while the March against Fear campaigned through the Mississippi Delta. Shields came to Humphreys County over a year after the march, by which time it was clear that Shields and Charles Evers had severed their political relationship. Shields, along with two representatives from the

Humphreys County Black community, presented eighteen demands to Belzoni mayor Hank Gantz on February 1, 1968. Shields stated that if the demands were not met by February 8th, a boycott would be initiated the next day.[45]

Rudy Shields was invited to Belzoni by Humphreys County NAACP leader Willie Hazelwood. Hazelwood hoped Shields's participation could spark momentum for the Humphreys County Movement. Humphreys County had experienced a significant decrease in Black voter registration after White terrorists murdered Reverend George Lee and Gus Courts was forced into exile in 1955 (see chapter 2). SNCC organizers, affectionately called "Freedom Riders" by the local population, began organizing in Humphreys County in 1964. When SNCC workers organized a COFO project in Humphreys County, only twenty registered Black voters remained from the four hundred that existed when Lee and Courts were organizing in the county in 1955. Several Humphreys County registered Blacks had been threatened by local White supremacists to take themselves off the voting rolls. Some had resisted, but other had relinquished their registration.[46]

A local farmer, Aaron Hazelwood (Willie Hazelwood's father), was one of a few Humphreys County residents who would house the "Freedom Riders" during Freedom Summer. The Hazelwood family farmed cotton and beans in the Goat Hill community of Humphreys County, two miles south of Belzoni. The Hazelwood patriarch suffered consequences due to his decision to provide shelter for voter registration workers. Financial assistance provided to Hazelwood and other Humphreys County farmers was suddenly declined. According to his daughter-in-law, Luella Hazelwood, the family patriarch was told by a local official, "[You] can't get no more money 'cause y'all got those freedom riders housed up in there. . . . If y'all get rid of them god-damned freedom riders, I'll give you a loan to work your farm." Aaron Hazelwood defiantly responded, "I'll just do the best I can, cause they human just like we are. . . . I ain't running nobody nowhere." Local grocers and other merchants also refused to allow the Hazelwood family to purchase produce from their enterprises. The Hazelwood family continued to house "Freedom Riders," who ate what the family could provide from their farm or whatever family members or neighbors shared.[47]

In addition to the economic reprisals, terrorist violence was directed at the Hazelwood household. Crosses were burned on the lawn of the Hazelwood residence. Nightriders drove by the Hazelwood domicile and fired into the home. Regular raids on the Hazelwood home had become so common that the family became accustomed to sleeping on the floor with their son under the bed to better avoid gunfire from nightriders. The Hazelwood family had become so accustomed to responding to gunfire that Luella Hazelwood joked that her eight-year-old son once said, "Didn't President [John] Kennedy know you are supposed to duck when someone is shooting?"[48]

Willie Hazelwood became the director of the Children's Development Group of Mississippi (CDGM) for Humphreys County in 1965. As with other local Movement activists, COFO personnel selected Hazelwood to direct the program due to his previous activism. (Other Movement activists who suffered economic reprisal were also able to secure employment through CDGM.) The momentum of the local movement had waned in Humphreys County by 1968, when Willie Hazelwood invited Shields to Belzoni. Shields convinced Hazelwood and other local leaders to organize a consumer boycott to achieve the demands of the Movement. Hazelwood needed little convincing to boycott local merchants because for four years, ever since SNCC organizers had come to the county in 1964, his family had not been able to purchase from them.[49]

Willie Hazelwood and the local NAACP organized a mass meeting in Belzoni. That evening the Humphreys County boycott was announced. Shields also called for Black workers making below the minimum wage of $1.15 an hour to quit their jobs unless employers increased their pay. He also called for a voter registration drive in this Black-majority county. Shields's call for an increase in wages and for voter registration struck at the heart of White privilege and power in the Delta County. Humphreys County plantation owners were still dependent on cheap Black agricultural labor in the cotton economy. White political power was also maintained if the Black majority did not participate in the electoral process. Black people constituted 65 percent of the county's population of approximately ten thousand residents.[50]

In previous civil and human rights campaigns in Humphreys County, activists had frequently been terrorized by White supremacist violence. Shields deterred White violence by making it known that he and his colleagues were armed and would respond to any conflict. He was quite aware of the presence of informants in mass meetings and would make statements he knew would get back to the White power structure. At a February 14th mass meeting, Shields proclaimed, "[V]iolence follows me. We will not start violence in Belzoni, but we will not run from it either." He implied in other meetings that the Deacons for Defense were ready to respond if needed in Humphreys County.[51]

Unlike the Natchez boycott and other boycotts in southwest Mississippi, there was no paramilitary formation established utilizing the name "Deacons for Defense." Nonetheless, Shields and local Blacks maintained a visible armed defense presence. It was also spread around the Black community that violence against the Movement would result in retaliatory violence. Robert "Fat Daddy" Davis, who had returned to Belzoni after participating in the Meredith March two years earlier, remembered, "For the first time, I think there was fear put in the Klansmen's hearts. They figured whatever you did to one of us we were gonna do to one of you. . . . We made it clear to them we wasn't to be messed with." One way that message was communicated was by "Da Spirit" painting graffiti in Belzoni neighborhoods proclaiming, "[E]ye for an eye . . . [I]f you kill one of us we'll kill one of you."[52]

Luella Hazelwood, whose household had earlier endured a series of nightriders' attacks, noted a sense of security in this period due to the willingness of forces in the Black community to defend themselves, as well as to retaliate. Even when she was arrested on one occasion, she did not fear being abused by Belzoni police because

> [t]hey never would hit nobody, when they pick them up like that. 'Cause they had a war going on. . . . 'Cause these folks [Black people] was ready to fight some. They wasn't like Martin Luther King. Get hit on this side and turn the other. Naw, we didn't turn no jaws. No lord![53]

Things had certainly changed in Humphreys County; thirteen years before the boycott, George Lee had been murdered on the street and Gus Courts exiled for organizing local Blacks to register to vote.[54]

Not two weeks after the boycott was initiated, Humphreys County officials reported to the Sovereignty Commission that the consumer boycott was 80 percent effective. A list of Belzoni enterprises that would not employ Blacks was created. Local Blacks were informed not to do business with any group on the list. Shields employed the enforcer squads "Da Spirits" (sometimes known in Belzoni as "The Black Spirits") to sanction Black people who did not adhere to the boycott. After a few examples were set, Humphreys County Blacks were clear that there were consequences for breaking the boycott. According to Luella Hazelwood, "They [violators of the boycott] got their tail whopped." Her sister Lorene Starks added,

"Them Spirits would get you. I didn't take no chances. I would go all the way to Jackson [over sixty miles away] just to get a box of salt."[55]

Municipal and county officials turned control of the boycott over to state officials. The Sovereignty Commission assumed the role of administrating the counterinsurgency campaign to suppress the boycott on February 19th, eleven days after the initiation of the boycott. Local and state officials both agreed that state police had experience attempting to counter Shields in previous campaigns in southwest Mississippi and Hattiesburg. The assignment to "put Shields and his goons out of business" was the responsibility of Sovereignty Commission official Lee Cole. The Belzoni police department was also placed under his command. A plan was developed to occupy Shields's energy and time with fighting charges that would ultimately neutralize his mobility in Humphreys County.[56]

The state Sovereignty Commission had been engaged in surveillance in Humphreys County before it took the primary counterinsurgency responsibility against the local boycott movement. State police observed armed guards at the routine NAACP mass meeting of the boycott on February 14th, five days before the Sovereignty Commission took over the case. Police detained a vehicle that they believed was driven by one of the young Black men who participated in the security of the meeting. Sovereignty Commission official Lee Cole seized two rifles from the vehicle. Cole refused to release the weapons when an attorney from the Lawyers Committee for Civil Rights under the Law contacted him the next day.

State surveillance and intelligence also revealed that Shields was driving a vehicle with an improper tag. State and local police planned to arrest Shields after the mass meeting on February 19th. Police noticed a crowd of approximately seventy-five people around Shields's car. While police officers were attempting to locate Shields, they failed to notice Willie Hazelwood preventing an armed Black man in the crowd from firing his weapon. Hazelwood purposely stood between Reverend Eddie "Bull" Harper and the police. Harper was known in the community for traveling with his "sawed off" shotgun in his overalls and was considered anxious to use it. Harper had pulled out his shotgun, but Hazelwood stood in his way, preventing him from firing. Harper said to Hazelwood, "All you got to do is step back. I'll take care of it." After Harper was persuaded to yield, Hazelwood got in Shields's 1962 Ford Falcon and attempted to drive away. He was immediately stopped by police, who took him into custody. The crowd then surrounded the police car as it attempted to leave the church grounds with Hazelwood. After the police vehicle stopped due to the crowd's intervention, Bull Harper's brother Scott opened the police car door. The officers pulled their weapons and threatened to use tear gas to disperse the crowd so they could leave the scene. Hazelwood was taken to the Humphreys County jail and charged with resisting arrest.[57]

Shields came to the county jail the next morning to post bail for Hazelwood. He was promptly arrested for having an improper tag on his vehicle. The arrests of Shields and Hazelwood led to a demonstration of approximately twenty Humphreys County residents later that day. Local police arrested twelve of the demonstrators on charges of marching without a permit and obstructing the sidewalk. The arrested demonstrators included Luella Hazelwood, her son James, 67-year-old Reverend Scott Harper, and a group consisting primarily of teenagers. Twenty-two Black activists, including others arrested for activities related to the boycott, had been incarcerated in Humphreys County within a 24-hour period. Aaron Hazelwood, mortician E. B. Johnson, and other propertied members of the Black community bailed out Shields, Willie, Luella, and James Hazelwood and other arrested Black activists.[58]

The arrests of Shields continued. State and local authorities found more significant charges for him. He was arrested later in the week, on February 24th, on a felony charge for "threatening the use of force or violence to prevent a person from engaging in his lawful vocation." Gus Harris, a Black senior citizen, was encouraged by local police to bring charges against Shields. Harris made a statement to Humphreys County officials that Shields threatened him because he refused to register to vote and adhere to the consumer boycott. In July of 1968, Shields would plead guilty to charges of using threatening language and would be fined $250 and given a suspended sentence of thirty days. A Humphreys County judge warned that he would lift the suspended sentence if Shields violated the law in the county within the next six months.[59]

Shields avoided arrest in Humphreys County for months. An effective boycott was still maintained by "Da Spirit" and the county's Black youth, who maintained vigilance and demanded that the Black community not shop with the targeted enterprises. FBI reports reflected a series of acts of coercion to maintain the boycott. In March of 1968, three Black girls were arrested for threatening to whip another Black female "with a strap" for buying produce from a boycotted Belzoni grocery store. On April 1st, according to local police reports to the FBI, a Black female had been beaten "with a blunt instrument" by "The Spirits" because she and her father had violated the boycott.[60]

Shields used the assassination of Dr. Martin Luther King Jr. to strike more fear into the Humphreys County White power structure. He publicly proclaimed that the death of King made "fifty Rap Browns," a reference to the radical nationalist spokesperson of SNCC. Shields warned Belzoni mayor Hank Gantz that it would be difficult to prevent violence. He also announced that armed Deacons would come to the Belzoni memorial for King at the county courthouse on April 6th. Mayor Gantz declined Shields's invitation to speak at the courthouse, but spoke at a church service commemorating Dr. King. Shields and six carloads of Humphreys County residents went to King's funeral in Atlanta on April 9th.[61]

The Sovereignty Commission and Humphreys County authorities would have another opportunity to arrest Shields months later that year. On November 5th, an argument between Shields and a White store clerk, seventy-year-old Sam Shipley, at the Star Store in Belzoni resulted in both pulling guns. Shipley and Shields both signed affidavits against each other and were charged with "pointing and aiming." Shipley was released on one thousand dollars' bail. Shields was also charged with "carrying a concealed weapon" and two counts of "pointing and aiming." A warrant was later issued for the third charge: that he "did willfully and unlawfully in the presence of three or more persons exhibit a pistol in a rude and angry manner, not in necessary self-defense." Shields was released on November 7th on two thousand dollars' bail and faced trial the following day, when he was convicted of all charges concerning the November 5th incident. An additional two thousand dollar bond was posted for his release pending appeal. A successful appeal by Shields's lawyers warranted a retrial. On February 14, 1969, the new trial ended in mistrial. In this trial, the jury was composed of six Whites and six Blacks. After a two-hour deliberation, the jury reported to the judge that they were "hopelessly deadlocked," hung six to six.[62]

The momentum of the Humphreys County boycott had declined by 1969. Nonetheless, Shields's efforts were not interpreted by all as a failure. One informant, according to FBI agents, explained that the "boycott in Belzoni [was] a necessary thing for the Negro community." This informant claimed that the boycott "had been a success and that the white community is starting to wake up to the fact that the Negro is no longer good for only picking cotton."[63] Besides these successes, Shields made several efforts to intensify the boycott of Humphreys County enterprises. He also began to spend more time in Indianola and Yazoo City working with local boycott efforts.

The effort to integrate public schools created another opportunity for Shields's leadership and militancy in Humphreys County. In 1969, a federal court ordered Humphreys County public schools to transition from a segregated system to a scheme that reflected "unitary, non-racial geographic attendance zones for the assignment of students at all grades." The predominantly White Belzoni High School would be merged with the previously Black public schools, the McNair Attendance Center in Belzoni and the Montgomery High School in Louise. These three schools would be merged into one institution on the campus of Belzoni High, to be renamed "Humphreys County High School." Anger and concern in the Black community resulted from the proposed dismissal of McNair's principal, Payton Flagg, in the merger of the county's high schools. Shields attended a meeting of three hundred Humphreys County residents concerning school integration, held at the newly formed Humphreys County Union for Progress. Shields participated in a march of two hundred people on June 9th, where he presented a petition signed by 490 people calling for the restoration of Flagg as principal and for the Black community to be informed of changes in the Humphreys County school system during the integration process. If demands were not met by the beginning of the 1969-1970 school term, a boycott of the schools would be initiated.[64]

Willie Hazelwood formed the Humphreys County Union for Progress. This organization was an economic cooperative and advocacy vehicle for Black farmers. It also sought to form Black-owned enterprises in the county and provide assistance to working and poor households. The FBI, the Sovereignty Commission, and local authorities viewed the organization as a major base of support for Shields and a potential economic boycott.[65]

The FBI investigated Shields and the Humphreys County Union for Progress for violations of the Hobbs Act. Local informants claimed that Shields and the Humphreys County Union for Progress were obtaining "most of their funds by donations and money paid to them by merchants who have agreed to pay them not to boycott their stores." According to an FBI field report,

> These sources indicated the merchants paid about twenty percent of the gross proceeds to Shields for "protection rights." . . . [I]t would be extremely hard to prove any pay-off is taking place because much of the pay-off is in cash and in private, also the merchants are afraid if they inform on what was taking place their businesses would be destroyed.[66]

This report verifies the potential of Black violence to compel some local Whites to submit to demands of local activists.

Belzoni after Shields: The Struggle Continues on Campus

Shields began to spend more time out of Humphreys, ultimately changing residence to Yazoo County by July of 1969. Shields's decreasing presence in Humphreys County would not mean the end of racial conflict militant protest in Belzoni. A new generation of militant Black youth who came of age with the activism of "Freedom Riders" in their communities and participation in the Shields-organized consumer boycotts were going to be in the center of a developing local conflict. Militant Black teenagers were now being asked to attend desegregated institutions with Whites who believed that school integration had been imposed upon them. Without the guidance of Shields, young "Black Spirits" remained in Humphreys ready to continue the struggle from their own perspective. Segregationist attitudes would collide with the militancy of the young Spirits, who were students at the newly desegregated Humphreys County High School. In late March and early April of 1971, the tension between the segregationists and young Black militants erupted into a crisis. The crisis was highlighted by a "walkout," civil disobedience by African American students, and spontaneous attacks by Black students on teachers and police. This student activism was led by Shields's Spirits in Humphreys County. Students presented eleven demands, including reforms in student governance and discipline, and instruction in Black history. The local school board agreed to all of the demands. Militant Black students were also suspected of several incidents of arson at public school buildings in the county.[67]

FBI operatives surmised from the information given to them by local informants that Shields left Humphreys County for Yazoo due to his disappointment in the support for his boycott efforts there. However, the student walkout of 1971 and the role of young Spirits in the campaign of disobedience demonstrated Shields's continued influence and the presence of local militancy even in the absence of his physical presence and daily leadership. One of the youth arrested said of Shields's impact on Humphreys County, "[H]e made people aware they didn't have to be afraid." In fact, Humphreys County Black youth went beyond being afraid to organize their rage into a force to be feared.[68]

"Let the Spirit Ride": Boycott Rudy in Yazoo County

Yazoo County was another community that was inspired by the Meredith March. The year after the historic march came there, in 1967, Father

Malcolm O'Leary was assigned as an associate pastor and teacher at the predominantly Black Saint Francis Parish church and Catholic school in the county seat, Yazoo City. Saint Francis's head pastor, White priest Father John Gist, was sympathetic to the Civil Rights Movement, and Saint Francis was the meeting place of the NAACP in Yazoo City. O'Leary would assume the role of head parish priest in 1968. Born to a Black landowning family in neighboring Madison County, O'Leary had developed a strong sense of racial consciousness. The priest was concerned over the lack of employment for Blacks in municipal civil service positions. No Blacks were employed in the fire or police departments in the majority-Black city and county. O'Leary decided to remedy the exclusion of Blacks in the local public sector by running for alderman. O'Leary requested and received permission from the regional bishop to run for political office.[69]

O'Leary became the first African American to run for office in Yazoo City. After receiving the most votes in the primary, he was defeated in the runoff. A significant factor in O'Leary's defeat was the fact that the majority of Yazoo Black residents remained unregistered. Blacks were a slight majority out of a total population of nearly eleven thousand in Yazoo City and 53 percent of approximately twenty-seven thousand in the county. Even Blacks who were registered stayed away from the polls due to fear of economic or physical reprisals.[70]

The election loss did not deter O'Leary. He decided to join with the local NAACP in calling a boycott in Yazoo City with five demands, including employment of Blacks in civil service. A boycott was called in 1967 by Father Gist and local NAACP members, but was unsuccessful. A meeting was called at the Saint Francis gymnasium in May of 1969. To the surprise of O'Leary and the other organizers, approximately one thousand Yazoo County Black residents attended the meeting and overwhelmingly endorsed the call for a boycott. The initial demands included requests for two Black police officers, two Black firemen, two Black clerks in the city government, and employment of Blacks in White-owned stores in the city and county.[71]

Rudy Shields appeared in Yazoo City shortly after the call for the boycott. Yazoo County NAACP president George Collins invited the boycott organizer to Yazoo to play his typical role of enforcer and to provide leadership. Speaking of Shields's role, O'Leary remembered,

> As soon as we put it [the boycott] on, somehow Rudy Shields came
> on the scene. . . . Rudy Shields was supposed to be the marshal . . . the

enforcer. If he caught you downtown, you're in trouble. He was not going to be brutal. But he was to confront you. . . . He was just going to confront the people [violating the boycott].[72]

As had been seen previously in Natchez, Port Gibson, Crystal Springs, Hazlehurst, and Belzoni, after a few weeks, the Yazoo boycott proved to be effective. Shields's experience as a boycott organizer proved invaluable. The Yazoo City central business district became a "ghost town," as Shields was effective in recruiting approximately twenty local youth to serve as enforcers of "Da Spirit." As in Humphreys County, the Yazoo Spirits were composed primarily of teenagers.[73]

Blacks who shopped downtown suffered the wrath of "Da Spirit" for failing to adhere to the boycott. Punishment by "Da Spirit" ranged from public spankings to damage to home or vehicle to seizure of property. Blacks shopping at prohibited stores were confronted downtown in the initial weeks of the boycott. After Shields, Luther Trim, Joe Thomas, and other young Spirits were arrested downtown for confronting Blacks, a new tactic was employed. Rather than risking arrest for challenging Black shoppers downtown, young Blacks began to observe downtown stores to gather intelligence. A list of Blacks who violated the boycott was announced at the weekly meetings at Saint Francis. Those observed shopping at stores on the boycott list were given a week to come to the meetings and explain themselves. Often those who violated the boycott would come and apologize or offer reasons why they shopped at boycotted institutions. One could avoid punishment if the majority of the meeting's audience thought the shopper should be granted leniency. If not, Shields might publicly spank the violator. If the person did not come to the meeting to provide reasoning for boycott violations, "Da Spirit" was immediately dispatched to punish the responsible party. The victims of "Da Spirit's" chastisement served as examples to other Yazoo Blacks. Many decided not to break the boycott after hearing of the punishment rendered to other Yazoo County residents.[74]

Downtown Yazoo transformed into a virtual "ghost town" a few weeks after the initiation of the boycott. Some local Whites feared being in the midst of conflict and also avoided shopping downtown. Yazoo mayor Jeppie Barbour contacted O'Leary and other Black leaders to initiate negotiations on the five demands. To Barbour's dismay, local Black leaders were emboldened by the success of the boycott and increased the number of demands to ten. Within a month, the number of demands increased to twenty-four. An additional demand calling for the dismissal of Yazoo police officers for acts of police brutality brought the number to twenty-five in October of 1969.[75]

Shields made it clear to Blacks and Whites in Yazoo that he did not intend to "turn the other cheek." In a pattern set by the Deacons in Natchez, Shields openly displayed weapons as a means of deterring White violence. He visibly wore a handgun in a holster. Yazoo-born author Willie Morris noted that when he went to interview Shields in the Yazoo County NAACP office, he noticed an interesting contrast in the office. Morris wrote, "A semi-automatic carbine stands in the corner, and there is a picture of Martin Luther King over the gas heater in the fireplace." Shields also gave a public message that he was ready to protect himself by sitting on the porch of his Yazoo residence armed with his rifle. He would also sleep outside of his home concealed by hedges to surprise nightriders attempting to attack him in his sleep.[76]

Yazoo residents would eventually provide support for Shields. "Da Spirit" and armed adults combined to form a sentry around his residence. Local Blacks also secured the weekly boycott meetings sponsored by the NAACP at Saint Francis gymnasium on Sundays. Herman Leach remembered, "Rudy had those people with those guns controlling that area with their guns, so people didn't bother him either. Couldn't nobody get close to that place."[77]

On one occasion, Shields intentionally organized a collective action to demonstrate that there were Blacks in Yazoo armed to protect themselves. Shields led a group of fourteen men armed with rifles and shotguns to march single file from Saint Francis to the courthouse to register their weapons. This action was designed "to put something on the mind" of the local White power structure and White supremacists.[78]

Police brutality was one of the major issues faced by Blacks in Yazoo City and County. County sheriff Art Russell and the city police (headed by Homer Hood) both had a reputation with the Black community for "busting heads." Shields made an impression on Yazoo Blacks by confronting local police about brutality and his demands that African Americans be treated as citizens and human beings. Shields's confrontation of the police inspired Blacks and served as a spark for education about civil and human rights. On the other hand, Shields's agitation tactics confounded the police and the White power structure.[79]

On May 30, 1970, a White police officer slapped a seventeen-year-old Black female, Delores Woodward, while intervening in a fight between White male youth and a fourteen-year-old Black girl. Woodward was knocked unconscious and had to be checked by a physician. Police brutal-ity had previously become a major issue of the boycott, which was a year old at this point. The city administration swiftly suspended the officer, Phillip Dangelo. The officer resigned amidst an outcry of protest from the African American community.[80]

An editorial written by Yazoo County NAACP leader George Collins to the *Yazoo Herald* on June 4th served as public response to the striking of Woodward by a Yazoo City police officer. Collins's rhetoric modeled the militant style of Shields and the Black Power Movement. Speaking not for the NAACP but for himself, Collins stated,

> I am voicing the sentiment of the whole Black community when I say we do not intend to start any violence, but we Blacks are not going to stand by and see our Black women, girls and boys be beaten on the streets of Ya-zoo City. . . . We Blacks want it known that such acts must be stopped be-cause we here in Yazoo will escort our Black women, girls and boys down the street in this town and, if any white lays a hand on any one of them we will take matters into our own hands—no matter who that white may be.[81]

Collins's editorial also threatened to bring to Yazoo "some outsiders more militant than we [local Blacks] are, just as I brought in Mr. Shields."[82]

The Yazoo City boycott was finally called off in early September of 1970. Father O'Leary and a majority of the local leadership were satisfied that the White power structure was working to fulfill the twenty-five demands of the African American community. O'Leary was also concerned that the Black community could not maintain its vigilance much longer. George Collins and Shields were disappointed in the ending of the boycott. Col-lins would have preferred to maintain the boycott until the demands were completely fulfilled by the White power structure and commercial sector. Collins told author Willie Morris that "[w]e been over the barrel for two hundred years. . . . Now we've got the [White] man where we need him and we can't take no promises. Black people ain't going to be punched around anymore."[83]

While Shields also would have continued the boycott, several Yazoo Blacks attributed its success to his leadership. Decades later, one of the boycott negotiators, Arthur Clayborn, remembered,

> He had everything in control here until, I think he stayed about a year and a half, a year and 8 or 9 months, somewhere near two years the boycott

was on, but the result of it we came out with Black policeman, we came with Black firemen. These young ladies working behind these cash registers in all these stores and everybody had to have a Black cashier, and it just really opened up everything for us as far as jobs and respect.[84]

The Yazoo boycott lasted eighteen months. Some White enterprises were permanently put out of business. Progress was made on most of the demands made by the NAACP. Blacks were hired as police officers, firemen, and civil servants. Stores downtown agreed to hire Black clerks. Plans were made to pave streets and extend sewer lines in Black neighborhoods. Black representation was promised on the school board and housing authority. The NAACP was also granted the power to appoint representation on a biracial committee to manage progress toward desegregation. Shields's leadership also provided a new militancy and sense of empowerment in the African American community.[85]

Even though he would travel to organize in other parts of the state, Shields found a home in Yazoo. The boycott leader was embraced by a significant portion of the community, and the vigilance of the Yazoo Black community won his respect and admiration. In an interview, Shields exhibited his pride in the solidarity of Black Yazoo, stating, "I've seen greater black unity here than any place in the country with the exception of Port Gibson." Things had certainly changed in Yazoo, where three years prior to the boycott Blacks had to overcome fear to register or just go downtown to see King. The militant posture and example of Rudy Shields inspired Yazoo Blacks to keep pushing forward.[86]

7

"Black Revolution Has Come"

Armed Insurgency, Black Power, and Revolutionary Nationalism in the Mississippi Freedom Struggle

Dear Fellow Black Man & Woman:
The Killings at Jackson and Augusta have shown us that we must shoot back when we are fired upon.
WE HAVE ENTERED THE ERA OF SELF-DEFENSE.
Black Brothers who will defend you are nearby. Some of us are your neighbors. But when we do our work to defend you, you must do your part to defend us.
Remember:
Hear no evil   See no evil   Speak no evil

> *The Republic of New Africa*
> *Building an Independent Black Nation*
> *Henry Hatches, Minister of Defense*[1]

"The Black Panthers Are Here!" The Aberdeen Boycott and the Manipulation of White Fears

One NAACP lawyer told author Willie Morris, "Rudy Shields is one of the few Black radicals left who still believe in integration." While Shields led Mississippi Black communities in local campaigns to pursue civil rights and desegregation, his rhetoric and perspective began to reflect the insurgent nationalism of the Black Power Movement. Shields identified with radical forces within the Black Power Movement and attempted to link the continuing human rights struggle in Mississippi with those forces. In a letter to the editor in the *Yazoo Herald* on January 15, 1969, invoking Dr. King on the martyred leader's birthday, Shields promoted sentiments of revolutionary nationalism. Shields exhorted, "No doubt about it—the 'Black Revolution' has come to Mississippi! Black people in this state are becoming more united!"[2]

Those close to Shields noted his nationalist perspective. U.S. Army veteran Lewis Williams returned home to Yazoo City in 1969 as the boycott in that area gained momentum. The impact Shields had in transforming his hometown impressed Williams, who decided to work with the militant leader and did so from 1969 throughout the 1970s. Williams commented on Shields's nationalism: "Rudy felt like if we were separated, we were better and we were stronger, because when you have white people teaching your children, then what they get is the white concept of life."[3]

Rudy Shields would not identify himself as a worker or volunteer for the NAACP after the 1969-70 Yazoo boycott. FBI records on Shields revealed that he "terminated his official position with the NAACP in early 1969."[4] In Yazoo and Belzoni, Shields had used the NAACP identification as a means to connect with preexisting structures and resources in local communities. However, he was not loyal to a particular organizational form but primarily relied upon his militant, charismatic leadership style and ability to inspire the youth into action. Shields told Willie Morris, "People tend to rally around a man, not an organization. They'll follow him if they think he's got guts."[5]

After abandoning his position in the state NAACP in 1970, Shields began to organize recruits into a formation, the Black United Front (BUF), that fit his insurgent Black nationalist perspective and provided him with a new organizational vehicle. Shields first used this vehicle in late August 1970, when he traveled from Yazoo to Aberdeen to support a boycott that had already been initiated by the NAACP. Aberdeen, located in northeast Mississippi, is the county seat of Monroe County. The sixty-five hundred Blacks in Aberdeen comprised over 60 percent of its population.

The Aberdeen boycott was initiated after two Black police officers, William Walker and James Lockett, protested having to wear Confederate symbols on their police uniforms. In early May 1970, Aberdeen police chief Dan Adams distributed patches with the Confederate battle flag to his officers to be included on their uniforms. The two Black officers refused to wear the patches and also objected to patrolling in police vehicles displaying Confederate symbols that they considered to be "a badge of slavery." Walker and Lockett were not allowed to work as long as they did not wear their uniforms with Confederate symbols. The officers sued for reinstatement and back pay. The refusal of Walker and Lockett to submit to wearing Confederate symbols became the basis for protest by the Black community. On May 19th, the Aberdeen City Council ruled that the officers were not fired and were not required to wear Confederate symbols. The Aberdeen government refused to provide Walker and Lockett with back pay and stated that they had until

June 13th to return to work. Walker and Lockett's attorney did not receive notice of the date the city ordered them to return to work until the June 13th deadline. On July 14th, a U.S. district court judge refused to reinstate the officers, but granted them one month of back pay. The NAACP demanded that the officers be reinstated and that the police department remove the Confederate battle flag from uniforms and official vehicles. The NAACP also issued demands for Black personnel to be included in the local fire and county sheriff's departments. The NAACP also demanded the hiring of Blacks in "all stores with equal pay." As with other Mississippi Black Power Era boycotts, a demand for proportional representation on city and county boards (with representatives selected by the Black community) was included. Similar to the Yazoo boycott, a demand for the "ending of police brutality and the abuse of Black people" was also declared.[6]

By the time Shields arrived in Aberdeen in early August 1970, the boycott was underway. The local White power structure met with accommodationist Black leaders who agreed to end the boycott the month before his arrival. Other Black leaders maintained their stand and summoned Shields's assistance. He quickly organized groups of young Blacks to patrol city streets and to discourage Monroe County Blacks from shopping in downtown Aberdeen. White merchants in Aberdeen organized an effort to break the Black community boycott in late August. Late August had traditionally been an important commercial period since parents would shop downtown for clothing and supplies for their children for the upcoming school year. White merchants planned to entice Black shoppers to forego the boycott by offering to serve barbecue and watermelon downtown the weekend prior to the start of school.[7]

Shields came up with a tactic to disrupt the merchants' plans. He contacted Lewis Myers, a Rutgers law student working in Mississippi that summer with the Lawyers for Constitutional Change under the Law. Shields was aware that Myers was organizing Black males in other northeastern Mississippi towns, so he asked Myers to bring a contingent of Black males to Aberdeen on the Saturday prior to the opening of the Monroe County schools. Decades later, Myers recalled the weekend and how their presence was effective in disrupting the Aberdeen White commercial community's plans. Myers remembered,

> Rudy and the guys in the town had leaked word to the White people that the Black Panthers were coming to town. . . . We show up on a Saturday morning. . . . Everybody started whispering "the Black Panthers are in

town!" People started running off the sidewalk and White folks start closing their stores and locking their doors and stuff. . . . Rudy told us to walk
up and down the main street where everybody could see us. . . . The local
Black folk started peeping and they started hollering "The Black Panthers
are here!" Negroes were running from us faster than White people.[8]

With only two carloads of Black males unfamiliar to the local community,
Myers and his friends were able to strike fear in Aberdeen that day. Shields
effectively manipulated the perceptions and fears mainstream media distributed about the "gun-toting" Black Panther Party for Self-Defense for
the advantage of maintaining the boycott. The image of radical, militant
Black revolutionaries intimidated Black consumers and White storeowners
and effectively undermined plans to break the Aberdeen boycott.[9]

A dynamic display of collective armed resistance occurred in Aberdeen
on the evening of August 15, 1970. Rudy Shields was out of town as dozens of
Black Monroe County residents participated in the protection of a local family from White supremacist nightriders. Two months prior, nightriders had
shot into the residence of the Cole household, who had moved to Aberdeen
in 1969 from Baton Rouge, Louisiana. Sixteen-year-old Keith Cole, known as
"White Meat" by his peers due to his light complexion, was one of the youth
activists involved in the boycott. Keith Cole had a series of charges due to his
participation in the boycott. Nightriders targeted the Cole residence due to
the visible activism and leadership of the teenager in the Aberdeen Movement. Police responded and found evidence of shooting, but no charges or arrests were made. Police concluded that Keith Cole shot into his own home.[10]

Not satisfied with the local police investigation of the shooting at the
Cole residence, several Monroe County Blacks mobilized to protect the
Cole family from further reprisal. On August 15th, four city police and
one county sheriff responded to reports of shooting at the Cole residence.
They came on the scene to find "an estimated 150 to 200 Negroes shooting
up the place and shooting at everything and everybody." The police officers got out and took positions under their vehicles due to the amount of
gunfire, which was coming from the shooters on the street, behind bushes,
and at the back of the Cole residence. While the officers were able to con-
fiscate eight firearms, realizing they were outnumbered and outgunned,
they ultimately fled the area "to save their own lives." While the shooting at
the Cole residence reportedly lasted an hour, no casualties were reported.
Nightriders refrained from invading the Cole residence after this massive
exhibition of Black collective resistance.[11]

Rage Up in West Point: Community Organizing
and Righteous Retaliation

Rudy Shields was in nearby West Point, Mississippi, in Clay County on the evening of the shooting at the Cole residence. Shields joined forces with organizers there on August 15, one day after the shooting of a Black activist by a White male in West Point. Clay County had a total population of 18,840, with 9,306 Blacks in 1970. West Point's total population was 8,714, with African Americans at 3,783. When Shields arrived in August of 1970, there was no Black representation on the municipal or county government. West Point had become a center of the Mississippi Black Freedom Struggle years before Shields's arrival.

COFO began organizing in Clay County in 1964. John Buffington, a native of Buford, Georgia, was the COFO project director in Clay. After attending Morehouse College in Atlanta, he transferred to Roosevelt University in Chicago. Buffington joined the Nation of Islam (NOI) after moving to Chicago in the early 1960s but ultimately left the NOI and became a member of the Chicago Friends of SNCC. Buffington came to Mississippi for the Freedom Summer project and was assigned to Clay. He stayed in West Point after Freedom Summer, basing many of his activities out of Mary Holmes College—a historically Black, two-year liberal arts college founded in 1892 by the Presbyterian Church. According to historian John Dittmer, the Clay County project became the most active SNCC chapter in Mississippi by 1966. Clay County also had an active MFDP, in which Buffington was a central participant. Buffington launched a new organizational vehicle in 1968: the Clay County Community Development Corporation (CCCDC), which became the conduit through which antipoverty funds were funneled through to the county. In 1968, Buffington opposed MFDP's participation in the Mississippi loyalist delegation, which included Charles Evers and Aaron Henry. The loyalist delegation also included the Prince Hall Masons, the state AFL-CIO, and racial moderates like Hodding Carter. Not all of these forces had supported the MFDP challenge in 1964, so Buffington opposed MFDP colluding with them. He also launched a campaign for mayor of West Point in 1970 and came in second out of a field of five mayoral candidates during the August 4th primary. He lost to White candidate Barnes Marshall in the August 18th runoff election.[12]

Unlike in other places where Shields organized, in West Point the political situation had figuratively and literally exploded before he arrived. West

Point became embroiled in a hostile school desegregation effort in early 1970. The West Point school board decided to close the predominantly Black secondary and middle school since Whites did not want to attend there. One integrated secondary school remained and functioned on five-hour split sessions. The integrated school also had no lunch break and only two-minute breaks between classes. The Black community was outraged by the decisions of the West Point school board. Members of the African American community were also concerned about the closing of Black primary and secondary public school buildings and the lack of retention of African American administrators and faculty in the desegregation process. On January 23rd, Blacks met at Mary Holmes and organized a boycott demanding the establishment of an advisory board to the local school board. The advisory board would be appointed by the Black community and represent the African American interests in desegregation plans. The boycott called for local Blacks not to shop in West Point with the exception of pharmacy purchases for health reasons.[13]

The office of the CCCDC was firebombed on January 24th. Along with the damage to the office, it was estimated that six thousand dollars in uninsured office equipment was destroyed. Buffington declared that the arson was motivated by a desire to eliminate petitions containing twelve hundred signatures of Blacks protesting the recent decisions of the local school board. However, the petitions were not in the CCCDC office during the fire, and local Black representatives presented them to the board the day following the fire. To express their solidarity with the boycott, fifteen hundred Clay County Blacks responded to a rally at Mary Holmes that evening. State and local police as well as the media insinuated that Buffington had set the fires himself.[14]

The firebombing of the CCCDC received a swift retaliatory response. A dynamite explosion occurred at the Clay County courthouse at 9:50 p.m. on January 25th, eighteen hours after the fire at Mary Holmes. The dynamite blew a hole into the concrete foundation of the courthouse, and all the windows and glass doors on the north side of the two-story building were shattered. Glass doors and windows in at least ten offices within two blocks of the courthouse were also smashed from the blast. No injuries resulted from the explosion.[15]

A local White storeowner, Billy Wilson, was wounded by gunfire five minutes after the bombing of the courthouse. According to witnesses, a 1965 Chevrolet with three African American males drove by Wilson's store, nearly a half-mile from the county courthouse. Wilson had come outside of his store after the explosion to "see what had happened" and was in front of his store as a vehicle approached. One of the vehicle's passengers suddenly fired several shots from a handgun at Wilson, who was wounded in his right thigh and taken to a local hospital. Wilson had reportedly bragged about participating in the lynching of Emmett Till fifteen years earlier. It was rumored that Wilson was married to the former wife of Roy Bryant, one of the acknowledged murderers of Till.[16]

The alert was sounded immediately after these two events. The Mississippi Highway Patrol set up checkpoints at all highways leading from West Point. No one was apprehended that evening. The Highway Patrol deployed ten officers to assist the West Point police. The FBI joined the investigation within twenty-four hours. On the afternoon after the shooting, police seized an abandoned vehicle fitting the description of the one engaged in the drive-by shooting. The vehicle had been reported stolen the evening of the bombing. Two Blacks, Nathan Cunningham and Davis Fortson (from the nearby town of Egypt), connected with the vehicle were detained for questioning but were released without being charged.[17]

Buffington and five other Blacks—Clifton Sykes, Charles Williams, Frankie Free, John Brown, and John Thomas Jr.—were arrested months later on April 7, 1970, for "conspiracy to commit a crime, to wit, unlawful use of explosives" for the bombing of the courthouse. All of the men charged were associated with the CCCDC. John Buffington was at the rally at Mary Holmes when the bombing and shooting occurred. Clay County sheriff Virgil Middleton stated that the conspiracy charge did not mean the six activists charged actually planted the explosive but rather that they "allegedly had some part in the planning of that crime." Right after Buffington and the others were charged, activist attorney Jesse Pennington organized bail and the legal defense for the defendants. All defendants were released on bond immediately after being arrested. The arrests were based on the information provided to the police by an informant. Charges were ultimately dropped for lack of evidence when the informant recanted.[18]

No one ever took responsibility or was arrested for the shooting of Wilson. Local and state police suspected former SNCC activist Ralph Featherstone of playing a part in the events. Police believed Featherstone was in West Point on the evening of the bombing and shooting. One source claims that Wilson's shooting was organized by an armed clandestine unit formed by Movement activists who had experienced years of White supremacist violence and decided that there was a need for the capacity to retaliate against those who had engaged in White terror in Mississippi in particular. Ralph Featherstone and his comrade William "Che" Payne were reportedly participants in this group of armed, clandestine, African American freedom fighters. Payne was a Movement activist from Covington, Kentucky, who worked with the Lowndes County Freedom Organization in Alabama. Another participant stated,

> It [Featherstone and Payne's clandestine group] grew out of . . . people who were part of political organizations who got frustrated, fed up with the fact they were getting their asses kicked every day, who just may have just dropped out the organization altogether, decided to form a paramilitary group.

Activists who had been members of SNCC and other nonviolent formations decided to support the Movement by engaging in underground armed militancy. Not only would they retaliate against those who participated in White terrorist violence but also they would protect the public Movement and support its aims. The shooting of Wilson was planned as the first action of the group.[19]

Weeks after the explosion and the shooting of Wilson, on March 9, 1970, Ralph Featherstone and William "Che" Payne were killed in a mysterious explosion of their vehicle on a highway in Bel Air, Maryland. In death, Featherstone was acknowledged as a "Movement Soldier." Federal and state police argued that Featherstone and Payne died while transporting explosives to a Maryland courthouse where their comrade, H. Rap Brown, was to have appeared the next day. Movement forces proclaimed that Featherstone's death was the responsibility of a counterinsurgency campaign. A statement issued after his death argued,

> He was murdered by the powerful forces in America that in their fear have decided to behead the militant black movement. . . . Officials are committing the final obscenity of suggesting that the explosive that killed him was intended for someone else. Again they are blaming the victim for the crime, still acting as if they can blot out ugly truth by destroying the people who speak it.[20]

Those he left behind revered his memory as a committed participant and leader in the Black Freedom Struggle.[21]

Shields, the Black United Front, and the West Point Boycott

Rudy Shields joined forces with Buffington and West Point activists in August of 1970 after the shooting death of local activist John Thomas Jr. Thomas (one of the six charged in the courthouse bombing) was shot five times and killed by a local White male, 45-year-old Sonny Stanley, on August 15th. Thomas was a father of eleven, an antipoverty worker, and a staff member on Buffington's mayoral campaign. With the mayoral election two days away, the Black activist was shot while sitting in a sound truck that was being used for the Buffington campaign. One witness stated that Stanley said he shot Thomas after the Black activist "cussed" at him, but witnesses on the scene did not hear the men argue. The Clay County Black community was angered that its authorities took two days to charge Stanley, in spite of two individuals who witnessed the shooting. Mayor Marshall also refused to make a public statement condemning the shooting of Thomas.[22]

Once again, one thousand Blacks rallied at Mary Holmes the following day. Speakers at the rally included Buffington and Shields. Buffington solicited Shields to come to West Point because of his experience and success as an effective boycott organizer. Sovereignty Commission reports claimed that several speakers told the audience "to arm themselves." An economic boycott resulted from a popular vote at the rally. The initial demand of the boycott was that Stanley be "charged, prosecuted and sentenced to the fullest extent of the law." The rally agreed that only one shopping center would be patronized "for medicine, school supplies and whatever few things are not available from Black merchants." The message was clear: "No Black person has any business downtown except to take care of their bank accounts and the post office." Blacks were expected to make utility and other payments through the mail. A statement from the rally proclaimed, "No white man has been given a life sentence or life imprisonment for the killing of a Black man in Mississippi in the history of this violent country."[23]

The Black United Front (BUF) was the organizational vehicle that provided leadership for the West Point boycott. BUF served different functions. First, it provided an umbrella under which a variety of African American organizations with different agendas united to pursue common interests. BUF also attracted young people and activists who no longer identified with nonviolence. The growing attitude of young activists to nonviolence was, "No, I'm not taking that shit no more." Activists in the West Point BUF network were commonly armed, and a communications network was established with citizens band radios to respond to attacks from White supremacists.[24]

By late September, the Black United Front issued a list of twenty-one demands to the Clay County White power structure, specifically the Chamber of Commerce, the county sheriff and West Point police department, the West Point mayor and alderman, as well as the city and county Boards of Education. The BUF demands targeted a variety of issues, including employment, decision making, and human rights. BUF sought Black employment in the private sector—including positions as clerks and tellers in banks—and in the public sector—including positions as clerks in the courthouse and city hall, staff in the county welfare department, and laborers in public works. In terms of public education, BUF called for predominantly Black facilities closed by desegregation plans to be reopened and for the split schedule to be abandoned. BUF also reiterated the demand for the instituting of a Black advisory board to represent the interests of the African American community in desegregation plans and for the appointment of Blacks to the West Point Board of Education. Several demands focused on law enforcement, including a general one for the end to police brutality. BUF demanded the firing of two White West Point police officers (Officers Collins and Owens) and two deputy sheriffs (Deputies Collins and Banana) and their replacement by African Americans to be selected by "the Black Community." The organization also desired a civilian review board with "fifty percent" Black representation to monitor police activity. Finally, BUF sought improvements to service, infrastructure, recreation, and housing in the African American community.[25]

Some believed that the initiation of a boycott prevented a spontaneous rebellion after the shooting of Thomas. One Black activist commented, "This boycott was instituted at that time mainly to prevent a riot. Things would have been a bloody mess otherwise." The *Black Voice*, the publication of the CCCDC, echoed this perspective. In an article titled "Why We Boycott," the editors of *Black Voice* argued,

> There are only two ways to get through to the white man. One is by boycotts. A boycott is an effective way because you are taking the dollar out of the man's hands, and . . . rather than lose his dollar he listens. Violence is the other effective way . . . actually the most effective, but it causes innocent people to be killed in the process. In order not to take lives . . . we boycott.[26]

The *Black Voice* considered consumer boycotts and armed resistance to be the primary means of activism in the Black Power phase of the Mississippi

Freedom Struggle.[27] Another Movement publication, *The Southern Patriot*, reported, "Shootouts between groups of White and Black people resulted in several injuries, some serious." The economic boycott and the heightened conflict ultimately won concessions in the hiring of African Americans in the private and public sector in West Point and Clay County. Many other demands were eventually won through litigation. An all-White jury ultimately acquitted Stanley for the murder of John Thomas in 1971.[28]

After the murder of Thomas, Rudy Shields spent most of the rest of 1970 in West Point. Shields was effective in recruiting West Point youth into the Black United Front. As in other boycotts organized by Shields, downtown was monitored by Black youth and transportation was supplied to carry Black consumers to nearby towns not under the boycott. Police targeted several youth associated with BUF. The *Black Voice* reported that police raided the homes of West Point Black youth fifty times between September and December of 1970. BUF members were regularly arrested and harassed by local police.[29]

Shields had previously used the name "Black Panthers" to strike fear into Blacks not respecting the Aberdeen boycott and into the local White power structure. He possibly wanted to make the Black Panthers more than a rumor in Mississippi. In October of 1970, an informant revealed to the FBI that the Illinois chapter of the Black Panther Party (BPP) received a request from Shields to come to West Point. Shields planned a statewide convention of Black Power organizations to be held at Mary Holmes College in early November 1970. By this point, Shields had participated in the formation of the Black United Front (BUF) in West Point, which the FBI described as a "revolutionary group." Shields also contacted the national office of the Black Panther Party in Oakland to request that its leader, Huey Newton, attend the conference and make a keynote address. Shields's proposed conference never materialized. Local police and Sovereignty Commission officials feared that BUF members would soon join the Black Panther Party. The FBI as well as the state and local officials were also concerned about whether Shields was a BPP member.[30]

"All Power to the People": The Black United Front in Jackson

The West Point boycott continued after Shields left in December of 1970. During that time, Shields brought the BUF organization to Jackson, the state capital. His primary base was students from predominantly African

American Jackson State College (JSC). Jackson State had been the scene of a bloody conflict in May of the same year. Hundreds of students from Jackson State and Millsaps, a predominantly White college, and youth from the community that surrounded the Black college involved themselves in antiwar and antiracist protest on the evening of May 13, 1970. The shooting of student antiwar protesters at Kent State in Ohio nine days earlier also enraged students. Police also killed six Blacks the evening before the Jackson protests during a demonstration in Augusta, Georgia, on May 12th. Some students and youth engaged in spontaneous violence by pelting the passing vehicles of White motorists with rocks and bottles. Fires were set on campus as angry students attempted to burn the ROTC building. Jackson city and Mississippi state police quelled the "mini-riot."[31]

The following evening, local police, armed with a tank, and the National Guard responded to spontaneous protests on the campus and its surrounding Black neighborhoods. Earlier that day rumors circulated throughout the campus that Charles Evers and his wife had been victims of an assassin's bullets in Fayette. The rumor of the Everses' death sparked rage and disorder on campus. After midnight, state and city police fired hundreds of rounds into Alexander Hall, a female dormitory, from which officers claimed snipers had fired. Alexander Hall and other student residences were riddled with bullet holes, looking more like a war zone than a college campus. A 21-year-old Jackson State student, Phillip Lafayette Gibbs, and seventeen-year-old high school student, James Earl Green, lay dead from the assault of police officers on campus. Twelve students were wounded from the barrage of gunfire. Four female students had to be treated for hysteria as a result of being in the line of fire. Many students were peacefully studying or relaxing in their dorm rooms when struck by bullets of city and state police. Others were injured by glass that shattered from the attack.[32]

The Black community was outraged by the events at Jackson State. A statement from African American activist leaders declared, "[I]t is our opinion that the action of the Highway Patrol constitutes murder. . . . We cannot find justification for shooting fleeing students regardless of the supposed provocation." Charles Evers's statement to the press was stinging. He held the governor, Jackson's mayor, and city commissioners accountable for the deaths and shootings. Evers declared, "This was a bloodthirsty and trigger-happy murder. . . . If this was a White campus, this wouldn't have happened." Five hundred youth from three high and five middle schools in Jackson walked out of class and marched to the governor's mansion to protest the events at JSC. Degecha X, a JSC student, spoke at the demonstration in front of the governor's mansion. Degecha told the audience of Black youth, "You better get ready to die . . . eventually there is going to be a confrontation." Some JSC students openly considered arming themselves after what they viewed as a massacre and racist abuse of power and force. There was a surge of gun purchases by Blacks in Jackson in the days after the campus shootings. Some Black leaders called for a paramilitary "defense league" to protect African Americans from the police. More moderate forces encouraged Jackson State students to picket and boycott White-owned enterprises in protest of the shootings on their campus. A state-wide boycott of all White-owned businesses was called until May 24th, the day of graduation at JSC. Evers and Shirley stayed overnight the evening after the shooting to discourage violent reactions from students and further reprisals from police.[33]

Local and state leaders responded in a variety of ways. Mississippi activist and physician Dr. Aaron Shirley warned that in the future Blacks might offer more resistance than had occurred on the JSC campus. Aaron Henry called for pickets at an event where Attorney General John Mitchell was speaking. Mitchell arrived in Jackson to speak with Mayor Russell Davis and JSC president Dr. John Peeples. Charles Evers proposed a more conciliatory posture. Evers called on Black businesses to close for one day in memory of the slain students. Adam Clayton Powell called for a congressional investigation. Roy Wilkins and United States senator Edward Brooke of Massachusetts came to JSC to gather information on the shootings. Ultimately, no police officer was indicted, arrested, or convicted for the deaths of Gibbs, Green, as well as the students wounded and injured by the May 15th shootings at JSC.[34]

Militant students at JSC provided the organizational base for Shields when he began to organize BUF in Jackson in December of 1970. At this time, the FBI office in Jackson received information that Shields planned to have a demonstration at the meeting of the Jackson City Council, demanding disciplinary action against the officers involved in the deaths of Gibbs and Green. The Jackson Black United Front (JBUF) was primarily composed of college students and alumni from JSC and Tougaloo and other local people. JBUF possessed a self-defense orientation. After the May 1970 massacre at JSC, militant students felt the need for protection. JBUF advocated the creation of a paramilitary organization for the protection of the Black community. Shields rented a house near the JSC campus to serve as the JBUF office.[35]

Shields and a group of five males and three females in their twenties appeared at the City Council meeting on January 5, 1971. Mayor Davis did not place the group on the agenda but promised to allow them to address the council at its following gathering. The group passed out flyers opposing plans to relocate JSC in favor of building public housing where the campus was located. The flyer was from JSC students and evoked the slogan of the Black Panther Party, "All Power to the People."[36] A JBUF contingent of twenty-one returned the following week to present demands before Mayor Davis and the City Council for Black representation in municipal decision making and on the city school board, fair employment practices, and other reforms.[37] Mayor Davis and the council made James Johnson their first African American appointment to the school board on February 21st. This was the first appointment of a Black person to a previously all-White board in the city of Jackson. JBUF believed that its pressure forced the local White power structure to make a decision to appoint an African American. JBUF stopped appearing at City Council meetings after the appointment of Johnson.[38] Shields also again unsuccessfully called for Huey Newton to come to speak in Mississippi at a Jackson BUF event.[39]

Shields began to spend more time in Yazoo County after a few BUF militant challenges to the Jackson municipal administration. Yazoo City became his permanent residence and center of operations. Yazoo provided a base of support he did not have in Jackson or elsewhere in the state. BUF floundered in Jackson without Shields's day-to-day presence and inspirational leadership. He had failed to attract the BPP to Mississippi in a visible way with his insurgent approach to Black Power.

"Free the Land": The Mississippi Freedom Struggle and the Republic of New Africa

Shields attempted to develop a relationship with national formations, such as the Provisional Government of the Republic of New Africa (PGRNA). Whereas Mississippi proved not to be attractive enough for the Black Panther Party to send Huey Newton or one of its other visible personalities, the Provisional Government saw Mississippi as strategic in its plan to establish a sovereign Black republic in the southern United States.

The PGRNA was formed in late March of 1968. Two brothers, Milton and Richard Henry, were leaders of the Malcolm X Society in Detroit. The

Republic of New Africa founders at Provisional Government Conference (1969).
Seated, left to right: Mabel Williams, Robert Williams, Gaidi Obadele. *Standing in
second row*: Imari Obadele (*third from right*), Queen Mother Moore (*sixth from
right*). (Courtesy of Malika Obadele and the Obadele Project.)

brothers would ultimately change their names to Gaidi (Milton) and Imari
(Richard) Obadele. Gaidi Obadele was an associate of Malcolm X. He
had invited Malcolm X to Detroit and hosted him there for three major
addresses between 1963 and February 1965, one week before his assassination. Gaidi also traveled with Malcolm to Cairo, Egypt, to a session of the
Organization of African Unity. The Malcolm X Society was formed after
Malcolm's assassination to promote the Black leader's concepts of interna-
tionalization of the Black Freedom Struggle, armed self-defense, self-determination, and peoplehood.⁴⁰

The Malcolm X Society organized a Black Governmental Conference in
Detroit from March 29 through March 31, 1968. The conference attracted
leading Black nationalists from around the United States: Maulana Karenga
of the Us organization; Hakim Jamal (related to Malcolm by marriage)

of the Malcolm X Foundation from Los Angeles; Amiri Baraka from the Committee for a Unified Newark (New Jersey); spiritual leader and traditional African religious priest Nana Oserjiman Adefumi of the Yoruba Temple; and reparations activist Queen Mother Moore from Harlem, New York. Representatives from the Black Panther Party, the Revolutionary Action Movement, and the League of Revolutionary Black Workers attended the Black nationalist convention. Lawrence Guyot of the Mississippi Freedom Democratic Party also was present. Malcolm's widow, Betty Shabazz, not only gave her blessing but also was a participant in the conference.[41]

Over five hundred conference participants grappled over a program for Black sovereignty and self-determination. The conference resolved to form a provisional government in the United States for Blacks, who were viewed as a "subjugated nation." Five states in the Deep South—Mississippi, Louisiana, Alabama, Georgia, and South Carolina—were identified as the national territory of the oppressed Black nation. These states had the largest percentages and concentrations of Black population due to the legacy of chattel slavery and the production of cotton, rice, and sugar before and after emancipation. The provisional government demanded that the five states be relinquished to its authority as part of reparations that were due the Black nation for centuries of exploitation and degradation. Ultimately, one hundred participants in the conference signed a document declaring their independence from the United States.[42]

The convention approved the proposal by Queen Mother Moore that the Black nation be identified as the "Republic of New Africa" (RNA). A provisional government was selected, including a "who's who" of Black Power militants from around the United States. Exiled activist and advocate of armed resistance Robert F. Williams was selected as president. Williams and his wife Mabel were living in the East African socialist state Tanzania when the RNA was founded. Betty Shabazz requested an office in the government, and she and Gaidi Obadele were designated as vice presidents. Other associates of Malcolm X, Herman Ferguson and Obaboa Owolo (also known as Ed Bradley), were assigned as minister of education and treasurer, respectively. Karenga, Baraka, and Adefumi were identified as ministers of culture. SNCC chairman H. Rap Brown was named minister of defense. While Brown was not in attendance, he accepted the post in solidarity with this new formation. The Revolutionary Action Movement central organizer, Max Stanford, was appointed "Minister without Portfolio."[43]

The PGRNA ultimately had a national presence with "consulates" in major urban centers like Detroit, New York, Boston, Dayton (Ohio), San

Francisco, Los Angeles, Milwaukee, Las Vegas, and Gary (Indiana), as well as a governmental center in the "national territory" in New Orleans. In public ceremonies, thousands of young Blacks swore their allegiance to the Republic of New Africa and chose RNA citizenship. Many abandoned their "slave names" and chose African ones, particularly Yoruba and Ki-Swahili names, to signify their New African identity and citizenship.[44]

Mississippi was strategic to the vision of the Obadeles. They had previously envisioned an electoral strategy in the state to create zones of Black empowerment. The Obadeles and the Malcolm X Society originally planned to organize in the Mississippi Delta and other Black-majority counties in the state to achieve Black political representation and ultimately agitate and organize for independence. The organization of the PGRNA changed their strategy. They believed Mississippi Blacks could be convinced that their future was brighter under the leadership of the PGRNA than under the White-minority rule that was a reality in most of the Black-majority counties in Mississippi in the late 1960s and early 1970s. The PGRNA could win allegiance in Mississippi's Black Belt through organizing economic cooperatives as well as educational and medical institutions to serve poor communities in Black-majority counties. A United Nations plebiscite would be organized for Blacks to vote for independence, similar to some colonized nations in Africa during the 1950s and 1960s. Imari Obadele identified the "Kush district," a contiguous area of majority-Black counties in the western part of state running along the Mississippi River, as the place to organize for a plebiscite on independence.[45]

The PGRNA would declare independence if a majority of Mississippi Blacks in Kush voted for it. It would then call upon the international community to recognize the Republic of New Africa's sovereignty. The entrance of newly independent states in Africa and a growing number of socialist regimes in Africa, Asia, and Latin America sparked the hope that the RNA would have international allies. The emergence of the People's Republic of China as a nuclear power inspired New African nationalists. A possible ally with nuclear capacity could change the international balance of power.[46]

The PGRNA would also promote the development of "new communities" on "virgin land" in the Kush district. The New African new communities would be built primarily by urban Blacks relocating to the rural South. The new communities would allow New Africans to begin to establish institutions and relationships under their vision of a "new society." The new communities would be organized under New African Ujama, the RNA's

economic program. The name "Ujama" was borrowed from the African so-
cialism of Tanzania, under the leadership of its postcolonial leader, Julius
Nyerere. The PGRNA proposed economic development in the Kush district based upon cooperative and collective ownership. Socialist principles
were articulated in the RNA economic program:

> ALL industry and agriculture are owned by the people as a whole and ad-
> ministered by the Republic of New Africa. . . .
>   People are trained and assigned work in accordance with their prefer-
> ence, their ability and the NEEDS of the Community and the Nation. . . .
>   After community NEEDS are satisfied, wealth is equally divided
> among all workers. . . .[47]

Obadele hoped that New African Ujama and the new communities would
demonstrate the values of the independent nation. The new communities
would offer an alternative to White supremacy and economic exploitation
and assist the cause for independence.[48]

The PGRNA hoped that Blacks from urban centers in the northern,
midwestern, and western United States would migrate to the Mississippi
new communities they developed. The PGRNA's new communities were
marketed as zones of refuge from the racism and deprivation that historically plagued people of African descent in the United States. Imari Obadele asserted,

> We regard Mississippi as the Promised Land for Black people. . . . We
> who are tired of poverty and oppression, the crime, corruption and cyni-
> cism of American society are entitled to rest our heads and start anew. . . .
> There are no more Australias or Palestines in the world. But there is
> Mississippi.[49]

The PGRNA also believed in a visible self-defense presence. Boston activist Alajo Adegbalola (formerly known as Leroy Boston) emerged in 1970 as
PGRNA minister of defense under Imari Obadele's leadership. Adegbalola
formed the New African Security Force as the defense arm of the Provisional Government. He required that all government workers must have
paramilitary training in order to defend the Republic of New Africa from
White supremacist and U.S. intervention in its organizing in Mississippi
and after independence was declared. Unlike many Black nationalist formations, the New African Security Forces under Adegbalola's leadership

had women engage in military training and occupy positions of authority in the paramilitary chain of command. The PGRNA argued that its presence in Mississippi would be "peaceful." They intended to take a defense posture, arming themselves with firearms to protect themselves, a constitutional right accorded U.S. citizens. They would organize new communities and for the plebiscite within the framework of U.S. and international law. Obadele and other PGRNA leaders also saw a role for urban guerilla warfare. The Black underground, commonly called the Black Liberation Army (BLA), was very active in the late 1960s and early 1970s. The PGRNA claimed no control of the BLA or other underground radical formations, but hoped Black clandestine units in northern urban centers would provide a disruptive or "second strike" capacity if the RNA were attacked. Obadele's strategy was labeled the "Malcolm X Doctrine."[50]

The Obadele brothers differed on the timetable of organizing a plebiscite in Mississippi. The differences became antagonistic, and ultimately they split, which disillusioned some elements in the organization. Imari Obadele emerged from the split as the president of the PGRNA in 1970. He was surrounded by a dedicated group of young people and committed veterans in the Black Freedom Struggle who ventured to bring their brand of militant urban, and mostly northern, Black nationalism to Mississippi. Prior to their exodus to Mississippi, the PGRNA had only one base of membership in its "national territory." New Orleans, under the leadership of former UNIA member and human rights activist Dara Abubakari (formerly known as Virginia Collins), was the only Deep South center of the PGRNA prior to 1971.[51]

The Republic of New Africa and the Mississippi Black Power Movement

The Black Freedom Struggle had made tremendous strides in the state by 1971. Registration of Black voters increased from twenty thousand in 1965 to three hundred thousand by 1970. Some White politicians, recognizing the new political realities, began to take a more moderate racial posture. In spite of the progress, significant obstacles still remained for Blacks desiring political participation and human rights. By 1971, there were only ninety-four Black elected officials, with African Americans representing 37 percent of the state's population. Racist violence still remained as a factor in Mississippi's political culture. Terror, harassment, and intimidation were still employed against Black political campaigns throughout the state. Black communities and activists could not rely on federal intervention to combat White supremacist terror. The Nixon administration viewed segregationist U.S. senator James Eastland as an ally. Nixon's Department of Justice did not aggressively enforce the Voting Rights Act in the face of continuing terror in Mississippi. Some Mississippi Blacks looked for radical alternatives; the PGRNA would offer one.[52]

The PGRNA attracted a small number of militant Blacks looking for a radical Black Power alternative to reformist politics in the state. The first recruit of PGRNA in Mississippi was Henry Hatches, activist and organizer in the Hinds County FDP. Hatches's activism with the FDP started with advocacy around public assistance for the poor in Hinds County. He emerged as an activist and key leader along with the emergence of militant Black Power in the county FDP. By 1967, the Hinds FDP publicly embraced the politics of Black Power and openly advocated armed militancy. Hinds's FDP had a more militant Black Power stand than the statewide party. Its organ, the *Hinds County FDP News*, included excerpts of speeches from SNCC chairmen and Black Power advocates Stokely Carmichael and H. Rap Brown. The newsletter masthead abandoned the Democratic Party's symbol of a donkey for an image of a Black Panther in its October 6, 1967, issue. Overt appeals for racial solidarity were employed by the FDP in Hinds County in electoral campaigns. Slogans like "Vote Black Now" appeared in the organization's newsletter. Another article entitled "Did You Know: Negroes Still Voting White" sharply criticized African Americans for voting for White candidates. The article concluded, "There is no need for you to use an excuse why you voted for a white man. The only answer is that you are a damn Nigger." Hatches was clearly associated with the politics of Black Power. He decided to run for office as the FDP candidate for constable in Hinds in 1967. An advertisement for his candidacy in the election in the local FDP newsletter was complemented by an illustration of a bomb with a lit fuse and the slogan "Black Power" written on it.[53]

Hatches served as a delegate from Hinds in the MFDP delegation to the National Conference for New Politics (NCNP) in Chicago in the late summer of 1967. Hatches's participation and position in the conference reflected the growing Black Power sentiment in the Mississippi Black Freedom Struggle. The NCNP was an effort to form an alliance between New Left forces, particularly the antiwar movement, and grassroots Civil Rights and militant Black Power Movements. Hatches and other Hinds delegates were in support of the Black Power advocates' demand that African Americans possess 50 percent of the voting power in all committees of the convention. Three hundred and fifty of the Black delegates separated from the multiracial assembly to convene on their own. Four hundred of the remaining African American delegates formed a Black caucus that presented resolutions that NCNP was pressured to adopt if it wanted their participation in the conference. The Black Caucus resolutions included calling for the reinstatement of Adam Clayton Powell in the United States Congress, solidarity with national liberation movements, condemnation of Zionism, support for the program of the 1967 Newark Black Power Convention, and reparations. The NCNP accepted Black Caucus resolutions, and those who had walked out returned. Hatches and his colleagues saw the adoption of the Black Caucus resolutions as a victory. The September 8, 1967, Hinds FDP newsletter complemented its article on NCNP with an illustration titled "New Politics." The "New Politics" illustration described how to make a Molotov cocktail firebomb. The same issue of *Hinds County FDP News* featured an article titled "Firepower the Only Hope." The article closed with the slogan "Burn Baby, Burn," that was made popular during the 1965 Watts Uprising in Los Angeles. Urban rebellions were also supported in another article titled "Race Riots: Violence May Be the Answer."[54]

Another Hinds FDP activist, Carolyn Williams, was an early PGRNA worker in Jackson. A single parent of three, Williams was active in grassroots electoral politics and economic development in Hinds County. Williams actively campaigned for Hatches and other FDP candidates. She also identified with the Black Power Movement. In an editorial in *FDP News*, she stated,

> I believe in Black dignity, black pride, black knowledge—in a great human campaign to restore to ourselves the image of our own strength. I believe in my own people who are rising into power on stepping stones of oppression and defeat. I believe in the structure being raised by our own courage and matured with our own blood.[55]

She concluded the article with "I BELIEVE IN BLACK POWER." Williams and Hatches served as the field representatives of the Southern Consumer Education Foundation in 1967. The Southern Consumer Education Foundation was an advocacy organization addressing economic issues for working and poor people of African descent in Hinds County. Hatches's and Williams's associate Jesse Montgomery was another local supporter of

PGRNA in Hinds. Montgomery had previously been associated with the Hinds FDP and had run for county supervisor in 1967. While not an active PGRNA worker, Montgomery took the pledge for RNA citizenship.[56]

In April of 1969, Hatches was appointed the PGRNA's southern regional minister of defense and Williams the provisional government's consul for the city of Jackson. They attempted to build a network of support for the organization in Hinds County. In July of 1970, Hatches distributed a flyer in Jackson announcing, "We are now in the era of self-defense." Invoking the massacres in Jackson and Augusta, it called upon Black people to support armed freedom fighters committed to defending the community from racist violence. The leaflet identified Hatches as the minister of defense. Hatches would soon change his name to Jomo Kenyatta, after the Kikuyu nationalist in Kenya. Similar to Medgar Evers and several militant and nationalistic African Americans, he associated Kenyatta with the Kikuyu Land and Freedom Army, commonly known as the Mau Mau.[57]

Exodus: Imari Obadele and Northern New Africans Move South

Hinds County bordered the RNA's projected Kush District. Obadele and his colleagues saw developing a base in Hinds County as significant to their overall plans in Mississippi. The demographic changes of the previous decade informed the New African nationalists that Jackson was experiencing rapid Black population growth. During the 1960s, Hinds County experienced a Black population increase of thirty-five thousand and a White migration of nearly equal numbers. Hinds's population of 215,000, which was predominantly in the city of Jackson, was the largest of any county in the state. The PGRNA leadership agreed to develop a capital site for the provisional government in Hinds County.[58]

PGRNA had its first gathering in Mississippi at the Central Methodist Church in Jackson on July 31, 1970. The Peoples Center Council (PCC), representatives of PGRNA units from around the United States, assembled to report on progress and make plans for future organizing. The acquisition of land was a major agenda item for the PCC meeting. The PCC assigned Jomo Kenyatta (Hatches) the responsibility of locating land for purchase by the PGRNA in Hinds County. Kenyatta's residence was firebombed on December 27, 1970. He—along with his brother, sister-in-law, and their five children—escaped with only two rifles and the clothes they wore, as the house burned to the ground.[59]

Kenyatta continued his pursuit to acquire land. He made an inquiry to Hinds County resident Lofton Mason about selling some of his land to the PGRNA. Mason was a landowning Black farmer in the Hinds County town of Bolton, a small, Black-majority town with a population approaching two thousand. Mason had been an FDP candidate for county supervisor in 1967 and had been the target of harassment and threats due to his political involvement. Mason's home had been shot at by nightriders, his cattle had been poisoned, and his property had been vandalized. Kenyatta discussed the purchase of twenty acres with Mason. FBI agents received information about PGRNA's desire to purchase land from Mason and tried to convince the Bolton farmer not to sell. Kenyatta, Obadele, and PGRNA supporter and Hinds County lawyer Hermel Johnson continued dialogue with Mason to resist the FBI pressure not to sell the property. Subsequently Obadele and Mason reached an oral agreement for a lease purchase of the land. Obadele and Mason agreed that the PGRNA would pay twenty thousand dollars for the land, a two thousand dollar down payment, and five thousand per year. The PGRNA would build a school, a dining hall/community center, and ultimately a new community on the land in Bolton. This site would be renamed "El-Malik," after the martyr of the New African Independence Movement Malik Shabazz (aka Malcolm X).[60]

The PGRNA made plans to publicize the imminent acquisition of its land. In January 1971, Obadele announced that the PGRNA was on the verge of obtaining the land. It planned a major gala on Mason's land called Land Celebration Day, intended as an opportunity for the RNA to consecrate the land slated to be purchased and as a vehicle to encourage New African citizens to emotionally and financially support the effort to acquire the property. Workshops, cultural events, and rituals were all planned as part of the events slated for late March 1971. The primary advertisement for the event announced, "Join the DAY OF PRAYER . . . On Behalf of the REPUBLIC OF NEW AFRICA FOR JUSTICE & SUCCESS AND COME TO THE LAND for BLACK PEOPLE'S LAND CELEBRATION DAY." A contractor was hired to begin construction of the school building and the dining hall on the land designated to be purchased from Mason. PGRNA workers were sent from Boston, Milwaukee, and New Orleans in March of 1971 to assist Williams and Kenyatta in the preparations.[61]

Mississippi and Hinds County officials were threatened by and concerned about the possibility of the PGRNA establishing a base in the state. State attorney general A. F. Summers proclaimed that there would be no Land Celebration Day. Officials perceived the RNA celebration as intended to declare independence within their jurisdiction. Hinds County sheriffs, the FBI, and state police raided a house in Bolton where RNA citizens were residing on the evening of March 23rd. Surveillance by the county sheriff had determined that a vehicle on the Bolton property was stolen and had a stolen tag. This car was operated by a New Orleans resident, David Cobb, who had transported two RNA government workers to Bolton. The stolen vehicle gave the county, state, and federal authorities the probable cause necessary to raid the residence. Ten people, including Kenyatta and his wife, Okadele (aka Mary Alice Hatches), were arrested for one felony of a stolen automobile and misdemeanor charges of obstruction of justice and possession of stolen property. Neither Cobb nor the stolen automobile was present during the arrest. Cobb was never apprehended. All of the weapons and office equipment in the house were seized.[62]

Two PGRNA workers from Boston were arrested in their station wagon after arriving in Jackson on the day after the Bolton raid. Three handguns, four rifles, ammunition, and communication equipment were also seized. One of the Boston New Africans, Hassam Ali, was charged with carrying a concealed weapon. Hakim Abdullah was arrested for the possession of a marijuana cigarette. Ali was the only one of the twelve New Africans arrested on March 24th to be released in time to participate in the Land Celebration Day events.[63]

PGRNA leaders believed that the raid and arrests of their workers were designed to disrupt Land Celebration Day. They were determined to continue their plans despite the arrests. Obadele arrived in Mississippi the day after the arrests and held a press conference at the Jackson airport. He stated, "The whole effort against us is designed to destroy the republic, to prevent our meeting this weekend and to prevent the plebiscite." The New African president declared, "We have made no threats against the United States and the people of Mississippi. . . . Our people are carrying weapons for defensive purposes and our activities are legal and peaceful." Making reference to the second-strike capacity of the Black Power Movement, Obadele proclaimed that if the RNA were attacked, "then they will see war all over the nation." Obadele invited Black congressional representatives to attend and observe a performance by the Motown recording group, the Originals. However, the U.S. representatives, the Originals, and other Blacks declined the invitation and call to Mississippi for Land Celebration Day after the arrests of RNA workers. Bolton city councilman Bennie

Armed New African woman on security at March 1971 Land Celebration Day. New African women participated in armed security and were in the defense forces' chain of command. (Courtesy of the archives of Chokwe Lumumba.)

Thompson and state representative Robert Clark held a press conference condemning the police attacks and expressed their solidarity with the PGRNA. Thompson argued that the raid was designed "to stop the Republic from building its community." Clark stated that while he was not in complete agreement with the beliefs of the PGRNA, the group was "nonviolent" and had the constitutional right to peacefully organize since it had not broken any state or federal laws. Representative Clark seemed sympathetic to the PGRNA's new communities. He declared, "[T]he only thing that this group here is trying to do is establish communities where Black people can have jobs and dignity without discrimination. . . . I don't think that they should be subject to the harassment that we are beginning to see." The Jackson Black United Front opened its doors to the PGRNA in Jackson, providing transportation, housing, and logistical support.[64]

The initial PGRNA prediction of three thousand participants in the Land Celebration would be scaled down significantly. A much smaller crowd of PGRNA workers and Land Celebration Day participants gathered at the Mount Beulah Christian Institute in the Hinds County town of Edwards. Mount Beulah had been established in 1964 by the National Council of Churches (NCC) to support the Black Freedom Struggle in the state and for use during Freedom Summer. The Delta Ministries, another NCC project, administered Mount Beulah. New Africans and their supporters gathered at the twenty-acre Mount Beulah land and facility, since the construction of facilities had not begun in Bolton on their projected site. Mount Beulah was only a few miles from the site of Land Celebration Day.

The day prior to Land Celebration Day, Obadele and his comrades noticed a sign painted near the Mount Beulah property. It stated, "Niggers, there will be no meeting here Sunday. Free six-foot holes." The message was signed "KKK." Undeterred by this threat, Obadele and a caravan of several vehicles, including a busload of New Africans from northern California, proceeded from Mount Beulah to Lofton Mason's land on the afternoon of March 28th. There was also a concern that more participants would be stopped on highways leading into Hinds County. Obadele contacted Black U.S. congressman John Conyers from Detroit. Conyers and other Black U.S. representatives assured Obadele that he would be able to express concerns to the federal Department of Justice regarding the right of the PGRNA to conduct its Land Celebration Day without harassment.[65]

The PGRNA prepared for attack from civilian White supremacists and state and local police. An armed advance team was sent to the site of Land Celebration Day on Mason's land to guard against ambush. Armed security was also organized for a caravan of sixteen automobiles, two vans, and a bus that had transported New Africans and their supporters from California. The PGRNA military command sent out scouts to determine whether there was any opposition along the route to the event location. The scouts reported that local and state police formed a barricade at the entrance of the Mount Beulah property. PGRNA defense minister Alajo Adegbalola, the consul from Detroit, Chokwe Lumumba, and RNA citizen and Jackson attorney William Miller were in the lead vehicle of the caravan. Observing the police barricade, they anticipated a confrontation with the police. As Adegbalola and Lumumba's vehicle approached the entrance of Mount Beulah, to their surprise, the police barricade opened to make way for the caravan. The caravan traveled five miles to the proposed RNA land site without incident. The RNA security formed an armed defense perimeter around the Land Celebration site, and federal, state, and local police monitored the events from remote locations.[66]

Land Celebration Day had 150 participants. Only twelve Black residents of Hinds County (who were not PGRNA workers) attended. Activities included a naming ceremony for fourteen Blacks who adopted "New African" names and a wedding ceremony for Adegbalola's daughter Fulani and New York activist Ahmed Obafemi. Obadele performed the "New African wedding" ceremony. Fifteen Blacks took the oath of allegiance to the New African nation. Lofton Mason and his wife were among those who pledged their allegiance to the RNA. Participants enthusiastically chanted the RNA slogan "Free the Land!" While the arrests and harassment had discouraged more participation, the PGRNA interpreted Land Celebration Day as a victory. They had survived the attempts of the FBI and state and local authorities to intimidate them and prevent the event from occurring.[67]

Few journalists were allowed to cover the event. Local reporters Jack Hobbs and Cliff Farrier, Jan Hillegas of the Movement periodical *The Southern Patriot*, and a few members of the local Black press were allowed to enter the site of the activities. Local broadcast media did not choose to interview New African press liaisons, but featured local White responses to Land Celebration Day. Hinds County sheriff Fred Thomas made it clear that Land Celebration Day would be monitored by local police. Thomas stated, "We'll make an arrest where we see crime violated in our presence. Other than that we'll travel on court orders, but other than that we do intend to keep the peace in the state of Mississippi." Local media also covered the response of the state White Citizens' Council leader, Medford Evans. Evans painted the RNA as a communist conspiracy, stating, "Somewhere or other they got big financing and it's got connections with Red China and Castro's Cuba. And obviously what they say they gonna do, they can't do, but they're doing something revolutionary and it should be taken very seriously."[68]

Mississippi attorney general A. F. Summers made an open appeal to U.S. attorney general John Mitchell days after the Land Celebration. Summers expressed concern over the RNA's separatist goals. The Mississippi politician asserted that the people of Mississippi were "justifiably disturbed over the fact that a group of people can proclaim . . . a new nation carved out of our state . . . without any intervention from the federal government nor any effort by the government to expel them." He was also perplexed by the open display of weapons. Summers expressed to Mitchell that the PGRNA was "heavily armed with rifles and side guns which were openly brandished in a menacing fashion." The Mississippi attorney general also claimed that the PGRNA had distributed literature instructing Blacks in the use of incendiary devices and in urban guerilla warfare. He argued that the RNA efforts in his state constituted an "armed insurrection." Summers requested federal assistance and intervention in preventing the PGRNA from pursuing its agenda in Mississippi. He concluded, "We would therefore request you at once advise the state of Mississippi as to your proposed course of action, if any, in this serious matter."[69]

Tension existed between Mississippi state officials and the federal government on how to handle the PGRNA. The state wanted to swiftly attack the New African nationalists. Some White supremacists had historically feared an armed Black uprising in the state, and the sight of armed Blacks during Land Celebration Day increased those fears. The federal government also wanted to neutralize the PGRNA, but wanted to create a legal pretext for their actions. A Jackson FBI agent told reporters, "We'd love to go down there and run them off . . . but so far they haven't broken any Federal laws."[70]

The official response of White Mississippians was unified in its condemnation of the RNA, but the African American community had a variety of perspectives on the New African nationalists. A small group of Mississippi Black Power militants like Williams and Kenyatta were recruited into the PGRNA. Rudy Shields, in search of a national Black Power organization with which to associate his organizing efforts, welcomed the nationalist politics of the RNA and openly associated with Obadele and his comrades. Shields's Jackson Black United Front served as the PGRNA's closest allies in Mississippi. Moderate leaders like Aaron Shirley, Thompson, and Clark defended the New African nationalists' right to organize, but never actively participated. Shirley spoke at PGRNA meetings and on one occasion covertly provided medical care to Obadele after a gun accident during the PGRNA's first Jackson gathering in the summer of 1970. In spite of his support, however, Shirley did not embrace the ideology and political goals of the RNA. The Jackson doctor reflected, "The Republic of New Africa didn't come across as a local movement; it came across as something on the fringes." Other Blacks feared that the PGRNA posture and rhetoric would incite White supremacist violence and reprisals against Mississippi Blacks. Land Celebration Day occurred ten months after the state and local police shootings at Jackson State, and some Blacks were sure that White authority in Mississippi would not tolerate the PGRNA and would force a military confrontation.[71]

PGRNA plans to establish a new community in Hinds County were undermined when in late April 1971 Mason reneged on his oral commitment to sell land to the nationalist formation. They were to close on the deal on April 30th, and Obadele had provided one thousand of the two thousand dollar down payment, withholding the rest of the down payment until Mason had produced a land survey and results of a title search. Obadele claimed that White supremacists had convinced Mason not to sell while Mason stated that Obadele had failed to come up with the down payment. The local authorities and media highlighted the failure of the PGRNA to acquire land in Bolton. The PGRNA held a "people's court" on July 19th to determine its right to the land. The PGRNA court ruled that Mason should honor the "gentlemen's agreement" and turn over the property to them. Hinds County authorities issued an injunction against the New Africans, forbidding them to occupy Mason's land. State Attorney General Summers filed an injunction to prevent the PGRNA from occupying Mason's land. Hinds County district attorney Jack Travis also offered Mason protection from the New Africans. Charles Evers joined with Travis, promising security for Mason. In the middle of a gubernatorial race, Evers framed PGRNA as outsider, charging, "[I]f they think they're going to come in here and run over my folks they've got another thing [sic] coming."[72]

War in America: The Ordeal of the Republic of New Africa 11

The PGRNA had established the custom of an audience standing for the RNA president when the officer entered the room. On August 5th, at a PGRNA press conference reporting on the RNA people's court, a reporter, David Smith of the Jackson *Daily News*, refused to stand for the RNA president, whereupon RNA security pushed him out of the PGRNA headquarters. Jackson police lieutenant William Skinner witnessed Smith being forced away from the PGRNA headquarters, and according to Obadele, Skinner promised to come back and "clean that place out." Skinner was the head of the Jackson police intelligence unit assigned to monitor the PGRNA. Obadele and PGRNA security braced themselves for an attack as police circled their residence/office. Obadele was arrested by Skinner the next day without incident and tried on a charge of simple assault. He was convicted in Jackson Municipal Court the following week and fined one hundred dollars.[73]

The tension between the federal, state, and local governments and the PGRNA climaxed on August 18th. A force of sixty FBI agents and Jackson police officers joined together in a predawn raid on the PGRNA Jackson headquarters, accompanied by the same tank used the previous year in the raid on the Jackson State campus. The PGRNA raid was predicated on a fugitive murder warrant for Jerry Steiner, who was wanted for murder in Michigan and had been transported by an FBI informant to Jackson to work and live with the RNA. The informant, Thomas Spells, told the FBI that Steiner was a fugitive, and the FBI allowed Spells to take Steiner to Mississippi before deciding to arrest him. During the week prior to the raid, Steiner had been expelled from the PGRNA headquarters for lack of the discipline required of their government workers. His presence in Jackson served the purposes of the FBI, even without him being in the headquarters on the morning of the raid. Police also had misdemeanor warrants for PGRNA southern regional defense minister Jomo Kenyatta and two other individuals. Neither Kenyatta nor the others named in the warrants were in the headquarters on the morning of the raid.[74]

The FBI and Jackson police contingent of approximately forty officers announced their presence with a bullhorn and gave sleeping residents of the PGRNA headquarters seventy-five seconds before firing tear gas into the domicile. Occupants of the house counterattacked after tear gas canisters and bullets by police were fired into the headquarters. A twenty-minute gun battle ensued before the New Africans signaled surrender. When the smoke cleared, Jackson police lieutenant Skinner was found to have been fatally wounded. Skinner had been shot in the head as he had risen above the cover of an automobile to shoot at the New Africans in the headquarters. Another Jackson police officer and an FBI agent were also wounded. Seven New Africans emerged from the house without serious injury. The PGRNA members arrested at the headquarters were Offogga Quddus (aka Wayne Maurice James of Camden, New Jersey) and his wife Njeri Quddus (Toni Austin, also of Camden); Hekima Ana (aka Thomas Norman, a Milwaukee resident raised in Charlotte, North Carolina) and his wife Tamu Ana (aka Ann Lockhart of Milwaukee); Addis Ababa (aka Dennis Shillingford of Detroit); Chumaimari Askadi (aka Robert Charles Stallings of Milwaukee); and Karim Njabafudi (aka Larry Jackson of New Orleans, Louisiana). The seven PGRNA workers were able to escape the barrage of gunfire aimed at their headquarters by descending to a tunnel beneath the house that was being prepared in anticipation of an attack but was not yet completed. Tamu Ana remembered being escorted in the tunnel along with Njeri Quddus by the nineteen-year-old Askadi. Askadi then placed his body over the two New African women to shield them from the gunfire of the police. The captured New Africans were beaten and badgered outside the PGRNA residence by the police in attempts to gain information because the police thought there were more nationalists inside the residence. Police continued to fire tear gas and bullets into the house after the New African nationalists surrendered. Police fired over three hundred rounds into the residence. When they surrendered, the New Africans were in the rear of the house, but they were taken to the front of the residence where their neighbors could witness their treatment. Several of the New African males were kicked and brutally butted with shotguns. Three months pregnant, Njeri Quddus was kicked in the side. Tamu Ana remembered a police officer threatening to "blow" her "head off" after she raised her head off the ground in reaction to an insect on the ground near her. Hekima Ana believed the only reason why he and his comrades were not killed in retaliation was that police believed there were dead New Africans and survivors in the residence. Police also believed the nationalists possessed an automatic weapon in the defense of their headquarters and wanted to know who was in possession of it.[75]

Obadele and three other New Africans were arrested at another residence in a nearby Jackson neighborhood. These arrests took place without shooting. Those arrested with Obadele included PGRNA minister of information Aisha Salim (of Philadelphia), Tawwab Nkrumah (George Matthews of Birmingham, Alabama), and Spade de Mau Mau (aka S. L. Alexander of New Orleans). All eleven arrested PGRNA workers were charged with the murder of Skinner, assault with intent to kill, and assault on a federal officer. Obadele, Salim, Nkrumah, and de Mau Mau were also charged with murder even though it was clear they were not at the scene of the combat. Hinds County district attorney Jack Travis applied Mississippi law to bring murder charges against the PGRNA members who had not been involved in the defense of the headquarters. Travis stated that under state law "those who aid, abet, assist or encourage a felony" are "as guilty as the principal." Obadele, in particular, was charged with "accessory before the fact of murder." The prosecution argued that Obadele's direction of and orders to New African security personnel led to the shooting death of Skinner. Travis later charged the PGRNA defendants with treason, stating that their actions constituted "levying war against the state of Mississippi." The charge of treason carried the maximum penalty of death.[76] Federal prosecutor would charge Offogga and Njeri Quddus, Hekima and Tamu Ana, Njabafudi, Obadele, Ababa, and Askadi with conspiring to interfere with federal officers, conspiring to use a firearm in commission of a felony, and conspiring to possess unregistered firearms. Offogga Quddus was also charged with possession of an unregistered automatic weapon. The FBI claimed that Quddus's semiautomatic AR-180 assault rifle was converted into an automatic weapon.[77]

RNA citizen and Jackson attorney William Miller served as co-counsel for what was to be known as the Republic of New Africa 11 (RNA 11). Miller had earlier that year been appointed as the PGRNA minister of justice. From the outset of the case, Miller argued that the New Africans were acting in self-defense. Miller expressed condolences for the death of Skinner, while arguing that the New Africans had only responded to an unprovoked attack by the FBI/Jackson police contingent. Miller worked to organize a legal team and political support for the RNA 11.[78]

White Mississippi officials immediately condemned the PGRNA and memorialized Lieutenant Skinner in the aftermath of the raid on the RNA headquarters and the arrests of the eleven defendants. Governor John Williams described Skinner as a "courageous officer" and used the moment to attack the liberal federal government and national media. The Mississippi governor framed the events of the current "law and order" debate. Williams stated, "With their hands shackled by these federal court decisions and in the face of constant antipolice propaganda barrages of the national media, we should thank God that we still have dedicated officers willing to risk their lives in enforcement of the law and the preservation of peace."[79] U.S. senator James Eastland also applauded the FBI and Jackson police and expressed sympathy for the death of Skinner. Eastland also took the time to attack the PGRNA, whom he characterized as "outlaws and hoodlums." The pro-segregationist politician had previously made assaults on the PGRNA on the floor of the United States Senate, accusing the New African nationalists of being part of an international communist conspiracy. Eastland declared, "These outrageous characters invaded our state, attempted to seize private property, gathered a sizeable cache of arms and waved guns in the face of our lawmen."[80]

Moderate Black leaders called for calm in the aftermath of the August 18th gun battle. Gubernatorial candidate Charles Evers took a conciliatory tone, offering condolences to Skinner's family and appealing to Black and White Mississippians, saying, "[W]e have come too far in the efforts for racial harmony to allow this tragedy to deter us." NAACP state president Aaron Henry was also conciliatory, but questioned the attacks on the PGRNA in Mississippi. Henry stated, "This event, any way you look at it, will not aid race relations in Mississippi." The state NAACP leader also called for a federal Department of Justice investigation.[81]

Some Jackson activists directly placed responsibility for the violent August 18th battle on the FBI and Jackson police. Jackson physicians Aaron Shirley and William Miller assembled a group of professionals and politicians under the umbrella of Black Jacksonians for Justice. Black Jacksonians for Justice held a press conference on August 27th condemning the police attack on the PGRNA. While expressing sympathy for the fatal loss of Lieutenant Skinner, Shirley stated,

> [W]e think it was just as unfortunate that law enforcement found it necessary to use tanks, shotguns and massive forces of men to serve simple warrants on Black people. . . . [I]t was clear that their mission was as it has been too many times in the past and as it was in Jackson State. . . .
>
> It was through no compassion of the officers for Blacks that none of the Blacks was killed. They were out to kill some niggers, just this time they were outsmarted.[82]

Shirley identified the "kill some niggers attitude" on the part of state and local police as responsible for the death of Skinner. He was joined at the press conference by Bolton city councilman Bennie Thompson, NAACP field secretary Alex Waites, and other Black leaders. Shirley claimed to have the support of "90 percent" of the Black population in Jackson. Dr. Shirley also visited pregnant Njeri Quddus and other captured RNA members to check on their medical status. Shirley was angered by the police attacks on the PGRNA. Interviewed decades later, he remembered, "After the shootout occurred everybody was mad . . . because those kids [the PGRNA members] were shot for doing nothing." After visiting Quddus, he went home and told his wife, "If I had some gasoline and a can, I would probably start a fire."[83]

The PGRNA defined the RNA 11 as "prisoners of war." They argued that the PGRNA was peacefully organizing a United Nations supervised plebiscite and that the attack on organizers was illegal under U.S. and international law. The PGRNA articulated that the captured New Africans were not only political activists but part of the defense forces of the provisional government of a national liberation movement. Like captured combatants of anticolonial movements in Africa and Asia, the RNA 11 should be treated as prisoners of war under the Geneva Convention.[84]

The RNA 11 went through state and federal trials. Hekima Ana was the first of the eleven New Africans to be tried on state murder charges. Ana was the Midwest regional vice president of the PGRNA. He and his wife Tamu had been visiting their comrades in Jackson and were to leave for North Carolina on the morning of the FBI/Jackson police raid. The prosecution contended that he fired the shot that was fatal to Skinner. Ana's defense argued that he acted in self-defense against the FBI/Jackson police raid, which did not give the occupants of the PGRNA headquarters adequate time to respond before firing tear gas projectiles and bullets. Ana delivered the opening statement of his defense. Establishing the basis of the self-defense argument, Ana told the jurors,

> August 18, 1971. What happened that day was the kind of thing and situation that would make an innocent person hurt someone in the defense of his own life. The police came to this house in the early hours of the morning, at a time when people are asleep, gave us a few seconds to come out, and after those seconds started shooting into the house . . . [M]y wife and I had just gotten out of bed when this shooting started, and let me say that I was frightened and didn't know what to do.[85]

The jury in Ana's trial was composed of eleven Whites and one African American male. Ana was convicted and sentenced to life. After his trial, Ana stated,

> My entire struggle up to date in Mississippi courts has convinced me and others that the defense in a case where a white police or any white person is involved is no defense at all. To say it another way, the natural right of self-defense is not natural and is not a right in Mississippi and if we are honest with ourselves no place else in the good ole U.S. of A.[86]

Ana's conviction was met by protests from Black activists and human rights supporters throughout the United States.

In separate state trials, Offogga Quddus and Karim Njabafudi were also convicted and sentenced to life for the murder of Skinner. Addis Ababa was sentenced to two concurrent ten-year sentences (of which he served seven years) on charges of assault and battery with intent to shoot a police officer. The Mississippi charge of treason was dropped against Obadele. Murder and assault and battery charges were dropped against Salim, de Mau Mau, Tamu Ana, and Njeri Quddus.[87]

In the federal trial, RNA defendants were faced with a series of charges, including conspiracy to assault federal officers, assault on federal officers, and use of firearms to commit felonies. Charges were ultimately dropped against Tamu Ana after it was proven that she was in Africa when the alleged conspiracy to assault and kill police officers was constructed. The firearms charge was predicated on the prosecution charge that the RNA manipulated a legal semiautomatic rifle to fire as an automatic weapon.

During the trial a federal weapons expert was unable to get a semiautomatic rifle found in the RNA residence to fire as an automatic weapon with the court, defendants, and jury observing. Tamu Ana remembered the FBI expert telling the judge, "Your Honor, I can't make this thang fire automatically to save my life." Despite this failure in the prosecution case and the protests of the defense attorneys, the judge still allowed the firearms charge to stand. On the federal trial, the jury found eight RNA defendants guilty on all counts, and Obadele, Hekima Ana, Offogga Quddus, and Ababa were all sentenced to twelve years. Njeri Quddus received a three-year sentence in the federal prosecution. Nkrumah went underground after being released on his own recognizance in 1971. He was captured years later and received a five-year sentence in the federal case.[88]

The convictions of the PGRNA were understood in the activist Black community as a message that White power in Mississippi would not tolerate Black self-determination or respect Black people's right to defend themselves. After the conviction of Hekima Ana, Delta Ministries director Owen Brooks stated,

> All power is in the hands of the white community, and that power was used to its fullest extent to attempt to destroy the Republic of New Africa. The RNA symbolizes for us the right of the Black community to raise issues of our own determination. . . . Jackson and the state have served notice on the Black community that they will not permit us to protect ourselves and determine the boundaries of our own freedom.[89]

In their capacity as the steering committee of the National Black Political Convention, Gary, Indiana, mayor Richard Hatcher, U.S. congressman Charles Diggs (of Michigan), and activist writer Imamu Amiri Baraka condemned the convictions and called for freedom for the RNA 11. NAACP state field director Emmet C. Burns criticized Blacks who sat on the juries of the RNA 11. One Black sat on Hekima Ana's jury, four on Quddus's, and two on that of Njabafudi. Burns stated that the Blacks on these juries allowed their White counterparts to "do their thinking for them."[90]

Rudy Shields, the RNA, and the End of Black Power in Mississippi

The PGRNA became the national Black Liberation Movement connection Rudy Shields had been seeking. He was one of the staunchest supporters of the PGRNA in Mississippi. Mississippi authorities believed that Shields was a PGRNA worker, and the FBI interrogated Shields about his relationship with the formation. He denied being a member, while stating that he shared their philosophy. Years later, Obadele revealed that Shields was a covert member of the PGRNA. Other PGRNA members in Mississippi confirmed that Shields's relationship with the organization was very close.

Shields was an active participant in PGRNA activities in Mississippi from 1971 to 1975. He attended a PGRNA Legal Conference in New Orleans on February 21, 1971. The purpose of the conference was to propose new legal strategies, including strategies made available by international law, for Black political prisoners, draft resisters, and the Black Liberation Movement. The PGRNA utilized the Jackson Black United Front office Shields rented as its temporary headquarters during Land Celebration in March of 1971. He considered organizing a boycott in Hinds County after the arrests of Kenyatta and other PGRNA workers the week prior to Land Celebration Day. Shields was not in Mississippi during Land Celebration Day in March of 1971 or when the August 18th gun battle occurred. One Yazoo City associate stated that Shields regretted not being in Mississippi to provide the RNA 11 support during and immediately after the FBI/Jackson police raid. He actively sought bail for Obadele and the RNA 11. Without success, he traveled to Yazoo and Humphreys counties soliciting the support networks he had utilized in previous boycott campaigns to acquire funds for bond. The FBI visited potential sponsors after Shields convinced them to financially contribute to the bail of the RNA 11, effectively delaying Obadele's ability to accumulate funds for bail. He was also present at the hearings and trials of the RNA 11. State officials feared that Shields and other Black Power militants would disrupt the proceedings.[91]

Shields also attempted to convince the PGRNA to move its headquarters to Yazoo County. He also made an inquiry with Yazoo Black farmers about acquiring land for the PGRNA after the deal with Mason was nullified. The PGRNA delivered copies of their newspaper, The New African, to Shields in Yazoo City. Rudy Shields was also an organizer of the International African Prisoner of War (APOW) Solidarity Day in Jackson in 1973. APOW Solidarity Day was an effort to support the RNA 11 and other Black Liberation Movement political prisoners in the United States, including the Wilmington Ten, H. Rap Brown, Muhammad Ahmad (aka Max Stanford), and several captured Black Liberation Army members. Federal, state, and local officials attempted to prevent APOW Solidarity events from occurring.[92]

Jackson City council and police would not approve a request by APOW Solidarity Day organizers for a parade permit. The permit was denied on the basis that PGRNA workers would participate in the parade. Jackson mayor Russell Davis argued that this type of assembly had the potential for disorder. The Jackson mayor stated,

> [T]his is a case where there is evidence that groups of people throughout the United States, including the [Black] Panthers and the SDS are being encouraged to come to Jackson. . . . It's entirely possible that this proposal would put a burden on public safety . . . that would exceed our capability.

Legal counsel for the Solidarity Day organizers, Lewis Myers, argued that the failure to issue a permit violated the "constitutional right to free assembly." Myers's efforts to seek an injunction against the city of Jackson could not be obtained prior to APOW Solidarity Day. Shields was also unsuccessful in obtaining a Yazoo City church for the APOW Solidarity Spiritual Rally. The APOW Solidarity Day committee was able to hold workshops, spiritual and cultural rallies, and a jazz concert at locations in Jackson. In spite of obstacles, the APOW Solidarity Day mobilized three thousand participants, the largest turnout for an activist event in Mississippi during the Black Power Movement. APOW Solidarity Day featured a significant array of the Black Power Movement personalities. Owusu Sadaukai (Howard Fuller) of the African Liberation Support Committee, Safiya Bukari (Bernice Jones) of the Black Panther Party (*Right On* faction), Reverend Ben Chavis of the Wilmington Ten, Nelson Johnson of the Youth Organization for Black Unity, Imamu Sukumu and Amiri Baraka of the Congress of African People, Charles Koen of the Cairo Black United Front, as well as Africana Studies Professor James Turner of Cornell University were featured speakers at the APOW Solidarity events. Shields served as master of ceremonies for the Spiritual Rally at a Jackson church on March 30th. Obadele was released on twenty-five thousand dollars bond after the APOW Solidarity events were over.[93]

Shields was vocal about his support for the PGRNA and Obadele and the RNA 11. He openly expressed his solidarity with the PGRNA in an interview with FBI agents on March 29, 1973. The FBI contacted Shields on several occasions, and the activist consented to an interview. Shields told the agents that while he disagreed with the tactics of the PGRNA, "he did believe in the philosophy of RNA and would assist the RNA in all of their activities." The veteran activist also stated that while he would not "resist arrest or encourage violence," he believed that the PGRNA and other Black Power militants "had a right to defend themselves against unfair attacks by authorities." He also began to support African Liberation Movements in Angola, Mozambique, and Guinea Bissau and identified with the growing Pan-Africanist trend in the Black Power Movement.[94]

Shields became disenchanted with the PGRNA by 1974. He continued to attend activities through January but was not as active. PGRNA activity declined in Mississippi after the 1973 APOW Solidarity Day. The RNA 11 ordeal and arrests, along with harassment of other members and supporters, seriously compromised the formation's effectiveness and capacity in Jackson. The FBI and state and local governments instituted an effective counterinsurgency campaign against the PGRNA, incorporating media disinformation, infiltration, and violent terror to isolate and decisively attack the organization's efficacy. Most of the human and material resources of the PGRNA were concentrated on the legal defense of its incarcerated members. Recruitment declined to a small number of the most militant Mississippi Blacks. The repression of the PGRNA even terrorized some militant elements away from associating with New African nationalism in a meaningful way. The intense ideological and violent repression of the organization prevented the formation from becoming a significant radical alternative for Black Power in the state.

Shields's health also declined as the PGRNA's effectiveness and capacity to organize in Mississippi decreased. The veteran activist began to suffer from a brain tumor that affected his ability to walk and speak clearly. Shields's spirit also waned after he was defeated in a 1974 election campaign for alderman in Yazoo City. He was disappointed in the Black voter turnout in the election. Shields began to move away from more militant tactics and thought that African Americans "in the South should pursue their objectives through the courts and the election of blacks to positions." He remained politically active in Yazoo County electoral campaigns and a small contingent of young Blacks continued providing protection for the elder organizer.[95]

Shields's changing perspective reflected the waning of the Black Power Movement in the mid-1970s, which represented the decline of this Movement in Mississippi. Some considered it an impossibility to have a successful Black Liberation Movement in the United States. Shields even considered the possibility of relocating to Africa.[96] While the efforts of the PGRNA and other revolutionary Black Power nationalists were defeated, the Mississippi Black Freedom Struggle and the use of armed resistance in that Struggle were not finished.

8

"No Longer Afraid"

The United League, Activist Litigation, Armed Self-Defense, and Insurgent Resilience in Northern Mississippi

Skip Robinson had just been released from jail, having been arrested on Election Day for disorderly conduct. All the Movement folk thought Skip had been arrested to destabilize the United League's electoral efforts. I was standing next to him when his primary security person came down the stairs of the Legal Services Office. The young bodyguard said he needed to go home and check on his family. He wanted Skip to come upstairs so he could give Skip his .357 Magnum. Standing on the north side of the main square of the city of Holly Springs, Skip said, "Give it to me right here. I want them [the White supremacists] to know I have a gun!" The young man hesitantly passed Skip the .357 right there on the street.[1]

The 1970s saw a resurgence of Ku Klux Klan and other White supremacist activity in the South and throughout the United States. The Anti-Defamation League of the B'nai B'rith identified the late 1970s as a "minor renaissance" for the Klan, which "almost tripled its national membership" in the decade of the 1970s. Klan leader David Duke received eleven thousand votes, one-third of the electorate, in a state senate race in Baton Rouge, Louisiana, in 1975. This demonstrated the continued base of White supremacy in some White communities during the decade. A contingent of seventy-five White supremacists, including Klansmen and Neo-Nazis, violently attacked an anti-Klan protest organized by the Community Workers Party in Greensboro, North Carolina, on November 3, 1979. The White supremacist raid left five anti-Klan activists dead and eleven wounded. Although the incident was videotaped, an all-White jury acquitted all six of the only members of the contingent who were prosecuted in a criminal proceeding.[2]

Local chapters of the NAACP in the state of Mississippi were seriously compromised by a legal offensive from White merchants in Port Gibson.

Tupelo armed KKK demonstration, 1978. An upsurge of Klan activity occurred in the late 1970s. (Courtesy of Jim Alexander.)

In 1969, the Mississippi legislature passed an antiboycott bill making it il-legal to conspire to "prevent a citizen from exercising a 'lawful trade.'" Port Gibson's White merchants filed a lawsuit for loss of income after a 1969 boycott and won a series of victories in state and federal appellate courts. A Mississippi state judge ruled in favor of Claiborne County merchants in 1976, ordering the state NAACP to pay $1.5 million for a "secondary boycott." The Claiborne County merchants argued that Black activists maliciously disrupted their enterprises through instituting economic co-ercion against them, while their grievances were with the municipal (not commercial) authorities. Consumer boycotts had served as the primary weapon used to fight for civil and human rights and empowerment for Black Mississippians after 1964, so the legal victories of the Port Gibson White commercial community placed the Mississippi NAACP activists on the defensive and crippled the national organization financially. The national office of the NAACP ordered its affiliates in Mississippi "not to engage in any kind of economic pressure" that could be considered in vio-lation of the court order.[3]

The radical trend of the Black Power Movement had also been serious neutralized by the middle of the 1970s. The effects of internal dissension and political repression greatly weakened the Black Liberation Movement. FBI counterinsurgency campaigns against SNCC, the Black Panther Party, RAM, and the PGRNA resulted in hundreds of political prisoners and exiles and significantly decreased the human and material resources available to sustain insurgent Movement activity. In spite of these compromises, Black activism continued in what Black Liberation Movement participants labeled a "lull" period. Historians Sundiata Cha-Jua and Clarence Lang characterized this time as "a moment of retreat, reconceptualization and regrouping."[4]

A dynamic Black social movement emerged in northern Mississippi, serving as a challenge to local White power structures and as an inspiration to Black-liberation, radical, and progressive forces around the United States. Originating in predominantly Black Marshall County, the United League utilized previous traditions of the Mississippi Black Freedom Struggle, including economic boycotts, armed self-defense, aggressive litigation, and bold rhetoric, to serve as the organizational vehicle for Black insurgency in northern Mississippi and other regions of the state in the middle to late 1970s. The United League also projected a visible and confrontational Black response to the Klan and open White supremacy in northern Mississippi.

Marshall County and the Black Social Movement

Black-majority Marshall County was a center of the Mississippi Black Freedom Struggle years before the United League emerged as a dynamic organizational vehicle. In 1970, African Americans comprised 62 percent of its population of 24,027. Marshall had possessed a large Black majority ever since slavery times, when the county had the fourth-largest population of enslaved persons of African descent in the state of Mississippi. The county seat, Holly Springs, also possessed a Black majority. The Black majorities in Holly Springs and Marshall County were subject to White minority rule, consistent with the general status of predominantly African American jurisdictions in the state.[5]

Civil rights activity intensified in Marshall County in the early 1960s. Activist faculty and students at Rust College spearheaded much of the early activism. Rust was a four-year, historically Black college located in Holly Springs. Faculty member S. T. Nero was in the center of the leadership of Mississippi's and Marshall County's Civil Rights Movement. Nero served as a board member of the Regional Council of Negro Leadership in its last days. He was also Marshall County's NAACP president. Nero and his colleagues focused on voter registration efforts. Students at Rust engaged in sit-ins and desegregation efforts targeting three local drug stores in 1962.[6]

Marshall County became the center of COFO activity in northern Mississippi during Freedom Summer. The Holly Springs Movement was organized by COFO and SNCC activists for the purpose of coordinating activity throughout northern Mississippi. A voter registration effort, freedom schools, and the Freedom Democratic Party were organized under the leadership of SNCC activists Ivanhoe Donaldson (the project director), Cleveland Sellers, and Hardy Frye. Faculty and students from Rust College provided workers and supporters for the campaign.[7]

While Marshall County had the reputation for being racially moderate, Black disenfranchisement, apartheid segregation, police harassment, and White supremacist violence were institutionalized much as they were in other Black-majority counties in Mississippi. In 1965, FDP activists organized a petition campaign against Holly Springs mayor Sam Coopwood for the purpose of demanding basic civil rights for the Black citizens of Holly Springs. The preamble of the petition stated,

> A small minority of whites has for a hundred years been able to maintain a ruthless system of social, economic, and physical tyranny and exploitation over Holly Springs. We shall no longer submit to this system. We have waited long enough for the freedom that has been due us since 1776. . . . We want the city to have an atmosphere of respect for the human dignity of every last one of its citizens, black and white.

The demands of the petition called for the "immediate and full integration" and "upgrading" of Holly Springs public schools; desegregation of "tax-supported public facilities . . . including three federally-supported housing projects" and "restaurants and service station washrooms"; the removal of "'White' and 'Colored' signs" at restrooms in the county courthouse; and the construction of a biracial committee "of concern to establish a frank, open, and permanent dialogue between the white and Negro citizens of Holly Springs." The petition also called on the city administration to condemn the acts of violence by state troopers on a civil rights demonstration in Selma, Alabama.[8]

Birth of the United League of Marshall County

Two of the local activists who were drawn into the COFO and FDP activity in the county were Henry Boyd Jr. and Alfred "Skip" Robinson, both of whom emerged as leaders of the local Movement in the late 1960s. Boyd had participated in Movement activity as a college student at Rust College in the early 1960s. Like his parents, he worked in the Holly Springs public schools immediately after graduating from Rust in 1962. Robinson was a local brick mason and contractor from Red Banks, a small Marshall County farming community. Robinson joined the Movement in 1960 after he met Medgar Evers in Jackson. Both Boyd and Robinson participated in the local Movement under the general leadership of elders in their community. Robinson's home in rural Marshall County was firebombed in 1965. He believed his home was bombed by White supremacists due to his political activity. Boyd and Robinson both participated in the local NAACP, the FDP, and the Marshall County Citizens for Progress, which was headed by local minister A. G. Pegues. Both Robinson and Boyd were active members of the Citizens for Progress, which organized a boycott of downtown Holly Springs in 1966.[9]

Robinson and Boyd were recognized as the central organizers in Marshall County by 1967, as S. T. Nero, Pegues, and other elder activists "passed the torch" to younger, more militant Movement advocates. Robinson and Boyd sought to unite the various human rights formations in the county, including the NAACP, the FDP, and Citizens for Progress. Unlike the FDP or the NAACP, the Citizens for Progress organization was not a local affiliate of a state or national group. Citizens for Progress was renamed the United League of Marshall County. All the county's local civil rights groupings were united under the umbrella of the United League (UL). Robinson served as the UL president and Boyd as the executive secretary; they coordinated Marshall County Civil Rights Movement activity in the UL headquarters in Holly Springs.

The UL developed as a mass membership organization, with membership dues of one dollar per year. The county was divided into five districts, each with its own chairperson, secretary, and treasurer. The district leadership was responsible for recruitment and mobilization in its area. In 1969, the United League organized its first boycott in Holly Springs around the desegregation of the city's public schools and the maintenance of Black teaching and administrative positions in the transition.[10]

United League president Skip Robinson speaking at a 1978 rally in Tupelo, Mississippi. (Courtesy of Jim Alexander.)

Robinson and Boyd participated in state and national politics. They remained active in the MFDP and were involved in the attempt to resurrect the MFDP in 1969 to unite the "poor of the state." Robinson and Boyd were a part of a 25-person policymaking committee, along with activists Fannie Lou Hamer, E. W. Steptoe, Robert Clark, Annie Devine, and Unita Blackwell. The same year, they both attended the historic Black Economic Development Conference in Detroit. In 1970, the United League distributed food, clothing, and medicine to Marshall's indigent populations through a relationship established with the Black Economic Union (BEU). The BEU was an organization of Black athletes spearheaded by the Cleveland Browns' Hall of Fame running back and activist Jim Brown. Brown's BEU campaigned around the United States to supply material support to working and poor Blacks in Mississippi. The BEU campaign found a receptive audience with city officials and the academic community in Boulder, Colorado. The BEU served as a liaison among the city of Boulder, the University of Colorado, and the United League. Philanthropic efforts in Boulder mobilized money and "four truckloads of food and clothing" to the United League for distribution to Holly Springs residents. Marshall County's and Mississippi's White power structure were concerned with the image of the county and the state projected by the campaign. Governor John Bell Williams, Holly Springs mayor Sam Coopwood, and other state and local officials visited Boulder to convince its officials that there were no "starving people" in Holly Springs. They argued that the erroneous picture created of the city had harmed its commercial progress. Coopwood identified Jim Brown and the UL as being responsible for "false propaganda." City, county, and state officials also believed the League utilized the aid to build its membership. Sovereignty Commission officials investigated whether Marshall County Blacks were required to have UL membership cards in order to receive aid.[11]

Another important relationship for the development and success of the United League of Marshall County was that between the organization and Northern Mississippi Rural Legal Services (NMRLS). NMRLS originated as Lafayette County Legal Services (LCLS) based on the campus of the University of Mississippi (Ole Miss) in Oxford. The program was initiated by faculty of Ole Miss Law School in 1966. It was funded through the Legal Services Corporation, a wing of the federal Office of Economic Opportunity. Robinson and Boyd established a relationship with the institution from its inception as members of the community advisory board. A branch of the organization was established in Holly Springs in 1967. LCLS was forced to leave the Ole Miss campus when it became involved in activist litigation, particularly advocacy for desegregation of Marshall County schools. The organization took on the title of "North Mississippi Rural Legal Services" after moving its headquarters to the campus of Mary Holmes in West Point in 1968. Robinson became chairman of the NMRLS board in 1970. That same year Boyd was hired as the assistant director of the NMRLS office in Holly Springs. The United League would benefit from the relationship with NMRLS, as NMRLS lawyers provided essential litigation for the organization, including providing defense in criminal and civil action as well as filing injunctions against government officials attempting to violate the United League's constitutional rights. NMRLS attorney Lewis Myers became one of the United League's principal spokespersons. A graduate of Rutgers Law School, Myers had participated in the Mississippi Black Freedom Struggle during his summers as a law student. Myers and other NMRLS members were active participants in the National Conference of Black Lawyers (NCBL), which was formed in 1968 to serve as the "legal arm of the movement for Black Liberation." The UL routinely utilized NMRLS office space and equipment. NMRLS also served as a place of employment for UL members. This relationship was a critical resource for the UL's activism.[12]

United League (UL) fe-
male supporter wearing
UL t-shirt at 1978 rally in
Tupelo, Mississippi. (Courtesy of Jim Alexander.)

Robinson emerged as a charismatic spokesperson for African American resistance in Mississippi. His bold rhetoric was inspirational to Black
youth and working people. Robinson did not conceal the fact that he and
the United League were armed and willing to shoot. He proved his resis-
tant nature on one occasion in Holly Springs. In 1974, a local Movement
activist, Bernice Totten, was the first Black to be elected to the Marshall
County Board of Supervisors. The United League was actively involved in
Totten's campaign. A small group of young White supremacists assembled
near the United League office after the election. As Robinson, Boyd, and
other UL members were leaving their office, one of the members of the
mob opened fire on them. Robinson returned fire, dispersing the mob.
Robinson remembered this event in a 1980 interview:

> We was ambushed when we came out of the office in Holly Springs. There
> were six Klans standing across the street and when four of us came down

the stairs they started shooting. I jumped over my brother's car and got my gun out of the briefcase. When I started shooting, they took off and one of them dropped his rifle. I was hit in the leg, but not bad. The bullet just glanced off my leg.[13]

Henry Boyd, also remembering that day, stated, "Skip had a .45 . . . and it was loud too. When he fired that gun, them white boys cleared the scene." Boyd and other UL members got into a vehicle and pursued the White supremacists who had fired on them. The UL contingent caught the fleeing vehicle with the White supremacists and made a "citizen's arrest." Remembering that day, Boyd recalled,

> We got in our car and caught the man that did the shooting. It was the chief of police son. And we caught him and put a gun on him and made an arrest and took the gun from him, the gun he had. We caught ourselves . . . that's the way we protected ourselves.[14]

While local police were aware of and near the scene of this incident, no arrests were made. Local media also ignored the shootout and the apprehension of the White supremacists, including the son of the Holly Springs police chief. The chief's son left the county, and the Klan was no longer visible in Marshall County after this incident.[15] Robinson's stature rose to legendary heights in Marshall County and other African American communities in northern Mississippi after he proved himself able to scatter the Klan in downtown Holly Springs.

Boycott in Byhalia

The United League gained national and regional attention after the boycott it initiated in the northern Mississippi town of Byhalia in 1974. Byhalia was a small Marshall County town of 750 people. It was 70 percent African American, but its mayor, its municipal leadership, and all of its merchants were White. Journalist and UL member Joseph Delaney said that the UL campaign in Byhalia was the organization's "first intensive protest effort." The campaign was sparked after 21-year-old Black laborer Butler Young was shot by a White police officer on June 28, 1974. Young was arrested by two Byhalia police officers for an alleged hit-and-run driving incident and was placed in the back seat of the police vehicle. The officers were also accompanied by a Black deputy sheriff from neighboring De Soto County. Young never made it to lockup. The three police officers claimed that on the way to jail, Young escaped from the back of the police vehicle (which had no handles on the doors or windows) and died of a broken neck as he ran into a fence.[16]

The United League engaged in demonstrations to demand an investigation of Young's death. The death of Young also served as a catalyst for the United League to invite young Blacks in the county to join the organization. By 1974, the UL leadership claimed that it possessed a membership of four thousand Black citizens of Marshall County. Osborne Bell, a Marshall County coroner, determined that Young's death was due to a wound caused by a gunshot from a police officer's weapon "at close range"; there was no evidence of a broken neck. Bell's investigation revealed that Byhalia police officer Morris Hanna fired the fatal shot that killed Young. Both officers were suspended and ultimately Hanna was charged with manslaughter, after an all-White county grand jury ruled Young's death a "tragic accident." Outrage emanated from Byhalia's African American community as a result of Hanna not being charged with the premeditated murder of Young. UL began a boycott of Byhalia's White businesses on July 10, 1974. The UL boycott not only called for Hanna and his colleagues to be indicted for murder but also included demands for representation of Blacks on the town's Board of Aldermen, Marshall County's Board of Supervisors, and the public utility company; further development of the local sewage system; hiring of Black police officers on the municipal force and in the town's private sector; and pursuit of efforts to bring a physician to Byhalia.[17]

The United League boycott initiated a legal response on behalf of Byhalia merchants and the Marshall County District Attorney's Office. The Marshall County district attorney, Tallmadge Littlejohn, filed an injunction in state court to prevent the UL from organizing a boycott. A Marshall County judge ruled in favor of Littlejohn's injunction on September 6, 1974. The same evening, a Byhalia store caught fire and burned to the ground. Local officials suspected that UL recruit and Vietnam War veteran Sandy Ealy was responsible for the store burning but could not prove it. Ealy had been a demolitions expert in the United State Army.[18] NMRLS attorney Lewis Myers began to work with the UL in response to its need for litigation as a result of an injunction by Littlejohn and the Byhalia merchants. Myers and other NMRLS lawyers challenged Littlejohn's injunction, ultimately receiving a federal court order allowing the UL to "engage in peaceful protest and boycotts." The Fifth Circuit Court of Appeals also ruled against a suit brought by Byhalia White merchants that called for an injunction against the United League boycott.[19]

Marshall County prosecutors also reconstituted the same grand jury impaneled to investigate Young's death to focus on the activities of the UL. Prosecutors presented a UL leaflet to a Marshall County judge to justify the grand jury investigation. The leaflet argued that the murder of Young was motivated by racism and condemned the grand jury investigation of his death as a "farce." The leaflet also proclaimed that Littlejohn was "acting as defense attorney for the officers rather than as prosecutor" in the grand jury investigation of Young's death. On September 6, 1974, the grand jury ordered that the court subpoena UL leadership and organizational records and minutes. Guided by local prosecutors, a Marshall County grand jury ordered United League leaders to appear at the county courthouse on September 7th. This session was highly unusual since it was being held on a Saturday. The UL had planned a demonstration for the same day as the hearing. The demonstration went on as planned, despite the fact that UL leadership were all in court that morning. The noise emanating from hundreds of demonstrators caused a Marshall County judge to postpone the hearing for one day.

When the hearings continued, the UL leadership decided to resist the order to provide the grand jury with information, as the activists perceived the order to be part of a counterinsurgency campaign to destroy the organization. UL secretary Boyd refused to present UL documents, and Boyd, Robinson, and other UL leaders were held for contempt of court. The NMRLS lawyers filed an injunction arguing that the grand jury investigation was in violation of the organization's First Amendment rights. The UL lawyers were ultimately successful in thwarting the grand jury subpoenas through litigation charging Marshall County prosecutors with violating First Amendment rights to assembly and free speech through its grand jury investigation.[20]

After the United League's organized campaign extended eight months, national media declared that the Byhalia boycott was "nearly 100 percent effective." Six downtown entrepreneurs claimed bankrupt status by March of 1975. Sales at Byhalia's Carrington Market declined from thirty thousand dollars a month to six thousand dollars. *Time* magazine reported that business in Byhalia had experienced a 75 percent decline due to the boycott. UL secretary Henry Boyd proclaimed, "The town just died. . . . Every store in town shut down."[21]

The Byhalia campaign relied on the tradition of boycotts that had been established in the state since Natchez in 1965. An aggressive team of enforcers was an essential part of the formula. Young, "street"-oriented Black males would be employed as boycott enforcers, as was the case with the Black consumer vigilance campaigns organized by Rudy Shields. Henry Boyd offered, "We did have some thuggish folks with us, who didn't mind whipping somebody." NMRLS lawyer and UL spokesperson Lewis Myers and the organization's vice president, Howard Gunn, and other UL members had previously worked with Rudy Shields on consumer boycotts. Gunn later acknowledged that Shields "laid the foundation. He mapped out strategy by which we could go by and have a successful boycott." The United League believed that the White power structure encouraged some Blacks to shop in downtown Byhalia to break the boycott, and the UL enforcers determined to make examples of Blacks who attempted to break the boycott. Boyd recalled, "Some of these thugs would whip these Toms real good." On one particular occasion, the media helped to communicate the United League message not to shop downtown. Boyd reiterated, "[T]hey [the White power structure] sent one of the Toms in there and they [UL enforcers] whooped him real good. The camera people there showed him getting a whooping. And from that day on we didn't have no trouble with people coming to town."[22] The UL was aware of the suits of Port Gibson merchants versus the NAACP, which was incorporated with the federal government, but since the UL was not an incorporated organization, it was difficult to target for litigation by local merchants in state and local courts.

Armed self-defense was an essential part of the United League's organizing. The United League assumed a posture of being prepared to respond to White supremacist violence with armed resistance. Robinson stated that when a UL chapter was formed in Byhalia in 1974, local residents "took their guns . . . and we laid it out to them. We told them that if any more people were killed, it would be a life for a life. We said the last Black had been killed in Byhalia."

Snipers shot at UL leaders. The United League increased its security organization and presence in response to the heightened threat level. Robinson was always armed and routinely assigned a personal security team. The UL provided Robinson with a team of five bodyguards who traveled with him and focused on his safety. NMRLS lawyer and UL spokesperson Lewis Myers also received individual protection.[23]

The United League also established a communication network utilizing citizens band radios. The communication network would enable a team of armed members to respond if there was an attack. The UL also had covert armed security at rallies and demonstrations. Henry Boyd stated, "We would always have security. . . . [I]f someone came in shooting we were going to have defense for that." The United League was not conciliatory about its practice of armed protection. Boyd proclaimed, "'through any means.' That was our motto."[24]

The United League was also confronted with challenges from federal officials. The League did not see the federal government as reliable allies in their fight in Marshall County. UL believed that U.S. senator James Eastland of the Senate Judiciary Committee utilized his influence to break the boycott. Department of Justice officials failed to take Byhalia police officers to federal grand jury in spite of the FBI uncovering evidence of police misconduct. The Community Relations Service (CRS) of the Department of Justice was dispatched to Marshall County to manage the conflict. CRS officials claimed that the UL was intimidating "elderly citizens" of Byhalia in enforcing the consumer boycott. The UL viewed the CRS as the "domestic intelligence branch of the Justice Department" engaging in a counterinsurgency campaign against them.[25] NMRLS lawyers filed a suit on behalf of Skip Robinson that was successful in forcing the CRS to leave Byhalia.[26]

The Byhalia boycott proved the UL's effectiveness in coordinating an insurgent campaign that utilized consumer vigilance, mass demonstrations, armed self-defense, and activist litigation. The UL was not able to force the Byhalia municipal government to fire the officers involved in Young's death, but several concessions were won on behalf of the African American community due to the UL boycott. These included the hiring of Black police officers in the Byhalia police department and Black cashiers in the Byhalia central business district, as well as school desegregation. Litigation filed by NMRLS lawyers was effective in countering obstacles that the UL leadership saw as being presented by local, state, and federal governments. Young's mother also won a settlement as the result of a wrongful death suit filed against the city of Byhalia submitted by UL-affiliated attorneys. The UL also won a concession from Marshall County with the hiring of an African American sheriff's deputy. Robinson selected a UL member, Robert Lay, to take this position, and Lay's presence within the sheriff's department became a vital asset for UL security. Robinson received daily death threats, which Robinson and Boyd reported to the police, but the information they provided was often not investigated or responded to by local police. Sympathetic White coworkers informed Lay about potential threats to Robinson and other UL leaders, and additional protection was placed around Robinson and Boyd based on the information provided by Lay.[27]

The United League boycott in Byhalia was ultimately perceived as successful by Blacks locally and in the region. Myers summed up the significance of the Byhalia campaign, stating,

> Byhalia put them [the UL] "on the map." . . . Cause out of Byhalia came national press coverage. And out of the national press coverage . . . the whole UL phenomenon came into public awareness and consciousness all over the state of Mississippi because Byhalia was a national news story. . . . Byhalia gave them national and statewide attention.[28]

The Byhalia campaign proved to be the most dynamic campaign in the state since the Rudy Shields–organized boycotts of the middle 1960s and early 1970s. Byhalia provided the momentum necessary to break the malaise in the Mississippi Freedom Struggle that had been in place since the legal victories of the Port Gibson merchants versus the NAACP. Unlike the NAACP, the UL was an "unincorporated body that ha[d] no legal organizational base." Robinson offered, "If you sue the United League, there ain't nobody going to get nothing, 'cause ain't nobody in it got nothing." The UL also included specific demands for the private sector to circumvent the charges of a secondary boycott. The UL would replace the NAACP as the organizational vehicle for local militant Blacks in Mississippi in the late 1970s.[29]

The Tupelo Boycott and United League Confrontation with the KKK

The success of the United League in Marshall County in general and Byhalia in particular resulted in a demand for its leadership in African American communities in Mississippi. The UL's activist attorneys, its organizing and mobilization experience, as well as its possession of the firepower to counter White supremacist violence appealed to Black activists in other northern Mississippi communities, who began to attend United League meetings in Holly Springs and to request assistance in their communities. This generally began the process of the United League spreading from Marshall County to other jurisdictions. Robinson stated, "I never just go someplace. I wait until someone calls me with a problem." Another UL member, George Williams, added, "Usually one or two people contact Skip when they have a problem. . . . And usually every town in Mississippi has the same problems—police brutality, the Klan, thefts of Black-owned land." Skip Robinson and a team of organizers would travel to the local community and work with local activists to build a United League chapter.[30]

The city of Tupelo was one of the cities where the United League was invited to come and organize. Robinson and the United League were invited to Tupelo after an angry response from the Black community in the city sparked by the brutal treatment of a Black prisoner by White police officers. Tupelo's inhabitants numbered twenty-one thousand in 1978, with only 21 percent of its residents being African American. Known as the birthplace of popular music star Elvis Presley, the northeast Mississippi urban center boasted the largest population in that part of the state. Tupelo was the county seat of rural Lee County, named after Confederate general Robert E. Lee. Lee County did not experience the activism that characterized other parts of the state like the Delta, McComb, Hattiesburg, Jackson, or southwest Mississippi in the 1960s.[31]

The incident that sparked the increase of UL activity in Tupelo was the assault on a Black male by White Tupelo police officers. The officers implicated were Dale Cruber and Roy Sandifer, captains of Tupelo's detective division of the city police department. Cruber, Sandifer, and other officers beat Eugene Pasto of Memphis in the Tupelo jail in March of 1976. Pasto had been arrested on a check forgery charge after driving through Tupelo with a White woman in his vehicle. Pasto unsuccessfully pursued a criminal investigation against Cruber and Sandifer with the Tupelo police department and the FBI. Pasto ultimately sued the Tupelo police department and the officers in federal court. NMRLS attorney Kenneth Mayfield represented Pasto in the federal lawsuit. Pasto asserted that Cruber, Sandifer, and other Tupelo officers beat him while he was in custody and coerced him to sign a confession that he had forged checks. Photographs exhibiting Pasto with "a severely damaged right eye" before Tupelo police turned him in to the county jail served as key evidence in proving the officers' abuse. On January 25, 1978, federal district judge Orma Smith overturned Pasto's conviction and ordered that Cruber and Sandifer pay twenty-five hundred dollars to Pasto for the abuse and violations of his rights.[32]

Black community activism increased after Judge Smith's ruling. Tupelo's lone African American alderman, Boyce Grayson, attempted without success to secure sanctions against the officers from his colleagues on the Board of Aldermen. The Board of Aldermen did agree to a two-week suspension after a large turnout from the Black community demanding the officers' dismissal at the February 7th board meeting. Black community leaders also called for a biracial committee to review civilian complaints of police brutality. The city administration and the Tupelo police chief, Ed Crider, tried to resolve the issue by demoting Cruber and Sandifer from the rank of captain to lieutenant and forming a "biracial committee of police officers to study future complaints." Crider also transferred Cruber to arsons investigations and Sandifer to the crime laboratory.[33]

Black leaders were not satisfied with the Tupelo White power structure's proposal to resolve the police abuse of Pasto. Tupelo alderman Grayson was skeptical of the demotions of Cruber and Sandifer. Grayson stated, "All the chief gave is his word on what the men will be doing. I'm not too trustworthy of his word." The NAACP and the UL were in agreement on the demands to fire the officers and form a biracial committee, but differed on tactics. Lee County NAACP president John Thomas Morris called for Tupelo to be denied federal funds if the officers were not fired. Morris stated, "If you hit a man's billfold he'll listen better." Lee County UL chairman Walter Stanfield called for demonstrations to protest the city's response to the uncovered police brutality. Morris and local NAACP leaders preferred negotiations with Tupelo's White power structure as opposed to demonstrations. In response to Black protests, the city administration offered to transfer Cruber and Sandifer to the fire department. Activists still pursued the officers being fired.[34]

Hundreds of Blacks participated in a demonstration—organized by Robinson, Stanfield, and the UL—on March 11th in Tupelo. The UL demanded that Cruber and Sandifer be dismissed from the Tupelo police department and their positions filled by Black officers. The UL also demanded that Cruber and Sandifer not be transferred to any other unit of municipal government. Stanfield stated that the firing of the two White police officers was a nonnegotiable demand. The march started with about three hundred protesters, but hundreds of local Blacks joined during the demonstration. A surprised police officer was overheard saying, "Look at them all come out."

Demonstrators beckoned to Black onlookers, "Come on in. . . . It may be your head next week." Robinson argued that this initial Tupelo march would encourage more participation, saying, "People are still scared, conditioned not to protest." The UL president predicted, "Now that they see this, we'll have twice as many people." Black prisoners of the Lee County jail shouted out, "We're with you," as the march passed the facility. Robinson publicly expressed disagreement with the Tupelo NAACP's preference for negotiation as opposed to demonstrations. Robinson criticized local NAACP president John Morris, predicting, "He's going to find out you cannot negotiate with the White man without a base of strength."

Morris did not participate in the march but attended the culminating rally at the courthouse steps. The Lee County NAACP president indicated that he would join subsequent protests if Cruber and Sandifer were not fired. No confrontations occurred during the march with police or local Whites. Robinson argued, "You can only get Black folks together through a crisis. . . . This will be the day when the merchants downtown know we mean business." Demonstrators assembled at a local church after a two-hour demonstration to discuss further actions. The meeting produced a list of demands, including bringing the employment of Lee's African American population in accordance with their numbers in the county and the establishment of a civilian review board, with the UL selecting two members of the body. The UL demanded that Blacks receive 30 percent of the jobs downtown, arguing that Blacks constituted 30 percent of Tupelo's population. The city administration and merchants challenged the UL's estimate, citing U.S. census figures of a 21 percent African American population. Robinson called for a second march and boycott of White-owned businesses in Tupelo.[35]

The UL marched again on March 18th. As Robinson predicted, the number of marchers doubled from the previous week. Morris did not join the march and continued negotiation with city administrators, but publicly the local NAACP and the UL denied any dissension between the two organizations. In spite of Stanfield being invited to participate in the negotiations, the UL declared that it would not attend negotiations with city government and called for dialogue with representatives from the local White commercial leadership and municipal government. UL spokespersons said they would call for a boycott of Tupelo if their demands were not met. The Tupelo Board of Aldermen issued a policy statement identifying "outside interference" and "efforts of outsiders" as the factors intended to "destroy . . . good race relations and to divide the city." The lone African American Tupelo alderman, Boyce Grayson, refused to join his colleagues in endorsing the statement, which was clearly intended to isolate Robinson and the militant UL forces from Marshall County in Tupelo. Robinson and his comrades were labeled outside agitators, though a local UL chapter had been formed with its own local leadership.[36]

The Tupelo Board of Aldermen and moderate local Black leaders announced an agreement on March 23rd. The accords stated that Cruber and

Sandifer would be dismissed as officers in the police department and receive new assignment in the city government. Cruber was assigned a position as an arson investigator in the fire department and Sandifer to the position of crime lab technician in the police department. The settlement also called for the suspension of a third march by the UL. UL organizers responded immediately. On the same evening as the announcement of the agreement, the UL leadership, speaking before a mass rally of three hundred at a local community center, denounced the agreement and announced their intentions to conduct the march. Over 350 Blacks marched and held a rally on the Lee County courthouse the next day, which was also Good Friday. That specific day was targeted by the UL to initiate the boycott since Blacks "do a lot of buying that day." The UL announced the initiation of the Tupelo economic boycott and Robinson pledged to continue the demonstrations until Cruber and Sandifer were no longer employees of municipal government. Over 125 Black citizens participated in pickets that were established at White-owned businesses and city hall after the demonstration and rally on Easter weekend. The UL planned to picket daily until demands were met.[37]

UL popularity and membership rapidly increased in Tupelo and Lee County. A significant portion of Tupelo's working-class and poor Black community identified with the bold action, rhetoric, and economic demands of Robinson and the UL. Tupelo had experienced an economic boom since the 1950s, and Lee County possessed the third-highest concentration of industrial jobs in the state of Mississippi. However, only a small percentage of African Americans in Tupelo benefited from the gains of the period. In 1978, Black unemployment was 7.8 percent (as compared to 4.5 for Whites), and Black median family income was $4,365 (as compared to $7,706 for Whites). A 1978 *Washington Post* article described the landscape of Tupelo's poor African American community as "shanties and the heavily littered, fly-infested housing project." The UL's articulation of economic demands for Black employment resonated with Tupelo's Black low-income and working-poor community. The grassroots and militant UL filled a vacuum of leadership for the majority of Lee County's Blacks, whom the middle-class African American leaders and local organizations had long abandoned. Working-class and poor Blacks constituted the bulk of the local participants in UL demonstrations and new recruits in its local chapter. The UL claimed that its Lee County membership increased from one hundred to twelve hundred within two months. One journalist observed that the UL "virtually dethroned the town's traditional Black leadership."[38]

White reaction to the rise in Black protests intensified in Tupelo. Threats against the UL leaders increased due to their activism in Tupelo. UL attorney and spokesperson Lewis Myers stated that "a lot of threats have been coming in." At the request of Myers, federal observers came to observe the protests and consumer boycott in Tupelo. Grand Dragon Douglass Coen of the Mississippi Invisible Empire of the Ku Klux Klan announced a "counter demonstration" in Tupelo "in support of white businesses." Coen was a resident of Harrison County in south Mississippi. The Invisible Empire claimed a membership of twenty-five hundred and was thought to be prone to violence. This faction of the Ku Klux Klan was headed by Bill Wilkinson, who had formerly been an electrical contractor from Denham Springs, Louisiana. He traveled on a private plane throughout the United States to speak at White supremacist rallies and recruit members. Wilkinson split with David Duke's Knights of the KKK to form the Invisible Empire, his own Klan organization, in 1975. Coen announced that Klansmen from southern Mississippi and Louisiana would converge on Tupelo in response to an invitation by local residents. The Mississippi Invisible Empire spokesman said the purpose of the Klan counterdemonstration was "to refamiliarize White people with the fact they have organizations to stand up for them."[39]

Local officials feared a confrontation between armed UL members and supporters and Wilkinson's KKK city officials and merchants. The officials called for the suspension of all demonstrations as part of a "cooling off" period. An editorial in the *Northeast Mississippi Daily* argued, "Time Has Come for Reason." The editorial labeled both the UL and the Klan as outside agitators. The editors of the Tupelo newspaper extolled racial moderation and declared that "we don't need the help of any from outside our area, black or white. Their presence is upsetting to the tranquility and precludes a reasoned approach to the solution." The Tupelo Board of Aldermen echoed a similar theme. The aldermen unanimously voted on a declaration requesting that "all marches on that date [April 8, 1978] be called off." The aldermen's statement implied that competing demonstrations by the UL and the KKK could lead to violence and "result in a highly flammable situation which could disturb the peace and good order of the City of Tupelo." Tupelo merchants met in response to Coen's announcement. The merchants announced that they possessed "no resistance to hiring qualified blacks" in response to the UL demands. As a reaction to the announced Klan counterdemonstration, the Tupelo merchants offered, "We haven't had any contact with the KKK, we don't want them to march in Tupelo. We haven't heard from them, we don't need them, and we don't want them."[40]

Coen and the Invisible Empire yielded to the requests of White Tupelo municipal and commercial leaders and held a rally at a Tupelo hotel convention center, as opposed to marching down the streets of Tupelo on April 8th. Coen, Wilkinson, as well as other Invisible Empire and Klan leaders spoke to a group of seventy-five at the rally. The audience included plainclothes police officers, city employees, and local youth. Coen announced the formation of a Lee County contingent of the Invisible Empire and that he would remain in the area the following week to help consolidate the new chapter. Wilkinson led a cross-burning ceremony that evening on locally owned private property. The next morning, young Blacks tore down the remnants of the burnt cross.[41]

The UL planned to march on April 8th. Lewis Myers forwarded a letter to Mayor Whitaker requesting clarity on whether the city intended to prevent the UL from marching. Myers made it clear that he would seek a federal injunction to ensure that the UL could exercise its right to demonstrate. In response to Myers's letter, Tupelo police chief Crider declared that the participants in the UL march would not be arrested if they didn't "violate the law." Approximately four hundred Blacks demonstrated in Tupelo on April 8th. The UL leaders expressed a militant tone at a culminating rally. Chickasaw County UL leader Howard Gunn made it clear that the organization would not be intimidated by the presence of KKK organizing and White supremacist opposition in Tupelo. Gunn proclaimed that the UL "would not dodge anybody. If we have to, we'll walk on you; we'll walk through you."[42]

UL attorneys subsequently filed a lawsuit against the city of Tupelo requesting that the federal government withhold federal revenue designated to the municipality due to racial discrimination. Boyce Grayson and two other Tupelo aldermen met with Robinson and the UL leaders and offered to fire Cruber and Sandifer if the UL would call off pickets and protests. Robinson replied that the municipal government should dismiss the two officers as an "act of good faith" before UL would consider entering into negotiations. Robinson argued that the demand to fire Cruber and Sandifer was not the primary issue of the boycott. The demand to increase employment of African Americans in Tupelo was of highest priority for the UL.[43]

Mayor Whitaker and the Board of Aldermen announced the resignations of Cruber and Sandifer at their meeting on April 18th. The pressure

KKK demonstration at Tupelo Police Station. The United League argued that a conspiratorial relationship existed between the Klan and the Tupelo Police Department. (Courtesy of Jim Alexander.)

of the UL demonstrations and consumer boycott clearly motivated their decision to retire. In a joint public letter, the former officers stated, "We are submitting our resignations as employees of the city of Tupelo effective May 1 and with the hope that demonstrations by the United League of North Mississippi be terminated." The mayor and aldermen also announced the formation of a provisional biracial committee established to create a permanent group. These announcements did not deter the continuation of the UL boycott and plans for future demonstrations.[44]

Tensions in Tupelo increased as Coen announced plans in early May 1978 for Klan patrols of the city as "a volunteer supplement to the police." The Mississippi Invisible Empire's leader proclaimed that the KKK would be on alert for "any felony violations, such as raping or looting." Tupelo Blacks were also infuriated after the city attorney stated, in response to media inquiry about the KKK plans, that citizen arrests were "allowable in certain cases under the law." UL said it would not be intimidated by the KKK presence in Tupelo. Myers condemned the response of the Tupelo city attorney. The UL legal counselor declared that the city administration was responsible for a dangerous environment, stating that it possessed a "lawless attitude." He also explained that "[t]his is a once-in-a-lifetime confrontation and we are not going to back down. . . . We have to assume our lives are in danger, and we will encourage marchers to act accordingly." Myers and other UL activists proclaimed that they were "prepared for trouble"—a conciliatory way of saying they would be armed.[45]

The UL increased its armed security of demonstrations in Tupelo. The organization established the practice of sending armed scouts or "spotters" in vehicles and on foot to locate or neutralize White supremacist snipers or armed personnel monitoring Black protests in Tupelo. UL leader Henry Boyd explained,

I remember one time we were marching in Tupelo, and we would have spotters go out before the . . . real big crowd gets there. It was myself, Robert Lay and a bunch others. We saw three white men sitting in a car in the path where we were going to be coming. At that time we would always carry our guns and stuff. . . . We slipped up behind them. . . . We pulled our guns out. [Boyd said,] "If he sneezes now you send him to the Promised Land."

Black participants in the protests also brought their weapons in anticipation of an armed confrontation with the Klan in Tupelo. This practice of Black protesters carrying guns would also continue in UL-organized demonstrations later in the year in nearby Okolona, Mississippi. UL security team member Ernest Cunningham remembered, "Women and men armed themselves. . . . Everybody was armed." Due to the volatile potential of dozens of armed Black demonstrators outside of the UL chain of command, the organization assigned Sandy Ealy and other local Korean and Vietnam War veterans to serve as marshals for the protest, providing direction and discipline. The veterans could "keep their people in line." These veterans also helped provide military training to other UL security. The organization's security also included Black police officers like Lay and Ernest Cunningham, who obtained their positions due to the organized consumer boycotts led by the UL.[46]

The UL sponsored a demonstration on May 6th. The demonstration included well over four hundred Blacks with a contingent of thirty Whites in solidarity with the UL demands. Security forces, with communication equipment and "two pickup trucks displaying rifles," were clearly visible. UL spokesmen made it clear that the organization would not back down to threats of KKK patrols in Tupelo. The KKK did not confront the UL marchers, but organized a thirty-car motorcade and rally of 150 people in the downtown area and a cross burning at a city-owned park in Tupelo. Former Tupelo police captain Cruber, once the center of the controversy, was introduced by Mississippi Grand Dragon Coen at the end of the KKK rally. At subsequent Klan rallies, local police officers would reveal their membership in the White supremacist organization by taking off their hoods at the gathering.[47]

Following these potentially volatile demonstrations, on May 18th, the Tupelo Board of Aldermen passed an ordinance directed at the UL and the KKK that banned demonstrations for ninety days. Mayor Whitaker argued that the racial conflict in Tupelo possessed the potential for "public insurrection." The ordinance set penalties of ten days in jail and/or a one hundred dollar fine for "anyone who boycotts, pickets, marches or burns a cross" for a ninety-day period. The Board of Aldermen also banned the use of city property by the organizations after the KKK used a municipal facility for a cross burning. Grayson again voted against the ordinance. UL attorneys immediately challenged their constitutional right to assemble and demonstrate, as they had done in previous years in Marshall County. U.S. district court judge Orma Smith agreed with UL counsel that the Tupelo ordinance was unconstitutional. Smith asserted that citizens had the right to peaceful protest and proposed that the situation in Tupelo be resolved

Rifles in the back of a United League armed truck at a 1978 demonstration in Tupelo, Mississippi. (Courtesy of Jim Alexander.)

through negotiations between the city administration and protest leaders, including the UL.[48]

UL and KKK demonstrations were planned again for June 10th in downtown Tupelo after negotiations proved unsuccessful. With the resignations of Cruber and Sandifer, Robinson emphasized the economic demands of the UL as the motivation of the demonstration. Bill Wilkinson called for a national KKK rally to assert its White supremacist agenda. National media—including the *New York Times*, the *Washington Post*, the *Chicago Tribune*, and ABC television—traveled to Tupelo anticipating a showdown between the UL and the KKK. Local authorities mobilized the National Guard, the state highway patrol, and the local riot police to monitor the demonstrations and ward off a violent confrontation.[49]

The UL and KKK mobilizations of June 10th took place without the anticipated violent confrontation. Verbal assaults, some brawling, and a few arrests occurred without a race war being initiated. At 12:30 p.m., the UL proceeded downtown from the Springhill Missionary Baptist Church located in a Tupelo Black neighborhood. The marchers followed a pickup truck with rifles openly exhibited. The Black protest linked the UL economic demands to the struggle against the KKK. Marchers carried signs

United League (UL) spokesman and attorney Lew Myers (*third from right*). Also in the picture are Republic of New Africa activist and National Conference of Black Lawyers attorney Chokwe Lumumba (*second to right*) and UL security Sandy Ealy (*far right*). Ealy is an example of the Vietnam War veterans who made up security for the UL. (Courtesy of Jim Alexander.)

proclaiming "Death to the Klan" and "Smash White Supremacy." The UL and several local Blacks prepared for violence that day by bringing guns to the protest. Henry Boyd remembered, "But it just happened that nobody got shot that day. . . . It was very tough. That was the first time I thought it was going to be a shootout in Tupelo, because all the Blacks had their guns." The UL mobilized greater numbers, with seven hundred answering their call to rally and demonstrate, well more than double the KKK gathering, estimated to be no more than three hundred.

The KKK counterdemonstration started downtown at 2:30 p.m. and approached the area after the UL rally ended. Most of the KKK demonstrators were from out of town. Local Blacks were emboldened by the greater numbers of the UL protesters and took the opportunity of the Klan counterprotest to unleash verbal assaults at White supremacists for years of racial intimidation and terror. Dozens of Black observers surrounded nearly equal numbers of KKK marchers and heckled and cursed the White supremacists. Sixty-four-year-old Jack Clark, a Black Tupelo resident, became a local celebrity for his vocal battles with Klansmen. Clark told reporters, "We used to have to get off the sidewalks for White folks . . . and them Klansmen, wooie boy, you didn't go messin' with them. But now, I tells 'em to go to hell." The knowledge of the presence of armed Blacks combined with the numbers of Black protesters was a significant factor in overcoming the White supremacist intimidation. The UL's Ernest Cunningham recalled, "They had guns under their robes" but "it's no telling how many guns we had. . . . They were more afraid than we were."[50]

Negotiations resumed months after the June 10th demonstrations. In late September, UL leaders agreed to meet with elements of the Tupelo White power structure, including Mayor Whitaker, Chief Crider, newspaper publisher George McClean, and commercial leader Felix McClean. The negotiations were brokered by Charles Evers, who was in the middle of a campaign for U.S. Senate (as an independent candidate). Tupelo city officials and commercial leaders agreed to develop a new affirmative action program focused on employment equity for African Americans. The Tupelo affirmative action plan would be overseen by Kenneth Mayfield, NMRLS lawyer and the attorney of Eugene Pasto. The UL agreed to temporarily suspend demonstrations and picketing of White-owned enterprises, but maintained the boycott. Both the UL and the Tupelo White power structure credited Evers's role in brokering the talks.[51]

The UL's effective boycott in Tupelo and its steadfast posture in the face of KKK intimidation won it notoriety in African American communities across the state of Mississippi. Robinson claimed that the UL possessed sixty-two thousand members and organized in thirty-three counties in the state after the June 10th march in Tupelo. On August 5th, Myers announced that the UL would "send demands to all cities in northern Mississippi" and that "United League chapters would start protests if demands were not met." While UL claims and proclamations may have been exaggerated, the organization's presence and activity in other counties increased significantly in the summer of 1978. The UL coordinated boycotts in five Mississippi counties by August; Lee, Chickasaw, Holmes, Alcorn, and Marshall counties. The UL also announced that the organization was expanding statewide and officially changing its name to the "United League of Mississippi." The increased resources of the organization also allowed Robinson to work for the organization full-time in the summer of 1978. Robinson made public plans to conduct a statewide organizing tour weeks after the greatly publicized "showdown" with the Klan on June 10th.[52]

November 1978 national march organized by the United League. (Courtesy of Jim Alexander.)

The momentum the UL developed from the Tupelo boycott made it more attractive to militant Mississippi Blacks than the NAACP. Some print media began to assert that the UL was assuming leadership of the Mississippi Black Freedom Struggle. State NAACP officials and the UL diverted media inquiries about competition between the two organizations. While there was obviously tension between the two groups, one bridge was that Robinson was still a card-carrying NAACP member. Mississippi state NAACP president Aaron Henry publicly applauded the expansion of the UL to a statewide organization. Henry declared, "I feel good about it. . . . Skip has been a dutiful member of the NAACP and there is no conflict between us." Henry acknowledged the significance of the UL role in leading the state's freedom struggle while the NAACP was faced with litigation in response to its boycotts in Port Gibson and other parts of the state. Henry offered, "What Skip Robinson has done is picked up that void until the question of the secondary boycotts has finally been resolved by the U.S. Supreme Court." Robinson stated that the United League "serves as a shelter over the NAACP. We work together. . . . God . . . has chosen us to go out into the field and do civil rights work." On other occasions, the UL president was less conciliatory about the relationship between the two organizations. Robinson spoke from the position of an insider when he offered why it was necessary to build the UL in spite of the existence of the NAACP: "I felt the NAACP was not really militant enough. I felt the NAACP was too hung up on integration and was not even thinking about human rights."[53]

United League in Okolona: Returning Bullet for Bullet

The most visible campaign for Robinson and the UL after Tupelo was in nearby Okolona, located twenty miles south of Tupelo in rural Chickasaw County. An economic boycott and militant demonstrations in Okolona would, in the summer and fall of 1978, become a primary focus of the UL fight against police brutality, economic injustice, and White supremacist terror. UL vice president Dr. Howard Gunn was also a local activist in Chickasaw County. Gunn had been born in 1941 in the Chickasaw County hamlet of Egypt, where he spent the early years of his life. He would spend most of his adult life in Okolona, one of two Chickasaw County capitals (the town of Houston being the other). Okolona possessed a population of three thousand, approximately 60 percent of whom were African American.[54]

Gunn was the Chickasaw County president of the NAACP in the late 1960s. He organized an economic boycott in Okolona with the support of Rudy Shields in 1970. The Okolona activist was involved in the development of social programs in northeast Mississippi and for the state, including NMRLS. In 1978, Gunn simultaneously served as the board chairman of NMRLS and as president of the Ministerial Institute and College, a small, historically Black college in West Point, Mississippi. He met Robinson when the UL came to Tupelo to meet with activists in northeast Mississippi. Gunn immediately identified with the UL president's militant message and thought that Robinson "sound[ed] like the man I should associate myself with." Robinson had heard of Gunn's history of activism and vigorously recruited the Okolona leader into the UL. Previous to joining the UL, Gunn had developed a close political and personal relationship with Lewis Myers, who came to describe Gunn as his "godfather." Gunn was an unashamed advocate of armed self-defense, and Myers credited Gunn with convincing him that he needed to own a .45 handgun (as opposed to a .38) to have more firepower to respond to White supremacists. Gunn would become one of the UL's primary spokespersons. Gunn's oration was particularly distinguished by his militant advocacy of armed resistance.[55]

The UL began organizing in Okolona in July of 1978. The Mississippi-based activist organization initiated protest marches and a consumer boycott initially in response to charges of assault being dropped against four White males accused of attacking a Black male in Okolona on July 4th. Okolona police chief Travis Sullivan was actually on the scene observing as Wardell Ford, a 22-year-old Black man, was injured in the brawl with four Whites: De Van Hanna and three brothers, David, Tom, and Joe Moore. Sullivan eventually broke up the fight and Ford filed complaints, charging the White males with assault. Hanna and the Moore brothers were arrested and released on bond, but charges were dropped within weeks. Sullivan publicly described the melee as a clash between "white boys and niggers." Tensions were also raised locally as young Black males attacked a young White male, Ronnie Palmer, on July 8th. Sullivan arrested one of the Black men, Harvey Moore Jr., and charged him with assault. The Okolona police chief stated that the July 8th fight was retaliation for the beating of Ford.[56]

The UL initiated protests in Okolona within weeks of the July 4th incident. Robinson and Gunn presented nine demands to Okolona's municipal government, one of which was a call for the resignation of Sullivan. The UL argued that Sullivan could have acted in a more expedient manner to protect Ford. Demands focusing on Black employment were also emphasized, as in the Tupelo campaign. Gunn argued that while "Blacks here [in Okolona] are on the threshold of advances into better jobs and management positions," there was White "resistance" to Black economic progress. In support of a UL call to march, 350 Blacks mobilized on July 15th. The UL threatened to boycott if their demands were not met. Nearly four hundred White Okolona residents gathered at a local community center to demonstrate their support for Sullivan and opposition to the UL campaign. Municipal leaders proposed that a biracial committee be formed to facilitate resolution of the potential crisis. Elements of Okolona's local government and commercial leadership feared a Black consumer boycott in the majority-Black town. The example of Tupelo and the boycott organized by Gunn eight years earlier served as incentive to discourage a Black economic coercion campaign.[57]

The UL marched again with a contingent of three hundred on July 22nd. Two weeks later, Gunn and Robinson led a march of four hundred on August 5th. The marchers assembled at Gunn's house, located in a Black neighborhood, and proceeded downtown for a rally near the Okolona

City Hall and Chickasaw County courthouse. UL spokespersons maintained the same militant posture as the UL exhibited in the Tupelo campaign. Robinson proclaimed that the UL demonstrations would continue throughout the state until "we [Blacks] get the same thing you [Whites] got." The UL president went on to say, "We'll march nine times, nine times, nine times—we'll be around here marching a long time." In what would become a common theme for him, Gunn announced that the UL would retaliate against the Klan if the group "impose[d] itself" or attacked the UL or members of the African American community. Gunn declared, "Because we came here peacefully, we don't want the KKKs to impose on us. But if you [the KKK] are going to impose on us we are going to retaliate. We are not going to throw up our hands and go behind closed doors."[58]

The initial UL marches occurred in Okolona without any violent reaction by White supremacists or law enforcement. White supremacists did organize a counterprotest to the August 5th UL demonstration and rally, however. The August 5th UL protest was preceded downtown by a White supremacist motorcade of twenty cars riding under the banner of the "Mississippi Citizens' Council." The participants in the White supremacist caravan made no statements other than waving Confederate and U.S. flags as they drove downtown.[59]

An incident occurred nearly a month after the UL-initiated protests in Okolona that put the local town in the center of the resistance against Klan resurgence. Gunn and five other UL members engaged in a gun battle with six White youth on an Okolona highway on the evening of August 13th. That evening, a Black Okolona female resident alerted Gunn that White supremacists were riding through her neighborhood armed and recklessly shooting. Gunn summoned his son, Willie Frank Gunn, and other local UL activists to join him for the purpose of providing him security as he investigated the shootings. The UL contingent traveled together downtown in Gunn's station wagon to assess the situation and to inform Chief Sullivan about the disturbances. The group accompanying Gunn was well armed since there had been reports of gunfire. The UL vice president could not find Sullivan downtown, but an Okolona police officer assured Gunn that law enforcement had matters under control. Gunn and his party returned to his home after communicating with the police officer. They were confronted and harassed by a group of White youth after stopping at an intersection on Highway 45 in Okolona. Gunn and his associates recognized the White youth as being affiliated with the local Klan group. According to Gunn, one youth held up the noose of a rope and shouted, "We gonna hang some niggers tonight." Shooting started after one of the White youth smashed the window of Gunn's vehicle with a staff with a Confederate battle flag attached to it as the UL spokesman attempted to pull off. Gunfire from the UL contingent scattered the group of young Whites, who returned fire as they retreated. One young White male was struck by the barrage of bullets and had to be hospitalized, and another four of the White youth were treated for gunshot wounds. None of the UL security party was injured, in spite of the fact that Gunn was nearly shot. Seventeen rounds penetrated Gunn's station wagon and shattered its front and rear windshields.[60]

Gunn and his sentry went back to his residence after the engagement. He immediately grabbed his .22 high-powered rifle and prepared for retaliation from the Klan. Willie Gunn also readied for nightriders seeking revenge. The young Gunn declared, "Let's go and get some ammo and come back and kill them all." Thirty minutes after Gunn and his party arrived at his home, nearly two hundred local armed Blacks assembled at the Gunn residence "ready to go to war." Gunn convinced his son and those who mobilized at his home for an armed confrontation to wait in the neighborhood for an attack from the White supremacists. Armed Blacks set up road blocks in the area around the Gunn family domicile. The elder Okolona activist remembered, "We didn't allow any white man to come down that strip and if you were light skinned you better watch it!" There was no White supremacist invasion in Okolona's African American neighborhoods that evening.[61]

The UL demanded a federal investigation of the incident. Local law enforcement and media ignored the gun battle. Gunn identified some of the Whites who attacked him and his party on August 13th, but no one was arrested. The UL organized a press conference on August 15th, two days after the incident. UL attorney Myers stated, "We feel there has been a total breakdown of law enforcement in the area. The U.S. attorney has refused to prosecute any White in the past seven years for incidents against Blacks." Myers again called for the removal of Police Chief Sullivan. The attorney advocated the right of self-defense in a hostile environment. Myers declared, "There are no prosecutions. . . . We have told Blacks they have no choice but to defend themselves." The FBI and Justice Department investigated the case, but no arrests followed.[62]

On the other hand, while the UL condemned federal and local law enforcement for its failure to respond, the organization gained momentum from the August 13th shootout. The fact that Gunn and his group escaped harm and one of the White supremacists was hospitalized was interpreted as a victory by the UL and their allies. This victory was often recounted by Gunn, Robinson, and other UL spokespersons. At a UL rally weeks after the August 13th gun battle, Gunn stated, "If you [White supremacists] should impose upon us, then we will certainly retaliate with all available forces. I don't have to tell you that. Evidence of that speaks for itself." The victory of surviving a shooting confrontation with White supremacists and of injuring an adversary in battle provided evidence of the UL's ability to retaliate against White racial imposition.[63]

One local criminal justice official did respond to the accelerating conflict in Okolona. Chickasaw County justice of the peace H. D. Ross ordered that marchers in the city be searched for weapons. This order was clearly directed at the UL and the fear of armed Blacks at protests in Okolona. Ross constructed regulations that "marchers be searched for weapons as well as 'suspicious-looking' observers of the demonstrations"—the latter tactic being particularly designed to neutralize the practice of armed sentinels monitoring from the periphery of the protest. Marchers possessing weapons would be arrested. Myers immediately responded by filing suit to prevent Ross's order. The UL lawyer declared Ross's ruling "insane" and argued that the judge was acting "in conspiracy with the [Okolona] police," whom the League viewed as adversaries. The suit on behalf of the UL was filed by the NMRLS and supported by the Mississippi chapter of the American Civil Liberties Union. The UL litigation team argued that Ross and Okolona officials were acting in conspiracy to limit the effectiveness of the UL demonstrations and harass Okolona Blacks. On August 24, U.S. district judge Smith declared that Judge Ross's order was unconstitutional. Smith argued that the Chickasaw judge's order limited the right of association of people participating in the UL marches.[64]

The overturning of Ross's ruling did not prevent local law enforcement from attempting to disarm UL members and constituency before they assembled at events. As previously mentioned, Blacks commonly came to UL protests in Tupelo and Okolona anticipating conflict with the Klan. Police roadblocks attempted to disarm Blacks en route to the march and rally. UL members traveling from Marshall County to Tupelo and Okolona used ingenuity to make sure they would still have guns to answer an attack from White supremacists. UL security team member Robert Lay described one of these tactics:

The first thing the police would do, if he comes . . . he [would] get one gun. We carried two guns. Because . . . they just take our guns. . . . They'd take the guns, but see we had one gun, but they get one gun and they gone. They think they took our guns. Everybody on the bus had two guns, because them police they get one gun, well they think the brother ain't got no other gun man. We have two guns every time man. That's how we done.

Black women in Okolona concealed weapons so as to provide the capacity to strike back on an assault from White supremacists. Howard Gunn recalled, "Our ladies were very smart. They would allow them to search their pocket books. They would always say it was hot when we were marching. They would have towels wrapped up in their hands and guns were wrapped up in their towels." Debra Jackson, a young attorney working on the NMRLS staff, noticed that a local minister hid a pistol in his Bible. The pages of the reverend's Bible were cut out so that a pistol could be inserted in the book.[65]

A Black minister carrying a weapon was not an unusual occurrence at a UL rally. The UL had significant participation from Black clergy and laity in northern Mississippi communities. UL spokespersons often utilized biblical characters and scriptures in their oratory, and the organization described itself as a "church on wheels." It was common for clergy to speak at UL rallies and publicly advocate armed self-defense. Some preachers even displayed their weapons while speaking from the podium at UL rallies. Ernest Cunningham expressed the League's perspective on guns, religion, and nonviolence when he stated,

Nonviolence is good . . . and they teach that nonviolence has its place . . . in religion and you shouldn't carry weapons. But I always quote that particular scripture where Peter has a sword. . . . He had to have a weapon. That was equivalent to a pistol during his day. . . . It nothing wrong with Christians and religious people carrying guns. It's what you do with the weapon. You carry it as a protection, for defensive purposes. Not to go out there and assault nobody. . . . They're for protection. That's basically why we carried them. We wasn't out there reckless.[66]

The UL's theology challenged stereotypes of the Black church taking a nonviolent posture in the southern Black Freedom Struggle.

The boycott feared by Okolona's civic and commercial leaders would not be avoided. The UL called a boycott of the Okolona business district on August 19th. On August 26th, 350 Blacks marched in Okolona, two days after Ross's order was reversed. Mississippi grand dragon Coen and thirty-six Klansmen watched behind a line of Chickasaw County deputies and Okolona police. Coen told the press that the Klan was present at the UL march "merely . . . as spectators to aid the law enforcement officers if necessary." He also claimed that other White supremacists were deployed near the march as reinforcements if needed. Robinson told the crowd at the rally that the UL's greatest accomplishment was "awakening our people. . . . We no longer have fear of the Klan."[67]

The Okolona boycott was similar to other UL campaigns and those organized by Rudy Shields in other Mississippi towns. Boycotts were enforced by the threat of coercive violence against Black consumers violating the call not to shop downtown. Gunn recalled the role of the enforcers, whom he called "Spirits" in the tradition of a Shields-organized economic coercion effort: "We had the Spirit in Okolona. Sometimes the ghosts would come out at night. Of course, whatever had to be done, the Spirit would do it in the name of love. [In UL boycotts] [t]he Spirit got a lot of people. After the Spirit got to them, they would come around."[68]

The UL also supported a student who initiated a boycott of the combined secondary/middle school in Okolona on September 8th. The majority of the students enrolled at the Okolona junior/senior high school were African American. Sixty Black students walked out of class, demanding a Black history course, Black cheerleaders for athletic events, and more African American faculty. The following day three hundred African American students, 80 percent of the Black student population, were absent from the school. Additionally, 195 elementary school students were absent, presumably in solidarity with the protest at the junior/senior high school. The students presented their demands to the Okolona school superintendent. During the first weeks of the boycott, 125 picketers, including students and parents, routinely protested near the entrance of the school. On September 14th, a temporary restraining order was placed on demonstrators at the school to "prevent loud displays." School officials charged that the singing and chanting of the students, parents, and UL activists served as "threats of physical violence to administrators as well as to black students who remained in school." U.S. district judge William Keady ordered that the demonstrators be moved three blocks from the school.[69]

Violence began to erupt in Okolona as racial tensions accelerated in late September and early October 1978. For several weeks, reports of shootings in the domiciles of Okolona's Blacks and Whites proliferated. Two White men affiliated with the Klan beat a 75-year-old Black man on October 5th. Eight men were arrested that evening for carrying concealed weapons during a curfew presumably imposed to prevent violence in Okolona. The White supremacists were alleged to have assaulted the elderly African American with brass knuckles. There was another exchange of gunfire into residences "on both sides of the tracks" on October 6th. Nearly four hundred Blacks assembled at the Gunn residence that evening, while Klansmen gathered in a White neighborhood in Okolona. Robinson called for federal marshals to intervene in Chickasaw County. The Okolona police force was only composed of seven men and did not possess the personnel to control a major disturbance.[70]

State officials and the local White power structure recognized that a volatile situation existed that had the potential to accelerate into greater hostility. UL leaders met in private dwellings with elements of state government and the Okolona municipal power structure to agree upon resolution of the shooting. These negotiations led to a process that brought Judge W. W. Brown from neighboring Calhoun County to Chickasaw to adjudicate the arrests of Black and White males suspected of the offenses. The Calhoun County judge supervised a three-month grand jury investigation of the racially motivated shootings that resulted in the indictments and convictions of six local men. Brown sentenced the men on January 30, 1979. After pleading guilty, two White males, Chuck Tackett and Spencer Griffin, were charged and convicted for shooting into homes in an African American neighborhood. Four Black men—Walter Smith, Randall Wallace, Harvey Moore Jr., and Billy Copperwood—all pleaded guilty to charges related to shooting into White-owned residences. Griffin, Smith, Wallace, and Cooperwood received suspended eight-year sentences with five-year terms of probation. Judge Brown sentenced Tackett and Moore to two years in prison and ordered them to pay restitution for damaged residences. Willie Gunn and Obbie Buchanan were also charged with assaulting a Chickasaw County sheriff's deputy after the arraignment of Smith, Wallace, Moore, and Cooperwood on October 7th. Sheriff's deputy Toby Craig was struck while attempting to break up a fight between young Blacks and Whites outside the county courthouse. Gunn and Buchanan each received a three-year suspended sentence and a five hundred dollar fine with three years of probation. Certainly the mobilization of hundreds of armed local Blacks gave the UL bargaining power at the negotiating table as state and local officials desired to avoid a race war in Okolona.[71]

The shootings in October 1978 would not calm the rhetoric of UL orators. Robinson emphasized the necessity of self-defense and told a rally after a UL demonstration in Okolona, "We are going to change Mississippi and push the Klan aside." He also appropriated the image of Martin Luther King Jr. and the rhetoric of nonviolence, but qualified it. The UL president declared at an October 18th rally at a Chickasaw County church,

> We still believe very deeply in what Dr. King meant when he said that love and understanding can overcome hate and killing. But we don't feel he meant that we should be cowards. If the Klan moves into my neighborhood and shoots at my neighbor, shoots at my house, I'm not going to fall on my knees and say "O Lord, stop him." God stops man through man. If the Klan shoots into my home, if I do anything I'm going to say "O Lord help me to aim straight."

Howard Gunn made no reference to nonviolence but continued his theme of "returning bullet for bullet" at the rally. Gunn proclaimed, "If a person fires upon us, we aren't going to tuck our tales and run. We going to retaliate with every available resource we have. If any person fires upon any Black person in this community, we're going to blow their doggone head off."[72]

The protest activity declined in the months after October of 1978, but the UL increased activity in Okolona after the winter months of 1979. The 1979 UL demonstrations in Okolona were not without incident and potential for racial explosion. Downtown merchants suspended business as two hundred marched with the UL on Saturday, March 17th. Robinson announced that this march was the first of many leading to a "long, hot summer" in Okolona. The UL president stated, "We're going to march and be in Okolona until every business goes out of business." The march was marred by one incident as local police arrested White Okolona resident Richard Clark for reckless driving and Ronnie Evans and Shaw Robbins for accessories in the incident. Clark was driving a vehicle that struck a marcher, 22-year-old Melvin Adams of the nearby town of Nettleton, during the demonstration. Adams was hospitalized for minor wounds on his legs and wrists.

State Highway Patrol and local police arrested 115 Blacks, including Robinson, in a UL protest on April 14th. The march started over two hours late after UL organizers were delayed in arriving from another northern Mississippi protest in Grenada. The officers arrested the UL contingent for marching without a permit and escorted their prisoners to the Chickasaw County–Okolona Jail, where they were searched for weapons. A report by Memphis *Commercial Appeal* journalists Elizabeth Fair and William Fuller noted that "some men with partially concealed guns and sticks" were observed as their comrades were arrested by law enforcement. A local Justice Court judge released the 115 marchers on their own recognizance within thirty minutes of their arrests. U.S. district judge William Keady issued a restraining order preventing local officials from arresting demonstrators on the basis of an ordinance created to limit the perimeters of the protests. UL lawyers challenged the constitutionality of the ordinance, and Keady ruled that local officials should refrain from arresting UL demonstrators until federal courts had ruled on its constitutionality. County and municipal police defied Keady's order and arrested 177 demonstrators at a march on April 28th on charges of marching without a permit and obstructing traffic. The arrests came after local officials declined the UL request for a permit to demonstrate. Myers filed a suit charging Okolona city officials and Chief Sullivan for violating the civil liberties of the marchers.[73]

The UL continued to challenge local officials in Okolona by organizing demonstrations. Federal officials intervened between local officials and UL leaders to negotiate the march route and perimeters. On June 2nd, 150 demonstrators marched in the Okolona central business district and picketed White-owned stores. Some of the businesses closed in response to the picketing. Gunn reiterated UL demands for more African American teachers and Black history courses in the public schools, and the employment of Blacks by county and municipal governments. UL leaders again called for the firing of Chief Sullivan and also the dismissal of Okolona school superintendent Jimmy Anderson. Robinson openly taunted White supremacist onlookers, stating, "Whoever points a gun at us will not draw it down alive!" Journalists covering UL marches noted the potential for violence, as White observers of demonstrations and UL security were both armed. The local police were also targets of Robinson's fiery rhetoric, especially Chickasaw County deputy sheriff Hansel Rogers, who led the mass arrests of April 14th and 28th. Rogers fired shots in the air prior to arresting the demonstrators in April. Robinson responded, "[P]raise God that you fired in the air. Otherwise, you would not be here today." Rogers also pulled his weapon and aimed it at UL member Herbert Trice after a heated exchange between the two men during the April 28th march.[74]

Tensions increased again when a Black teenager was killed in an Okolona jail. On June 5, 1979, Deputy Sheriff Rogers shot an eighteen-year-old Black inmate, Lee Carouthers, the cousin of Lee County UL president Walter Stanfield, when he was in the Chickasaw County jail awaiting transfer to the Parchman state prison after being convicted for burglary. Carouthers was shot when Rogers and an African American Okolona police officer, Tony Ivy, were taking the prisoner back to his cell after interrogation. Rogers claimed that he pulled Ivy's gun and shot Carouthers after the inmate threatened the two police officers with a knife. UL leaders refused to believe the scenario presented by Rogers, whom they publicly accused of being a member of the Klan. Gunn and Robinson both stated that Rogers had a history of harassment of local Blacks as well as possible cooperation with, and ignoring the illegal activities of, White supremacists. The FBI and officials from the civil rights division of the federal Department of Justice came to Okolona to investigate the death of Carouthers. Robinson also stated that the UL would initiate armed patrols of Black neighborhoods in Okolona.[75]

The UL leaders were suspicious of the FBI's willingness to prosecute White law enforcement in Mississippi. They believed that the involvement of federal officials was designed to divert the insurgent activism of the grassroots movement. The UL asserted that Mississippi Blacks could not depend on the FBI for justice, but must rely on their own initiative to obtain redress. Myers argued,

> In nine years, there has never been a prosecution of a White law enforcement officer . . . who violated the civil rights of Blacks. . . . This [the involvement of the FBI] has the effect of killing the momentum of any serious community reaction toward an incident. Let's quit begging for Washington to come help us. . . . The FBI is not accountable to us. It's time to make our local officials more accountable.[76]

The UL called for an African American special prosecutor to investigate Rogers's actions, as well as, ultimately, for the prosecution of the deputy sheriff and the dismissal of Officer Ivy. The businesses of Ivy and his wife Hazel were also targets of the UL protests. Officer Ivy owned two ice cream carts, and his spouse owned a nursery. While the organization questioned the will of the federal government to intervene in a just way, the UL did appeal for federal officials to institute martial law in Okolona since "[l] aw and order" had "completely broken down." The militant activists did not rely on federal protection to defend themselves from White suprema-cist violence. The UL sponsored a demonstration in response to the death of Carouthers on June 9th, and four hundred demonstrators participated in the march. While marchers were told not to come armed to the demon-stration, according to Robinson about fifteen armed security protected the march. Some security also visibly carried batons for protection. NBC tele-vision news reported that the UL "encouraged Blacks to beat up Klansmen in Black neighborhoods in Okolona." At a rally on the evening following Carouthers's death, the League appealed to local residents to "form neigh-borhood patrols to protect the Blacks citizens of Okolona from harass-ment and death." Gunn reported that armed patrols composed of "50 to 60 armed Blacks" were established to ward off the Klan and other nightrid-ers.[77] Deputy Sheriff Rogers resigned in the midst of the protests. Rogers's resignation came after both a Chickasaw County grand jury and a federal grand jury failed to indict him for murder.[78]

Decline of the United League

Okolona was the League's most visible hot spot in the summer of 1979. The organization was involved in demonstrations and boycotts in other parts of the state at the same time. The UL continued its protest activities in Holly Springs and Tupelo, in spite of the decline in the momentum of the insur-gency previously initiated in these cities. The League chapter in Holmes County organized a consumer boycott in the city of Lexington in April in response to charges of brutality by municipal police against a young Afri-can American female. The local UL chapter mobilized demonstrations to complement the boycott after the arrests of local Black and White activists by Lexington police in September of 1978. The Black-majority Lexington was the seat of Holmes County. The Holmes County UL boycott demands centered on police conduct and employment for African Americans in the private and public sector. In Madison County, the local UL coordinated marches and a consumer boycott in Canton in response to charges result-ing from the beating of a Black youth by sheriff's deputies in November of 1978. In addition, League organizers asserted that the deputies placed a noose around the youth's neck and threatened to hang him. The UL also established a chapter in the town of Indianola in the Mississippi Delta in 1979. The expansion of the League's activity throughout the state sig-nificantly increased demands on the human and material resources of the organization, which was also engaged in protests and economic resistance in Mississippi towns like Corinth, Ripley, Goodman, and Mendenhall.[79]

United League activity declined significantly after several opponents targeted its relationship with the federally funded NMRLS. Local and state officials called for investigation into the role of the NMRLS in UL protests. Tupelo officials filed a formal complaint to the federal Legal Services Corporation (LSC), the parent body of NMRLS, in May 1978. The Tupelo complaint charged that NMRLS attorneys actively participated in demonstrations and initiated "legal action solely for the purpose of harassment of the City of Tupelo." Tupelo's city attorney, Guy Mitchell Jr., accused the NMRLS of being "a Black racist organization rather than a responsible law office." Mississippi congressional representatives John Stennis, James Eastland, and Trent Lott all demanded an investigation of the relationship between the NMRLS and the UL. In response to the complaints from Tupelo and federal officials, LSC began an investigation of the NMRLS. Allies of the NMRLS and the UL, including the NCBL, the National Lawyers Guild, the National Organization of Legal Service Workers, and the Delta Ministry, led a protest at the LSC offices in Washington, D.C., to protest the investigation in January of 1979. The protest charged that the LSC investigation was an "attempt to limit the First Amendment rights of legal services attorneys." In March of 1979, the LSC ultimately ruled that there was no wrongdoing by NMRLS attorneys.[80]

A debate occurred within the NMRLS concerning the agency's relationship with the UL. NMRLS director Wilhelm Joseph sought to distance the institution from UL protests and not to engage organizational resources in support of League-organized boycotts. Despite the LSC investigation finding no wrongdoing, the federal body placed pressure on Joseph to create more distance between the organizations. NMRLS attorney Leonard McClellan argued that the NMRLS mandate prevented the agency's attorneys from defending UL protesters in criminal defense efforts, particularly the 327 defendants arrested in the April 1979 demonstrations in Okolona. Myers and other activist-oriented attorneys and UL members on the agency's board of directors desired to maintain institutional assistance and advocacy for UL campaigns. In July of 1979, the NMRLS Board of Directors settled on a resolution declaring that the NMRLS and the UL were "separate organizations." Robinson also moved the UL office in Holly Springs from the Marshall County NMRLS office to an adjacent location.[81]

Myers also officially resigned from his position with the NMRLS due to health reasons and left the state in July 1979. The absence of Myers from the UL was a significant blow to the organization's activist campaigns. Myers not only served as legal counsel and litigator but also was an organizational spokesperson and key strategist. Gunn commented that Myers's resignation would mean that the NMRLS would "not have as much community involvement as . . . before." The Okolona activist also acknowledged Myers's role as an advisor to Robinson and himself.[82]

A major rupture between the UL and the NMRLS was apparent when Robinson publicly called for Joseph to resign as NMRLS director in June of 1980. Robinson argued that Joseph was too "conservative" and lacked the grassroots orientation necessary for an organization that served as an advocate for the poor. The UL leader also charged that Joseph prioritized increasing attorneys' salaries over hiring paralegals and staff that would better reflect the organization's concerns and communicate with the indigent population. Robinson accused Joseph of "wasting taxpayers' money to set up a dictatorship that is used to by-pass the needs of the client community it [the NMRLS] is designed to service." Joseph and his supporters countered by citing the agency's growth and evidence of clients' support since his appointment in 1975.[83]

The final chapter to the activism of the United League occurred after Robinson announced in March of 1981 that he was a member of the Nation of Islam (NOI) under the leadership of Minister Louis Farrakhan. Robinson was named minister of the NOI for the state of Mississippi and was henceforth to be identified as Minister Alfred X. Robinson continued his public advocacy of armed self-defense and retaliatory violence as an NOI minister, declaring, "We will no longer pray for those who persecute us. . . . We will get them back." However, Robinson denounced the boycott strategy and protest marches. According to Robinson, the UL "gradually phased out" protests as a tactic because they were not "accomplishing anything." Denouncing confrontational tactics and insurgent activism, the UL primary spokesman asserted that the organization would no longer "be the aggressor or impose on anyone." His new philosophy instructed him that Blacks must "do for yourself and not depend on any government." He went on to say, "I will no longer teach my people to sit around and wait for a handout." African Americans should "no longer want to be part of their [the Whites'] world," which was on its "way out." The Mississippi activist now advocated the NOI dietary and cultural lifestyle and

Black autonomous institutional and economic development, particularly through agriculture.[84]

Robinson's denunciation of staple tactics of the UL confused other organizational leaders like Gunn and Boyd and much of the constituency of the organization. The UL was still engaged in boycotts in Tupelo, Okolona, Lexington, and Holly Springs. While the momentum of these boycotts had significantly declined, some local UL leaders considered Robinson's new position a betrayal of the sacrifices and efforts of the organization and local people who engaged in and supported UL-led campaigns. On the other hand, Robinson recruited some of his family members and close comrades in Marshall County into the ranks of the NOI, promoting its self-help economic philosophy and race-conscious theological orientation. The UL did not survive the division created in its ranks by the conversion of Robinson and his associates to the NOI and their repudiation of insurgent activism.[85]

The Legacy of the League and Armed Insurgency

The UL represented the most dynamic expression of grassroots activism in the post–Civil Rights/Black Power Movement era in Mississippi. The UL continued the strategy of economic coercion and armed resistance fashioned in the state by Rudy Shields. Its dynamic campaigns won significant concessions for Blacks in Byhalia, Holly Springs, Okolona, and Tupelo and sustained insurgent activity in those and other Mississippi towns. It kept Mississippi in the attention of Black and social justice activists throughout the United States in the late 1970s. UL spokespersons Robinson and Myers participated in national speaking tours throughout the United States in 1978 and 1979. The United League also received attention in national mainstream and left media during that time. Robinson was invited to be a part of national efforts to rebuild the Black Liberation Movement. He addressed a rally of thousands adjacent to the United Nations in New York in early November 1979. Robinson shared the platform with legendary Black activist Queen Mother Moore, activist clergyman Herbert Daughtry of Brooklyn, New York, as well as representatives of the Black United Fronts of Cairo, Illinois, and Philadelphia, Pennsylvania, the Provisional Government of the Republic of New Africa, the Palestinian Liberation Organization, and the Zimbabwean African National Union. Robinson was also one of the founders of the National Black United Front in June 1980.

The use of armed resistance by the UL and its supporters to combat White terrorist violence and intimidation marks a significant moment in the Mississippi freedom struggle. The ability of armed Blacks to march in the streets of Tupelo and Okolona in the face of the Klan represented a different day in the struggle of Blacks in the South. No longer would White terrorists intimidate Black communities in Mississippi from asserting their rights. Blacks believed they had the firepower to stand up to and even defeat the Klan.

Conclusion

Looking Back So We Can Move Forward

I grew up in Compton, Watts, and South Central Los Angeles, California. I embraced the Black Power Movement as a teenager. Malcolm X, George Jackson, Robert Williams, Max Stanford, and the Black Panthers were my heroes. I was recruited into the African Peoples Party and the House of Umoja, two successor organizations of the Revolutionary Action Movement, after graduating from high school in 1972. One of my first introductions to the armed resistance tradition of the southern Black Freedom Struggle was in 1976, when I traveled to Atlanta for a national Black student activist assembly. One of the advisors for our student association was Dara Abubakari (who was called Sister Dara) of the Provisional Government of the Republic of New Africa. Sister Dara was the child of members of Marcus Garvey's UNIA and a veteran activist in the Movement from New Orleans. I "bummed" a ride from Atlanta to New Orleans with Sister Dara, her son Walter Collins, and a mutual friend, Joe Taylor. Walter was a former political prisoner due to his resisting the Vietnam War–era draft, a SNCC activist, and a leader of the Southern Conference Education Fund. Taylor was serving as the driver and security for Sister Dara. When we drove from Atlanta through Birmingham, Sister Dara and Walter began to reminisce about the campaigns there. They told me that caches of weapons had been buried outside of the city by defense networks. Sister Dara and Walter also explained how armed sentries protected people from the periphery of marches and demonstrations in the early 1960s. I was amazed hearing their stories.

In 1978, my comrades and I invited Skip Robinson and Lewis Myers to come to Los Angeles to speak about the work of the United League of Mississippi. We organized a tour for Robinson and Myers at colleges and universities, churches, and community events in Southern California. I went to Atlanta the following year for a meeting and decided to catch the

Greyhound to northern Mississippi to observe the work of the UL. Most of the UL members were either armed or had security.

My comrades and I believed that self-determination for the descendants of enslaved Africans in the United States would be manifested in the southern Black Belt, counties in the region where Blacks were the historic majority. One Sunday, we participated in a forum hosted by another Black nationalist organization in Los Angeles. Our hosts disagreed with our belief that a self-determining Black nation could rise up in the South. One of their leaders and spokespersons berated the lack of militancy of Black southerners. He harangued, "[H]ow y'all going to build a nation in the South? Black people down there are so passive and nonviolent." One customary stereotype that young Black militants in the northern and western urban centers embraced was that our elders and people in the South, particularly in rural areas, were docile and intimidated. Additionally, there was a misconception that the southern Movement was solely "nonviolent." I responded on the basis of my limited study and experiences listening to Sister Dara and Walter as well as observing Skip and the UL.

I countered that the notion of southern Blacks being docile and passive was a myth. The southern Black Freedom Struggle produced Robert Williams and the Deacons for Defense. Skip Robinson and the UL were the latest manifestation of this tradition. The principal leader of the host organization intervened in the debate to acknowledge the tradition of armed self-defense in the South and their organization's familiarity with Robinson's advocacy and practice of armed self-defense. The organization had a photo of Robert Williams displayed prominently in its building. However, the stereotype of Black submissiveness to White supremacy overcame the historical reality of armed resistance in the southern Black Freedom Struggle in the minds of many northern, urban Blacks and nationalists. Challenging this stereotype is one of the motivations for this work.

Much of the recent literature on armed resistance in the South focuses on the utilization of armed self-defense in the early to mid-1960s. This work describes the use of armed force by Black activists in Mississippi until 1979, during the Black Power Era (1965-1975), and after the decline of the national Black Power Movement. Some scholars who write about armed resistance after the Civil Rights Movement do not see its efficacy. As mentioned in the introduction, historian Simon Wendt has asserted that organized Blacks committed to armed resistance "outlived their usefulness" after 1967 due to federal intervention and the acquiescence of White racists.

Wendt argues that during the Black Power era, armed resistance existed as "a gendered symbol of male psychological empowerment."[1]

We Will Shoot Back demonstrates the organization of armed resistance by Black activists in Mississippi for over a decade after 1967. After that year, Blacks in Jackson, Yazoo City, Belzoni, Aberdeen, West Point, Marshall County, Okolona, and Tupelo all participated in collective armed defense of their communities, leaders, and institutions. The retaliatory attack and guerilla warfare organized by Ralph Featherstone in West Point in 1970 was consistent with other clandestine networks that developed in the Black Power Movement of the 1970s. These radicals believed that the Black Freedom Struggle needed more "teeth" to address the violence of White supremacists and the very state itself. They employed clandestine organization and guerilla warfare to respond to state repression, White supremacist forces, as well as criminal and antisocial elements of the African American community. The most documented expression of this trend is the Black Liberation Army.[2]

While gender and the construction of Black masculinity certainly played a role, political repression and "low intensity warfare" against Black Power activists by local police and federal agencies through vehicles such as the FBI's COINTELPRO program makes the organization of self-defense during that period more than "symbolic"; it was a means of survival. The militant Black Power Movement saw armed self-defense as necessary to protect their leadership, members, and the community itself from White racist police and paramilitary groups, as well as federal agents dedicated to the destruction of the Movement. If the New Africans had not prepared to respond to violent attack, one can only speculate whether the occupants of the Republic of New Africa residence in 1971 would have met the same fate as Fred Hampton and Mark Clark, who in 1969 were murdered by a Chicago police raid designed to kill Black Panthers.[3] The 1979 massacre of anti-Klan activists in Greensboro, North Carolina, by a White supremacist coalition of Klan and neo-Nazi terrorists demonstrates that armed self-defense was still a necessity over a decade after 1967. Subsequent evidence revealed the complicity of federal and local law enforcement in this massacre, which resulted in the murders of five left activists. The awareness of FBI agents of the possibility of a violent confrontation and the lack of police protection on that day confirms the belief on the part of late 1960s and 1970s Black activists who prepared to protect themselves from White supremacist violence.[4]

Large numbers of grassroots Black activists and youth were convinced of the necessity of armed self-defense after the assassination of Martin

Luther King Jr., the popular, nonviolent warrior and spokesperson of the Black Freedom Struggle. The violent demise of King would certainly convince grassroots leaders of the necessity for protection from racist police and White supremacist civilian organizations. They were definitely expendable if an internationally known personality with a relationship with federal officials, including the president, could be assassinated. The assassination of King also contributed to a growing radicalization of the Black Freedom Struggle and Black youth. The politically motivated murder of King sparked more than one hundred spontaneous uprisings across the United States and is considered a factor in the rapid expansion of the Black Panther Party from a regional organization on the West Coast to a national organization.[5]

To attribute the decline of armed insurgency in the Black Freedom Struggle solely to federal intervention or the acquiescence of Whites is to fail to consider the agency and internal dynamics of the Civil Rights and Black Power Movements and the nature of repression of the Struggle. Other factors must be considered when one examines the decline of armed self-defense and resistance in the southern Black Freedom Struggle, as well as the national Black Liberation Movement, in the middle to late 1970s and early 1980s. In some communities where the Deacons were active, such as Natchez and Fayette, paramilitary organization declined with the achievement of Black political representation in municipal and county government. The recruitment and elevation of African Americans in law enforcement complemented the presence of Blacks in local government. In these communities, many Blacks saw less need for organized defense formations with these reforms in place. Black voting power also made some policymakers more sensitive to the security needs of Blacks.

On the other hand, radical elements of the Black Liberation Movement still felt the need for armed self-defense, which continued through vehicles like the PGRNA and other Black Power organizations. Ultimately, these elements were neutralized through the COINTELPRO program and other counterinsurgency campaigns, with the leadership as well as rank and file members of radical organizations incarcerated and more cynical about the potential of the Black Liberation Movement. The disillusionment of Rudy Shields with insurgent movements by the middle years of the 1970s is consistent with the decline of the Black Power Movement due to political repression and internal contradictions. The impact of the influx of drugs in the national Black community on the decline of the Black Power Movement in the United States in the late 1960s and 1970s can also not be underestimated. The persistent use of armed self-defense in the United League–led campaigns in Byhalia, Tupelo, and Okolona demonstrates that armed resistance was an important part of political resistance by the most dynamic social movement campaigns in Mississippi, the region, and the United States for years after the decline of the national Black Power Movement.

The numbers of Blacks coming armed to protests in Okolona and Tupelo demonstrate that Black activists and their constituency had little confidence in federal intervention to ensure their security. They also felt threatened by White supremacist violence in response to their open demands for justice. The fact that hundreds of Mississippi Blacks were armed during demonstrations in the late 1970s also testifies to the role of weapons as a tool to overcome fear and intimidation for the purpose of demanding justice and human rights. Furthermore, the efficacy of retaliatory violence is shown in the negotiated settlement in Okolona after drive-by shootings in White neighborhoods by Blacks who responded to nightriders' raids in Black neighborhoods.

The confrontation of White supremacy by the Black Freedom Struggle and its allies as well as the changing political environment regionally, nationally, and globally provided different political opportunities. A variety of tactics and campaigns contributed to a different political reality in the 1970s than that faced by Joe Pullen in 1923 and other lone resisters in the Nadir period of apartheid Mississippi. The mass organizing strategies employed by the Regional Council of Negro Leadership, the NAACP, SNCC, and CORE were all complemented by some form of armed self-defense by the local people. After 1964, economic boycotts were complemented by a more aggressive defense posture and the open advocacy of armed resistance. Security was provided for Movement spokespersons, activists, supporters, and whole communities, which allowed Mississippi Blacks to challenge the fear that had crippled many sustainable political insurgencies from the end of Reconstruction to the emergence of the Civil Rights Movement in the 1950s.

In many Mississippi Black communities, efforts to protect themselves with weapons were intrinsic to the initiation of activities in the Black Freedom Struggle. Armed resistance must be included with litigation, mass organizing, nonviolent demonstrations and protests, as well as other forms of insurgent challenge to force federal intervention and a change in White attitudes and behavior toward Black humanity. Moreover, armed resistance contributed to giving activists and communities the confidence to challenge White supremacist terror even when the federal government did not have the capacity or will to protect them. Without due attention to the role of armed resistance in Mississippi, either the agency of Blacks in the Civil Rights and Black Power Movements is denied or an inaccurate account of the Struggle is offered.

I remember the feeling I had as a young man when Sister Dara and Walter told me the stories of Black people defending the Movement and the community, as well as how that information affected my consciousness. I remember how I was inspired when I observed Skip Robinson and the United League carrying guns for protection in northern Mississippi in the late 1970s. This was a history that was not a part of my formal education and was not well represented in popular culture when I was growing up. In spite of the recent scholarship, the awareness of armed resistance in the southern Black Freedom Struggle is not a part of the contemporary popular narrative about the various movements. I hope that this book plays a small part in correcting the narrative and inspires youth like myself to uncover their ancestors' stories of struggles and encourages them to fight for social justice.

Notes

Acknowledgments

1. James Baldwin, *The Fire Next Time* (New York: Vintage Books, 1993).
2. Alex Haley and Malcolm X, *The Autobiography of Malcolm X: As Told to Alex Haley* (New York: Ballantine Books, 1987).

Introduction

1. Emilye Crosby, "'It Wasn't the Wild West': Keeping Local Studies in Civil Rights Historiography," in *Civil Rights History from the Ground Up: Local Struggles, National Movement*, ed. Emilye Crosby (Athens: University of Georgia Press, 2011), 194.
2. John Dittmer, *Local People: The Struggle for Civil Rights in Mississippi* (Champaign: University of Illinois Press, 1995).
3. Charles M. Payne, *I've Got the Light of Freedom* (Berkeley: University of California Press, 2007).
4. Adam Fairclough, *Race and Democracy: The Civil Rights Struggle in Louisiana, 1915-1972* (Athens: University of Georgia Press, 2008).
5. David T. Beito and Lynda Royster Beito, *Black Maverick: T. R. M. Howard's Fight for Civil Rights and Economic Power* (Champaign: University of Illinois Press, 2009).
6. Emilye Crosby, *Common Courtesy: The Civil Rights Movement in Claiborne County, Mississippi* (Bloomington: Indiana University Press, 1995).
7. Hasan Kwame Jeffries, *Bloody Lowndes: Civil Rights and Black Power in Alabama's Black Belt* (New York: New York University Press, 2009).
8. Wesley C. Hogan, *Many Hearts, One Mind: SNCC's Dream for a New America* (Chapel Hill: University of North Carolina Press, 2007).
9. Timothy B. Tyson, *Radio Free Dixie: Robert F. Williams and the Roots of Black Power* (Chapel Hill: University of North Carolina Press, 2001).
10. Lance Hill, *The Deacons for Defense: Armed Resistance and the Civil Rights Movement* (Chapel Hill: University of North Carolina Press, 2006).

11. Christopher Strain, *Pure Fire: Self-Defense as Activism in the Civil Rights Era* (Athens: University of Georgia Press, 2005).

12. Simon Wendt, *The Spirit and the Shotgun: Armed Resistance and the Struggle for Civil Rights* (Gainesville: University of Florida Press, 2007).

13. Wendt, *Spirit and the Shotgun*, 6.

14. Strain, *Pure Fire*, 5-6.

15. Akinyele Umoja, "Eye for an Eye: The Role of Armed Resistance" (Ph.D. diss., Emory University, 1996), 16-18.

16. Colin Palmer, *Passageways: An Interpretive History of Black America*. Vol. 1, *1619-1865* (Fort Worth, TX: Harcourt Brace, 1998), x.

17. Michael Gomez, *Exchanging Our Country Marks: The Transformation of African Identities in the Colonial and Antebellum South* (Chapel Hill: University of North Carolina Press, 1998), 9-10.

18. John K. Thornton, *Warfare in Atlantic Africa, 1500-1800* (London: UCL Press, 1999), 139-47; Walter Rucker, *The River Flows On: Black Resistance, Culture, and Identity Formation in Early America* (Baton Rouge: Louisiana State University Press, 2006), 6-10.

19. Geronimo ji Jaga, interviewed by Bakari Kitwana, "A Soldier's Story," *The Source*, February 1998, 132.

20. Gomez, *Exchanging Our Country Marks*, 101.

21. Gomez, *Exchanging Our Country Marks*, 291-22; Cedric J. Robinson, *Black Movements in America* (New York: Routledge, 1997), 96-97.

22. Sundiata Cha-Jua and Clarence Lang, "Long Movement as Vampire: Temporal and Spatial Fallacies in Recent Black Freedom Studies," *Journal of African-American History* 92, no. 1 (Winter 2007): 272-73. Cha – Jua and Lang distinguish between the Civil Rights Movement and the Black Power Movement in this provocative historiography.

23. Crosby, "'It Wasn't the Wild West,'" 218.

Chapter 1

1. Lerone Bennett, *Black Power U.S.A: The Human Side of Reconstruction, 1867-77* (Baltimore, MD: Pelican, 1967), 359.

2. Ibid.

3. Ibid., 360; James Loewen and Charles Sallis, *Mississippi: Conflict and Change* (New York: Pantheon, 1974), 160; Ken Lawrence, "The Story of Charles Caldwell," Charles Caldwell Centennial March, Souvenir Map, 1975 Bolton (Mississippi) Bicentennial Project (October 11, 1975), Mississippi Department of Archives and History (MDAH).

4. W. E. B. Du Bois, *Black Reconstruction in America, 1860-1880* (New York: Atheneum, 1962), 431; Julius Thompson, *Lynching in Mississippi* (Jefferson, NC: McFarland, 2001), 3.

5. Du Bois, *Black Reconstruction*, 438.

6. Herbert Aptheker, *To Be Free: Pioneering Studies in Afro-American History* (New York: Citadel, 1991), 171; Lawrence, "Charles Caldwell."

7. John Lynch, *The Autobiography of John Lynch*, ed. John Hope Franklin (Chicago: University of Chicago Press, 1970), 166.

8. Ibid., 167.

9. James W. Garner, *Reconstruction in Mississippi* (Baton Rouge: Louisiana State University Press, 1968), 375-77; Aptheker, *To Be Free*, 177.

10. Garner, *Reconstruction*, 378.

11. Aptheker, *To Be Free*, 179-80. The other U.S. senator from Mississippi, Blanche K. Bruce—a Black man—appealed to President Grant for federal intervention. Lynch, *The Autobiography of John Lynch*, 167.

12. George Washington Albright, interview in *The American Slave: A Composite Autobiography, Mississippi Narratives (Part 1)*, eds. George Rawick, Jan Hillegas, Ken Lawrence (Westport, CT: Greenwood Press, 1977), 11.

13. Garner, *Reconstruction*, 384.

14. Thompson, *Lynching in Mississippi*, 11-12.

15. Du Bois, *Black Reconstruction*, 670.

16. Loewen and Sallis, *Mississippi*, 141.

17. Mary Francis Berry, *Black Resistance/White Law: A History of Constitutional Racism in America* (New York: Allen Lane/Penguin, 1994), 98.

18. Stewart E. Tolnay and E. M. Beck, "Rethinking the Role of Racial Violence in the Great Migration," in *Black Exodus: The Great Migration from the American South,* ed. Alferteen Harrison (Jackson: University Press of Mississippi, 1991), 22.

19. Neil McMillen, *Dark Journey: Black Mississippians in the Age of Jim Crow* (Champaign: University of Illinois Press, 1990), 49.

20. Ibid., 41-42; Loewen and Sallis, *Mississippi*, 183-88.

21. Ibid., 293-95. In 1904, five African American communities initiated boycotts in response to the state legislature ordering streetcars to establish segregated facilities for it patrons. The boycotts were short lived and represented the only documented direct action campaign in the state during this period.

22. McMillen, *Dark Journey*; Mary G. Rolinson, *Grassroots Garveyism: The Universal Negro Improvement Association in the Rural South, 1920-1927* (Chapel Hill: University of North Carolina Press, 2007), 173-74.

23. McMillen, *Dark Journey*, 314.

24. Nan Woodruff, *American Congo: The African-American Freedom Struggle in the Delta* (Cambridge, MA: Harvard University Press, 2003), 117.

25. Ibid., 117; Rolison, *Grassroots Garveyism*, 98.

26. Rolison, *Grassroots Garveyism*, 112, 173-78.

27. Tunica uprising described in John C. Willis, *Forgotten Time: Yazoo–Mississippi Delta after the Civil War* (Charlottesville: University Press of Virginia,

2000), 132-33. The story of the LeFlore County rebellion of 1889 in William
F. Holmes, "The Leflore County Massacre and the Demise of the Colored
Farmers Alliance," *Phylon* 4 (1973): 267-74; Willis, *Forgotten Time*, 129-37;
Woodruff, *American Congo*, 22; McMillen, *Dark Journey*, 288.

28. Paul Gilje, *Rioting in America* (Bloomington: Indiana University Press, 1996),
104-5; Thompson, *Lynching in Mississippi*, 72; McMillen, *Dark Journey*, 140.

29. *Baltimore Afro-American*, April 15, 1921, quoted in Frederick G. Detweiler, *Negro Press in the United States* (Chicago: University of Chicago Press, 1922), 84;
McMillen, *Dark Journey*, 139-40.

30. *Negro World*, December 12, 1923, 2; Rolinson, *Grassroots Garveyism*, 135;
Woodruff, *American Congo*, 138-39.

31. *Negro World*, January 19, 1924, 2.

32. *Negro World*, August 19, 1922, 8.

33. Ibid.

34. Lawrence Levine's *Black Culture and Black Consciousness: Afro-American Folk
Thought from Slavery to Freedom* (Oxford: Oxford University Press, 1977),
367-440, discusses a variety of heroic archetypes in the African-derived culture in the United States. These archetypes include the "Bad Man," "merciless toughs and killers confronting and generally vanquishing their adversaries without hesitation and without remorse"; "the moral hard man" (a variation of the Bad Man), admired because he possessed "the strength, courage,
and ability to flout the limitations imposed by white society"; and the "tricksters," who were "weak, relatively powerless creatures who attain their ends
through the native wit and guile rather than power and authority." Levine
only ties the trickster archetype to West African origins, but the "moral hard
man" has its predecessor in the warrior in African folk culture. See Clyde W.
Ford's *Hero with an African Face* (New York: Bantam, 1999), 68-94, for a description of the warrior in traditional African folklore.

35. Allison Davis, Burleigh Gardner, and Mary Gardner, *Deep South: A Social Anthropological Study of Caste and Class* (Chicago: University of Chicago Press,
1941), 23, 249, 534.

36. Ed Cole, in discussion with the author, July 25, 1994, Jackson, MS.

37. Ibid.; Lillian Brown, in discussion with the author, July 29, 1994, Fayette, MS.

38. Cole, discussion.

39. MacArthur Cotton, in discussion with the author, July 23, 1994, Jackson, MS.

40. C. O. Chinn, in discussion with the author, July 19, 1994, Canton, MS.

41. "Annie Colton Reeves" is a pseudonym created for an informant who for personal reasons, particularly security concerns, did not desire to be identified
in print.

42. Annie Colton Reeves, in discussion with the author, July 18, 1994, McComb,
MS.

43. T. C. Johnson, interview in Youth of the Rural Organizing and Cultural

Center (ROCC), *Minds Stayed on Freedom: The Civil Rights Movement in the Rural South; An Oral History* (Boulder, CO: Westview Press, 1991), 11, 154; Hazel Brannon Smith, "Separate and Unequal," *APF Reporter* 6, no. 6 (1983), http://www.aliciapatterson.org/APF0606/Brannon_Smith/Brannon_Smith.html.

44. Smith, "Separate and Unequal."
45. Smith, "Separate and Unequal."
46. T. C. Johnson, interview in *Minds Stayed on Freedom*, 156.
47. Richard Wright, *Black Boy: A Record of Childhood and Youth* (Cleveland, OH: World Publishing, 1945), 227.
48. McMillen, *Dark Journey*, 284.
49. Rolinson, *Grassroots Garveyism*, 134.
50. David Beito, *From Mutual Aid to the Welfare State: Fraternal Societies and Social Services, 1890-1967* (Chapel Hill: University of North Carolina Press, 2000), 20-21; Woodruff, *American Congo*, 83-84.
51. The case of a clandestine lodge network aiding Black sharecropper Henry Loury evading a lynch mob in the Arkansas Delta is documented in Woodruff, *American Congo*, 110-12.
52. Several Black families, including my own, have stories of relatives who escaped the South, fleeing lynch mobs, as a result of confrontations, whether verbal or physical, with White people.
53. "Publisher Who Fled Mississippi in Casket Undergoes Eye Surgery," *Jet*, February 27, 1958.

Chapter 2

1. "The New Fighting South: Militant Negroes Refuse to Leave Dixie or Be Silenced," *Ebony*, August 1955, 69.
2. Amzie Moore, quoted in James Forman, *Making of Black Revolutionaries* (Seattle, WA: Open Hand, 1990), 279.
3. Linda Royster Beito and David Beito, "The Unknown Black Leader," *Journal of Intercultural Disciplines* 2 (2004): 824, http://www.naaas.org/2004%20 monograph-II.pdf.
4. Mary Dudziak, *Cold War Civil Rights: Race and the Image of American Democracy* (Princeton, NJ: Princeton University Press, 2000), 12.
5. John Dittmer, *Local People: The Struggle for Civil Rights in Mississippi* (Champaign: University of Illinois Press, 1994), 3–9.
6. Charles Payne, *I've Got the Light of Freedom: The Organizing Tradition and the Mississippi Freedom Struggle* (Berkeley: University of California Press, 1996), 27; Neil McMillen, *Dark Journey: Black Mississippians in the Age of Jim Crow* (Champaign: University of Illinois, 1990), 314.
7. Payne, *Light of Freedom*, 25–27.

8. David Beito, *From Mutual Aid to the Welfare State: Fraternal Societies and Social Services, 1890–1967* (Chapel Hill: University of North Carolina Press, 2000), 182–88.

9. T. R. M. Howard, quoted in Hodding Carter, "He's Doing Something about the Race Problem," *Saturday Evening Post,* February 23, 1946, 30.

10. Beito, *Mutual Aid to Welfare State,* 188.

11. Aaron Henry with Constance Curry, *Aaron Henry: The Fire Ever Burning* (Jackson: University Press of Mississippi, 2000), 79–80; Linda Royster Beito and David Beito, "The Unknown Black Leader: T. R. M. Howard," *Journal of Inter-Cultural Disciplines* 2 (2004): 820–21, http://naaas.org/2004%20mono-graph-II.pdf.

12. Henry, *Aaron Henry,* 80–81.

13. Charles Evers, interview by David Beito, tape recording, September 2, 1999, Oakwood College Library.

14. Robert M. Ratcliffe, "Time for That Tent Again," *Pittsburg Courier,* March 20, 1954, 23.

15. Robert M. Ratcliffe, "Behind the Headlines," *Pittsburg Courier,* May 14, 1955, 17.

16. Reverend George Lee, quoted in Simeon Booker, *Black Man's America* (Englewood Cliffs, NJ: Prentice Hall, 1964), 161.

17. Reverend George Lee, quoted in Julian Bond, "The Movement: History from the Bottom Up," *Black Issues in Higher Education* 12, no. 23 (1996): 32.

18. *Ebony,* August 1955, 72

19. *Ebony,* August 1955, 73.

20. "12,000 Jam 'Rights' Confab in Mississippi's All-Negro Town," *The Louisiana Weekly,* May 7, 1955, 2.

21. Marjorie McKenzie, "Democracy in Action," *Pittsburg Courier,* January 29, 1955, 24.

22. *Ebony,* August 1955, 69.

23. John Dittmer, *Local People: The Struggle for Civil Rights in Mississippi* (Champaign: University of Illinois Press, 1995), 47.

24. Myrlie Evers with William Peters, *For Us the Living* (New York: Ace Books, 1970), 140; "The New Fighting South," 71. The *Ebony* article provides photos and brief biographical information on activists named on the list.

25. "The New Fighting South," 70; Booker, *Black Man's America,* 162–63.

26. T. R. M. Howard, quoted in "New Fighting South," 70.

27. Booker, *Black Man's America,* 163; "The New Fighting South," 70; Dittmer, *Local People,* 53–54.

28. Gus Courts, interview by John Britton, February 22, 1968, Ralph Bunche Oral History Collection, Howard University; Dittmer, *Local People,* 54.

29. Courts, interview; Dittmer, *Local People,* 54; Evers, *For Us the Living,* 156.

30. Courts, interview, 2.

31. Booker, *Black Man's America,* 166; Mamie Till-Mobley and Christopher Benson, *Death of Innocence: The Story of the Hate Crime That Changed America* (New York: Random House, 2003), 156.

32. Robert M. Ratcliffe, "A Man's Family. . . ," *Pittsburg Courier,* December 31, 1955, A13; Evers, interview.

33. Evers, interview.

34. "He Rode Highways with Hidden Gun . . . Always Cocked! Has Dr. Howard Given Up Ghost?" *Pittsburgh Courier,* September 1956, B6.

35. Benjamin Hooks, interview by David Beito, tape recording, June 15, 2000, Oakwood College Library.

36. Till-Mobley, *Death of Innocence,* 156.

37. Booker, *Black Man's America,* 166.

38. Ratcliffe, "A Man's Family," A13.

39. Dittmer, *Local People,* 47.

40. David Houck, "Killing Emmett," *Rhetoric and Public Affairs* 8, no. 2 (2005): 226–28.

41. Carolyn P. DuBose, *The Untold Story of Charles Diggs: The Public Figure, the Private Man* (Arlington, VA: Barton, 1998), 52; Houck, "Killing Emmett," 230.

42. Ruby Hurley, quoted in Howell Raines, *My Soul Is Rested: The Story of the Civil Rights Movement in the Deep South* (New York: Penguin Books, 1983), 134.

43. Houck, "Killing Emmett," 248; Mamie Till-Mobley, interview by David Beito, tape recording, September 28, 1999, Oakwood College Library.

44. Till-Mobley, interview.

45. Till-Mobley and Benson, *Death of Innocence,* 153–54.

46. DuBose, *Charles Diggs,* 51; Till-Mobley and Benson, *Death of Innocence,* 156.

47. Till-Mobley, interview.

48. Ibid.; Till-Mobley and Benson, *Death of Innocence,* 156.

49. Till-Mobley and Benson, *Death of Innocence,* 158-91.

50. "Dr. Howard Sells Home, Farm," *Pittsburg Courier,* December 24, 1955, 6; Ratcliffe, "A Man's Family," A13.

51. Ratcliffe, "A Man's Family," A13.

52. Arrington High, as told to Marc Crawford, "I Escaped from Mississippi in a Casket," *Jet,* February 27, 1958, 11.

53. "Situation in Mississippi Extremely Serious: Tension Is Continuing to Mount," *Pittsburg Courier,* October 8, 1955, 1–2.

54. Charles Evers, with Grace Halsell, ed., *Evers* (Fayette, MS: privately printed, 1976), 93–96; Charles Evers, *Have No Fear: A Black Man's Fight for Respect in America* (New York: Robert Beinstein, 1997), 60–64.

55. Evers, interview; Evers, *Have No Fear,* 72–73.

56. Payne, *Light of Freedom,* 50; Evers, *For Us the Living,* 89–92.

57. Payne, *Light of Freedom;* Evers, *For Us the Living,* 102–3, 105–6.

58. Henry, *Aaron Henry*, 91–92.
59. "Memorandum to the Branch and Budget Committees from Mr. Current," October 8, 1954, Part 17, National Staff Files, Reel 26, 1940–55 (microfiche), Emory University Library.
60. "Memorandum to Mr. Wilkins from Current," December 1, 1954, Part 17, National Staff Files, Reel 26, 1940–55 (microfiche), Emory University Library.
61. Evers, *For Us the Living*, 115–19.
62. "To All members of the Branches Department Staff from Gloster Current," May 17, 1955, Part 17, National Staff Files, Reel 26, 1940–55 (microfiche), Emory University Library. Georgia was the only other Deep South state with an increase in NAACP membership. The Georgia NAACP increase of 1897 was attributed primarily to the city of Atlanta, where race relations had the reputation of not being as violent as in the rest of Georgia and the Deep South.
63. Donald Barnet and Karari Njama, *The Mau Mau Within: An Analysis of Kenya's Peasant Revolt* (New York: Modern Reader, 1966), 51–55, 74–75, 492. According to Barnett and Njama, the designation "Mau Mau" was never the chosen name of the Kikuyu insurgent movement. The movement operated in decentralized cells often utilizing Ki-Swahili and Kikuyu terminology to identify themselves. The "Mau Mau" designation seems to have come from the British colonial press and counterinsurgency forces. Forces under the command of the Kenyan Defense Council, the coordinating body of the Kenyan insurgent movement, were identified as the Land and Freedom Army.
64. Evers, *For Us the Living*, 82–84; Ruby Hurley, interview by John Britton, January 26, 1968, Howard University Civil Rights Documentation Project, Howard University, Washington, DC; Evers, *Have No Fear*, 75–76.
65. Robert Carl Cohen, *Black Crusader: A Biography of Robert Franklin Williams* (Secaucus, NJ: Lyle Stuart, 1972), 129.
66. Timothy Tyson, *Radio Free Dixie: Robert F. Williams and the Roots of Black Power* (Chapel Hill: University of North Carolina Press, 1999), 148–65; Cohen, *Black Crusader*, 128–31.
67. Hunter Gray (John Salter), correspondence with the author, December 25, 2007.
68. Hurley, interview.
69. Evers, *For Us the Living*, 124.
70. John Salter, *Jackson, Mississippi: An American Chronicle of Struggle and Schism* (Hicksville, NY: Exposition-Banner, 1979), 39–46.
71. Medgar Evers to Gloster Current, correspondence, November 17, 1959, Papers of NAACP, Part 20, Reel 14; Mississippi State Conference of NAACP Branches Press Release, November 17, 1959, Papers of NAACP, Part 20, Reel 14, Emory University
72. Mississippi NAACP Press Release, November 17, 1959.

73. Evers, *For Us the Living,* 194.

74. Salter, *Jackson, Mississippi,* 24; Hurley, quoted in Raines, *My Soul Is Rested,* 271.

75. Carolyn Tyler-Guidry, in discussion with the author, December 30, 2007, Decatur, GA.

76. Sam Bailey, in discussion with the author, July 14, 1994, Jackson, MS.

77. Bailey, discussion.

78. Tyler-Guidry, discussion.

79. Salter, *Jackson, Mississippi,* 24, 43; Evers, *For Us the Living,* 237–38; Adam Nossiter, *Of Long Memory: Mississippi and the Murder of Medgar Evers* (Reading, MA: Addison-Wesley, 1994), 48.

80. Evers, *For Us the Living,* 232–36; Nossiter, *Of Long Memory,* 61.

81. Tyler-Guidry, discussion.

82. Nossiter, *Of Long Memory,* 62; Bailey, discussion.

83. Booker, *Black Man's America,* 166.

84. Myrlie Evers-Williams and Manning Marable, *The Autobiography of Medgar Evers: A Hero's Life and Legacy Revealed through His Writings, Letters, and Speeches* (New York: Basic Civitas Books, 2005), 11–12.

Chapter 3

1. MacArthur Cotton, in discussion with the author, July 23, 1994, Jackson, MS.

2. August Meier and Elliot Rudwick, *CORE* (New York: Oxford University Press, 1973), 4-10.

3. Ibid., 10

4. Ibid., 18.

5. Bayard Rustin, *Down the Line* (Chicago: Quadrangle Books, 1971), 102.

6. Ibid., 102.

7. Marcellus Barksdale, "The Indigenous Civil Rights Movement and Cultural Change in North Carolina: Weldon, Chapel Hill, and Monroe: 1946-1965" (Ph.D. diss., Duke University, 1977), 368; James Forman, *The Making of Black Revolutionaries* (New York: Macmillan, 1972), 275; David Garrow, *Bearing the Cross: Martin Luther King, Jr. and the Southern Christian Leadership Conference* (New York: William Morrow, 1986), 477, 485.

8. Clayborne Carson, *In Struggle: SNCC and the Black Awakening in the 1960s* (Cambridge, MA: Harvard University Press, 1981), 23.

9. Ibid., 23.

10. Ibid., 39-42; Bob Moses in discussion with the author, June 26, 1994, Jackson, MS.

11. Forman, *Making of Black Revolutionaries,* 147-49.

12. Ibid., 174; Mary King, *Freedom Song: A Personal Story of the 1960s Civil Rights*

Movement (New York: Quill, 1987), 103-4. In Forman's autobiographical account of his involvement in SNCC, he recalls participating in an armed watch of the home of Robert Williams.

13. Timothy B. Tyson, *Radio Free Dixie: Robert F. Williams and the Roots of Black Power* (Chapel Hill: University of North Carolina Press, 1999).
14. Michael Flug, in discussion with the author, June 24, 1994, Jackson, MS.
15. King, *Freedom Song*, 90-91.
16. Rustin, *Down the Line*, 74-77; Charles M. Payne, *I've Got the Light of Freedom* (Berkeley: University of California Press, 2007), 44-45.
17. Howell Raines, *My Soul Is Rested: The Story of the Civil Rights Movement in the Deep South* (New York: Penguin Books, 1983), 236.
18. Payne, *Light of Freedom*, 44.
19. Tracy Sugarman, *Stranger at the Gates: A Summer in Mississippi* (New York: Hill and Wang, 1966), 75.
20. Lawrence Guyot, quoted in Raines, *My Soul Is Rested*, 239.
21. Raines, *My Soul Is Rested*, 234; Eric Burner, *And Gently He Shall Lead Them: Robert Parris Moses and Civil Rights in Mississippi* (New York: New York University Press, 1994), 29-31.
22. Raines, *My Soul Is Rested*, 234-35; Burner, *And Gently He Shall Lead*, 29-30.
23. Moses discussion; John Dittmer, *Local People: The Struggle for Civil Rights in Mississippi* (Champaign: University of Illinois Press, 1995), 106.
24. Timothy Jenkins and Lonnie King, interview by Raines, *My Soul Is Rested*, 227-31; Payne, *Light of Freedom*, 108-9.
25. Dittmer, *Local People*, 119-20; Jesse Harris, in discussion with the author, July 27, 2009, Jackson, MS.
26. Burner, *And Gently He Shall Lead*, 37; Dittmer, *Local People*, 103; Jack Newfield, *A Prophetic Minority: A Probing Study of the Origins and Development of the New Left* (New York: Signet Books, 1966), 52.
27. Ibid.; Jack Mendelsohn, *The Martyrs Who Gave Their Lives for Racial Justice* (New York: Harper and Row, 1966), 23-24.
28. Mendelsohn, *The Martyrs*, 24-25; Cotton, discussion.
29. Cotton, discussion; Watkins, in discussion with the author, July 13, 1994, Jackson, MS.
30. Newfield, *A Prophetic Minority*, 50.
31. Eldridge W. Steptoe Jr., interview by Jimmy Dykes, University of Southern Mississippi Digital Collections, University of Southern Mississippi, Center for Oral History, September 6, 2008, http://www.lib.usm.edu/legacy/spcol/crda/oh/steptoe.htm; Payne, *Light of Freedom*, 113.
32. Charles Cobb, interview by Tom Dent, Washington, DC, February 11, 1983.
33. King, *Freedom Song*, 148, 318; Seth Cagin and Phillip Dray, *We Are Not Afraid: The Story of Goodman, Schwerner, and Chaney, and the Civil Rights Campaign for Mississippi* (New York: Nation Books, 2006), 147.

34. Newfield, *A Prophetic Minority*, 59; Joe Martin, in discussion with the author, July 18, 1994, McComb, MS.

35. Chuck McDew, interview by Katherine M. Shannon, 1967, Washington, DC, Howard University Ralph Bunche Oral History Collection, 104-5.

36. "A Mississippi Negro Is Finally Registered after 11 Trying Years," *The Worker*, State of Mississippi Sovereignty Commission Files, Document: E. W. Steptoe (10-13-0-4-1-1-1), Mississippi Department of Archives and History (MDAH); Cagin and Dray, *We Are Not Afraid*, 152.

37. Cobb, interview; Payne, *Light of Freedom*, 114.

38. McDew, interview; Cotton, discussion.

39. E. W. Steptoe Jr., quoted in Carolyn Rickerd, "Amite Farmer Fought for Something 'Worth Dying For,'" *McComb Enterprise-Journal*, December 9, 1984, 10-B.

40. McDew, interview.

41. Steptoe Jr., interview.

42. Ibid.; Moses, discussion; Dittmer, *Local People*, 106; King, *Freedom Song*, 318; Payne, *Light of Freedom*, 114.

43. McDew, interview.

44. Bob Moses, quoted in King, *Freedom Song*, 318.

45. Rickerd, "Worth Dying For," 1-B.

46. Ibid.; "Mississippi Negro Is Finally Registered"; Steptoe Jr., interview; M. Susan Orr-Klopfer, *Where Rebels Roost: Mississippi Civil Rights Revisited* (Lulu. com, 2005), 310; Mendelsohn, *The Martyrs*, 25; Newfield, *Prophetic Minority*, 60.

47. Orr-Klopfer, *Where Rebels Roost*, 310.

48. Mendelson, *The Martyrs*, 29-38; Dittmer, *Local People*, 109-10.

49. E. W. Steptoe, interview by Miriam Feingold, Miriam Feingold Papers, Wisconsin Historical Society, Tape 1, Side 1.

50. Ed Cole, in discussion with the author, July 24, 1994, Jackson, MS.

51. J. F. Nobles, in discussion with the author, July 20, 1994, McComb, MS; Watkins, discussion.

52. J. F. Nobles, discussion; Watkins, discussion; Carson, *In Struggle*, 78; Dittmer, *Local People*, 101.

53. J. F. Nobles, discussion.

54. Watkins, discussion; Watkins interview by Tom Dent, November 3, 1979, Jackson, MS; Dittmer, *Local People*, 107-8.

55. Joe Martin, in discussion with the author, July 18, 1994, McComb, MS; Watkins, discussion; Watkins, interview; Dittmer, *Local People*, 110-15.

56. Watkins, discussion.

57. Ibid.

58. Ibid.

59. Howard Zinn, *SNCC: The New Abolitionists* (Boston: Beacon Press, 1965),

102-3; Sandra Adickes, *The Legacy of a Freedom School* (New York: Palgrave Macmillan, 2005), 13-14.

60. Dittmer, *Local People*, 179-80; Adickes, *Legacy of a Freedom School*, 8.

61. Vernon Dahmer Memorial, July 26, 1986, Vernon Dahmer file, University of Southern Mississippi (USM) archives; "Black Community Leader Killed in Klan Bombing," Vernon Dahmer file, USM archives, Hattiesburg, Mississippi; Adickes, *Legacy of Freedom Schools*, 12.

62. Payne, *Light of Freedom*, 128-29; Watkins, interview.

63. Watkins, discussion.

64. Ibid.; Ellie Jewel Dahmer, in discussion with the author, July 27, 1994, Kelly's Settlement, MS.

65. Douglas Martin, "Sam Block, 60, Civil Rights Battler Dies," *New York Times*, April 22, 2000; Wazir Peacock, "Sam Block: Memories," Veterans of the Civil Rights Movement, October 12, 2008, http://www.crmvet.org/mem/samblock.htm; Payne, *Light of Freedom*, 141-42; Dittmer, *Local People*, 128; Zinn, *SNCC*, 83.

66. Payne, *Light of Freedom*, 133-34; Dittmer, *Local People*, 128-29; Orr-Klopfer, *Where Rebels Roost*, 323; Zinn, *SNCC*, 84.

67. Payne, *Light of Freedom*, 133; Zinn, *SNCC*, 83.

68. Peacock, "Sam Block"; Payne, *Light of Freedom*, 141-42, 144-45; Dittmer, *Local People*, 128-32.

69. Dittmer, *Local People*, 129-31; Payne, *Light of Freedom*, 145.

70. Sam Block, quoted in James Forman, *Making of Black Revolutionaries*, 283; Zinn, *SNCC*, 86.

71. Payne, *Light of Freedom*, 147.

72. Bob Moses, quoted in Zinn, *SNCC*, 84.

73. Dittmer, *Local People*, 132.

74. Ibid., 133; Luvaughn Brown, quoted in Forman, *Black Revolutionaries*, 284-85.

75. Dittmer, *Local People*, 133.

76. Jimmy Travis, quoted in Forman, *Black Revolutionaries*, 294-95; Zinn, *SNCC*, 89-90; Taylor Branch, *Parting the Waters: America in the King Years, 1954-63* (New York: Touchstone, 1988), 716-17.

77. Dittmer, *Local People*, 147-48; Zinn, *SNCC*, 90; Branch, *Parting the Waters*, 717.

78. Payne, *Light of Freedom*, 130; Dittmer, *Local People*, 118-20, 148.

79. Carson, *In Struggle*, 79, 80-81, 84-86; Willie Peacock, interview by Tom Dent, November 2, 1979, Greenwood, MS.

80. Forman, *Black Revolutionaries*, 296; Peacock, interview by Dent; Carson, *In Struggle*, 86.

81. Branch, *Parting the Waters*, 718; Dittmer, *Local People*, 150-51; Forman, *Black Revolutionaries*, 296; Payne, *Light of Freedom*, 221.

82. Payne, *Light of Freedom*, 221.

83. Forman, *Black Revolutionaries*, 296.

84. Branch, *Parting the Waters*, 719; Forman, *Black Revolutionaries*, 297; Dittmer, *Local People*, 151. Moses was reticent about Forman's call to go to protest at city hall. His experience in McComb made him hesitant about engaging in direct action in Greenwood.

85. Watkins, discussion.

86. Branch, *Parting the Water*, 719-20; Dittmer, *Local People*, 151-52.

87. Cagin and Dray, *We Are Not Afraid*, 194-95; Dittmer, *Local People*, 150-51; Forman, *Black Revolutionaries*, 296; Payne, *Light of Freedom*, 168, 205, 221.

88. Dittmer, *Local People*, 155.

89. Payne, *Light of Freedom*, 208-9; Peter Levy, *The Civil Rights Movement* (Westport, CT: Greenwood Press, 1998), 113.

90. Ibid., 209.

91. Watkins, discussion.

92. Branch, *Parting the Waters*, 724-25; Dittmer, *Local People*, 155-56.

93. Jay MacCleod, introduction to Youth of the Rural Organizing and Cultural Center (ROCC), *Minds Stayed on Freedom: The Civil Rights Movement in the Rural South; An Oral History* (Boulder, CO: Westview Press, 1991), 10; Dittmer, *Local People*, 190-91.

94. MacCleod, introduction in ROCC, *Minds Stayed on Freedom*, 13; Payne, *Light of Freedom*, 278.

95. Hartman Turnbow, interview in Raines, *My Soul Is Rested*, 261; Payne, *Light of Freedom*, 279; Dittmer, *Local People*, 192.

96. Reverend J. J. Russell, interview by Kenneth Sallis, William Williams, and Jennifer Dixon, in ROCC, *Minds Stayed on Freedom*, 23.

97. Hartman Turnbow, interviewed in Raines, *My Soul Is Rested*, 262-63; Russell interview in ROCC, *Minds Stayed on Freedom*, 24-25; Payne, *Light of Freedom*, 204; Burner, *And Gently He Shall Lead*, 106.

98. J. J. Russell, interview in ROCC, *Minds Stayed on Freedom*, 25-27; Turnbow, interview in Raines, *My Soul Is Rested*, 24-25; Burner, *And Gently He Shall Lead*, 107; Branch, *Parting the Waters*, 781-82.

99. Cobb, interview; Watkins, discussion; Turnbow, interview in Raines, *My Soul Is Rested*, 265-66.

100. Payne, *Light of Freedom*, 279.

101. Ibid., 178-79; Dave Dennis, interview with Tom Dent, October 8, 1983, Lafayette, LA, Dent Collection, Tougaloo College.

102. Ann Moody, *Coming of Age in Mississippi* (New York: Dell, 1968), 286-88; Dittmer, *Local People*, 186-88; Meier, *CORE*, 271.

103. Dennis, interview with Dent.

104. Ibid.; Rudy Lombard, in discussion with the author, June 25, 1994, Jackson, MS.

105. C. O. Chinn, in discussion with the author, 19 July 1994, Canton, MS; Lombard, discussion.

106. Dennis, interview with Dent; C. O. Chinn, discussion; Meier and Rudwick, *CORE*, 272.
107. Minnie Chinn, in discussion with the author, July 17, 1994, Canton, MS.
108. Matthew Suarez, interview by Tom Dent, July 8, 1977, New Orleans, LA, Dent Collection, Tougaloo College; Lombard, discussion.
109. Dennis, interview with Dent; Moody, *Coming of Age*, 303.
110. Lombard, discussion.
111. Ibid.; Dennis, interview with Dent; Moody, *Coming of Age*, 302-3; 327-29.
112. Dittmer, *Local People*, 189-90; Meier and Rudwick, *CORE*, 272; Moody, *Coming of Age*, 300-304.
113. Moody, *Coming of Age*, 317-20, 327-29.

Chapter 4

1. Margaret Block, in discussion with the author, June 23, 2010, Cleveland, MS.
2. Charles Cobb, interview by Tom Dent, Washington, DC, February 11, 1983, Dent Collection; Charles Cobb, in discussion with the author, August 19, 1994, Washington, DC.
3. Doug McAdam, *Freedom Summer* (New York: Oxford University Press, 1988), 38.
4. James Forman, *The Making of Black Revolutionaries* (New York: Macmillan, 1972), 354-71; Clayborne Carson, *In Struggle: SNCC and the Black Awakening in the 1960s* (Cambridge, MA: Harvard University Press, 1981), 96-98; Eric Burner, *And Gently He Shall Lead Them: Robert Parris Moses and Civil Rights in Mississippi* (New York: New York University Press, 1994), 112-13, 114-24.
5. Carson, *In Struggle*, 77.
6. Ibid.
7. Ibid., 98; Dennis, interview with Dent.
8. Hollis Watkins, interview in Henry Hampton and Steve Fayer, *Voices of Freedom: An Oral History of the Civil Rights Movement from the 1950s through the 1980s* (New York: Bantam Books, 1990), 182-83; MacArthur Cotton, in discussion with the author, July 23, 1994, Jackson, MS; Hollis Watkins, in discussion with the author, July 13, 1994, Jackson, MS; Charles Payne, *I've Got the Light of Freedom: The Organizing Tradition and the Mississippi Freedom Struggle* (Berkeley: University of California Press, 1995), 297-98.
9. Often Black workers, particularly domestics, who had close proximity to the White power structure supplied information to the Movement about what segregationists were planning. This informal network was essential to the security apparatus of local community activists.
10. Cobb, interview; Cobb, discussion.
11. Cotton, discussion; Watkins, discussion.
12. Carson, *In Struggle*, 99-100; Forman, *Black Revolutionaries*, 372-73.

13. "Staff Meeting Minutes," June 10, 1994, SNCC Papers, Box 7, Folder 7, archives of Martin Luther King, Jr. Center for Nonviolent Social Change, Atlanta, GA.

14. Ibid.

15. Ibid.

16. Ibid.; Charles Cobb referred to Liberty County NAACP activist E. W. Steptoe.

17. "Staff Meeting Minutes"; Mary King, *Freedom Song: A Personal Story of the 1960s Civil Rights Movement* (New York: Quill, 1987), 323; Cobb, discussion.

18. King, *Freedom Song*, 324; Forman, *Black Revolutionaries*, 374-75; Cobb, discussion.

19. "Staff Meeting Minutes."

20. Max Stanford, "Towards a Revolutionary Action Movement Manifesto," quoted in "The Colonial War at Home," editorial, *Monthly Review* 16, no. 1 (May 1964): 5-6; Robert Brisbane, *Black Activism: Racial Revolution in the United States, 1954-1970* (Valley Forge, PA: Judson Press, 1974), 181-82; Robert Carl Coher, *Black Crusader: A Biography of Robert Franklin Williams* (Secaucus, NJ: Lyle Stuart, 1972), 211-13, 223-24, 225-26.

21. Donald Freeman, "Black Youth and Afro-American Liberation," *Black America* (Fall 1964): 15-16, Martin Luther King Center Archives, Atlanta, GA, Box 1, File 3; Muhammad Ahmad, *We Will Return in the Whirlwind: Black Radical Organizations, 1960-75* (Chicago: Clark Kerr, 2007), 102, 117, 123.

22. Freeman, "Black Youth," 15-16; Ahmad, *We Will Return*, 117-19; Muhammad Ahmad (Max Stanford Jr.), in discussion with the author, November 20, 2011, Atlanta, GA; Askia Ture (Roland Snellings), in discussion with the author, September 3, 1994, Atlanta, GA.

23. Ahmad, discussion; A. Ture, discussion; Ahmad, *We Will Return*, xi-xviii, 119.

24. Ahmad, discussion; A. Ture, discussion; Ahmad, *We Will Return*, 118, 121; Roland Snellings, "The Long Hot Summer," *Black America* (Fall 1964): 13-14, Martin Luther King Jr. Center for Nonviolent Social Change Archives, Black Revolutionary and Black Power Organizations 1964-68, Box 1, File 3.

25. "Staff Meeting Minutes"; A. Ture, discussion.

26. Ahmad, discussion; A. Ture, discussion; Ahmad, *We Will Return*, 54-55, 121-22; "The Colonial War at Home," 1-13.

27. Cotton, discussion; Ahmad, discussion; A. Ture, discussion; Ahmad, *We Will Return*, 121; "Staff Meeting Minutes."

28. Kwame Ture, in discussion with the author, February 6, 1994, Atlanta, GA; Forman, *Black Revolutionaries*, 375.

29. K. Ture, discussion.

30. Forman, *Black Revolutionaries*, 374-75.

31. August Meier and Elliot Rudwick, *CORE* (New York: Oxford University Press, 1973), 263-64.

32. M. S. Handler, "Militancy Grows, CORE Aides Warn: Convention Delegates Fear Negro Will Strike Back," *New York Times*, June 28, 1963, 12.

33. Ibid.; Meier and Rudwick, *CORE*, 296.

34. Meier and Rudwick, *CORE*, 116.

35. Ibid., 298.

36. Ibid.

37. Dennis, interview with Dent; Jack Mendelsohn, *The Martyrs Who Gave Their Lives for Racial Justice* (New York: Harper & Row, 1966), 112-28.

38. "FBI Director Tells Plans for Our State: No Protection Planned for Civil Rights Workers Here," *Jackson Clarion-Ledger*, July 11, 1964, 1A.

39. John Dittmer, *Local People: The Struggle for Civil Rights in Mississippi* (Champaign: University of Illinois Press, 1995), 248-51.

40. Ibid., 248-49; Dennis, interview in *Voices of Freedom*, 194; Dave Dennis, interview in Howell Raines, *My Soul Is Rested: The Story of the Civil Rights Movement in the Deep South* (New York: Penguin, 1983), 278.

41. Dennis, quoted in Raines, *My Soul Is Rested*, 278.

42. Dennis, interview in Raines, *My Soul Is Rested*, 278.

43. Dennis, interview with Dent; Dennis, interview in *Voices of Freedom*, 195; Dennis, interview in Raines, *My Soul Is Rested*, 277-78; Meier and Rudwick, *CORE*, 298. After Freedom Summer, Dennis returned to Louisiana, where he worked closely with the Deacons for Defense and Justice. The association of Dennis with the Deacons, considered by many after 1964 to be the armed wing of the southern Black Freedom Struggle, further demonstrates his disassociation with nonviolence and embrace of self-defense.

44. McAdam, *Freedom Summer*, 255-56.

45. Len Holt, *The Summer That Didn't End: The Story of the Mississippi Civil Rights Project of 1964* (New York: Da Capo, 1992), 12.

46. John Herbers, "School Test Nears in Harmony, Miss.," *New York Times*, August 16, 1964, 58.

47. Winson Hudson, interview by Tom Dent, August 1, 1979, Harmony, Mississippi, Dent Collection; John Herbers, "School Test Nears"; Dittmer, *Local People*, 256-57.

48. Hudson, interview by Tom Dent.

49. Ibid.

50. Jerome Smith, interview by Tom Dent, New Orleans, September 23, 1983, Dent Collection.

51. Nicholas Von Hoffman, *Mississippi Notebook* (New York: David White, 1964), 94-95. *Mississippi Notebook* has photographs by Henry Herr Gill of Harmony Blacks defending their community with guns, including Harmony youth participating in an armed watch of the Harmony Community Center.

52. Ibid.; Jerome Smith, interview.

53. Dovie Hudson, interview in Brian Lanker, *I Dream a World: Portraits of Black*

Women Who Changed America (New York: Stewart, Tabori, and Chang, 1989), 161.

54. Hudson, interview by Tom Dent.
55. Hudson, interview in *I Dream a World*, 161.
56. Payne, *Light of Freedom*, 279-82.
57. Ibid., 280.
58. Ed Brown, interview by Tom Dent, Atlanta, Georgia, July 2, 1979, Dent Collection.
59. Brown, interview.
60. Watkins, discussion.
61. Ibid.
62. Shadrach Davis, interview by Thomas Frazier and Nathaniel Spurlock in Youth of the Rural Organizing and Cultural Center (ROCC), *Minds Stayed on Freedom: The Civil Rights Struggle in the Rural South; An Oral History* (Boulder, CO: Westview Press, 1991), 124.
63. Brown, interview.
64. Lorenzo Wesley's poem in Peter B. Levy's *Documentary History of the Civil Rights Movement* (New York: Greenwood, 1992), 145.
65. King, *Freedom Song*, 319.
66. Martha Honey, in discussion with the author, August 26, 1994, Silver Springs, MD.
67. Ibid.
68. Ibid.; Abe Osheroff was a former member of the Communist Party and carpenter residing at the time in Los Angeles. Osheroff used his carpentry skills in the building of the Holmes County community center. Matt Herron, in discussion with the author, November 8, 2007, San Rafael, CA; Douglass Martin, "Abe Osheroff, Veteran of the Abraham Lincoln Brigade Dies at 92," *New York Times,* April 11, 2008, http://abeosheroff.org/NYTObituary.html.
69. Martha Honey, discussion.
70. Jodie and Virgie Saffold, in discussion with the author, July 1994, Old Pilgrims Rest, MS; Jodie Saffold, interview by Marques Saffold, Jefferey Blackmon, and Marvin Noel in ROCC, *Minds Stayed on Freedom,* 64-65; Vanderbilt and Cora Roby, interview by Marques Saffold in ROCC, *Minds Stayed on Freedom,* 48, 52-55.
71. Jack Nelson, *Terror in the Night: The Klan's Campaign against the Jews* (New York: Simon & Schuster, 1993), 104-7; Charles Young, in discussion with the author, October 3, 1994, Meridian, MS.
72. Ibid.; Nelson, *Terror in the Night,* 108-9.
73. Cotton, discussion; Watkins, discussion; Payne, *Light of Freedom*, 208-9.
74. Unita Blackwell, in discussion with the author, June 29, 1994, Jackson, MS.
75. Kwame Ture, in discussion with the author, February 9, 1994, Decatur, GA; Sundiata Acoli, letter to author, October 8, 1994.

76. Margaret Block, in discussion with the author, June 23, 2010, Cleveland, MS.
77. Tallahatchie County, Mississippi, Largest Slaveholders from 1860 Slave Census Schedules and Surname Matches for African-Americans on 1870 Census, http://freepages.genealogy.rootsweb.ancestry.com/~ajac/mstallahatchie.htm.
78. Block, discussion.
79. Ibid.; Fred Mangrum, interview by Robert Wright, July 8, 1969, Civil Rights Documentation Project, Bunche Collection, Moorland Spingarn Research Center, Howard University; Ed Brown, in discussion with author, October 8, 2009, Atlanta, GA.
80. WATS Report, August 5,1964, SNCC Papers, Box 38, Folder 2, MLK Center Archives; WATS Report, August 8,1964, SNCC Papers, Box 38, Folder 2, MLK Center Archives; WATS Report, August 10,1964, SNCC Papers, Box 38, Folder 2, MLK Center Archives, Atlanta, GA; Margaret Block, phone conversation with author, July 27, 2010.
81. WATS Report, August 11, 1964, SNCC Papers, Box 38, Folder 2, MLK Center Archives, Atlanta, GA; Block, discussion.
82. Block, discussion; Ed Brown, discussion; Brown, interview.
83. Block, discussion.
84. Block, discussion; Brown, discussion; Brown, interview.
85. Block, discussion.
86. Ibid.; Brown, discussion; Brown, interview.
87. Block, discussion.
88. Ibid.; Brown, discussion; Brown, interview.
89. Dittmer, *Local People*, 268.
90. Ibid., 266-68, 304.
91. Matthew Nobles, in discussion with the author, July 18, 1994, McComb, MS.
92. "Police Probing Blasts," *Jackson Clarion-Ledger*, June 24, 1964, 1, 5; Claude Bryant, in discussion with the author, July 1994, McComb, MS; Dittmer, *Local People*, 267, 306.
93. Dittmer, *Local People*, 306; Bryant, discussion.
94. J. F. Nobles, in discussion with the author, July 20, 1994, McComb, MS.
95. Ibid.; Dittmer, *Local People*, 268, 306.
96. The Reeves family name was changed at their request.
97. While in the minority, the openly defiant Blacks were often admired and raised to the status of folk heroes by the majority of the Black community. See Allison Davis, Burleigh Gardner, and Mary Gardner, *Deep South: A Social Anthropological Study of Caste and Class* (Chicago: University of Chicago Press, 1941), 2, 249, 534.
98. Annie Reeves, in discussion with the author, July 18, 1994, McComb, MS.
99. Ibid.; William Reeves, in discussion with the author, July 18, 1994, McComb, MS; Eddie Williams, in discussion with the author, July 18, 1994, McComb, MS.

100. M. Nobles, discussion.
101. Watkins, discussion; J. F. Nobles, discussion; M. Nobles, discussion.
102. M. Nobles, discussion; J. F. Nobles, discussion.
103. Peter Cummings, "Voting Drive Starts Despite Violence," *The Harvard Crimson*, October 1, 1964.
104. Dittmer, *Local People*, 267; Jesse Harris, in discussion with the author, July 23, 2009, Jackson, MS.
105. Ibid.
106. Ibid.; Dittmer, *Local People*, 304.
107. "Federal Inaction Challenged," *The Student Voice*, September 23, 1964, 3.
108. J. F. Nobles, discussion; Harris, discussion; Joe Martin, in discussion with the author, July 18, 1994, McComb, MS.
109. Martin, discussion.
110. J. F. Nobles, discussion.
111. Ibid.
112. Martin, discussion.
113. Ibid.; J. F. Nobles, discussion; Dittmer, *Local People*, 307.
114. Dittmer, *Local People*, 308-10.
115. Ibid., 310-11; "McComb Shaken by Over 20 Bombings," *Student Voice*, November 25, 1964, 1, 4.
116. Dittmer, *Local People*, 310-13; Payne, *Light of Freedom*, 316.
117. Acoli, letter to author.
118. Cobb, discussion.
119. Martin, discussion.
120. Bob Moses in discussion with the author, June 26, 1994, Jackson, MS.
121. Cleveland Sellers, *The River of No Return: The Autobiography of a Black Militant and the Life and Death of SNCC* (Jackson: University Press of Mississippi, 1990), 111; Forman, *Black Revolutionaries*, 386-96.
122. Lorne Cress, in discussion with the author, June 18, 1994, Jackson, MS; Cobb, discussion.

Chapter 5

1. Roy Reed, "Deacons in Mississippi Visits, Implores Negroes to 'Wake up,'" *New York Times*, August 30, 1965, 18, ProQuest Historical Newspapers.
2. J. Loewen and C. Sallis, *Mississippi: Conflict and Change* (New York: Pantheon Books, 1974), 18, 40, 80-82.
3. "Adams County, Mississippi," SNCC Research: Atlanta, Georgia, October 25, 1965, Freedom Information Service Archives, Jackson, Mississippi.
4. Ralph Jennings, interview by author, March 23, 2010, Natchez, MS; Paul Hendrickson, *Sons of Mississippi: A Story of Race and Legacy* (New York: Random House, 2003), 227; James Young, in discussion with the author, July 28, 1994,

Natchez, MS; John Bevilaqua, "The FBI Cointelpro-White Hate: The Decline of KKK Organizations in Mississippi," The Education Forum, available online.

5. Young, discussion; Bevilaqua, "FBI Cointelpro"; Hendrickson, *Sons of Mississippi*, 237.

6. "Cops, Race Strife Cut Tourist Trade in Natchez," *Muhammad Speaks*, September 25, 1964. Young, discussion; Bevilaqua, "FBI Cointelpro"; Hendrickson, *Sons of Mississippi*, 237.

7. "If a White Man Shoots at a Negro, We Will Shoot Back," *Nashville Runner*, February 17, 1964.

8. "Address in Nashville Distorted, Evers Says," White Resistance and Reprisals—1956-65, Papers of the NAACP, Part 20, Reel 14, Emory University.

9. Myrlie Evers, *For Us, the Living* (Jackson: University Press of Mississippi, 1976), 130-32; Milton Cooper, in discussion with the author, July 23, 1994, Jackson, MS.

10. C. Horowitz, *Natchez, Mississippi: Six Weeks of Crisis*, unpublished document, 1965, Freedom Information Service Archives, Jackson, Mississippi. "Desegregation Petition Filed," *Natchez Democrat*, August 20, 1965; John Dittmer, *Local People: The Struggle for Civil Rights in Mississippi* (Champaign: University of Illinois Press, 1994), 355-60; Young, discussion; "Car Bomb Injures NAACP Leader in Natchez, Miss.," *New York Times*, August 28, 1965, 49, ProQuest Historical Newspapers; Ser Sesh Ab Heter (Clifford M. Boxley), in discussion with the author, March 23, 2010, Natchez, MS.

11. "Natchez Bombing Is Laid to Whites," *New York Times*, September 27, 1964; "Police Push Investigations of Blasts That Hit Natchez," *Jackson Clarion-Ledger/Jackson Daily News*, September 27, 1964, sec. A; "Two More Burned Out Churches Dedicated," *Jackson Clarion Ledger*, March 22, 1965; "Leader Claims Five Slayings," *Jackson Daily News*, May 7, 1964.

12. "Natchez Police Car Stoned," *New York Times*, August 29, 1965, 51, ProQuest Historical Newspapers.

13. "Natchez Mayor Offers Reward for Bomber," *Jackson Clarion-Ledger*, August 28, 1965; Roy Reed, "Bombing Angers Natchez Negroes," *New York Times*, August 29, 1965, 51.

14. Charles Evers quoted in Drew Pearson, "The Negroes Are Fed Up," *The Washington Post*, September 1, 1965, B13, ProQuest Historical Newspapers, *The Washington Post* (1877-1993).

15. Ibid.

16. Gene Roberts, "NAACP May Oust Evers as Aide in Mississippi," *New York Times*, September 10, 1965, 22, ProQuest Historical Newspapers; Dittmer, *Local People*, 354.

17. James Stokes, in discussion with the author, August 1, 1994, Natchez, MS; Jesse Bernard Williams, in discussion with the author, July 24, 2009, Natchez, MS; Young, discussion.

18. Reed, "Bombing Angers Natchez," 51; Williams, discussion; Lance Hill, *Deacons for Defense: Armed Resistance and the Civil Rights Movement* (Chapel Hill: University of North Carolina Press, 2004), 192; "Deacons for the Defense and Justice, Incorporated," Federal Bureau of Investigation Racial Matters document, September 3, 1965, 1-6, Cointelpro Federal Bureau of Investigation (FBI); Roy Reed, "The Deacons, Too, Ride by Night," *New York Times Magazine*, August 15, 1965, 10, New York Times Historical Newspaper; Roy Reed, "White Man Is Shot by Negro in Clash in Bogalusa," *New York Times*, July 9, 1965, 1.

19. Stokes, discussion; Roy Reed, "Bombing Angers Natchez Negroes," *New York Times*, August 29, 1965, L51.

20. Stokes, discussion; Young, discussion

21. Horowitz, *Natchez, Mississippi.*

22. Stokes, discussion; Young, discussion.

23. Hollis Watkins, in discussion with the author, July 13, 1994.

24. Stokes, discussion; Young, discussion.

25. "Black Natchez," produced by Ed Pincus and David Neuman, Center for Social Documentary Film, 1967, University of Mississippi Library; Stokes, discussion.

26. Young, discussion; Charles Evers, with Grace Halsell, ed., *Evers* (Fayette, MS: privately printed, 1976).

27. Ser Sesh Ab Heter, discussion.

28. Stokes, discussion.

29. Federal Bureau of Investigation, *Deacons for Defense and Justice Inc.*, Field Office File 157-2466-59, FBI Files (Jackson, MS, 1967).

30. Young, discussion.

31. Watkins, discussion.

32. Young, discussion. Ed Cole, in discussion with the author, July 24, 1994, Jackson, MS; Lillie Brown, in discussion with the author, July 29, 1994, Fayette, MS; Stokes, discussion.

33. FBI, *Deacons for Defense.*

34. Stokes, discussion; Cole, discussion.

35. "Board Meets with Negro Delegation," *Natchez Democrat*, August 29, 1965; "Natchez Officials Meeting to Consider Racial Crisis," *Jackson Daily News*, August 30, 1965; "Board Rejects Demands," *Natchez Democrat*, September 3, 1965.

36. "Board Rejects Demands."

37. "Curfew Set from 10pm to 5am Effective Now," *Natchez Democrat*, September 1, 1965.

38. "National Guardsmen in City as Alderman Nix Demands," *Natchez Democrat*, September 3, 1965.

39. Dittmer, *Local People,* 355-58.

40. Ibid., 356; Evers, *Evers*, 134.

41. William Morris, *Yazoo: Integration in a Deep Southern Town* (New York: Harper Magazine Press, 1971), 62-63.

42. Young, discussion.

43. Cole, discussion.

44. M. Evers, *For Us*, 134.

45. Young, discussion; James Nix, in discussion with the author, September 20, 1994, Hattiesburg, MS; University of Southern Mississippi, "An Oral History with James Nix," Civil Rights in Mississippi Digital Archive, http:/www.lib.usm.edu/legacy/spcol/crda/oh/nix.htm. According to Forrest County activist James Nix, after the boycott campaign in Hattiesburg in 1966, the enforcer squad was called "Da Spirit."

46. Cole, discussion

47. Stokes, discussion

48. Stokes, discussion; L. Brown, discussion. Samuel Harden, in discussion with the author, October 30, 1994, Woodville, MS.

49. Emilye Crosby, "Common Courtesy: A Community Study of the Civil Rights Movement in Port Gibson, Mississippi" (Ph.D. diss., University of Indiana, 1995), 16-17. R. Devoual and J. Miller, *Freedom Lives in Mississippi* (pamphlet, n.p., n.d.), 5.

50. George Walker, in discussion with the author, September 29, 1994, Port Gibson, MS; Crosby, "Common Courtesy," 230-31.

51. Walker, discussion.

52. Ibid.

53. Stokes, discussion.

54. Ellie Dahmer, in discussion with the author, July 27, 1994, Kelly's Settlement, MS; "Malice toward Some," *Newsweek*, April 11, 1966, 39-40; "Night Riders Kill Mississippi Negro," *New York Times*, January 11, 1966.

55. "Night Riders Kill Mississippi Negro."

56. A. Hopkins, *Observation and Investigation in Hattiesburg, Forest County, Mississippi*. Mississippi State Sovereignty Commission Report, Governor Paul Johnson Papers, University of Southern Mississippi, 1966.

57. University of Southern Mississippi, "An Oral History with James Nix," in the Civil Rights in Mississippi Digital Archive, http:/www.lib.usm.edu/legacy/spcol/crda/oh/nix.htm; "Black Community Leader Killed in Klan Bombing," Vernon Dahmer, University of Southern Mississippi Archives.

58. Herman Leach, in discussion with the author, July 30, 1994, Yazoo City, MS; Earle Johnston, *Mississippi's Defiant Years, 1953-1973* (Forest, MS: Lake Harbor Publishers, 1990), 292-97.

59. Andrew Marx and T. Tuthill, "Resisting the Klan: Mississippi Organizes," *Southern Exposure* 8, no. 2 (Summer 1980): 73-76.

Chapter 6

1. Chester Higgins, "Meredith's Threat to Arm: Not Answer, Says Dr. King," *Jet Magazine,* June 23, 1966, 18.
2. "Mississippi Story," *New York Times*, June 12, 1966, ProQuest Historical Newspapers, 207; "Heat on Highway 51," *Time,* June 17, 1966, http://www.time.com/time/magazine/article/0,9171,899204,00.html; Carolyn Kleiner Butler, "Down in Mississippi: The Shooting of Protester James Meredith Thirty-Eight Years Ago, Seemingly Documented by a Rookie Photographer, Galvanized the Civil Rights Movement," *Smithsonian Magazine*, February 2005, http://www.smithsonianmag.com/history-archaeology/Down_In_Mississippi.html. Norvill was apprehended and charged with assault with intent to commit murder. He pleaded guilty before trial and received a five-year sentence of which he did eighteen months.
3. Roy Wilkins, with Tom Mathews, *Standing Fast: The Autobiography of Roy Wilkins* (New York: Viking Press, 1982), 315; Steve Lawson, *The Pursuit of Power: Southern Blacks and Electoral Politics 1965-1982* (New York: Columbia University Press, 1985), 51.
4. Lawson, *Pursuit of Power*, 51-52; Stokely Carmichael, with Ekwueme M. Thelwell, *Ready for Revolution: The Life and Struggles of Stokely Carmichael (Kwame Ture)* (New York: Scribners, 2003), 496-97.
5. Carmichael, *Ready for Revolution*, 493, 497; Jesse Harris, in discussion with the author, July 23, 2009, Jackson, MS; Lance Hill, *Deacons for Defense: Armed Resistance and the Civil Rights Movement* (Chapel Hill: University of North Carolina Press, 2004), 246; "Black Power," *Now: News of the Nation and the World* 2, no. 5 (Summer 1967): 5.
6. Carmichael, *Ready for Revolution*, 497-500; Henry Hampton and S. Fayer, *Voices of Freedom: An Oral History of the Civil Rights Movement from the 1950s through the 1980s* (New York: Bantam Books, 1990); Cleveland Sellers, with Robert Terrell, *The River of No Return: The Autobiography of a Black Militant and the Life and Death of SNCC* (Jackson: University Press of Mississippi, 1990), 162-63; Harris, discussion.
7. Carmichael, *Ready for Revolution*, 502.
8. Sellers, *River of No Return*, 165-66.
9. John Dittmer, *Local People: The Struggle for Civil Rights in Mississippi* (Champaign: University of Illinois Press, 1995), 392.
10. Gene Roberts, "Mississippi Reduces Police Protection for Marchers," *New York Times*, June 17, 1966, ProQuest Historical Newspapers, 33; Carmichael, *Ready for Revolution*, 506-7; Sellers, *River of No Return*, 166-67; Peniel Joseph, *Waiting 'Til the Midnight Hour: A Narrative History of Black Power in America* (New York: Macmillan, 2007), 140-43.

11. "Negro Baptist Aide Hits 'Black Power,'" *New York Times*, June 23, 1966, Pro-Quest Historical Newspapers, 24; Carmichael, *Ready for Revolution*, 513-14; Gene Roberts, "King Plans to Return," *New York Times*, June 22, 1966, Pro-Quest Historical Newspapers, 25.
12. Carmichael, *Ready for Revolution*, 513.
13. Gene Roberts, "Marcher Ranks Expand to 1200," *New York Times*, June 20,1966, ProQuest Historical Newspapers, 20; Luella Hazelwood, in discussion with the author, July 25, 2009, Belzoni, MS; Gene Roberts, "Rights Marchers Walk 16 Miles," *New York Times*, June 21, 1966, ProQuest Historical Newspapers, 30.
14. Roberts, "Marcher Ranks Expand to 1200," 20; Tyrone "Fat Daddy" Davis, in discussion with the author, June 17, 2009, Jackson, MS; Hondo Lumumba, in discussion with the author, June 17, 2009, Jackson, MS.
15. Nancella Hudson, in discussion with the author, July 30, 1994, Yazoo City, MS.
16. Arthur Clayborn, in discussion with the author, September 25, 1994, Yazoo City, MS.
17. Herman Leach, in discussion with the author, July 30, 1994, Yazoo City, MS.
18. James K. Cazalas, "Deacons Play Unannounced Role at March," *Commercial Appeal*, June 26, 1966, Deacons for Defense file, Sovereignty Commission, MDAH, 11-11-0-20-1-1-1; Dittmer, *Local People*, 395; Lawson, *Pursuit of Power*, 54.
19. Roberts, "Mississippi Reduces Police," 1; Dittmer, *Local People*, 395-96; Carmichael, *Ready for Revolution*, 504-5.
20. Gene Roberts, "Marchers Upset by Negro Apathy," *New York Times*, June 14, 1966, ProQuest Historical Newspapers, 19; Lester Sobel, *Civil Rights, 1960-66* (New York: Facts on File, 1966), 393.
21. Harris, discussion.
22. Sellers, *River of No Return*, 166; Roberts, "Marcher Ranks Expand."
23. Roberts, "Marcher Ranks Expand," 20.
24. Roberts, "Marchers Upset," 19.
25. Carmichael, *Ready for Revolution*, 504-5; Roberts, "Marchers Upset," 35.
26. Cazalas, "Deacons Play Unannounced Role at March"; Roberts, "Marchers Upset," 19.
27. "Dr. King Scores 'Deacons,'" *New York Times*, June 22, 1966.
28. Martin Luther King Jr., *Where Do We Go from Here: Chaos or Community?* (New York: Harper & Row, 1968), 26-27, 55-59.
29. Higgins, "Meredith's Threat," 18; King, *Where Do We Go*, 26-27, 55-59.
30. Andrew Young, quoted in Carmichael, *Ready for Revolution*, 497.
31. Robert Reed, "Philadelphia, Miss., Whites and Negroes Trade Shots," *New York Times*, June 22, 1966, ProQuest Historical Newspapers, 25; Roberts, "Marcher Ranks Expand," 20; Hill, *Deacons for Defense*, 248-49.

32. Paul Good, *The Trouble I've Seen: White Journalist/Black Movement* (Washington, DC: Howard University Press, 1974), 259-60; Reed, "Philadelphia, Miss.," 25; Robert Tyrone Davis, in discussion with the author, June 17, 2009, Jackson, MS; Memorandum to Erle Johnson from A. L. Hopkins, Sovereignty Commission, June 21, 1965, SCR ID # 2-112-2-40-1-1-1, Mississippi Department of Archives and History (MDAH); Carmichael, *Ready for Revolution*, 504-5.

33. Reed, "Philadelphia, Miss.," 1; Gene Roberts, "Mississippi Strife Studied by FBI," *New York Times*, June 23, 1966, ProQuest Historical Newspapers, 22; Sobel, *Civil Rights*, 394; Carmichael, *Ready for Revolution*, 505. Philadelphia had recently hired two Black police officers.

34. Reed, "Philadelphia, Miss.," 1; Roberts, "Mississippi Strife," 22.

35. "Civil Rights and Armed Struggle: Interview with a Southern Militant," *Urgent Tasks* 13 (Spring 1982): 30.

36. Ibid.; "New SNCC Officers," *SNCC Newsletter* 1, no. 4 (June–July 1967): 8; James Featherstone, in discussion with the author, August 25, 1994, Washington, DC; Chude Pam Parker Allen, "Would You Marry One," http://www.crmvet.org/info/marryone.htm.

37. Roy Reed, "Dr. King Bids U.S. Guard New March," *New York Times*, June 23, 1966, ProQuest Historical Newspapers, 23; "President Gets Assurance," *New York Times*, June 24, 1966, ProQuest Historical Newspapers, 20.

38. Reed, "Dr. King Bids," 23; "Report Received by Telephone June 23, 1966," Sovereignty Commission, file 9-31-5-45-1-1-1, MDAH; "Investigation in Canton and Madison County to Determine the Effectiveness of the Boycott and Whether or Not Threats Are Being Made to the Negro Citizens for Shopping at White Stores," Sovereignty Commission, September 27, 1966, File 2-24-4-40-1-1-1, 3, MDAH; Dittmer, *Local People*, 399.

39. Gene Roberts, "Mississippi Police Use Gas to Rout Rights Campers," *New York Times*, June 24, 1966, ProQuest Historical Newspapers, 1, 20; "The Major Events of the Day," *New York Times*, June 24, 1966, ProQuest Historical Newspapers, 39; Dittmer, *Local People*, 399-401; Hollis Watkins, phone conversation with author, March 1, 2010, Jackson, MS.

40. Davis, discussion; Roberts, "Mississippi Police Rout Campers," 20; Homer Bigart, "Accord by King Angers Marchers," *New York Times*, 25 June 1966, ProQuest Historical Newspapers, 1.

41. Bigart, "Accord Angers Marchers," 1; Laurence Henry, "Black Power," *Now: News of the Nation and the World* 2, no. 5 (Summer 1967): 6; Sobel, *Civil Rights*, 395.

42. Higgins, "Meredith's Threat," 16.

43. Ibid., 17; Gene Roberts, "Meredith Leads March on Eve of Rally in Jackson," *New York Times*, June 26, 1966, ProQuest Historical Newspapers, 40.

44. "The Nation," *New York Times*, June 26, 1966, ProQuest Historical Newspapers, E2.

45. Emilye Crosby, *A Little Taste of Freedom: The Black Freedom Struggle in Claiborne County, Mississippi* (Chapel Hill: University of North Carolina Press, 2005), 177; Report from Lee Cole to Erle Johnston, Mississippi State Sovereignty Commission, February 9, 1968, MDAH, 2-53-0-48-1-1-1, available online; "Belzoni, Mississippi," report from L. E. Cole, Mississippi State Sovereignty Commission, February 19, 1968, MDAH, 2-53-0-49-1-1-1, available online.

46. Hazelwood, discussion; WATS report, January 30,1965, SNCC Papers 39, King Center archives, Atlanta, GA, 1; "County Reports, Humphreys, Weaver, David ," n.d., Mississippi Freedom Democratic Party Papers, Box 8, File 30, Martin Luther King Jr. Center for Nonviolent Change archives. "County Reports, Humphreys, Weaver, David " contains testimony from Humphreys County Blacks who registered in 1955 before the assassination of George Lee and were harassed as well as threatened by local White supremacists.

47. Willie Owens, in discussion with the author, June 15, 2009, Jackson, MS; Hazelwood, discussion; Lorene Starks, in discussion with the author, July 25, 2009, Belzoni, MS.

48. Hazelwood, discussion.

49. Starks, discussion; Hazelwood, discussion; Report from Lee Cole to Erle Johnston.

50. "Rudolph Arthur Shields," FBI Racial Matters, February 2, 1968, Jackson, MS, 24, FBI Files; Report from Lee Cole to Erle Johnston; United States Department of Commerce, Bureau of the Census, *1970 Census of Population: Supplementary Report, Distribution of Negro Population by County* (Washington, DC: United State Department of Commerce), http://www2.census.gov/prod2/decennial/documents/31679801n1-40ch01.pdf .

51. "Rudolph Arthur Shields," 24, 27.

52. Davis, discussion.

53. Hazelwood, discussion.

54. Ibid.

55. Report from Lee Cole to Erle Johnston; Hazelwood, discussion; "Rudolph Arthur Shields," 2; Starks, discussion.

56. Report from Lee Cole to Erle Johnston.

57. "Belzoni, Mississippi," Report from L. E. Cole, Mississippi State Sovereignty Commission, February 20, 1968, MDAH, 1-112-0-27-1-1-1, available online; Hazelwood, discussion.

58. Ibid.; "Supplement to Report of February 26 1968," Mississippi State Sovereignty Commission, February 28, 1968, 1-112-0-30-1-1-1, MDAH, available online.

59. "Rudolph Arthur Shields," FBI, May 17, 1968, Jackson, MS, 28, FBI files; Lee Cole, "Belzoni, MS," Sovereignty Commission, February 29, 1968, MDAH, 2-53-0-51-1-1-1, 1-2, available online.

60. "Rudolph Arthur Shields," May 17, 1968, 30.

61. Ibid., 33-34; Hazelwood, discussion.

62. "Rudolph Arthur Shields," May 17, 1968, 2-4; "Rudolph Arthur Shields," FBI Memorandum From: SAC to FBI Director, November 14, 1968, Jackson, MS,157-8411, 1-2, FBI Files; "Rudolph Arthur Shields," Memo from Jackson SAC to FBI director, February 11, 1969, Jackson, MS, 2, FBI Files; James Mohead, Weekly Report, June 9, 1969, to June 13, 1969, Sovereignty Commission, MDAH, 2-53-0-63-1-1-1, available online.

63. "Rudolph Arthur Shields," February 11, 1969, 3, FBI Files.

64. "Rudolph Arthur Shields," FBI, Memorandum from SAC, June 11, 1969, Jackson-157-8411 to FBI director, Jackson, MS, 1-4, FBI Files; Mohead, Weekly Report.

65. Hazelwood, discussion; Starks, discussion; Lumumba, discussion; "Rudolph Arthur Shields," June 11, 1969, 4.

66. "Rudolph Arthur Shields," Unknown Merchants-Victim Belzoni and Yazoo City, Mississippi AR-Hobbs Act, SAC Jackson to Director, FBI, 1-2, December 30, 1969, FBI Files.

67. Correspondence from Toby Wood to W. Burk, March 20, 1970, Sovereignty Commission, MDAH, 2-53-0-72-1-1-1; Correspondence from Toby Wood to W. Burk, July 1,1970, Sovereignty Commission, MDAH, 2-53-0-73-1-1-1; Starks, discussion; Lumumba, discussion; "Racial Disorders at Humphreys County High School, Belzoni," Memorandum to Sovereignty Commission from James Mohead, March 31,1971, to April 9,1971, Sovereignty Commission, 2-53-0-77-1-1-1; "We, the Students of Humphreys County High School Hereby Request the Following Demands to Be Met," Sovereignty Commission, n.d., MDAH, 2-53-0-78-1-1-1, available online; "Student Rights," State Sovereignty Commission, n.d., MDAH, 2-53-0-78-1-1-1, available online; From S. N. Brown, April 8, 1971, Sovereignty Commission, MDAH, 2-53-0-80-1-1-1, available online; Writ of Injunction: Humphreys County School District vs. Terry Minnifield et al., April 8, 1971, Sovereignty Commission, MDAH, 2-53-0-81-1-1-1, available online.

68. "Rudolph Arthur Shields," FBI Cointelpro, Feburary 11, 1969, Jackson, MS, 3, FBI Files.

69. Malcolm O'Leary, in discussion with the author, July 23, 2009, Vicksburg, MS; Herman DeCell to Erle Johnson, November 21, 1967, Sovereignty Commission, MDAH, 99-48-0-341-1-1-1, available online; Tom Scarborough, "Yazoo County," November 28, 1967, Sovereignty Commission, MDAH, 2-13-0-58-1-1-1, available online.

70. O'Leary, discussion; United States Department of Commerce, *1970 Census*.

71. O'Leary, discussion; "Yazoo City," Sovereignty Commission, MDAH, 2-13-0-58-1-1-1, available online; Willie Morris, *Yazoo: Integration in a Deep Southern Town* (New York: Harpers, 1971), 60.

72. O'Leary, discussion.
73. Ibid.; Morris, *Yazoo*, 60; Herman Leach, in discussion with the author, July 30, 1994, Yazoo City, MS; Clayborn, discussion.
74. Leach, discussion; Hudson, discussion; Clayborn, discussion.
75. O'Leary, discussion; "Rudolph Arthur Shields," FBI, July 11,1969, Jackson, MS, 1-2, FBI Files; "Junior Auxiliary Stresses Positive Approach to Woes: Forum Takes Up Boycott, URC Urban Renewal, Few M.D.'s," *Yazoo Herald*, October 23, 1969, 2, 5.
76. Leach, discussion; Clayborn, discussion; Lewis Williams, in discussion with the author, September 25, 1994, Yazoo City, MS; Morris, *Yazoo*, 61.
77. Leach, discussion; Williams, discussion.
78. Leach, discussion.
79. Leach, discussion; Clayborn, discussion.
80. "City Policeman Resigns after Slapping Negro Girl," *Yazoo Herald*, June 4, 1970, 104, 3, 1.
81. George Collins, "Collins Comments," *Yazoo Herald*, June 4, 1970, 104, 3, 1.
82. Ibid.
83. "Boycott Now Over: City to Pave Streets," *Yazoo Herald*, September 3, 1970, 104, 16, 1; "Leaders Are Pleased with Business Surge: Return to Normal Signals Progress," *Yazoo Herald*, September 10, 1970, 104, 17, 1; O'Leary, discussion; George Collin, quoted in Morris, *Yazoo*, 61-62.
84. Clayborn, discussion.
85. Ibid.; Malcolm O'Leary, discussion; "Boycott Now Over."
86. Rudy Shields, quoted in Morris, *Yazoo*, 64.

Chapter 7

1. From flyer distributed in Hinds County, Mississippi (July 1970), signed
2. "Henry Hatches, Minister of Defense, Republic of New Africa," Sovereignty Commission, n.d., Mississippi Department of Archives and History (MDAH), available online.
3. William Morris, *Yazoo: Integration in a Deep Southern Town* (New York: Harper Magazine Press, 1971), 63; Rudy Shields, "Letter to the Editor: Words of Praise and Criticism from Bro. Rudy Shields," *Yazoo Herald*, January 15, 1970, 2.
4. Lewis Williams, in discussion with the author, September 25, 1994, Yazoo City, MS.
5. "Rudolph Arthur Shields," December 8, 1970, FBI, Jackson, MS, 6, Cointelpro, Federal Bureau of Investigation (FBI).
6. Rudy Shields, quoted in Morris, *Yazoo*, 64.
7. "Aberdeen Boycott," *Southern Patriot* 28, no. 7 (September 1970), Southern Conference Education Fund (SCEF) Papers, Southern Labor Archives,

Georgia State University, Atlanta, GA, 4; "Court Rules Two Police Offi-cers Not Be Reinstated," *Aberdeen Examiner,* July 16, 1970, 1; Fulton Tutor, "Weekly Report," Sovereignty Commission, May 4-9, 1970, MDAH, 2-67-0-39-1-1-1, available online; "The Boycott," *Aberdeen Examiner*, August 6, 1970, Sovereignty Commission, MDAH, 2-67-0-40-1-1-1, available online. "Aber-deen Boycott"; "The Merchants and the Boycott," *Aberdeen Examiner,* July 9, 1970, 7; "Anyone for Work," *Aberdeen Examiner,* July 23, 1970; "The Boy-cott," 7; Fulton Tutor, "Weekly Report," Sovereignty Commission, August 3-7, 1970, MDAH, 1-112-0-44-1-1-1, available online; Fulton Tutor, "Weekly Report," Sovereignty Commission, August 31 to September 5, 1970, MDAH, 1-112-0-45-1-1-1, available online; Lewis Myers, in discussion with the author, October 3, 2009, Chicago, IL.

8. Myers, discussion.

9. Ibid.; Jesse Pennington, in discussion with the author, June 21, 2010, Jackson, MS.

10. Pennington, discussion; Memorandum from Fulton Tutor to Sovereignty Commission, "Aberdeen, Mississippi, Monroe County," August 19, 1970, MDAH, available online; Report from Fulton Tutor, August 17 to 22 August 1970, Sovereignty Commission, MDAH, 8-19-2-13-1-1-1, available online.

11. Ibid.

12. John Buffington, interviewed by Robert Wright, August 12, 1968, Washing-ton D.C., Civil Rights Documentation Project, Moorland Spingarn Research Center, Howard University, Washington, DC; John Dittmer, *Local People: The Struggle for Civil Rights in Mississippi* (Champaign: University of Illinois Press, 1995), 408, 410, 421, 422; Correspondence from James Haddock to Governor John Williams, "Situation in West Point, Mississippi," February 3, 1970, 1, Sovereignty Commission, MDAH, 2-88-0-90-1-1-1, available online; Robert Analavage, "Mississippi: Split Beset Movement," *The Southern Patriot* (November 1968), Sovereignty Commission, MDAH, 2-163-0-23-2-1-1, avail-able online; Jan Hillegas, "West Point Campaign," *Southern Patriot* 28, no. 7 (September 1970): 4, SCEF Papers, Southern Labor Archives, Georgia State University, Atlanta, GA; Tombigee Council on Human Relations, *West Point, Mississippi: A Report* (Mississippi State College, 1971), 5, 23.

13. Jan Hillegas, "West Point 'Desegregation Produces Violent Reactions,'" *The Southern Patriot* 28, no. 2 (February 1970): 7, SCEF Papers, Southern Labor Archives, Georgia State University, Atlanta, GA; Pennington, discussion.

14. Hillegas, "West Point," 7; Haddock to Williams, "Situation in West Point, Mississippi," 1; William Street, "Red Tape, Opposing Attitudes Endanger OEO Program," *The Commercial Appeal*, February 1, 1970, 6-3; Lewis Nolan, "Courthouse Blast Shakes West Point," *The Commercial Appeal*, January 26, 1970, 3.

15. "City Is Rocked by Bombing, Shooting," *Daily Times Leader*, January 24,

1970, 1, 8; Nolan, "Courthouse Blast Shakes West Point," 3; Hillegas, "Desegregation Produces Violent Reactions"; Haddock to Williams, "Situation in West Point, Mississippi"; Street, "Red Tape"; Memorandum from Fulton Tutor to Sovereignty Commission Director, "Weekly Report 26-31 January 1970," February 5, 1970 , Sovereignty Commission, MDAH, 8-19-1-97-1-1-1, available online.

16. Mary Tom Watts, "Store Shot Up, Owner Wounded," *Daily Times Leader*, January 27, 1970, 1, 8; Nolan, "Courthouse Blast Shakes West Point," 3; Hillegas, "Desegregation Produces Violent Reactions"; Haddock to Williams, "Situation in West Point, Mississippi"; Street, " Red Tape"; Memorandum from Fulton Tutor to Sovereignty Commission Director, "Weekly Report 26-31 January 1970"; Pennington, discussion.

17. Watts, "Store Shot Up, Owner Wounded," 1; Tombigee Council on Human Relations, *West Point, Mississippi*, 5.

18. Mary Tom Watts, "Conspiracy Charges Filed against Six in Bombing Case," *Daily Times Leader*, April 8, 1970, 1; Nolan, "Courthouse Blast Shakes West Point," 3; Hillegas, "West Point Campaign," 4; Fulton Tutor, "Weekly Report 6-11 April 1970," Sovereignty Commission, MDAH, 8-19-1-122-1-1-1, available online; Pennington, discussion.

19. Charles Harris, in discussion with the author, June 8, 1994, Jackson, MS; "Charles Harris" is a pseudonym created for this informant. Harris was an African American activist born and raised in Mississippi. He declined to allow me to use his name, given the sensitive nature of his testimony. "Civil Rights and Armed Struggle: Interview with a Southern Militant," *Urgent Tasks* 13 (Spring 1982): 31-32; Fulton Tutor, "Weekly Report 9-14 March 1970," 2, Sovereignty Commission, MDAH, 8-19-1-116-1-1-1, available online; Paul Lee, "The FBI Conspiracy against H. Rap Brown," *The Michigan Citizen*, November 2009, http://sixties-l.blogspot.com/2009/12/fbi-conspiracy-against-h-rap-brown.html; "Blacks Say Bigoted Whites Planted," *Jet Magazine*, March 26, 1970, 6, available online.

20. "Death of a Movement Soldier," *Southern Patriot* 28, no. 3 (March 1970): 1, 4.

21. Ibid.; "Bombing a Way of Protest," *Time,* March 23, 1970, 3, http://www.time.com/time/magazine/article/0,9171,943178-1,00.html; James Featherstone, in discussion with the author, August 17, 1994, Washington, DC; Ed Brown, in discussion with the author, October 8, 2009, Atlanta, GA; Lee, "The FBI Conspiracy"; "Bigoted Whites Planted."

22. Mary Tom Watts, "Police Charge Local Man with Murder in Shooting," *Daily Times Leader*, August 17, 1970, 1; Mary Tom Watts, "Stanley Enters Innocent Plea; Held without Bail," *Daily Times Leader*, August 21, 1970, 1; Pennington, discussion.

23. Memorandum from Fulton Tutor to File, "West Point, Clay County, Mississippi," Sovereignty Commission, August 19, 1970, MDAH, 2-88-0-94-1-1-1,

available online; Flyer, n.d., Sovereignty Commission, MDAH, 2-88-0-92-1-1-1, available online.

24. Pennington, discussion.

25. Tombigee Council on Human Relations, *West Point, Mississippi*, 24-25.

26. Ibid., 7.

27. Ibid.

28. "News Briefs: West Point, Miss.," *Southern Patriot*, December 1971, 29, 10, 2, SCEF Papers, Box 288, Southern Labor Archives, Georgia State University, Atlanta, GA; Pennington, discussion.

29. "News Briefs," 6, 12; Memorandum from Fulton Tutor to File, "West Point, Clay County, Mississippi," Sovereignty Commission, August 19, 1970, MDAH, 2-88-0-94-1-1-1, available online; Flyer, n.d., Sovereignty Commission, MDAH, 2-88-0-92-1-1-1, available online; "West Point Trial in Slaying Delayed," *The Commercial Appeal*, April 6, 1971, Sovereignty Commission, MDAH, 99-102-0-28-1-1-1, available online; Hillegas, "West Point Campaign," 4.

30. Fulton Tutor, "Weekly Report," October 5-10, 1970, Sovereignty Commission, 1-112-0-56-1-1-1, MDAH, available online; "Rudolph Arthur Shields," December 8, 1970, 4-6.

31. Tim Spofford, *Lynch Street: The May 1970 Slayings at Jackson State College* (Kent, OH: Kent State University Press, 1988), 33-52; George Whittington, "Mobs Attacks Autos Here," *Clarion-Ledger*, May 14, 1970, Sovereignty Commission, MDAH, 10-105-0-62-1-1-1, available online.

32. Spofford, *Lynch Street*, 53-79; George Whittington, "Sniping Proceded Police," *Clarion-Ledger*, May 15, 1970, Sovereignty Commission, MDAH, 10-105-0-63-1-1-1, available online; Jan Hillegas, "Jackson's Night of Agony," *Southern Patriot* 28, no. 5 (May 1970): 8.

33. Hillegas, "Jackson's Night of Agony," 1, 8; Spofford, *Lynch Street*, 115; "Attorney General Talks with Mayor," *Daily News*, May 19, 1970, 1, 3; Davis Smith, "Varied Groups Probe Fatal Confrontation," *Daily News,* May 18, 1970, 1, 4 , Sovereignty Commission, MDAH, 10-105-0-65-1-1-1, available online; "Mitchell Meets Mississippi Aides," *New York Times,* May 19, 1970, ProQuest Historical Newspapers; Aaron Shirley, in discussion with the author, July 22, 2009, Jackson, MS.

34. Spofford, *Lynch Street*, 115; "Attorney General Talks with Mayor," 1; Hillegas, "Jackson's Night of Agony," 8; "Mitchell Meets Mississippi Aides," 35.

35. "Proposed Demonstration under Leadership Rudolph Arthur Shields at Jackson, Mississippi," FBI, Jackson, MS, December 28, 1970, 1-2; Spofford, *Lynch Street*, 115; "Rudolph Arthur Shields at Jackson, Mississippi," FBI, Jackson, MS, FBI Files July 13, 1971, 2; Shirley, discussion.

36. "Proposed Demonstration under Leadership Rudolph Arthur Shields at Jackson, Mississippi," 1-4.

37. "City Council," *Clarion-Ledger*, January 13,1971, Sovereignty Commission, MDAH, 1-112-0-59-1-1-1, available online; "Proposed Demonstration, December 22, 1970, under Leadership Rudolph Arthur Shields at Jackson, Mississippi," January 13, 1971, FBI, Jackson, MS, 1-4, FBI Files; Billy Skelton, "Mayor Responds to 'Racism' Complaint," *Clarion-Ledger*, January 27, 1971, Sovereignty Commission, MDAH, 1-112-0-60-1-1-1, available online; "Proposed Demonstration under Leadership Rudolph Arthur Shields at Jackson, Mississippi," January 29, 1971, FBI, Jackson MS, 1-3, FBI Files.

38. "Proposed Demonstration under Leadership Rudolph Arthur Shields at Jackson, Mississippi," March 2, 1971, FBI, Jackson, MS, 1, FBI Files.

39. Jimmy Ward, "Covering the Crossroads with Jimmy Ward," *Daily News*, February 1971, Sovereignty Commission, MDAH, 1-112-0-62-1-1-1, available online; "Rudolph Arthur Shields, Mississippi," July 13, 1971, FBI File, 2.

40. Imari Obadele, in discussion with the author, March 9, 2005, Baton Rouge, LA; "Malcolm Lives: The RNA," *The New African*, February 27, 1971, 7.

41. U.S. Congress. Senate. *Committee on Government Operations. Permanent Subcommittee on Investigations. Hearings on Riots, Civil and Criminal Disorders.* 90th Cong., 1st sess.–91st Cong., 2d sess, 1967–1970, 4177-92, 4246-70.

42. The Republic of New Africa (RNA), "The Republic of New Africa: A Short Chronological History," n.d., Republic of New Africa file, MDAH.

43. Ibid.

44. Assata Shakur speaks about receiving an African name in a New African naming ceremony in her autobiography *Assata: The Autobiography of a Revolutionary* (Chicago: Lawrence Hill, 1987), 183-85.

45. Imari Obadele I, *Foundations of the Black Nation* (Detroit: House of Songhay, 1975), xi-xii.

46. Ibid., 5.

47. "Building the New Community," *The New African*, February 27, 1971, 12; "RNA Buys Land for First Mississippi Community," *Michigan Chronicle*, January 16, 1971, Sovereignty Commission, MDAH, 13-25-2-16-1-1-1, available online.

48. "Building the New Community."

49. "RNA Buys Land for First Mississippi Community."

50. "Malcolm Lives: The RNA," 7; Imari Obadele, *Free the Land: The True Story of the Trials of the RNA-11 in Mississippi and the Continuing Struggle to Establish an Independent Black Nation in Five States in the Deep South* (Washington, DC: House of Songhay, 1984), 8-9, 17.

51. RNA, "The Republic of New Africa," 2-3.

52. Mike Honey, "Tensions Rise in Mississippi," *The Southern Patriot* 29, no. 8 (October 1971): 1, 5.

53. *Hinds County FDP News*, October 6, 1967, 1, MFDP Papers, Box 8, File 13, MLK Center Archives, Atlanta, GA; "Did You Know: Negroes Still Voting

White," *Hinds County FDP News*, August 11, 1967, 4, MFDP Papers, Box 8, File 13, MLK Center Archives, Atlanta, GA; "Vote Hatches," *Hinds County FDP News*, June 22, 1967, 4, MFDP Papers, Box 8, File 13, MLK Center Archives, Atlanta, GA.

54. "New Politics," *Hinds County FDP News*, September 8, 1967, 1, 3, Sovereignty Commission, MDAH, 2-165-6-101-1-1-1, available online; Simon Hall, "On the Tail of the Panther: Black Power and the 1967 Convention of the National Conference for New Politics," *Journal of American Studies* 37, no. 1: 59-78; "Firepower Only Hope," *Hinds County FDP News*, September 8, 1967, 4, Sovereignty Commission, MDAH, 2-165-6-101-4-1-1, available online; "Race Riots: Violence May Be the Answer," *Hinds County FDP News*, July 28, 1967, 1, MFDP Papers, Box 8, File 13, MLK Center Archives, Atlanta, GA.

55. Carolyn Williams, "A Guest Editorial," *Hinds County FDP News*, July 8, 1967, MFDP Papers, Box 8, File 13, MLK Center Archives, Atlanta, GA, 4.

56. Ibid.; Obadele, *Free the Land*, 29-30.

57. Obadele, *Free the Land*, 29-30; "The Republic of New Africa," November 3, 2009, Sovereignty Commission, MDAH, 13-25-1-57-3-1, available online; "Henry Hatches," n.d., Sovereignty Commission; Memorandum from Herman Glazer to Sovereignty Commission Director, "Republic of New Africa Conference of the Peoples Center Council, National Governing Body of RNA, Jackson, MS, 7-31-70 to 8-2-70," August 5, 1970, Sovereignty Commission, MDAH, 13-25-2-3-1-1-1, available online.

58. Obadele, *Free the Land*, 32-33.

59. RNA, "Republic of New Africa," 3; Memorandum from Herman Glazer to Sovereignty Commission Director, August 5, 1970; Obadele, *Free the Land*, 31, 39.

60. Obadele, *Free the Land*, 33-35, 41; "We Made It," *Hinds County FDP News*, June 10, 1967, 2; "Did You Know," *Hinds County FDP News*, June 22, 1967, 4, MFDP Papers, Box 8, File 13, MLK Center Archives; RNA, "Republic of New Africa," 3; Memorandum from W. Webb Burke to File, "Republic of New Africa," March 11, 1971, Sovereignty Commission, MDAH, 13-25-2-11-1-1-1, available online; Edgar Fortenberry, "Weekly Activity Report," December 7-11, 1970, Sovereignty Commission, MDAH 13-25-2-8-1-1-1, available online.

61. "RNA Buys Land for First Mississippi Community"; Memorandum from W. Webb Burke to File, March 11, 1971.

62. Davis Smith, "Local Cops Arrest Armed Militants," *Jackson Daily News*, March 24, 1971, Republic of New Africa Subject File, MDAH; Jean Culbertson, "Six RNA Members Are Released from Jail," *Clarion-Ledger*, March 31, 1971, Sovereignty Commission, MDAH, 13-25-2-19-1-1-1, available online; Jan Hillegas, "RNA Capital in Mississippi Consecrated," *The Southern Patriot* 29, no. 5 (May 1971): 1; Jon Nordheimer, "Black 'Nation' Vexes Mississippi," *New York Times*, April 10, 1971, ProQuest Historical Newspapers, 21, available online.

63. Jan Hillegas, "Republic of New Africa Meeting Harassed by Police," *Guardian*, April 10, 1971, Sovereignty Commission, MDAH, 13-25-2-24-1-1-1, available online; Obadele, *Free the Land*, 4, 21.

64. Charles Smith, "Black Nation Meet Here Still Planned," *Clarion-Ledger*, March 26, 1971, 1; Ron Harris, "RNA President Delays Session," *Times Picayune*, March 26, 1971, Sovereignty Commission, MDAH, 13-25-2-30-1-1-1, available online; "Republic of New Africa: Yes, Separation; No, Integration!" *Close Up* (March–April 1971): 12, Republic of New Africa File, MDAH; Obadele, *Free the Land*, 44-48; Hillegas, "RNA Capital in Mississippi Consecrated," 4.

65. "Black Republic Sets Dedication of Its 'Capital,'" *The Commercial Appeal*, March 28, 1971.

66. Joe Bonney, "Black Separatists Consecrate Land," *The Clarion-Ledger*, March 28, 1971, 1; Obadele, *Free the Land*, 56-59.

67. Jan Hillegas, "RNA Capital in Mississippi Consecrated," 1, 4; Obadele, *Free the Land*, 59.

68. Obadele, *Free the Land*, 59; Rondee Jeanette Gaines, "Race, Power, and Representation: Broadcast News Portrayal of the Republic of New Africa" (master's thesis, University of Alabama, 2003), 34-36.

69. "Summer Asked to Meet Black," *The Commercial Appeal*, April 11, 1971; "Summer Urges Position on RNA," *Times Picayune*, April 3, 1971; "State to Wait for Federal Action on RNA," *Jackson Daily News*, April 24, 1971, Sovereignty Commission, MDAH, 13-25-2-36-1-1-1, available online.

70. Nordheimer, "Black 'Nation' Vexes Mississippi," 21.

71. Shirley, discussion; Nordheimer, "Black 'Nation' Vexes Mississippi," 21.

72. Charles M. Hills Jr., "Travis, Evers Offer to Protect Mason," *Clarion Ledger*, May 23, 1971, Sovereignty Commission, MDAH, 13-25-2-57-1-1-1, available online; Correspondence from Imari Abubakrari Obadele I to Lofton Mason, July 14,1971, RNA Subject file, MDAH.

73. Obadele, *Free the Land*, 119-22; "Obadele Convicted of Assault," *Jackson Daily News*, August 12, 1971, 16a, Sovereignty Commission, MDAH, 13-25-2-58-1-1-1.

74. "RNA 11 Story in Brief," *The New Afrikan* 7, no. 19 (February 1979): 8.

75. Obadele, *Free the Land*, 138-44; Tamu Kanyama, in discussion with the author, April 21, 2012, Atlanta, GA; Hekima Kanyama, in discussion with the author, April 21, 2012, Atlanta, GA.

76. "Treason Added to RNA Charge," *The Commercial Appeal*, August 24, 1971, Sovereignty Commission, MDAH, 13-25-2-74-1-1-1, available online; Davis Smith, "FBI Specialist Ties Gun-RNA Case," *Jackson Daily News*, September 23, 1972, RNA Subject File, MDAH.

77. "June 18 Hearing Set for RNA Group," *Jackson Daily News*, May 31, 1973, 1A, RNA Subject File, MDAH.

78. "Eleven RNA Members Charged in Policeman's Death," *Commercial Appeal*,

August 20, 1971, Sovereignty Commission, 13-25-2-64-1-1-1, MDAH, available online.

79. Ibid

80. Ibid.

81. Ibid.

82. "Blacks Charge 'Kill' Attitude," *Times Picayune*, August 28, 1971, Sovereignty Commission, MDAH, 13-25-2-78-1-1-1, available online; Aaron Shirley, quoted in Obadele, *Free the Land*, 148.

83. Ibid.; Shirley, discussion.

84. Chokwe Lumumba, "The African Prisoner of War Movement and the International Prisoner of War Solidarity Day," *Black Collegian*, March–April 1973, 20-21, 49-51; Chokwe Lumumba, "Repression and Black Liberation," *The Black Scholar* 5 (October 1973): 34-42.

85. "Brother Hekima's Opening Statement," *The New African* 4, no. 8 (August 1972): 4.

86. Hekima Ana, "Hekima Writes from Mississippi," n.d., RNA files, MDAH.

87. "RNA 11 Story in Brief," 8-9; Alex Poinsett, "Where Are the Revolutionaries?" *Ebony* 31, no. 4 (February 1976): 92; RNA, "Republic of New Africa," 5-6; "Free the RNA-11," n.d., RNA file, MDAH; "Delay Granted in Trial of RNA Member James," *Jackson Daily News*, July 14, 1972, RNA Subject File, MDAH; "Third RNA Case Verdict Guilty," *Clarion Ledger*, September 26, 1972, RNA Subject File, MDAH.

88. T. Kanyama, discussion; H. Kanyama, discussion.

89. "And That Power Was Used to Destroy the Republic of New Africa," *The New African* 4, no. 8 (August 1972): 4.

90. RNA, "Republic of New Africa," 6.

91. Memorandum from Jackson SAC to Director, "Computerized Telephone Number File, New Left, Black, and other Ethnic Extremists; Quarterly Newsletter," July 12, 1974, FBI, 7-8, FBI Files; "Jackson, Mississippi," April 12, 1971, Sovereignty Commission, MDAH, 1-112-0-66-1-1-1, available online; "RNA-11 Story in Brief," 9; "Rudolph Arthur Shields," July 13, 1971, FBI, Jackson, MS, 3, FBI Files; Obadele, *Free the Land*, 189; "Rudolph Arthur Shields," May 22, 1972, FBI, Jackson, MS, 4, FBI Files; "Rudolph Arthur Shields," April 20, 1973, FBI, Jackson, MS, 11-12, FBI Files.

92. "International Prisoner of War Solidarity Day" (n.d.), RNA file, MDAH; "Rudolph Arthur Shields," April 20, 1973, FBI, Jackson, MS, 12, 15-16, FBI Files.

93. "Separate RNA Still Sought," *Times Picayune*, April 4, 1973, RNA Subject File, MDAH, 1-5; "Obadele Calls for His Release Big Victory for Blacks," *Jackson Daily News*, April 4, 1973, RNA Subject File, MDAH, 3b; "Rally Backers File Suit," *Times Picayune*, March 28, 1973, RNA Subject File, MDAH, 1-11.

94. "Rudolph Arthur Shields," April 20, 1973, 17; "Parade Permit Denial Upheld

by City Councilmen," *Jackson Daily News*, March 24, 1973, RNA Subject File, MDAH, 1.

95. "Rudolph Arthur Shields," July 31, 1974, FBI, Jackson MS, 2; Memorandum from Jackson MS SAC to FBI Director, "Rudolph Arthur Shields," July 31, 1974, FBI, Jackson MS, 2, FBI Files; Memorandum from Jackson MS SAC to FBI Director, "Rudolph Arthur Shields," March 18, 1975, FBI, Jackson MS, 1-2, FBI Files.

96. "Rudolph Arthur Shields," July 31, 1974, 2.

Chapter 8

1. This is a memory of the author from a visit to Holly Springs, Mississippi, in the summer of 1979 to observe and participate in United League activity.

2. David Chalmers, *Hooded Americanism: The History of the Ku Klux Klan* (Durham, NC: Duke University Press, 1987), 406, 412; Manning Marable, *Race, Reform, and Rebellion: The Second Reconstruction in Black America, 1945-1990* (Jackson: University Press of Mississippi, 1991), 174-75.

3. "The Law: The Siege of Port Gibson," *Time*, October 11, 1976, http://www.time.com/time/magazine/article/0,9171,946669,00.html; Wilson F. Minor, "League: Can It Destroy Stable NAACP?" *The Capitol Reporter*, September 14, 1978, United League Subject file, Mississippi Department of Archives and History (MDAH), 2.

4. Sundiata Cha-Jua and Clarence Lang, "Long Movement as Vampire: Temporal and Spatial Fallacies in Recent Black Freedom Studies," *Journal of African-American History* 92, no. 1 (Winter 2007): 272-73.

5. Marshall County, Mississippi: Large Slaveholders from 1860 Slave Census Schedules and Surname Matches for African Americans on 1870 Census, http://freepages.genealogy.rootsweb.ancestry.com/~ajac/msmarshall.htm; "Seven Blacks Win Primary Votes in Mississippi Election," *Jet*, October 4, 1979, 5, available online.

6. Henry Boyd, in discussion with the author, October 21, 1994, Holly Springs, MS.

7. Cleveland Sellers, with Robert Terrell, *The River of No Return: The Autobiography of a Black Militant and the Life and Death of SNCC* (Jackson: University Press of Mississippi, 1990), 94-99.

8. "A Petition to the Mayor of Holly Springs—March 13, 1965," MFDP Papers, Box 10, File 20, King Center Archives, Atlanta, GA.

9. Boyd, discussion; "United League Leader Speaks," *Southern Struggle* (September–October 1978), Box 288, Southern Conference Education Fund (SCEF) Papers, Southern Labor Archives, Georgia State University, Atlanta, GA; Ernest Cunningham, in discussion with author, December 2, 1994, Holly Springs, MS, 4.

10. Boyd, discussion; "1500 Demand Justice for All," September–October 1978, Box 288, SCEF Papers, Southern Labor Archives, Georgia State University, Atlanta, GA, 5; Cunningham, discussion.

11. "Freedom Democrats Widen Breach with Loyalist," *Clarion Ledger,* January 6, 1969, Sovereignty Commission, MDAH, 1-117-0-10-1-1-1; "Delegation Tries to Patch Torn Holly Springs Image," *Commercial Appeal*, May 5, 1970, Sovereignty Commission, MDAH, 2-20-2-81-1-1-1; "False Propaganda Refuted," *Southern Reporter*, n.d., Sovereignty Commission, MDAH, 2-20-2-83-1-1-1.

12. Boyd, discussion; Kris Shepard, *Rationing Justice* (Baton Rouge: Louisiana State University Press, 2007) 31-33, 208; "History of NMRLS," http://www.nmrls.com/History.htm; "National Conference of Black Lawyers," http://www.ncbl.org/default.htm.

13. Alfred "Skip" Robinson, quoted in Andrew Marx and Tom Tuthill, "Resisting the Klan: Mississippi Organizes," *Southern Exposure* 8, no. 2 (Summer 1980): 75.

14. Boyd, discussion.

15. Ibid.; Marx and Tuthill, "Resisting the Klan," 75; Cunningham, discussion.

16. Joseph Delaney, "Legal Workers Battle for Poor in Mississippi," *Southern Changes* 1, no. 4 (1979): 17; "Mississippi: Boycott in Byhalia," *Time*, March 10, 1975, http://www.time.com/time/magazine/article/0,9171,917174,00.html; Robert Lay, in discussion with the author, August 24, 2011, Holly Springs, MS.

17. "Mississippi: Boycott in Byhalia"; Cunningham, discussion.

18. "Mississippi: Boycott in Byhalia"; Donald Simon, "The Once and Future Mississippi," *The Harvard Crimson*, October 2, 1974, http://www.thecrimson.com/article/1974/10/2/the-once-and-future-mississippi-plast; Lewis Myers, in discussion with the author, January 4, 2010, Chicago, IL.

19. Sandy Ealy et al., Plaintiffs-Appellants v. Talmadge Littlejohn et al., Defendants-Appellees, United States Court of Appeals, Fifth Circuit, http://openjurist.org/569/f2d/219; Myers, discussion.

20. Ealy v. Littlejohn; Boyd, discussion; Shepard, *Rationing Justice*, 89-90.

21. "Mississippi: Boycott in Byhalia"; Boyd, discussion.

22. Boyd, discussion; Cunningham, discussion; Howard Gunn, in discussion with the author, March 18, 1998, Tupelo, MS.

23. Boyd, discussion; Cunningham, discussion; Lay, discussion; Myers, discussion.

24. James Young, "League Announces Plan for Statewide Branches," *Commercial Appeal*, July 30, 1978, 33; Myers, discussion.

25. "Mississippi: Boycott in Byhalia"; Shepard, *Rationing Justice*, 89-90.

26. Boyd, discussion; Shepard, *Rationing Justice*, 80.

27. Shepard, *Rationing Justice*, 80; Lay, discussion; Cunningham, discussion; Myers, discussion.

28. Myers, discussion; David Clary, "NAACP Leader OKs Statewide United League," *Clarion Ledger*, July 2, 1978, United League Subject file, MDAH, 3a; Alfred Robinson, quoted in "Behind the Struggle in Tupelo," *Southern Struggle*, September–October 1978, SCEF papers, Georgia State University Archives, Atlanta, GA, 5.

29. Boyd, discussion; Alfred "Skip" Robinson quoted in Marx and Tuthill, "Resisting the Klan," 73; George Williams, quoted in Marx and Tuthill, "Resisting the Klan," 74.

30. Frederick Tulsky, "Blacks in Tupelo Protest City Action," *Jackson Clarion Ledger*, March 12, 1978, Tupelo Boycott 1978, MDAH, 1A; Vaugn L. Grisham Jr., *Tupelo: Evolution of a Community* (Dayton, OH: Kettering Foundation, 1999), 150.

31. David Comer, "Federal Probe Begins in Alleged Inmate Beating," *Northeast Mississippi Daily Journal*, March 22, 1978, 1; Grisham, *Tupelo*, 152.

32. Frederick Tulsky, "Racial Tension Mounts in Tupelo," *Jackson Clarion Ledger*, February 24, 1978, Tupelo Boycott file, MDAH, 1A; "KKK/United League March," Mississippi Civil Rights Project History County by County, http://www.mscivilrightsproject.com/content/153.

33. Tulsky, "Racial Tension Mounts in Tupelo," 18A; Tulsky, "Blacks in Tupelo Protest City Action," 1A; "KKK/United League March."

34. Tulsky, "Blacks in Tupelo Protest City Action," 16A; "350 Blacks March in Tupelo, Second March Planned Saturday," *Northeast Mississippi Daily Journal*, March 13, 1978, 10; "KKK/United League March"; Grisham, *Tupelo*, 154.

35. Michael Kerr, "Alderman Issue Policy Statement," *Northeast Mississippi Daily Journal*, March 20, 1978, 1, 14.

36. Deborah Counce, "United League Presents Demands," *Northeast Mississippi Daily Journal*, March 20, 1978, 14; Michael Kerr, "City Awaits Local Black Response," *Northeast Mississippi Daily Journal*, March 23, 1978, 1; Michael Kerr, "Local Blacks Urge to Call Off Boycott," *Northeast Mississippi Daily Journal*, March 24, 1978, 1, 20; Michael Kerr, "Blacks Launch Economic Boycott," *Northeast Mississippi Daily Journal*, March 25-26, 1978, 1.

37. Warren Brown, "Tupelo: Black Boycott Stirs Klan-Led Backlash," *Washington Post*, June 26, 1978, A2; "KKK/United League March."

38. "The Klan Rides Again," *Time*, November 19, 1979, http://www.time.com/time/magazine/article/0,9171,948780-2,00.html; "Knights of the Ku Klux Klan," Southern Poverty Law Center, available online; Michael Kerr, "Statement Asks for No Marches," *Northeast Mississippi Daily Journal*, April 1-2, 1978, 1.

39. "Time Has Come for Reason," *Northeast Mississippi Daily Journal*, March 29, 1978; "Ku Klux Klan Demonstration Not Wanted in Tupelo," *Northeast Mississippi Daily Journal*, March 29, 1978, 1, 4; Kerr, "Statement Asks for No Marches," 1;

40. Michael Kerr, "Klan Won't March, Rents Hall," *Northeast Mississippi Daily Journal*, April 4, 1978, 2; Joe Rutherford and Michael Kerr, "Small Group Hears Klan Praise Racism," *Northeast Mississippi Daily Journal*, April 10, 1978, 2.

41. "Aldermen Ask League, Klan Cancel Marches," *Northeast Mississippi Daily Journal*, April 3, 1978, 2; Michael Kerr, "United League March Abbreviated under Midday Sun on Saturday," *Northeast Mississippi Daily Journal*, April 10, 1978, 3.

42. Joseph Shapiro, "United League President Rejects Bias Talks Proposal," *The Commercial Appeal*, April 15, 1978, 17; David Gray, "Racial Strife Resembles 1960s," *Jackson Daily News*, August 28, 1978, 1.

43. "Two Ex-Police Captains Quit Tupelo Jobs," *Jackson Daily News*, April 19, 1978, Tupelo Boycott 1978 Subject file, MDAH.

44. Frederick N. Tulsky, "KKK/League Prepare for Possible Clash," *Jackson Daily News*, Tupelo Boycott Subject file, MDAH, 3A; Candace Lee, "State Patrol Was Ready for Violence," *Jackson Daily News*, May 22, 1978, Tupelo Boycott Subject file, MDAH, 1C.

45. Boyd, discussion; Cunningham, discussion; Myers, discussion.

46. Tulsky, "KKK/League Prepare for Possible Clash"; Boyd, discussion; David Crary, "A Hard Rain Doesn't Cool Down Tensions in Tupelo," *The Clarion Ledger*, May 8, 1978, Tupelo Boycott Subject file, MDAH, 3H; Chalmers, *Hooded Americanism*, 436.

47. "Marches Banned in Tupelo," *The Clarion Ledger*, May 19, 1978, Tupelo Boycott 1978 Subject file, MDAH, 1A; Frederick Tulsky, "Judge Concerned for Blacks' Rights in Tupelo," *The Clarion Ledger*, May 23, 1978, Tupelo Boycott 1978 Subject file, MDAH, 3; Shepard, *Rationing Justice*, 215.

48. "KKK/United League March."

49. Ibid.; "Mississippi Blacks, Klansmen Hold Peaceful Marches," *Washington Post*, June 11, 1978, Tupelo Boycott Subject file, MDAH, A6H; Boyd, discussion; Brown, "Tupelo: Black Boycott Stirs Klan-Led Backlash," A2; Grisham, *Tupelo*, 155.

50. "Tupelo Mayor Plans Second Meeting on Racial Problems," *Jackson Daily News*, September 29, 1978, Tupelo Boycott 1978 Subject File, MDAH, 12D; "Tupelo Officials Work to End Racial Problems," *Clarion Ledger*, October 4, 1978, Tupelo Boycott 1978 Subject File, MDAH, 3A; Johnna Neuman, "Evers Credited with Bringing Both Sides Together in Tupelo Dispute," *Clarion Ledger*, October 5, 1978, Tupelo Boycott 1978 Subject File, MDAH, 3A.

51. Elizabeth Fair, "Racial Unrest Still Churning Despite Silence in Tupelo Streets," *The Commercial Appeal*, March 4, 1979, B-1; Elizabeth Fair, "March by 400 Blacks in Okolona Is Quiet," *Commercial Appeal*, August 6, 1978, A12; Shepard, *Rationing Justice*, 209.

52. Minor, "United League: Can It Destroy Stable NAACP," *The Capitol Reporter*,

September 14, 1978, United League Subject File, MDAH, 2; David Crary, "NAACP Leader O.K.'s Statewide United League," *The Clarion Ledger*, July 2, 1978, United League Subject File, MDAH; Aaron Henry, quoted in "Behind the Struggle in Tupelo"; Jo Ann Klein and David W. Kubissa, "Emerging Civil Groups Dispute 'Docile' NAACP Tactics," *The Clarion Ledger*, July 10, 1979, 3A.

53. Gunn, discussion; Elizabeth Fair and Michael Arnold, "Town May Face Race Conflict," *Commercial Appeal*, July 17, 1978, Okolona 1979 Subject File, MDAH.

54. Gunn, discussion; Myers, discussion.

55. Fair and Arnold, "Town May Face Race Conflict"; "Justice Department Probe Is Asked in Okolona Shooting," *Jackson Daily News*, August 16, 1978, Okolona 1979 Subject File, MDAH.

56. Fair and Arnold, "Town May Face Race Conflict."

57. Fair, "March by 400 Blacks in Okolona Is Quiet," A12.

58. Ibid.

59. Gunn, discussion; "Justice Department Probe Is Asked in Okolona Shooting"; "United League Requests U.S. Justice Department to Investigate Shooting," *Clarion Ledger*, Okolona Boycott Subject File, MDAH; Robert M. Press, "Racial Issues Still Vex Mostly Quiet South," *The Christian Science Monitor*, September 29, 1978, Okolona Boycott Subject File, MDAH, 6; Boyd Lewis, "A Tale of Two Towns," *The Jackson Advocate*, December 21-27, 1978, Okolona Boycott Subject File, MDAH, 3; Marx and Tuthill, "Resisting the Klan," 75; "League Repels Klan in Okalona [sic]," *Southern Struggle*, September–October 1978, SCEF Papers, Special Collections and Archives, Georgia State University Library, Atlanta, GA, 4-5.

60. Gunn, discussion.

61. "Justice Probe Is Asked in Okolona Shooting"; "United League Requests U.S. Justice Department"; "Blacks Promise Extended Boycott of Okolona's Business District," *Clarion Ledger*, August 27, 1978, Okolona Boycott Subject File, MDAH; "League Repels Klan in Okalona [sic]," 5.

62. "Race Trouble in Mississippi," August 27, 1978, http://tvnews.vanderbilt.edu/tvn-video-view.pl?RC=500365; "League Repels Klan in Okalona [sic]," 5.

63. "Justice Probe Is Asked in Okolona Shooting"; "United League Requests U.S. Justice Department"; "Okolona Ruling Thrown Out," *Daily News*, August 25, 1978, Okolona Boycott Subject File, M.

64. Robert Lay, discussion; Gunn, discussion; Debra Jackson, in discussion with the author, November 13, 2010, Stone Mountain, GA.

65. Cunningham, discussion.

66. "Blacks Promise Extended Boycott of Okolona's Business District."

67. Gunn, discussion.

68. "Boycott Continues," *Jackson Daily News*, September 18, 1978, 7; "Okolona School Boycott Enters Its Eighth Day," *Jackson Daily News*, September 20, 1978, Okolona Subject file, MDAH, 6d; "Okolona Black Students Continue Nine-Day Boycott," *Jackson Daily News*, September 20, 1978, Okolona Subject file, MDAH; George Pickens, et al., Plaintiffs-Appellants v. Okolona Municipal Separate School District et al., Defendants-Appellees, United States Court of Appeals, Fifth Circuit, May 3, 1979, http://ftp.resource.org/courts.gov/c/F2/594/594.F2d.433.78-3021.html.

69. Robert M. Press, "Racial Issues Still Vex Mostly Quiet South," *The Christian Science Monitor*, September 29, 1978, Okolona Boycott Subject file, MDAH, 6; Bob Zeller, "Blacks March through Tense Okolona," *Clarion Ledger*, Okolona Boycott Subject file, MDAH; "Okolona Officials Uneasy over Civil Rights March," *Jackson Daily News*, October 7, 1978, Okolona Boycott Subject file, MDAH; "Robinson Asks for Help in Okolona," *Clarion Ledger*, October 7, 1978, Okolona Subject file, MDAH, 2a.

70. Myers, discussion; Press, "Racial Issues Vex Mostly Quiet South," 6; Elizabeth Fair, "Okolona's Racial Turmoil Results in Sentences for 8," *Commercial Appeal*, January 31, 1979, Okolona Subject file, MDAH, 3; "Eight Sentenced in Okolona Violence," *Daily News*, February 1, 1978, Okolona Subject file, MDAH.

71. Alfred Robinson, quoted in Lewis, "A Tale of Two Towns," 3; Howard Gunn, quoted in Lewis, "A Tale of Two Towns," 3.

72. Elizabeth Fair and William Fuller, "115 Rights Marchers Arrested in Okolona," *The Commercial Appeal*, Okolona 1979 File, MDAH; Elizabeth Fair, "Parade Ordinance Raises Legal Questions," *The Commercial Appeal*, April 22, 1979, Okolona 1979 File, MDAH, 15B; "Okolona March Leads to Arrests," *Jackson Daily News*, April 29,1979, Okolona 1979 File, MDAH, 3B; "Okolona Arrests Draw Lawsuits," *The Clarion Ledger*, May 1, 1979, Okolona 1979 File, MDAH, 2B; "United League Lawyer Asks $200,000 Damage for Protestors," *Commonwealth*, May 1, 1979, Okolona 1979 File, MDAH.

73. Atlanta United League Support Coalition (UL Support), "Victorious March in Okolona," *Land, Jobs, and Justice* 1, no. 2 (June 1979): 2; Bruce Hansen, "Grievances Unheeded, Rights Leader Says," *The Commercial Appeal*, June 3, 1979, Okolona 1979 File, MDAH, 1B; "Okolona Sees Year's Fifth March," *The Clarion Ledger*, June 3, 1979, 4A, Okolona 1979 File, MDAH.

74. Atlanta United League Support Coalition (UL Support), "Followed by Police Murder," *Land, Jobs, and Justice* 1, no. 2 (June 1979): 1; Don Hoffman, "Group Asks for Special Prosecutor," *The Clarion Ledger*, June 8, 1979, United League File, MDAH; "Jail Shooting Fans Flames in Okolona," *Jackson Advocate*, June 7-13, 1979, 1A; Elizabeth Fair, "Special Prosecutor Requested for Probe of Inmate's Death," *The Commercial Appeal*, June 8, 1979, Okolona File, MDAH.

75. UL Support, "Followed by Police Murder"; Leon Rubis, "March in Okolona Hot, Peaceful," *The Clarion Ledger*, June 10, 1979, Okolona 1979 File, MDAH, 3; "Policeman's Wife: A Personal Struggle," *The Clarion Ledger*, June 10, 1979, Okolona 1979 File, MDAH, 3A; Racial Demonstrations, June 9, 1979, http://tvnews.vanderbilt.edu/tvn-video-view.pl?RC=505080,

76. Fair, "Special Prosecutor," B-1.

77. "Deputy Who Shot Black Okolona Inmate Resigns," *The Clarion Ledger*, June 13, 1979, Okolona File, MDAH, 3A.

78. Ibid.

79. "150 Demonstrators Show Support for Lexington Boycott," *Clarion Ledger*, September 3,1978, United League Subject File, MDAH, 3a; Art Toalston, "Civil Rights Opponents Meet, Term Due Tonight," *Jackson Daily News*, September 8, 1978, 1b, United League Subject File, MDAH; Don Hoffman, "Canton March Ends Quietly, Boycott Begins," *The Clarion Ledger*, November 12, 1978, 1b, 4b, United League Subject File, MDAH; "Rights Group Opens Office in Indianola, "*The Clarion Ledger*, March 22, 1979, United League Subject File, MDAH; Klein and Kubissa, "Emerging Civil Groups," 3a; Marx and Tuthill, "Resisting the Klan," 73-74.

80. Shepard, *Rationing Justice*, 217.

81. Ibid., 217-18; Elizabeth Fair, "League's Legal Aid in Jeopardy," *Commercial Appeal*, July 21, 1979, B11; "Legal Service Group Aid in United League Efforts May Soon Have to Halt," *The Clarion Ledger*, July 22, 1979, 3A.

82. Elizabeth Fair, "Myers' Resignation from Post 'Will Be Blow,' Gunn Laments," *Commercial Appeal*, July 18, 1979, B12.

83. "Robinson Asks Director of Legal Activity to Quit," *Commercial Appeal*, June 19, 1980, B19; "United League Seeks Ouster of Legal Director," *The Clarion Ledger*, June 19, 1980, United League Subject File, MDAH, 3b.

84. "Social Activist Has New Name as State's Minister for Islam," *Commercial Appeal*, March 24, 1981, United League Subject File, MDAH, B13; Lea Anne Hester, "Skip Robinson to Proselytize for Islam," *The Clarion Ledger*, March 26, 1981, United League Subject File, MDAH, 4a.

85. Gunn, discussion; Myers, discussion.

Conclusion

1. Simon Wendt, *Spirit and the Shotgun: Armed Resistance and the Struggle for Civil Rights* (Gainesville: University of Florida Press, 2007), 6.

2. Please see Akinyele O. Umoja, "Repression Breeds Resistance: The Black Liberation Army and the Radical Legacy of the Black Panther Party," in *Liberation, Imagination, and the Black Panther Party*, eds. Kathleen Cleaver and George Katsiaficus (New York: Routledge, 2001), 3-19.

3. Roy Wilkins and Ramsey Clark (Chairmen), "Search and Destroy: A Report

by the Commission of Inquiry into the Black Panthers and the Police" (New York: Metropolitan Applied Research, 1973), vii-xii. This book is the product of an independent inquiry into the Chicago predawn police raid on the Illinois State Chapter of the Black Panther Party that resulted in the deaths of Panthers Fred Hampton and Mark Clark and injury to several of their comrades.

4. "Agent Tells of '79 Threats by Klan and Nazis," *New York Times*, May 12, 1985, 26, ProQuest Historical Newspapers; Sally Avery Bermanzohn, "A Massacre Survivor Reflects on the Greensboro Truth and Reconciliation Commission," *Radical History Review* 97 (Winter 2007): 103, 102-9.

5. "On this day: April 4 1968," *BBC News*, August 29, 2011, http://news.bbc.co.uk/onthisday/hi/dates/stories/april/4/newsid_2453000/2453987.stm; Aline Carambat, "Black Panther Founder Discusses Role, Purpose of Controversial Organization," *The DM online*, October 15, 2009, available online.

Index

Mississippi Summer Project, 85, 89,
98–99
Mitchell, Guy, Jr., 250
Mitchell, John, 185, 199
Money, Mississippi, 45
Monroe, North Carolina, 53, 88, 90
Monroe County, Mississippi, 174, 175
Montgomery, Isaiah, 17
Montgomery, Jesse, 193–194
Montgomery Bus Boycott (1956-1957),
50, 51
Monthly Review (periodical), 93
Moody, Anne, 80, 82
Moore, Amzie: armed self-defense, 55;
financial assistance to, 55; financial
harassment by White Citizens'
Council, 55; Freedom Summer
(1964), 92–93; NAACP (National
Association for the Advancement of
Colored People), 55, 56; photograph
of, 56; RCNL (Regional Council
for Negro Leadership), 31; SNCC
(Student Nonviolent Coordinating
Committee), 56; targeting of, 86;
threats against, 55; Till case, Em-
mett, 37, 55; voter registration, 33, 56;
WWII veteran, 28
— and: Block, Margaret, 108; Block, Sam,
67; Evers, Medgar, 55; Guyot, Law-
rence, 55; Hurley, Ruby, 55; Moses,
Bob, 55–56, 67; Payne, Charles, 55;
Snellings, Roland, 92–93; Stanford,
Max, 92–93; Sugarman, Tracy, 55
Moore, Audley, 90
Moore, David, 239
Moore, Harvey, Jr., 239, 245
Moore, Joe, 239
Moore, Queen Mother, 187, 188, 252
Moore, Rachel, 19
Moore, Tom, 239
Morgan City, Louisiana, 5
Morris, John Thomas, 226, 227
Morris, Willie, 170, 171, 173, 174
Moses, Bob, 53–62, 83–88; Amite
County, Mississippi, 59–62; armed

self-defense, 87–88; beating, 60;
Black Nationalism, 93; COFO
(Council of Federated Organizations), 77, 84; FBI, 84;
Moses, Bob (cont'd): Freedom Summer
(1964), 83–88, 93; Leflore County
voter registration, 69–70; McComb,
Mississippi, 63; Mississippi Summer Project, 85; nonviolence, 57, 62,
87–88; SNCC (Student Nonviolent
Coordinating Committee), 53, 54–55,
57, 119; targeting of, 86; United States
Department of Justice, 84; voter registration, 53, 56–62; White northern
student volunteers, 99
— and: Baker, Ella, 55; Blackwell, Randall, 69; Block, Sam, 67, 68; Carmichael, Stokely (later Kwame Ture),
93; Cotton, MacArthur, 58; Dennis,
Dave, 85; Moore, Amzie, 55–56, 67;
Peacock, Willie, 69; Steptoe, E. W.
(Eldridge Willie), 60–62, 63; Turnbow, Hartman, 75
Mound Bayou, Mississippi: dedication
of, 27; founder, 17; mass rally (1955),
27; RCNL (Regional Council for Negro Leadership) tent meetings, 32
— and: Evers, Medgar, 40, 42; Howard,
T. R. M., 30–31
Mount Beulah, Mississippi, 198
murders. *See* assassinations
Myers, Lewis: Aberdeen boycott,
175–176; author's relation with,
254; Byhalia boycott, 220, 224; FBI,
241; International African Prisoner
of War (APOW) Solidarity Day,
208–209; Lawyers for Constitutional
Change, 175; National Conference
of Black Lawyers (NCBL), 217;
NMRLS (Northern Mississippi
Rural Legal Services), 217, 250–251;
Okolona, Mississippi, 241, 242, 247;
photograph of, 235; protection for,
222; speaking tours, 252; Tupelo,
Mississippi, 229, 230, 232, 236; UL

About the Author

Akinyele Omowale Umoja is an educator and scholar-activist. He is Associate Professor and Chair of the Department of African American Studies at Georgia State University, where he teaches courses on the history of the Civil Rights and Black Power Movements and other social movements. He has been a community activist for over forty years.